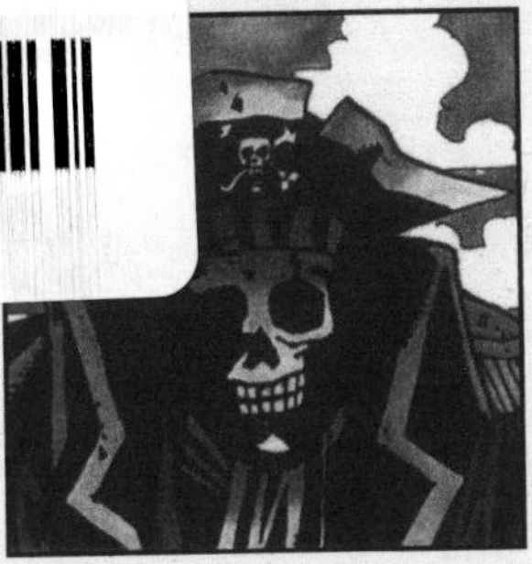

There's something I'd like to do if I had a whole year off. I would like to do a serious study of different drawing techniques and materials. Then I bet drawing would become even more fun. Whoever said it's a small world?

—*Eiichiro Oda, 1998*

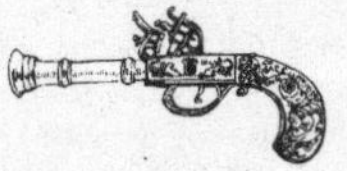

Eiichiro Oda began his manga career at the age of 17, when his one-shot cowboy manga **Wanted!** won second place in the coveted Tezuka manga awards. Oda went on to work as an assistant to some of the biggest manga artists in the industry, including Nobuhiro Watsuki, before winning the Hop Step Award for new artists. His pirate adventure **One Piece**, which debuted in **Weekly Shonen Jump** magazine in 1997, quickly became one of the most popular manga in Japan.

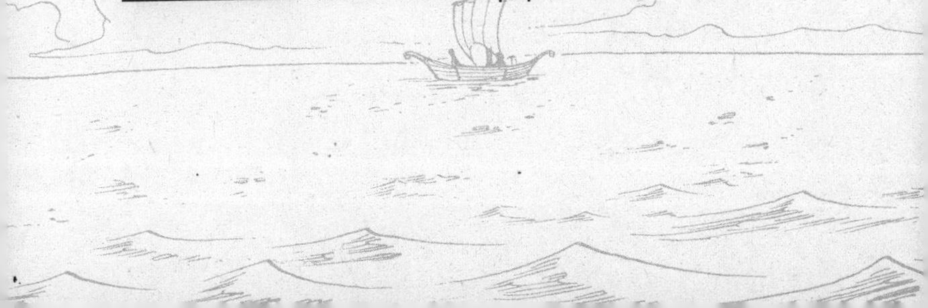

ONE PIECE VOL. 3
EAST BLUE PART 3

SHONEN JUMP Manga Edition

This volume contains material that was originally published in
English in **SHONEN JUMP** #10–13.

STORY AND ART BY EIICHIRO ODA

Translation/Andy Nakatani
English Adaptation/Lance Caselman
Touch-Up Art & Lettering/Bill Schuch, Walden Wong
Cover Design/Sean Lee
Graphics & Layout/Sean Lee
Supervising Editor/Jason Thompson
Editors/Megan Bates, Shaenon K. Garrity

Printed in the U.S.A.

Published by VIZ Media, LLC
P.O. Box 77010
San Francisco, CA 94107

27
First printing, February 2004
Twenty-seventh printing, January 2023

viz.com

ONE PIECE

Vol. 3

DON'T GET FOOLED AGAIN

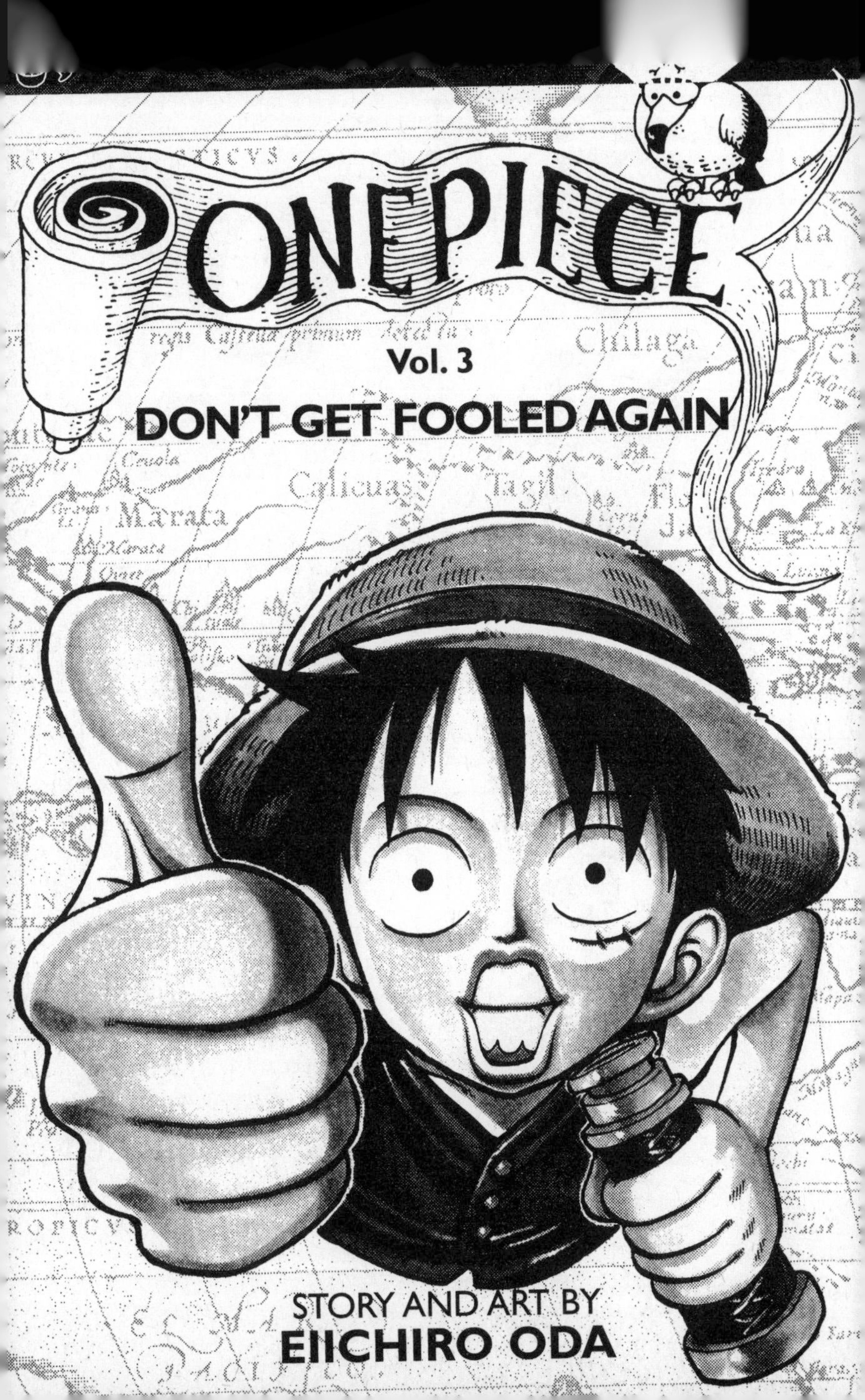

STORY AND ART BY

EIICHIRO ODA

THE STORY OF ONE PIECE
Volume 3

Monkey D. Luffy started out as just a kid with a dream – and that dream was to become the greatest pirate in history! Stirred by the tales of pirate "Red-Haired" Shanks, Luffy vowed to become a pirate himself. That was before the enchanted Devil Fruit gave Luffy the power to stretch like rubber, at the cost of being unable to swim – a serious handicap for an aspiring sea dog. Undeterred, Luffy set out to sea, where he found an unlikely partner in the fearsome pirate hunter Roronoa Zolo…

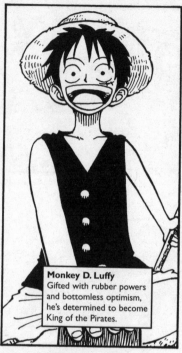

Monkey D. Luffy
Gifted with rubber powers and bottomless optimism, he's determined to become King of the Pirates.

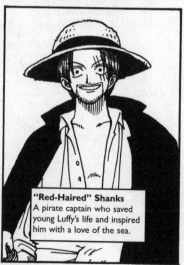

"Red-Haired" Shanks
A pirate captain who saved young Luffy's life and inspired him with a love of the sea.

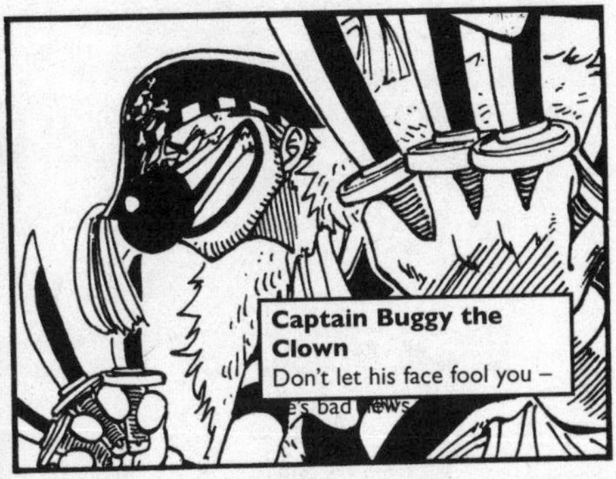
Captain Buggy the Clown
Don't let his face fool you – he's bad news.

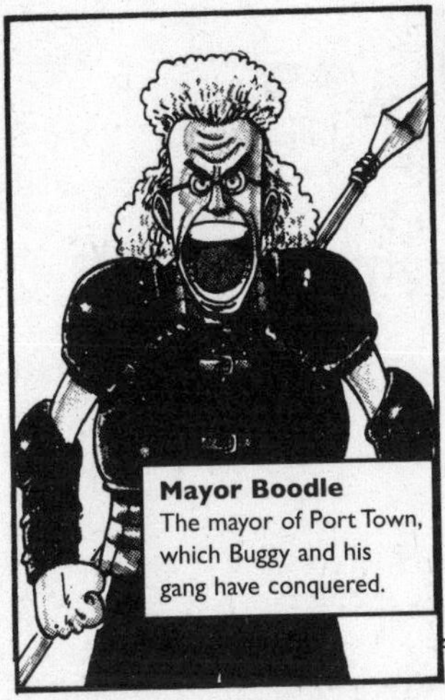
Mayor Boodle
The mayor of Port Town, which Buggy and his gang have conquered.

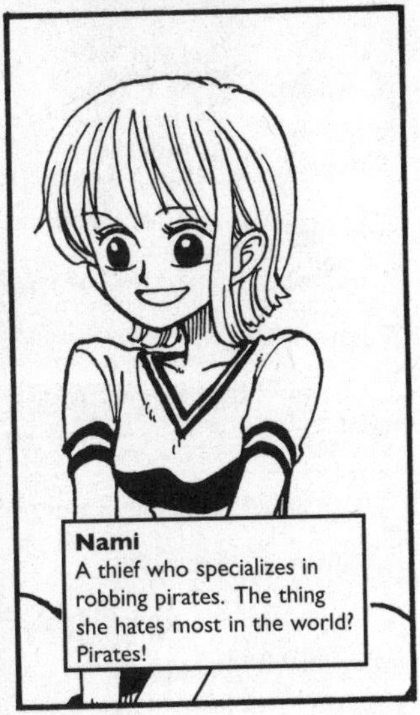
Nami
A thief who specializes in robbing pirates. The thing she hates most in the world? Pirates!

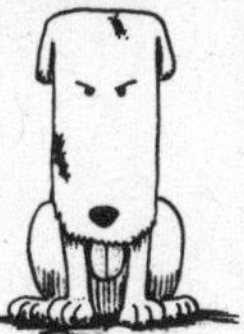
Chouchou
A dog.

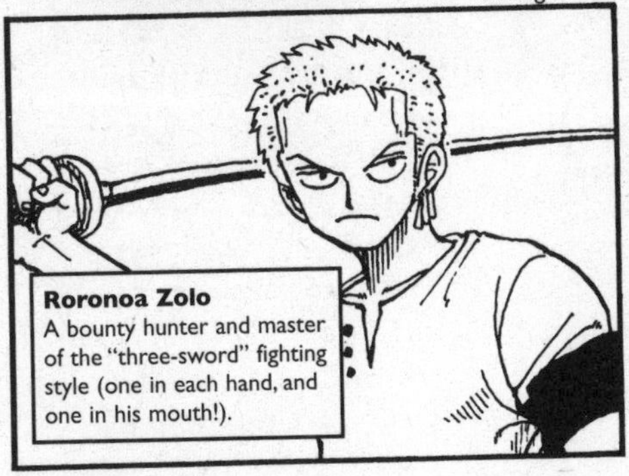
Roronoa Zolo
A bounty hunter and master of the "three-sword" fighting style (one in each hand, and one in his mouth!).

Now Luffy and Zolo are under attack by the ruthless pirate lord Buggy the Clown. Captain Buggy has also eaten the Devil Fruit – and gained the power to split his body into pieces like a jigsaw puzzle! How can Luffy fight a foe who's literally all over the place? And can he trust Nami, the fast-talking thief who stole Buggy's ship? As Volume 3 of ONE PIECE opens, the battle with Buggy is raging… and it's only the beginning of Luffy's problems.

Vol. 3
DON'T GET FOOLED AGAIN

CONTENTS

Chapter 18:

THE PIRATE BUGGY THE CLOWN

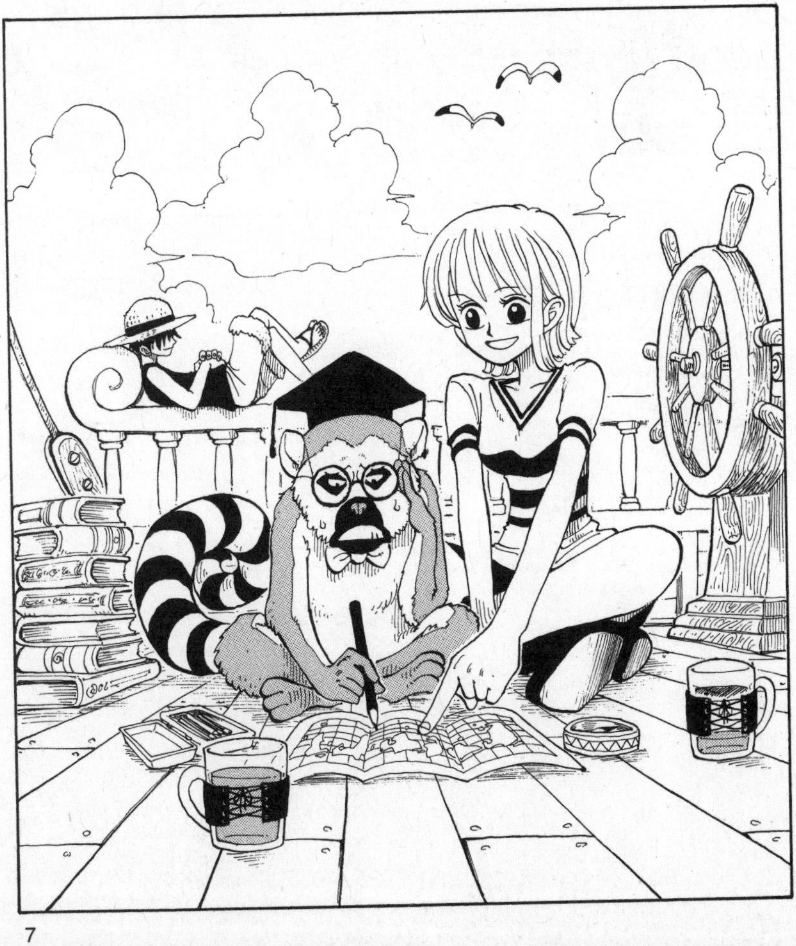

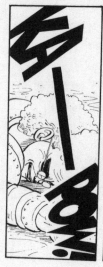

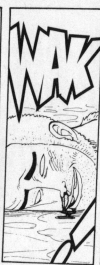

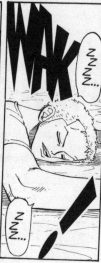

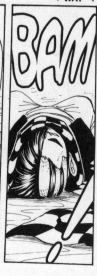

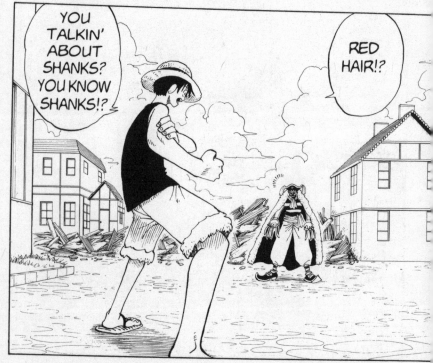

READ THIS WAY

BAM
WAK
ZZZZ...
ZZZ...
WAK
KA—BOOM!
RED HAIR!?
YOU TALKIN' ABOUT SHANKS? YOU KNOW SHANKS!?

READ THIS WAY

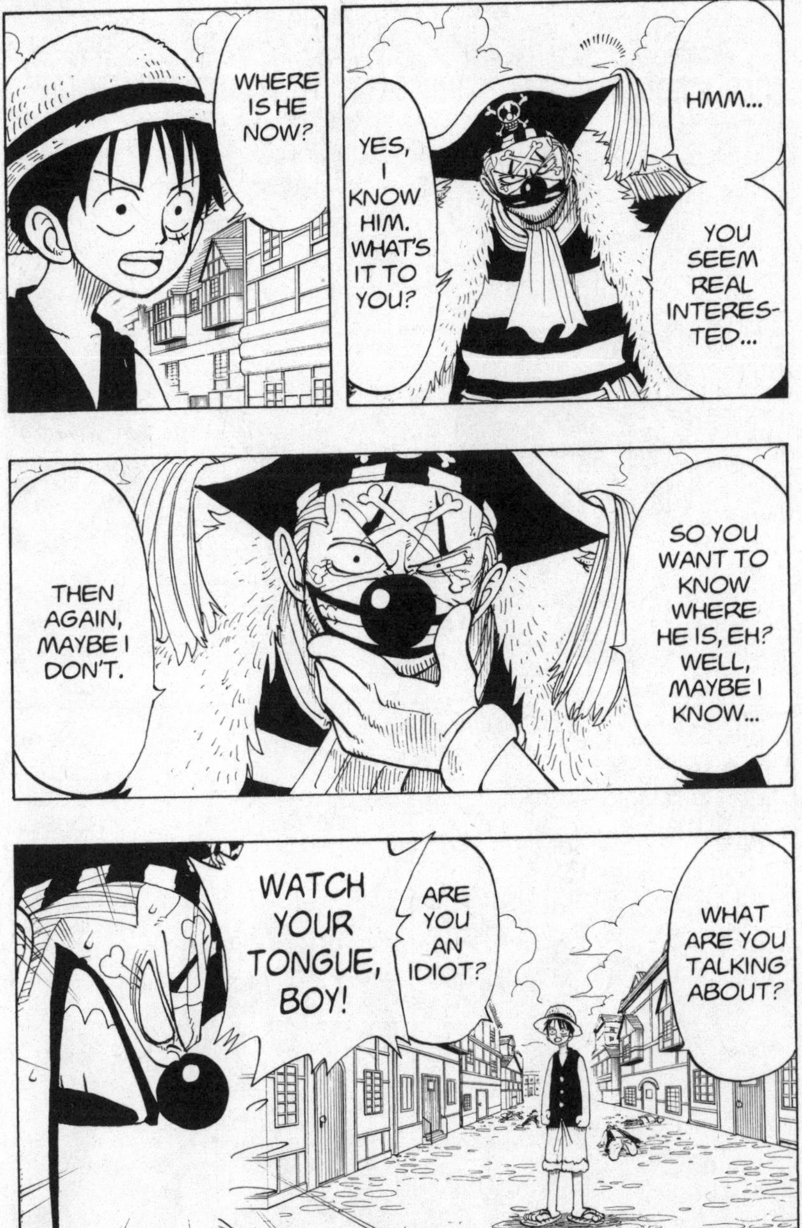
HMM...
YOU SEEM REAL INTERESTED...
YES, I KNOW HIM. WHAT'S IT TO YOU?
WHERE IS HE NOW?
SO YOU WANT TO KNOW WHERE HE IS, EH? WELL, MAYBE I KNOW...
THEN AGAIN, MAYBE I DON'T.
WHAT ARE YOU TALKING ABOUT?
ARE YOU AN IDIOT?
WATCH YOUR TONGUE, BOY!

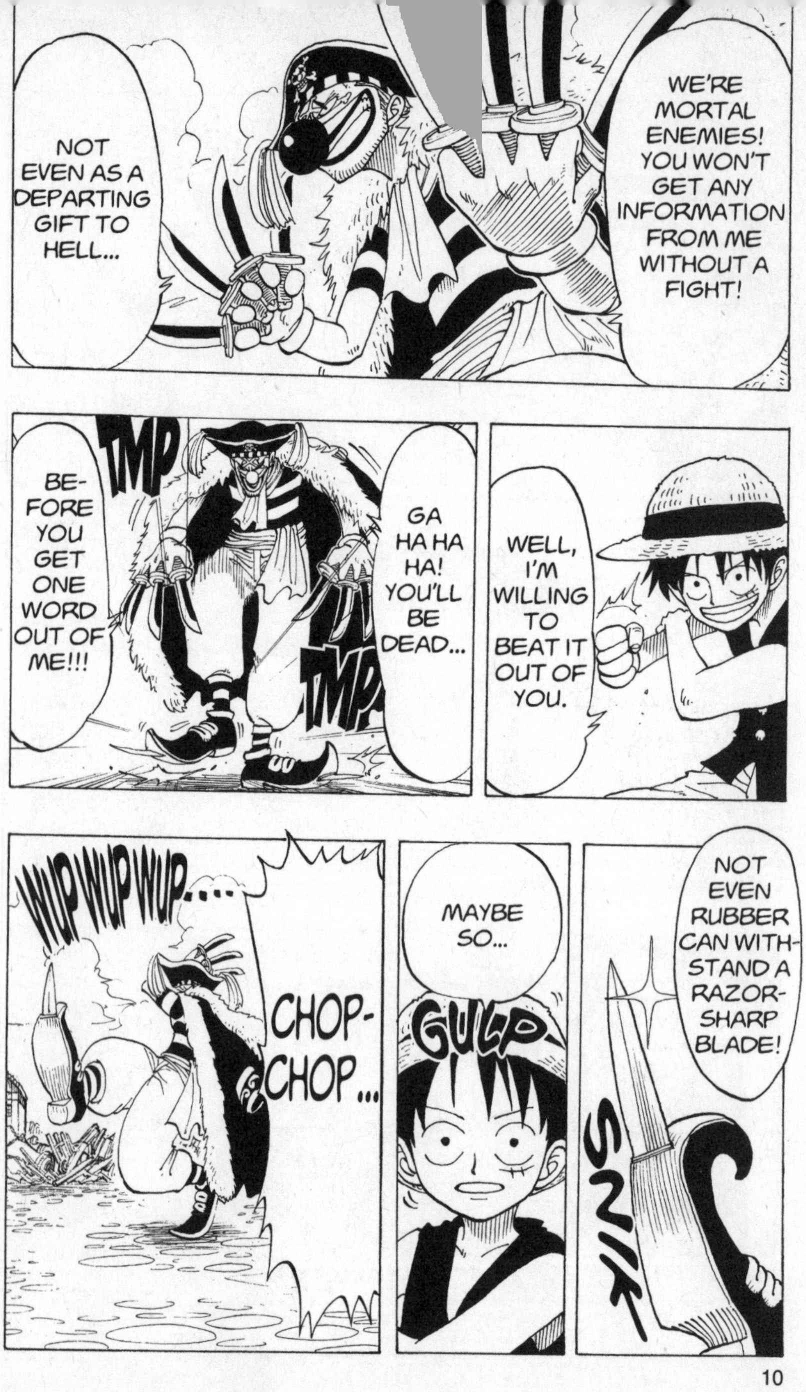
WE'RE MORTAL ENEMIES! YOU WON'T GET ANY INFORMATION FROM ME WITHOUT A FIGHT!
NOT EVEN AS A DEPARTING GIFT TO HELL...
WELL, I'M WILLING TO BEAT IT OUT OF YOU.
GA HA HA HA! YOU'LL BE DEAD...
TMP
BE-FORE YOU GET ONE WORD OUT OF ME!!!
TMP
NOT EVEN RUBBER CAN WITH-STAND A RAZOR-SHARP BLADE!
SNIK
MAYBE SO...
GULP
CHOP-CHOP...
WUP WUP WUP......

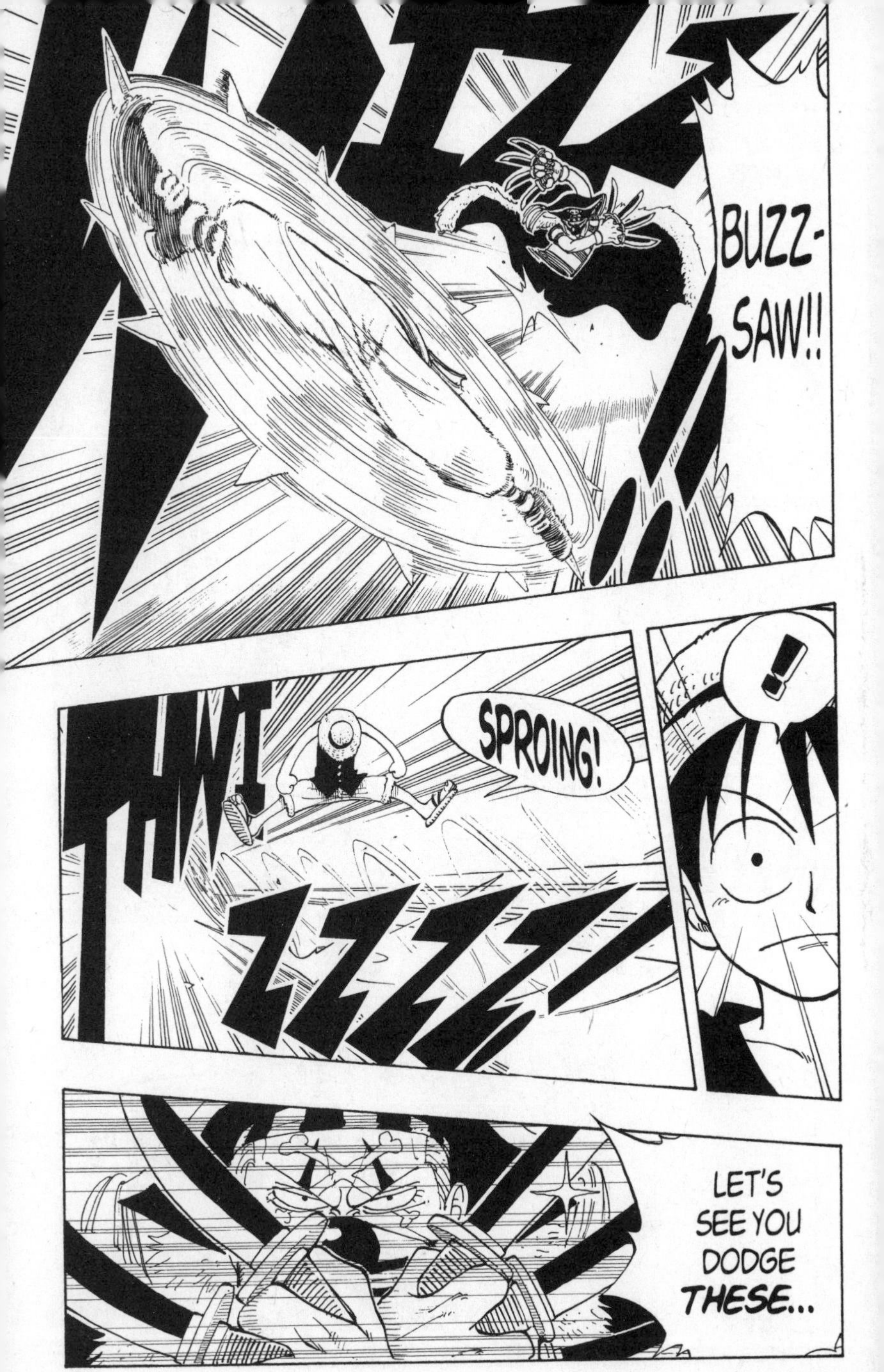
BUZZ-SAW!!
!
SPROING!
LET'S SEE YOU DODGE THESE...

READ THIS WAY

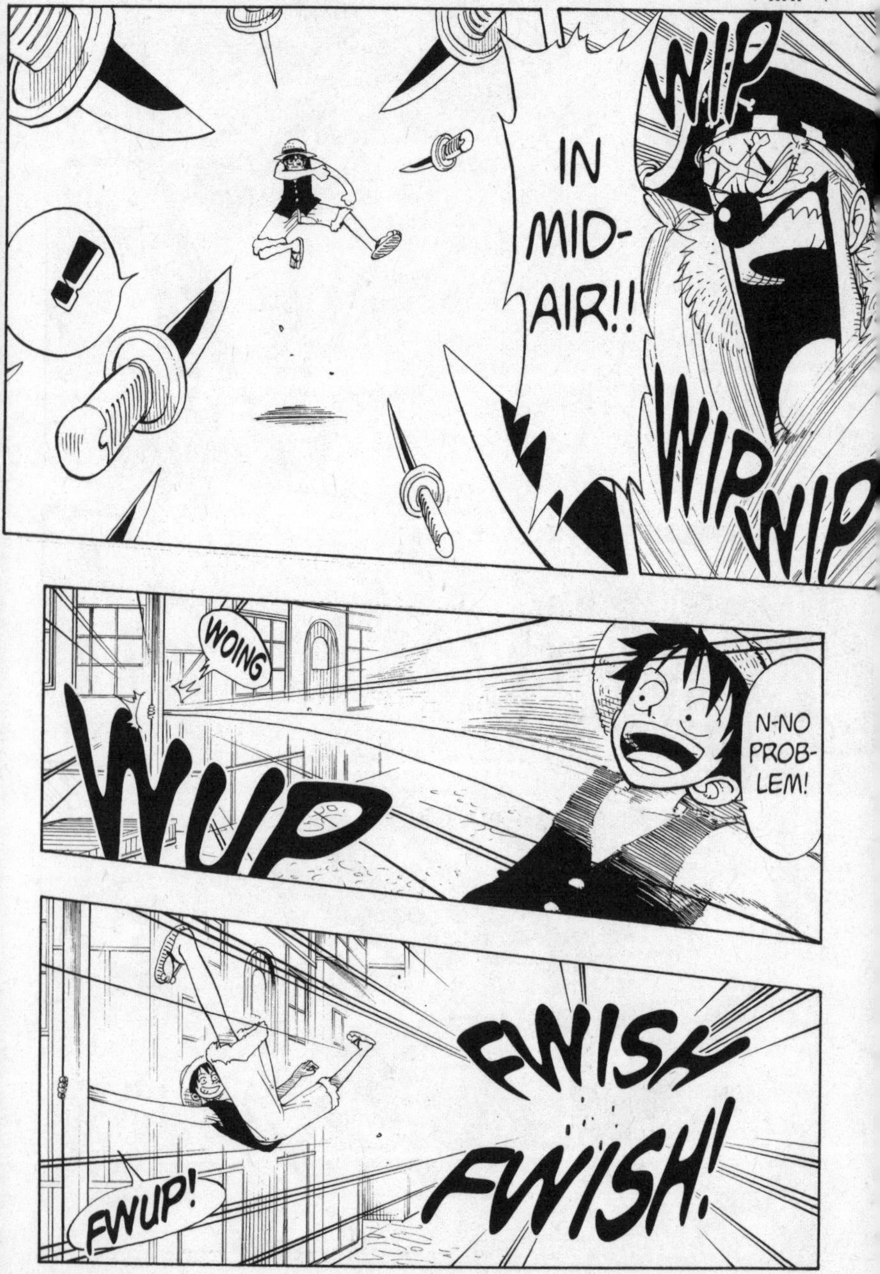

WIP
IN MID-AIR!!
WIP
WIP
!
N-NO PROBLEM!
WOING
WUP
FWISH
FWISH!
FWUP!

READ THIS WAY

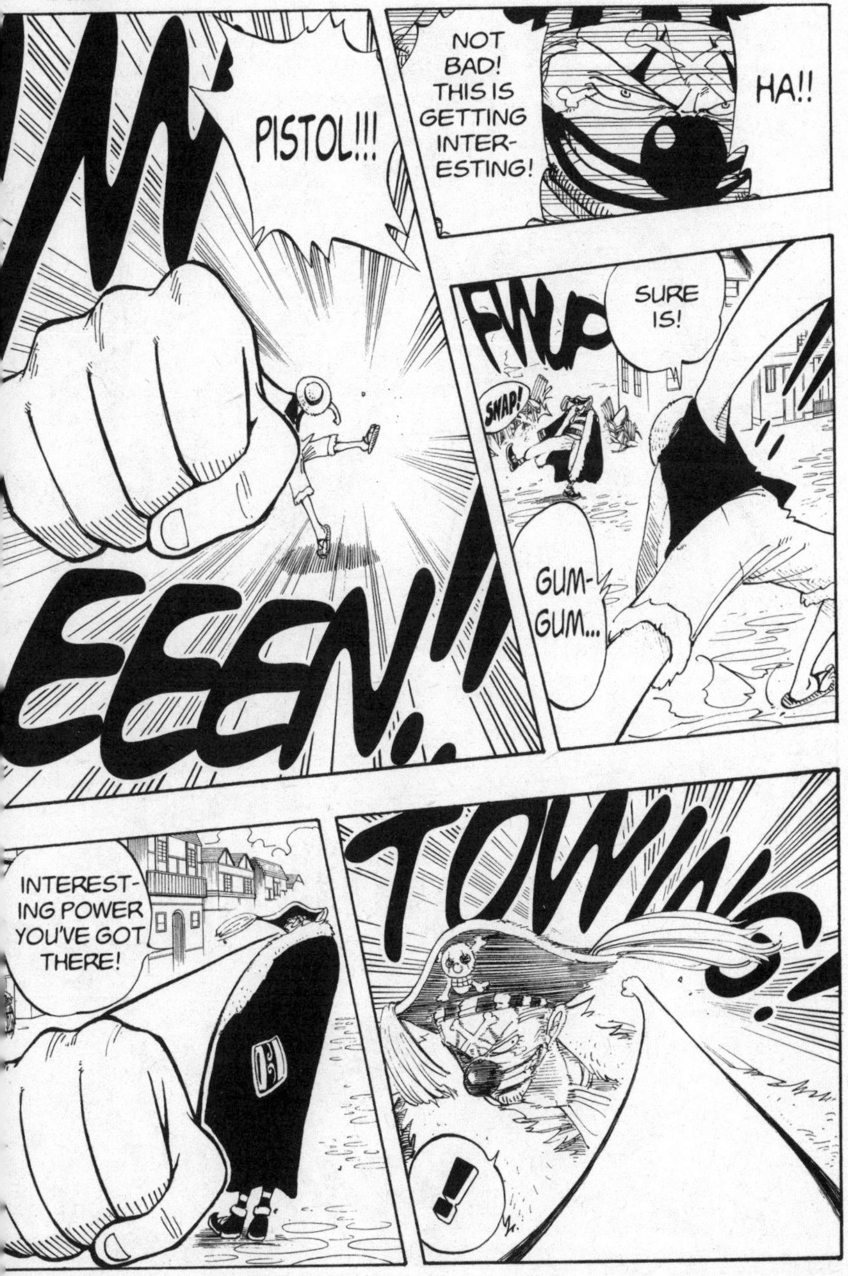
HA!!
NOT BAD! THIS IS GETTING INTER-ESTING!
SURE IS!
FWUP
SNAP!
GUM-GUM...
PISTOL!!!
!
INTEREST-ING POWER YOU'VE GOT THERE!

READ THIS WAY

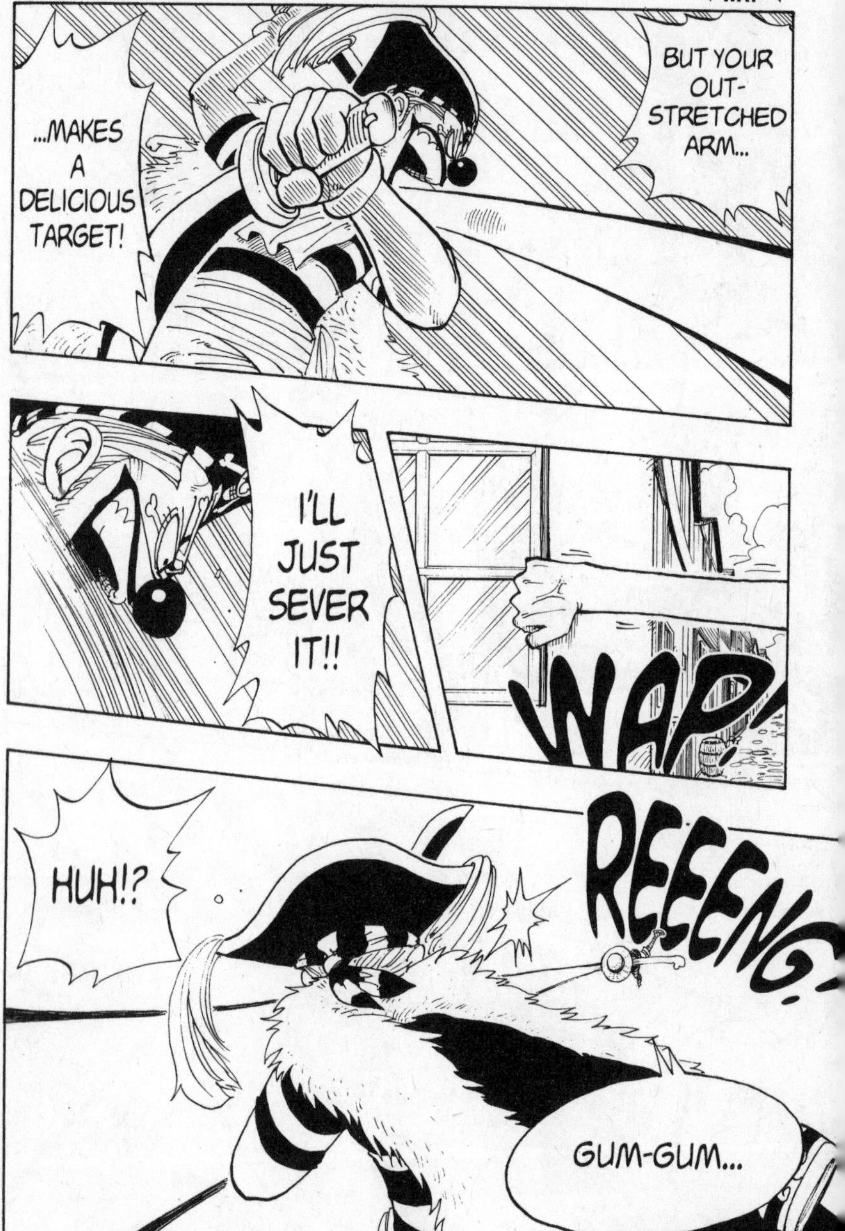
BUT YOUR OUT-STRETCHED ARM...
...MAKES A DELICIOUS TARGET!
WAP!
I'LL JUST SEVER IT!!
REEENG!
HUH!?
GUM-GUM...

READ THIS WAY

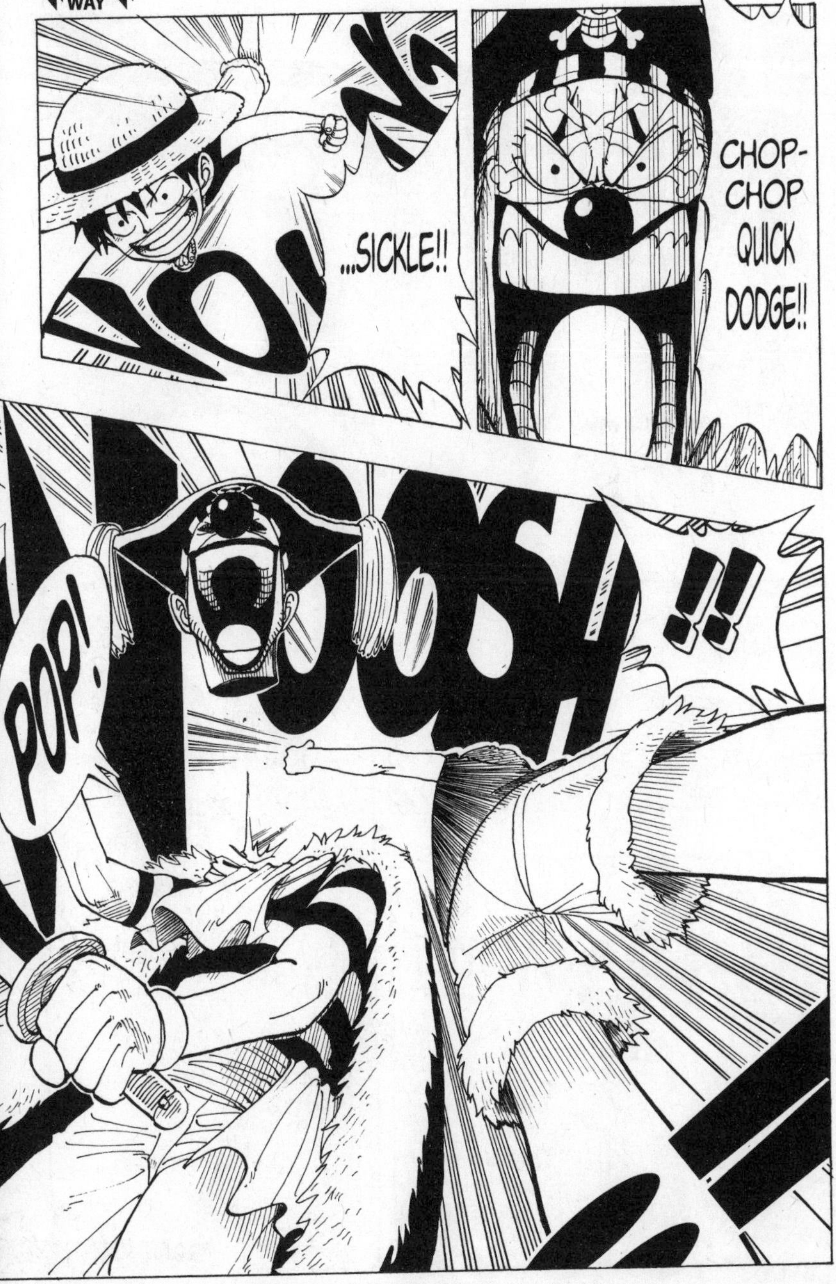
CHOP-CHOP QUICK DODGE!!
VOING
...SICKLE!!
OOSH!!
POP!

READ THIS WAY

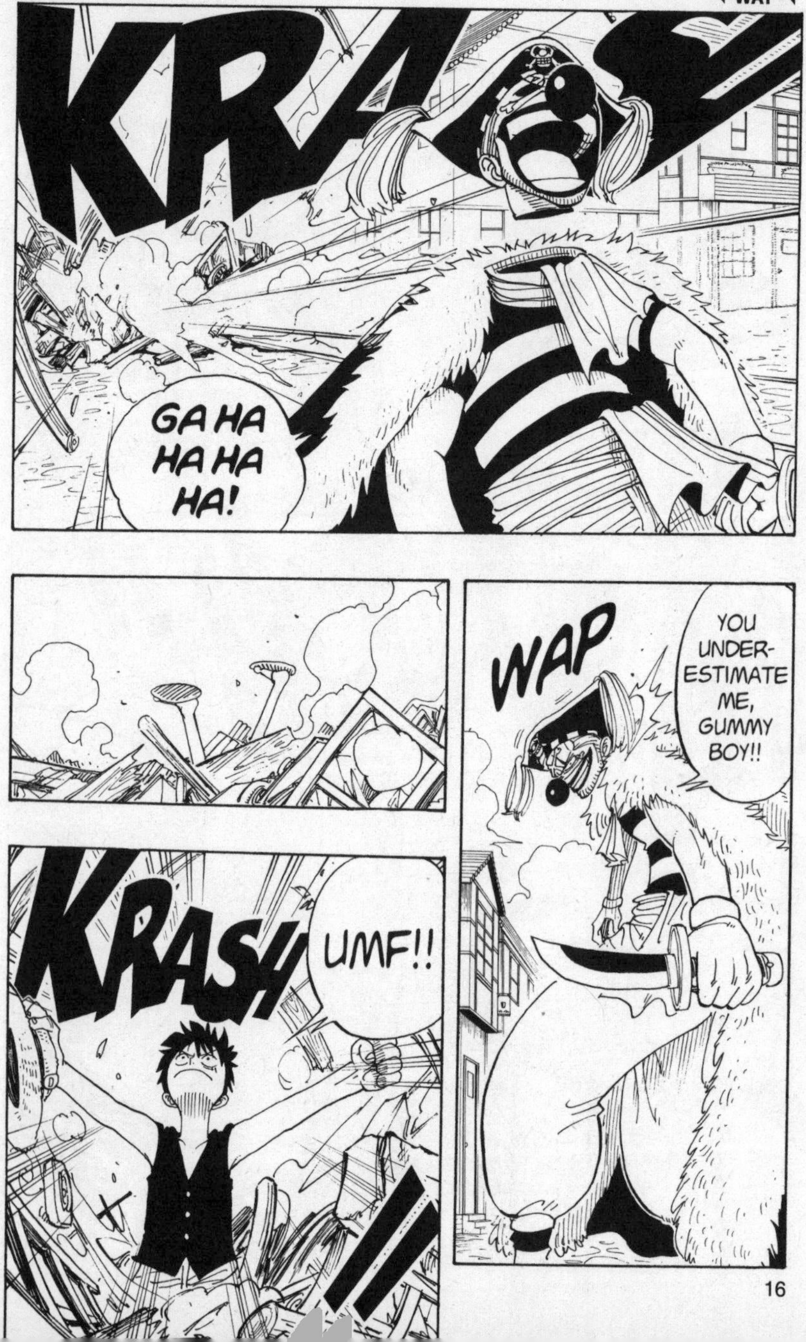
KRA
GA HA HA HA HA!
WAP
YOU UNDER-ESTIMATE ME, GUMMY BOY!!
KRASH
UMF!!

READ THIS WAY

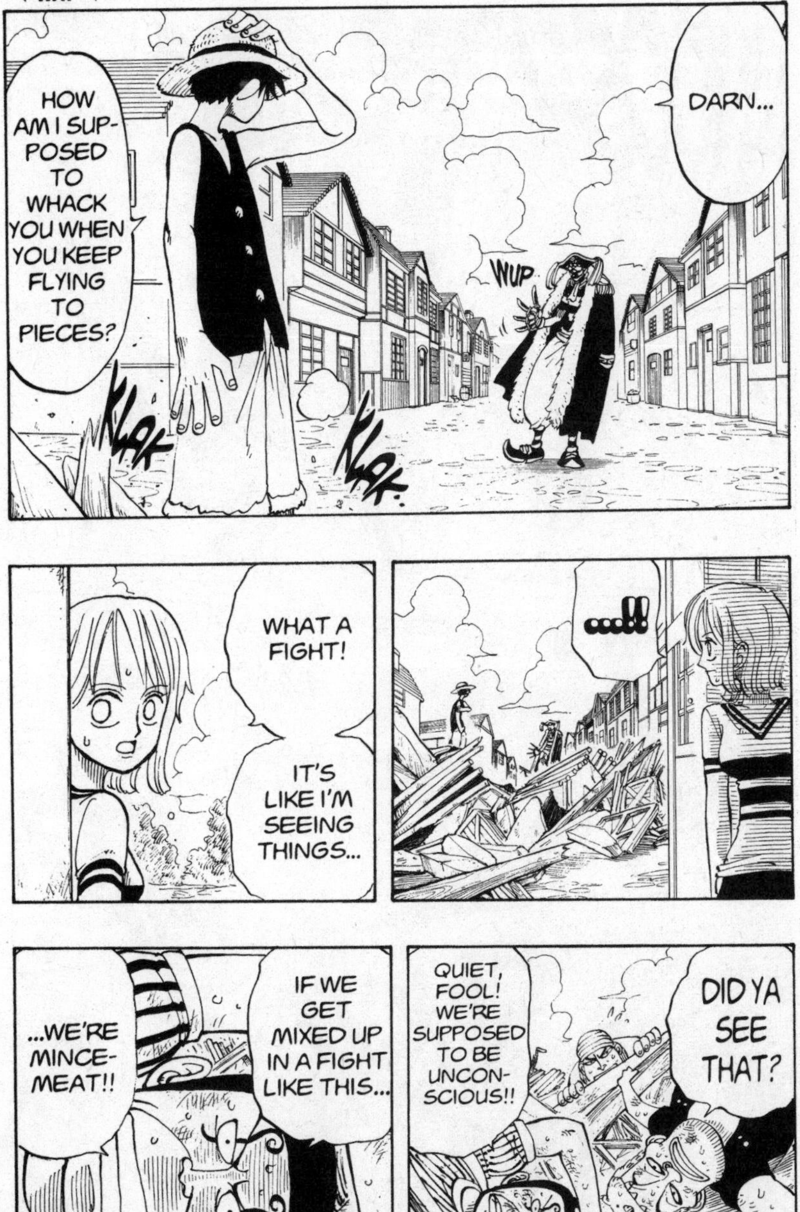
DARN...
WUP
HOW AM I SUPPOSED TO WHACK YOU WHEN YOU KEEP FLYING TO PIECES?
KLAK
KLAK
...!!
WHAT A FIGHT!
IT'S LIKE I'M SEEING THINGS...
DID YA SEE THAT?
QUIET, FOOL! WE'RE SUPPOSED TO BE UNCONSCIOUS!!
IF WE GET MIXED UP IN A FIGHT LIKE THIS...
...WE'RE MINCEMEAT!!

READ THIS WAY

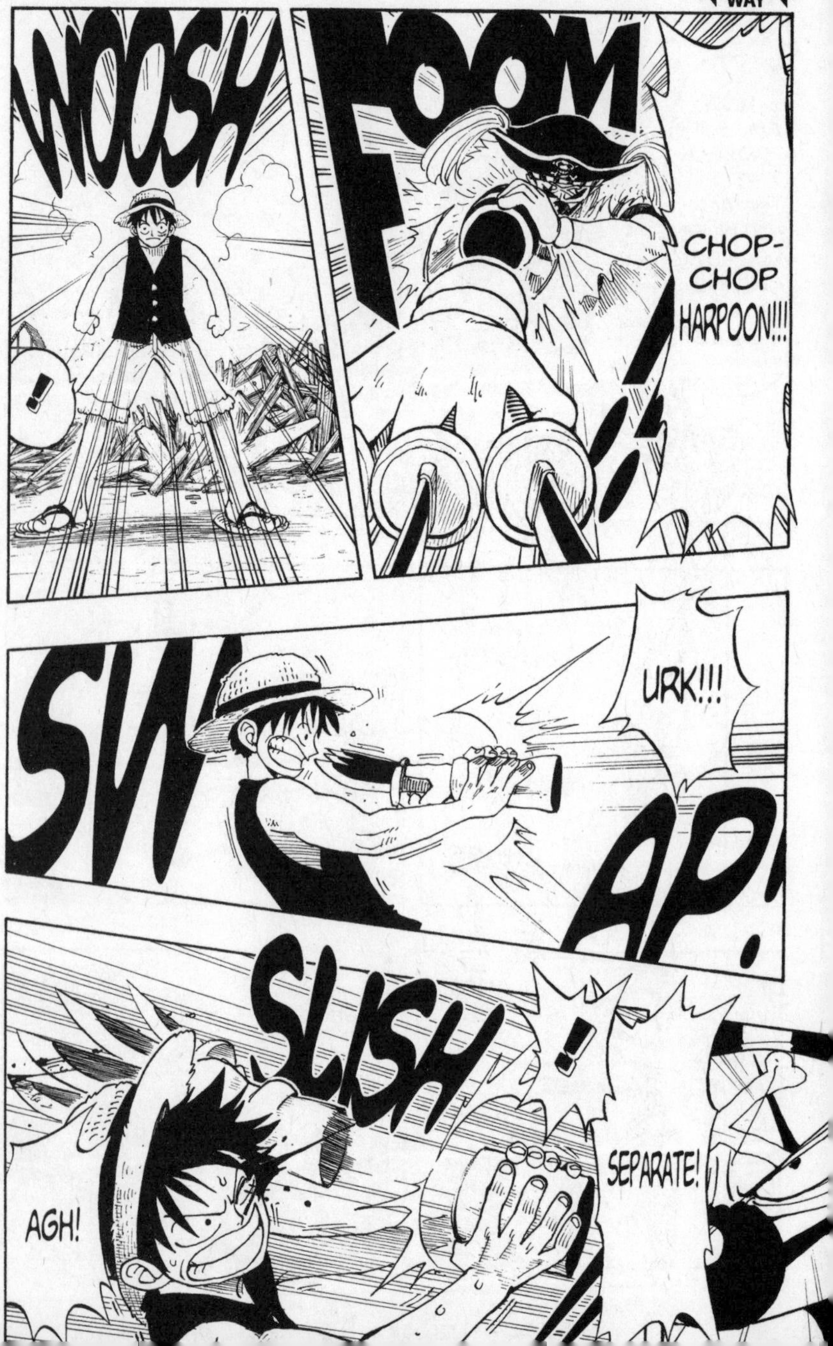
FOOM
CHOP-CHOP HARPOON!!!
WOOSH
!
URK!!!
SW
AP!
SLISH
!
SEPARATE!
AGH!

READ THIS WAY

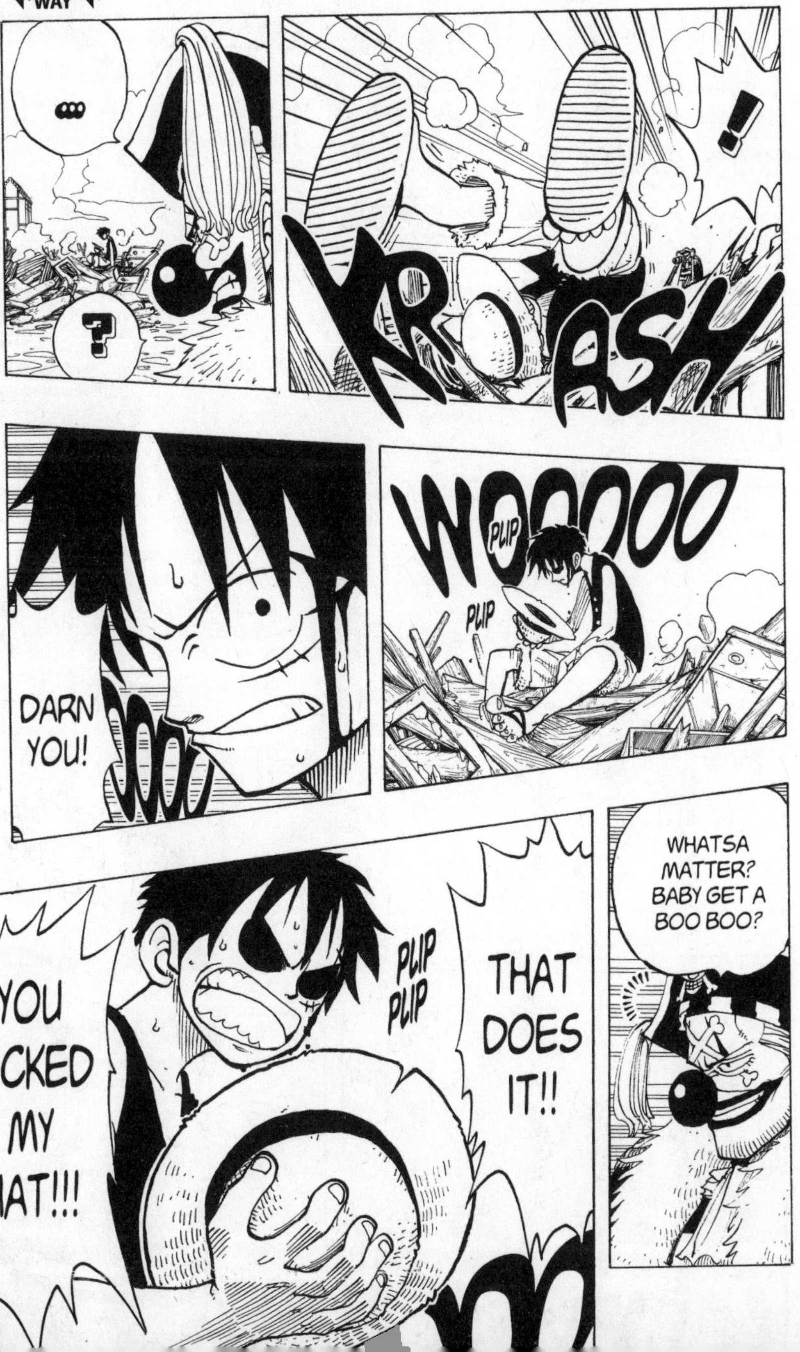
!
KRASH
...
?
WOOOOO
PLIP
PLIP
DARN YOU!
WHATSA MATTER? BABY GET A BOO BOO?
THAT DOES IT!!
PLIP PLIP
YOU NICKED MY HAT!!!

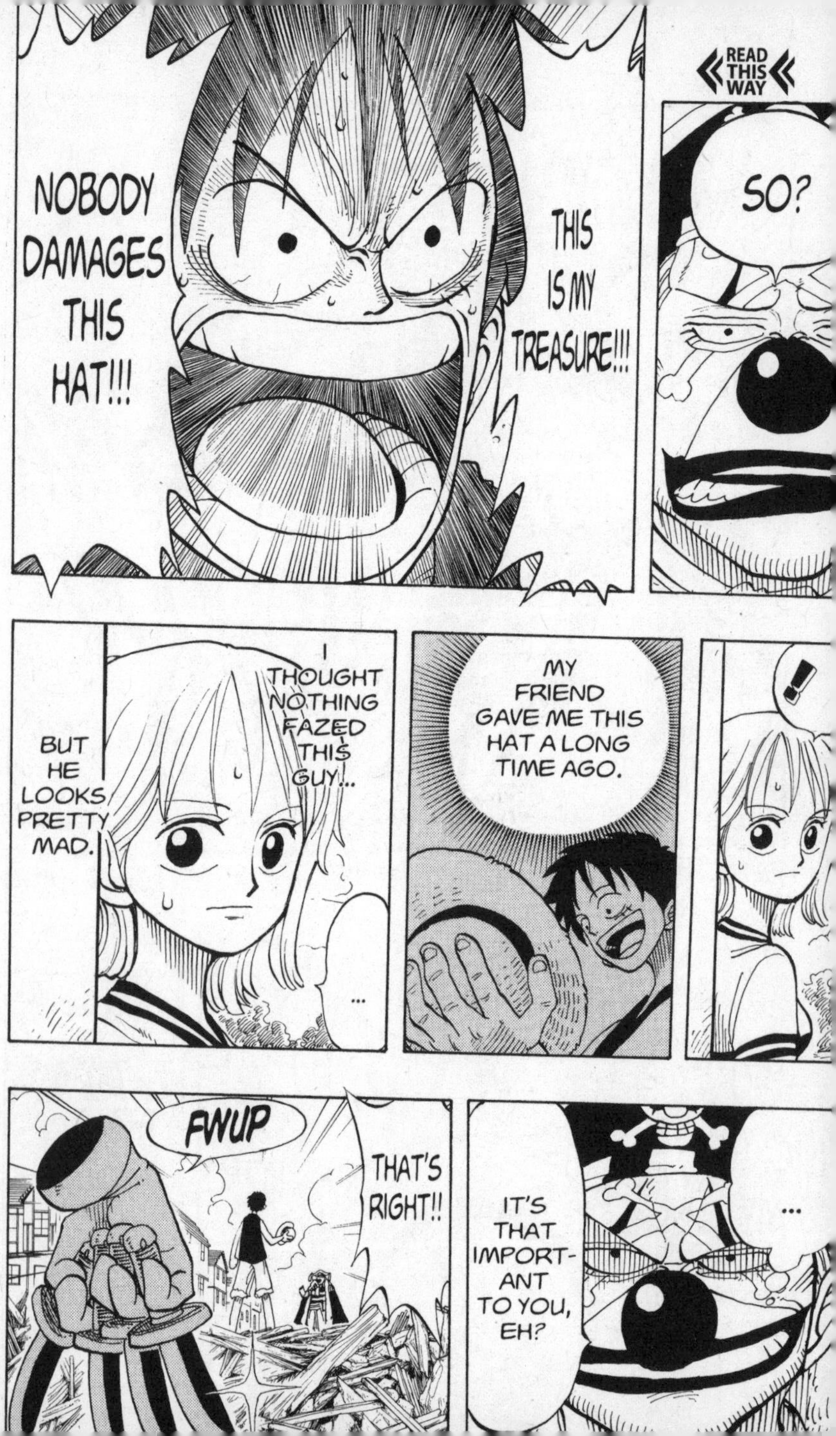
READ THIS WAY
SO?
NOBODY DAMAGES THIS HAT!!!
THIS IS MY TREASURE!!!
!
MY FRIEND GAVE ME THIS HAT A LONG TIME AGO.
I THOUGHT NOTHING FAZED THIS GUY...
BUT HE LOOKS PRETTY MAD.
...
...
IT'S THAT IMPORT-ANT TO YOU, EH?
THAT'S RIGHT!!
FWUP

READ THIS WAY

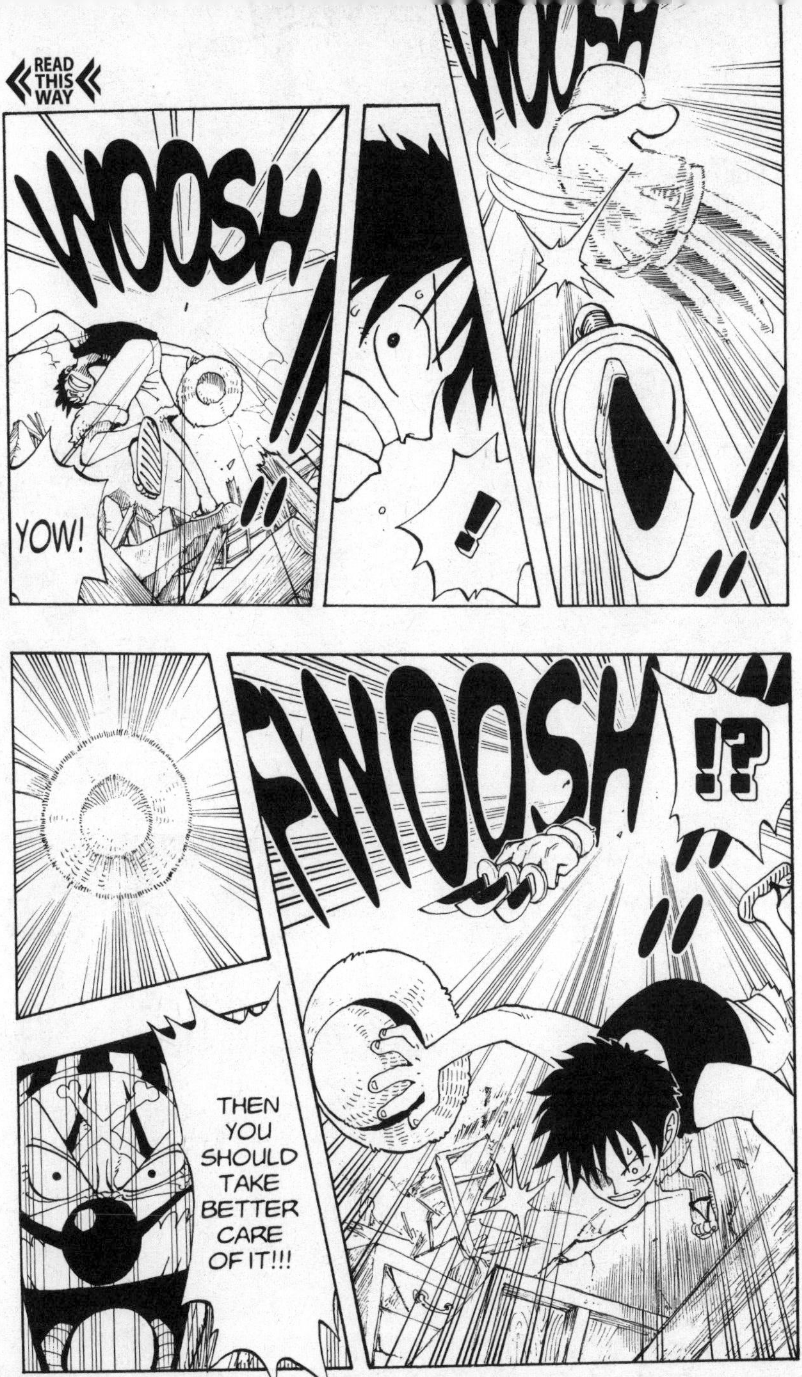
WOOSH
!
WOOSH
YOW!
FWOOSH
!?
THEN YOU SHOULD TAKE BETTER CARE OF IT!!!

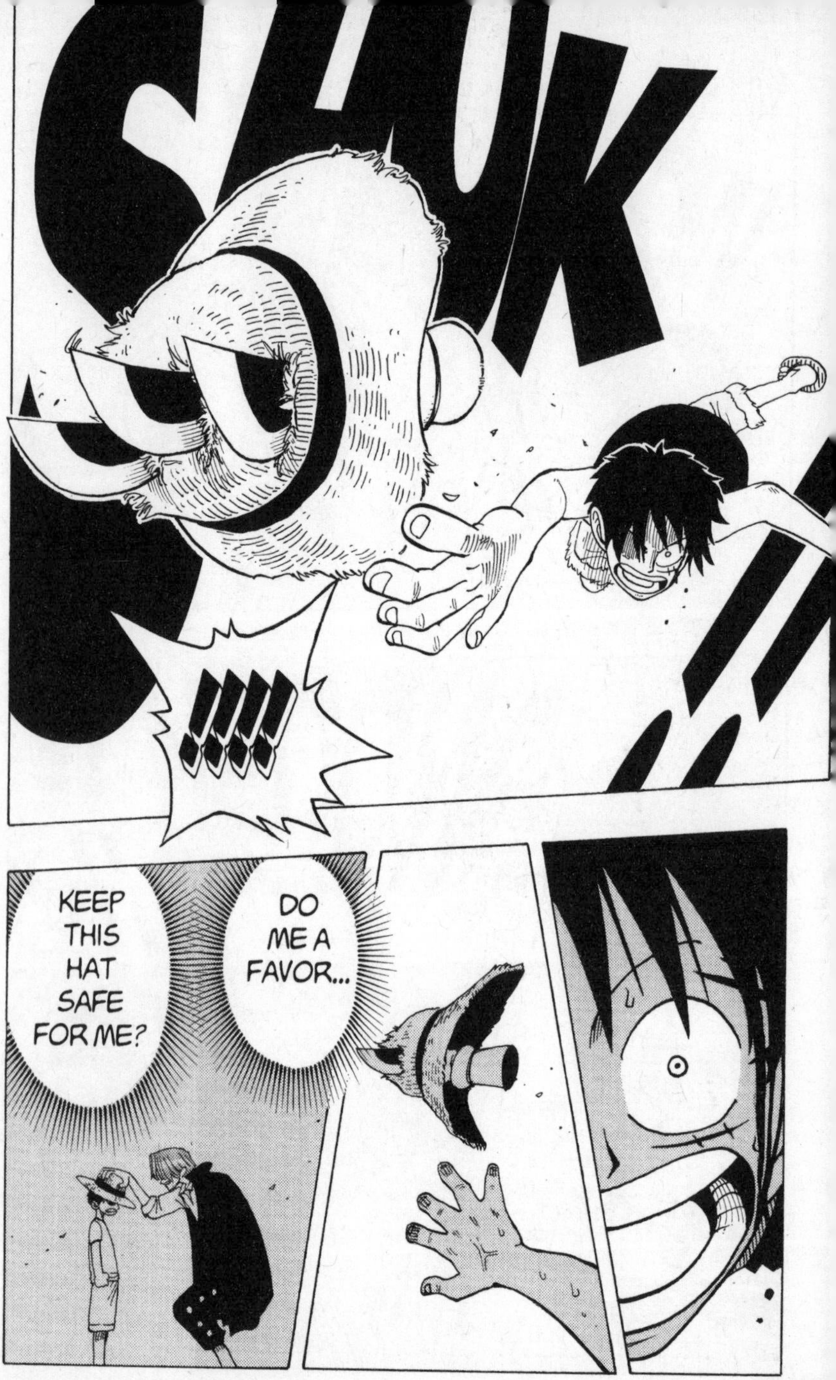
SHUK
!!!!
DO ME A FAVOR...
KEEP THIS HAT SAFE FOR ME?

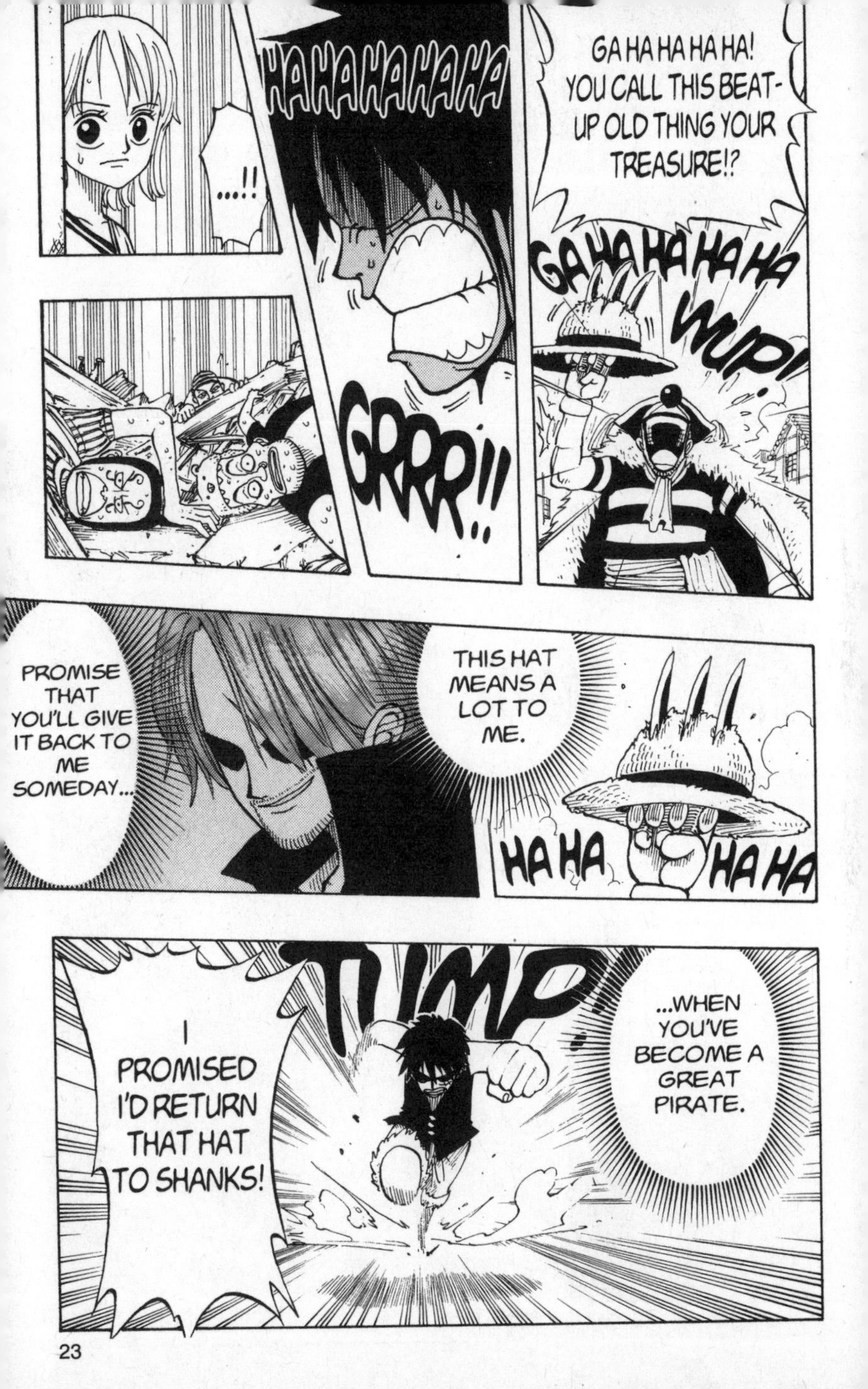

GA HA HA HA HA! YOU CALL THIS BEAT-UP OLD THING YOUR TREASURE!?
GA HA HA HA HA
WUP!
HAHAHAHAHAHA
GRRR!!
....!!
THIS HAT MEANS A LOT TO ME.
HA HA
HA HA
PROMISE THAT YOU'LL GIVE IT BACK TO ME SOMEDAY...
...WHEN YOU'VE BECOME A GREAT PIRATE.
TUMP
I PROMISED I'D RETURN THAT HAT TO SHANKS!

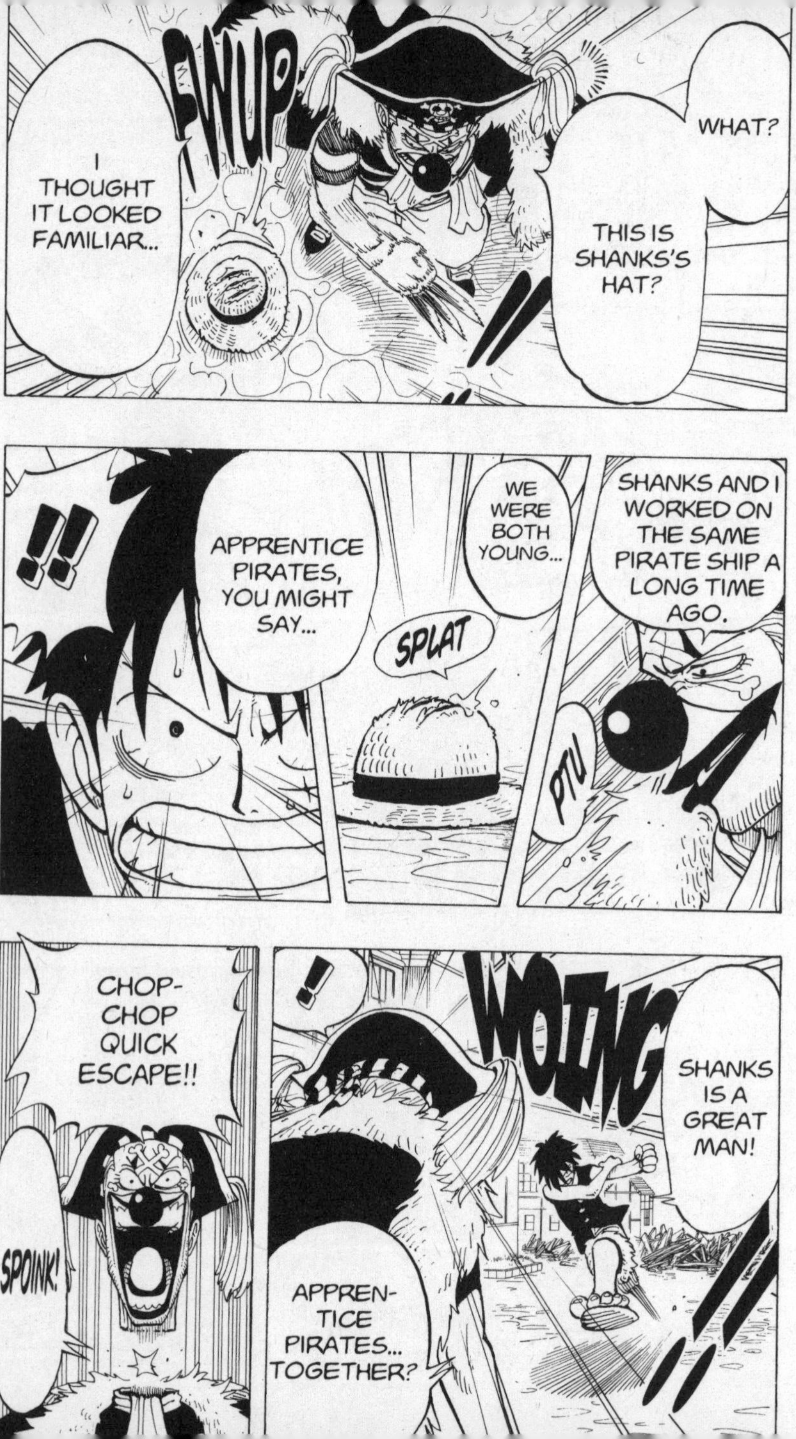
WHAT?
THIS IS SHANKS'S HAT?
FWUP
I THOUGHT IT LOOKED FAMILIAR...
SHANKS AND I WORKED ON THE SAME PIRATE SHIP A LONG TIME AGO.
PTU
WE WERE BOTH YOUNG...
SPLAT
APPRENTICE PIRATES, YOU MIGHT SAY...
!!
SHANKS IS A GREAT MAN!
WOING
!
APPREN-TICE PIRATES... TOGETHER?
CHOP-CHOP QUICK ESCAPE!!
SPOINK!

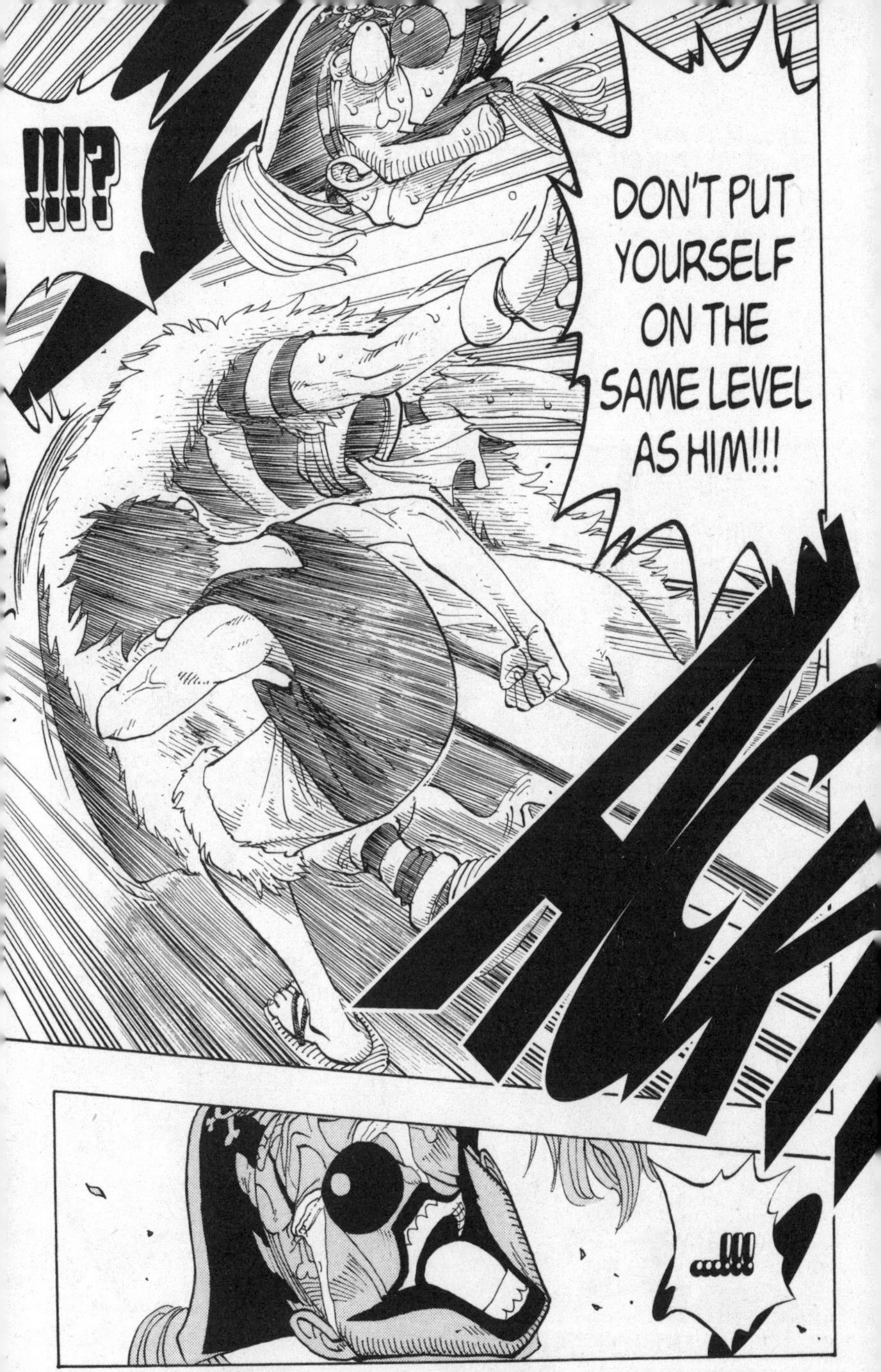
DON'T PUT YOURSELF ON THE SAME LEVEL AS HIM!!!
!!!?
...!!!

Early Sketch: Boogie the Clown!

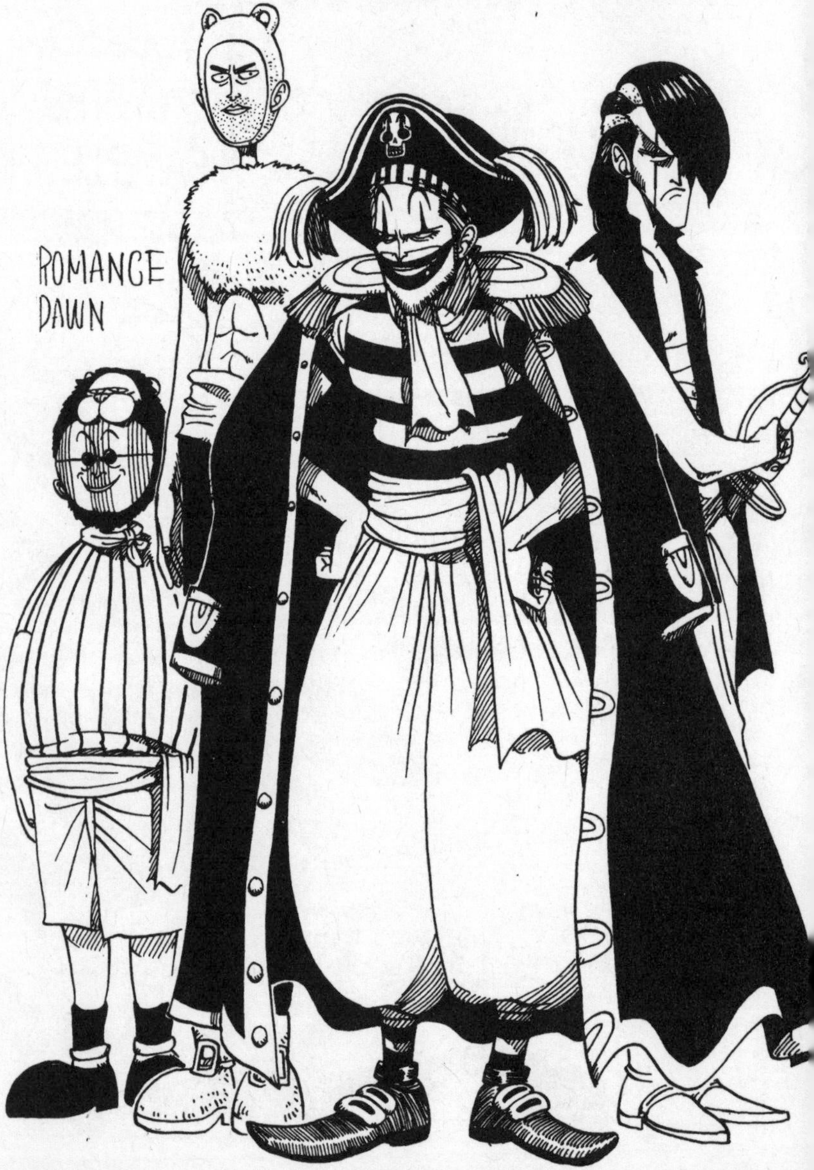
ROMANCE
DAWN

Chapter 19:

DEVIL FRUIT

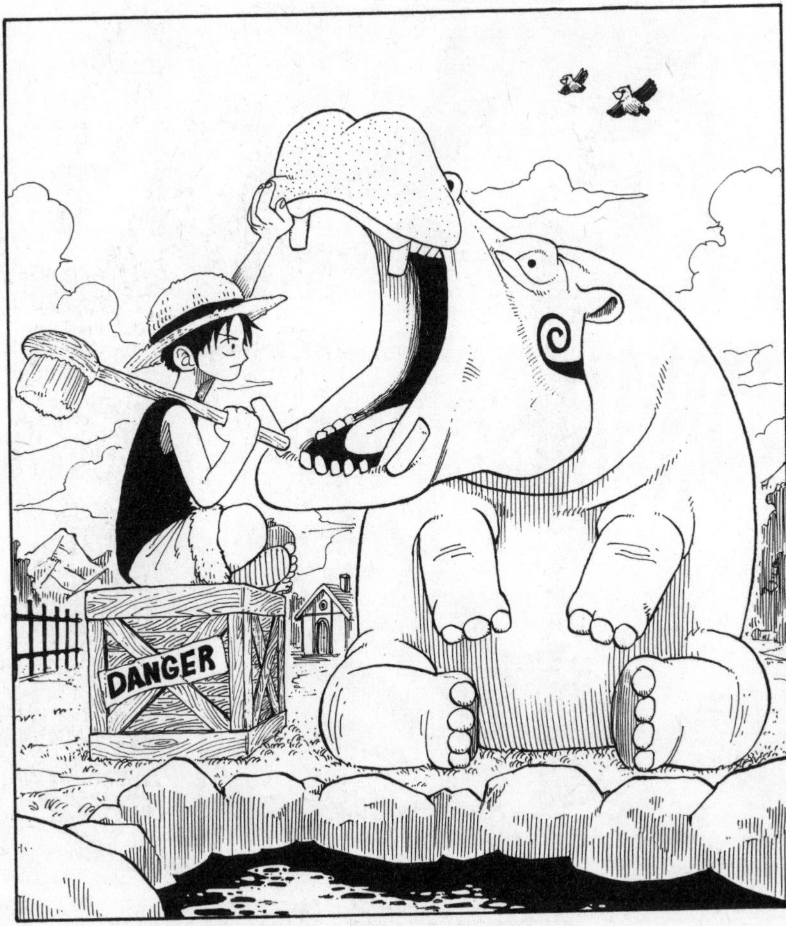
DANGER

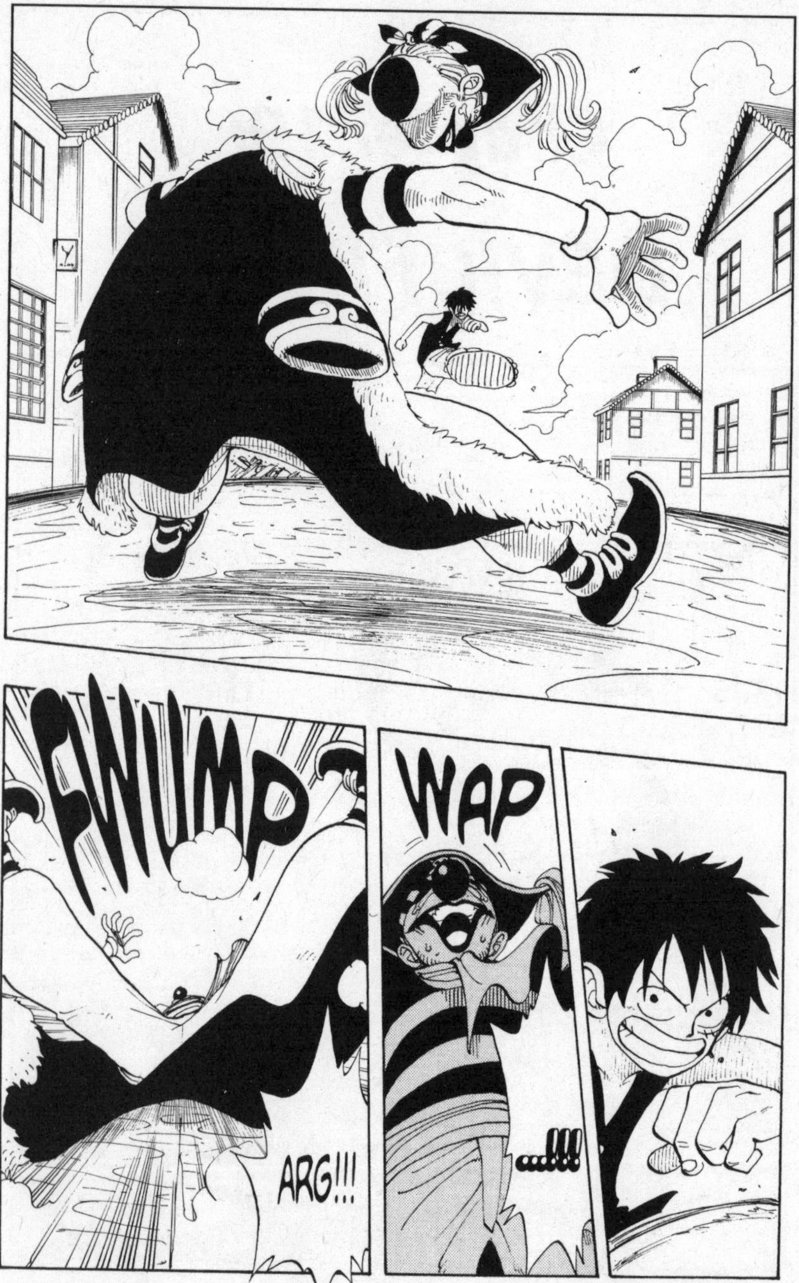
WAP
...!!!
FWUMP
ARG!!!

READ THIS WAY

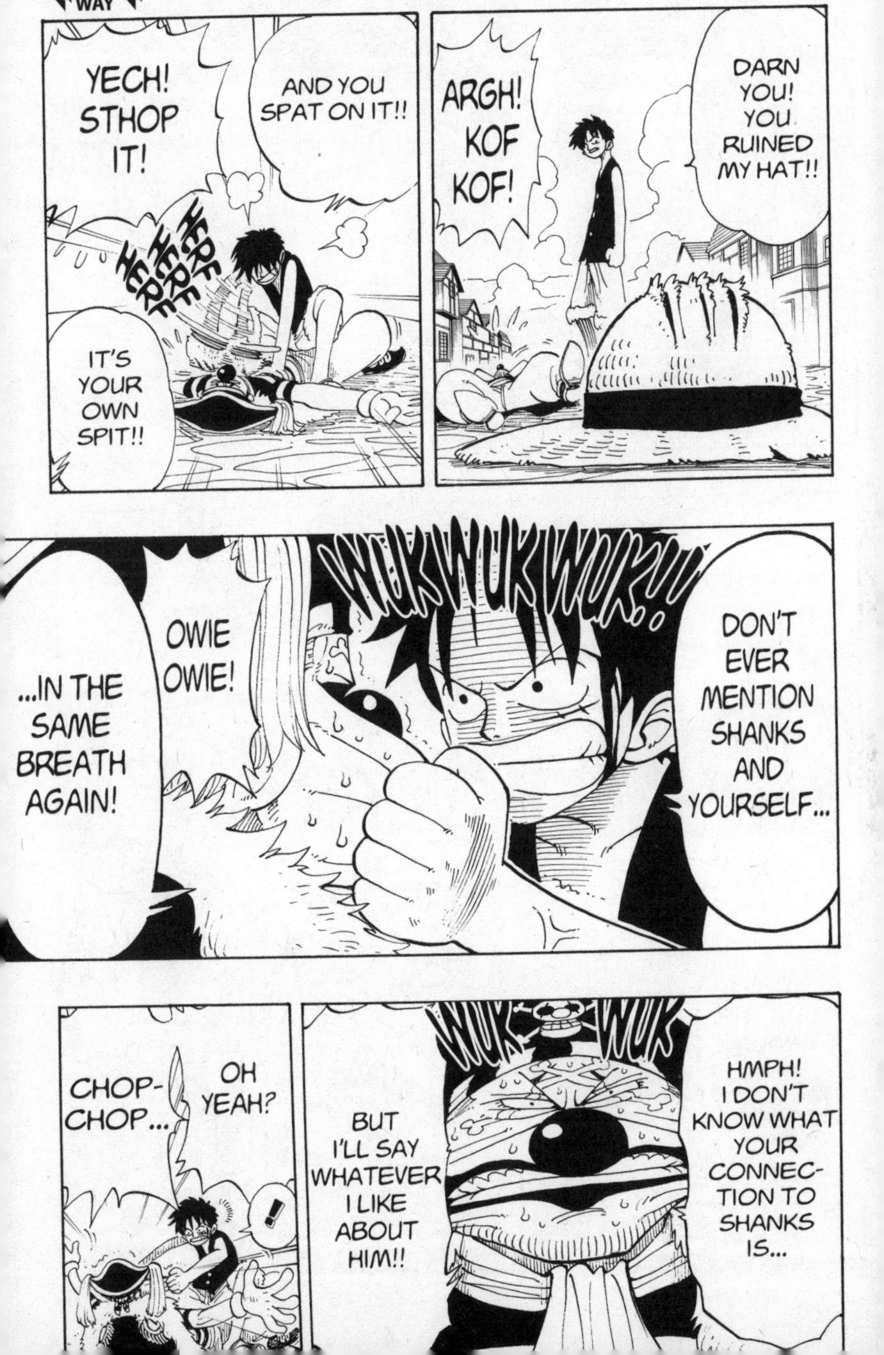
DARN YOU! YOU RUINED MY HAT!!
ARGH! KOF KOF!
AND YOU SPAT ON IT!!
YECH! STHOP IT!
HERF HERF HERF
IT'S YOUR OWN SPIT!!
WUK WUK WUK!!
DON'T EVER MENTION SHANKS AND YOURSELF...
OWIE OWIE!
...IN THE SAME BREATH AGAIN!
WUK WUK
HMPH! I DON'T KNOW WHAT YOUR CONNEC-TION TO SHANKS IS...
BUT I'LL SAY WHATEVER I LIKE ABOUT HIM!!
OH YEAH?
CHOP-CHOP...
!

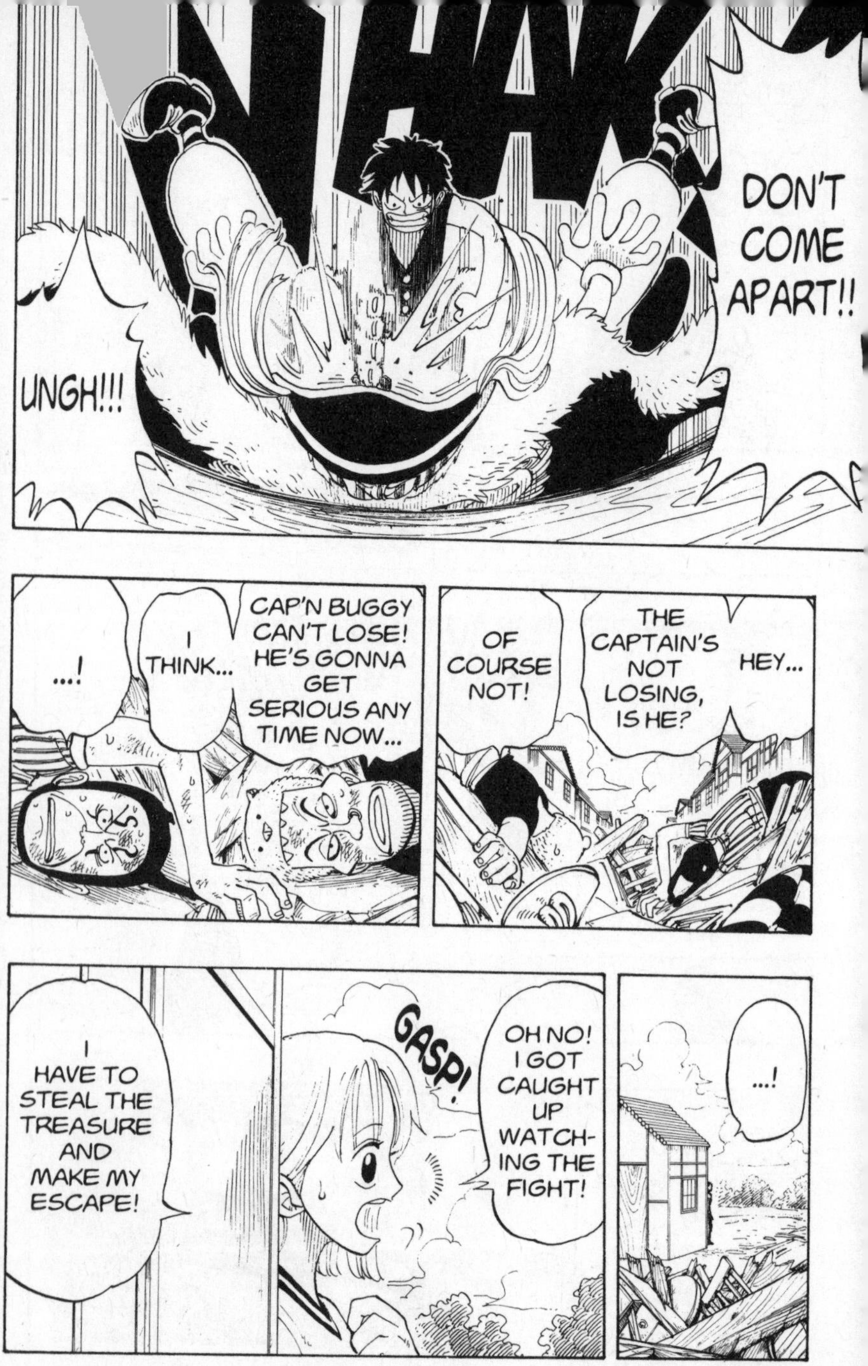
DON'T COME APART!!
UNGH!!!
HEY...
THE CAPTAIN'S NOT LOSING, IS HE?
OF COURSE NOT!
CAP'N BUGGY CAN'T LOSE! HE'S GONNA GET SERIOUS ANY TIME NOW...
I THINK...
...!
...!
OH NO! I GOT CAUGHT UP WATCH-ING THE FIGHT!
GASP!
I HAVE TO STEAL THE TREASURE AND MAKE MY ESCAPE!

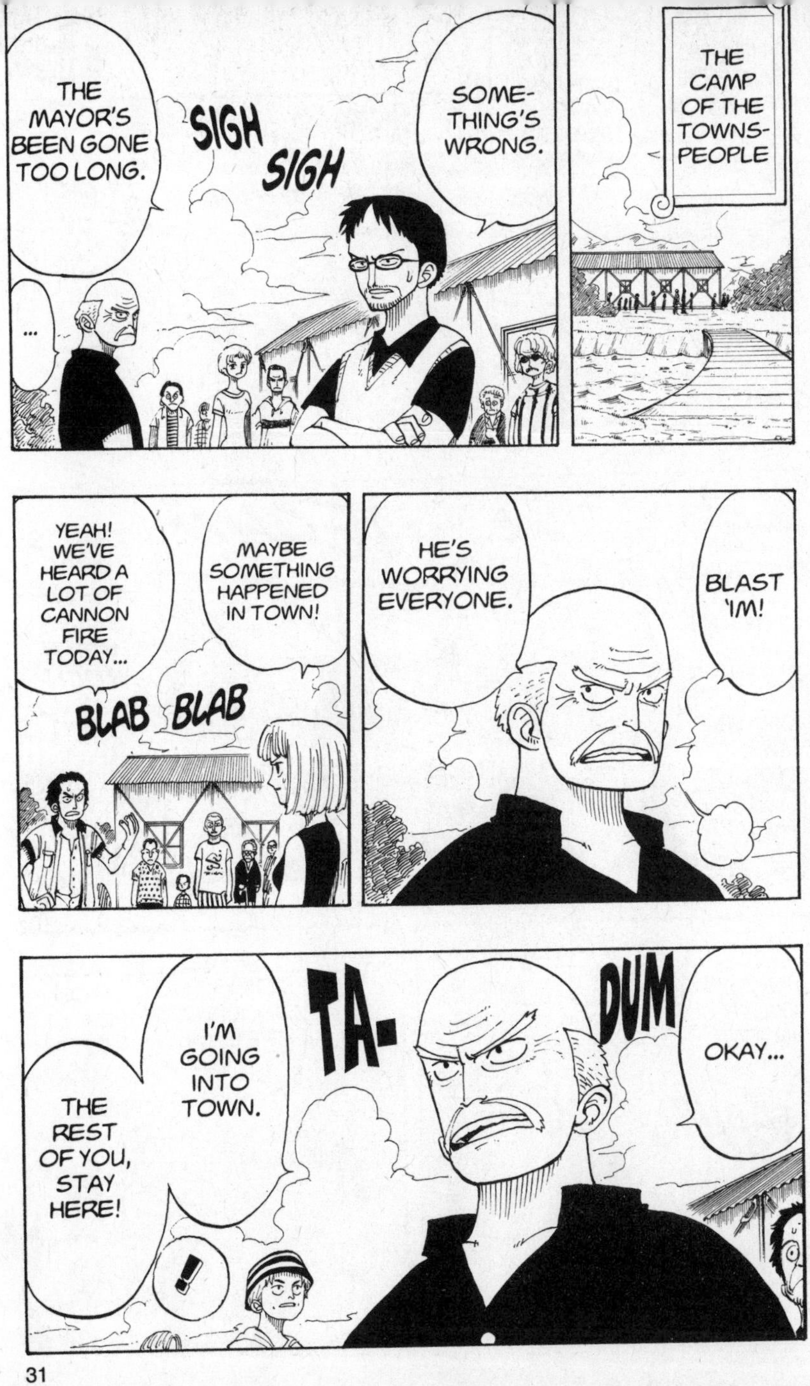
THE CAMP OF THE TOWNSPEOPLE
SOME-THING'S WRONG.
SIGH SIGH
THE MAYOR'S BEEN GONE TOO LONG.
...
BLAST 'IM!
HE'S WORRYING EVERYONE.
MAYBE SOMETHING HAPPENED IN TOWN!
YEAH! WE'VE HEARD A LOT OF CANNON FIRE TODAY...
BLAB BLAB
OKAY...
TA-DUM
I'M GOING INTO TOWN.
THE REST OF YOU, STAY HERE!
!

READ THIS WAY

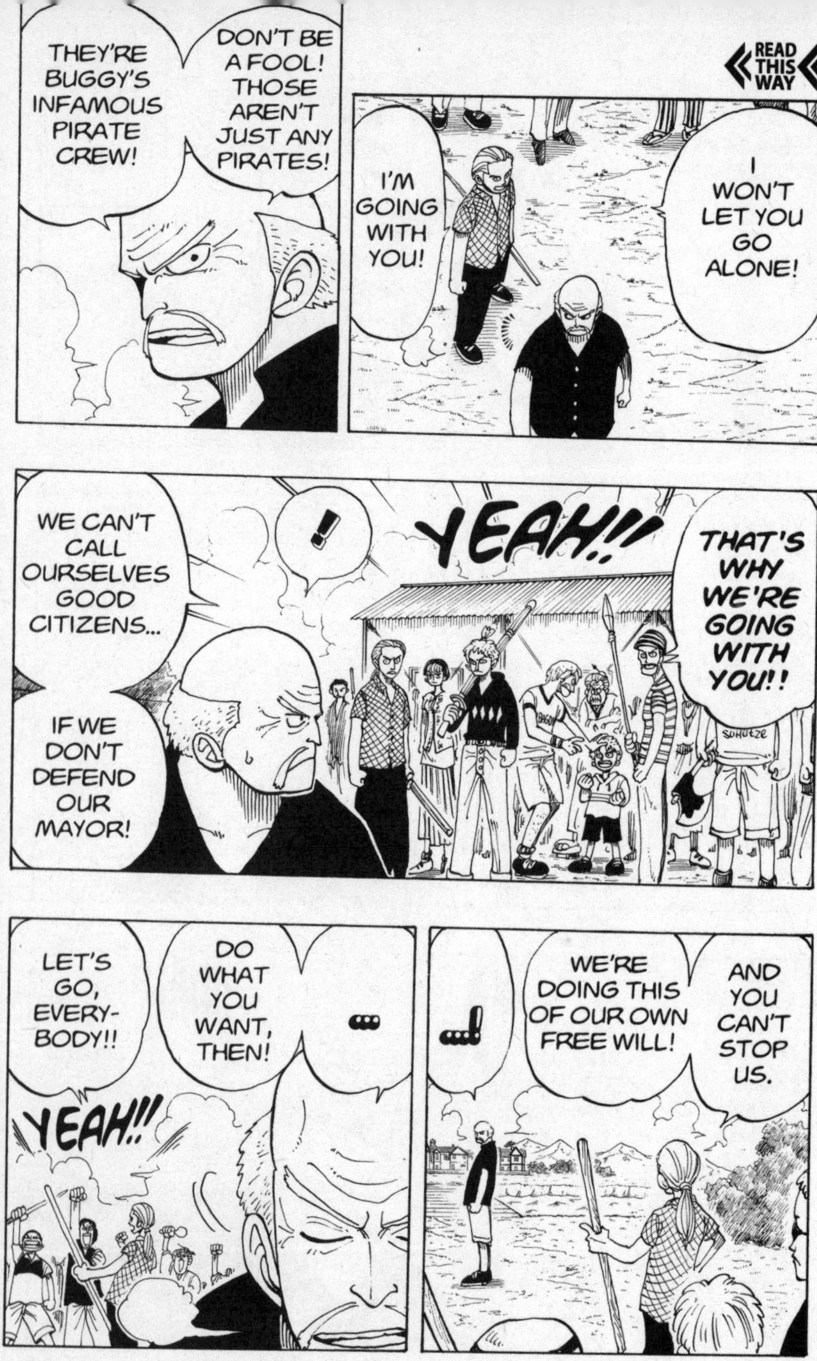
I WON'T LET YOU GO ALONE!
I'M GOING WITH YOU!
DON'T BE A FOOL! THOSE AREN'T JUST ANY PIRATES!
THEY'RE BUGGY'S INFAMOUS PIRATE CREW!
THAT'S WHY WE'RE GOING WITH YOU!!
YEAH!!
!
WE CAN'T CALL OURSELVES GOOD CITIZENS...
IF WE DON'T DEFEND OUR MAYOR!
AND YOU CAN'T STOP US.
WE'RE DOING THIS OF OUR OWN FREE WILL!
...!
...
DO WHAT YOU WANT, THEN!
LET'S GO, EVERY-BODY!!
YEAH!!

READ THIS WAY

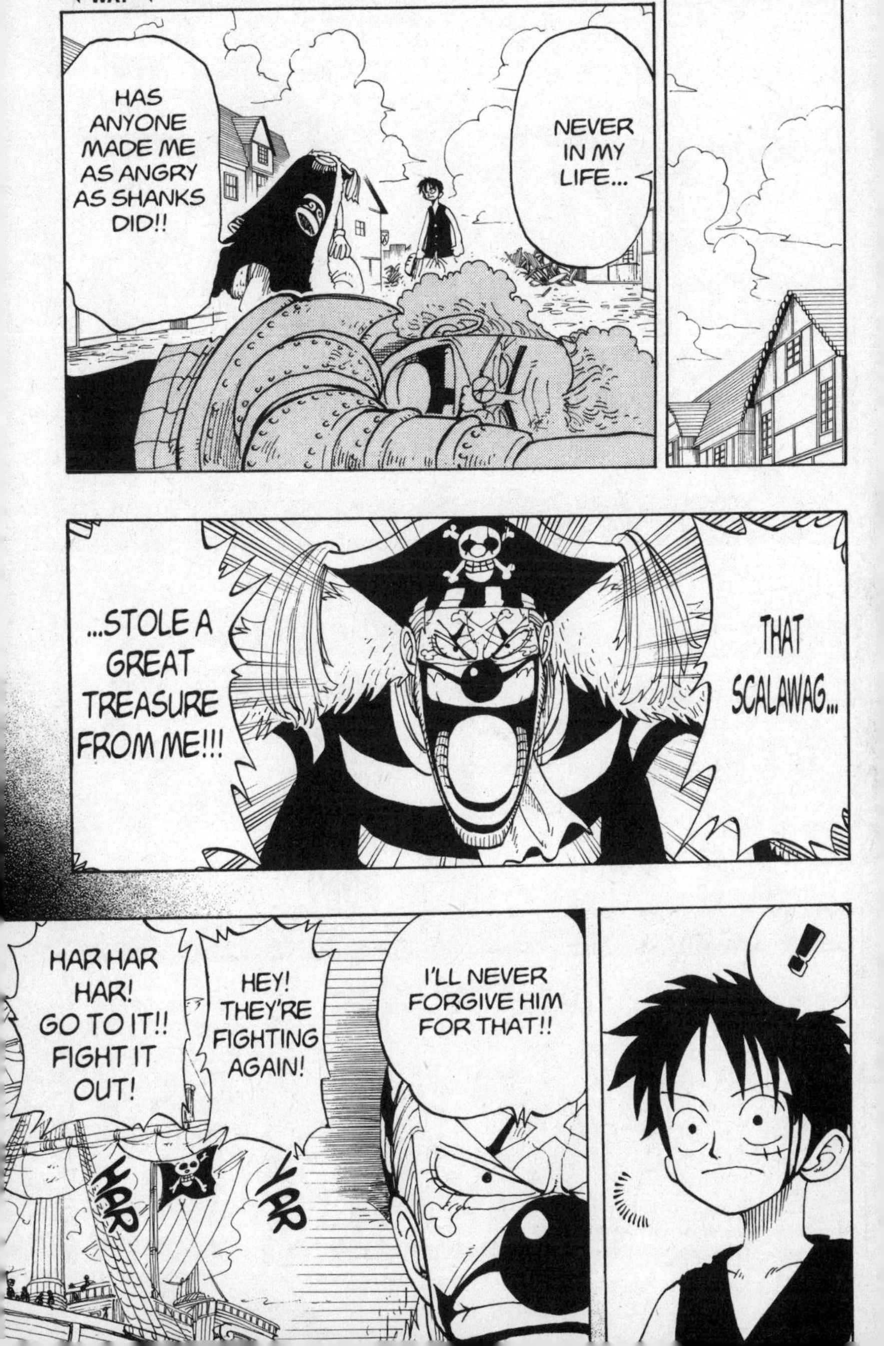
NEVER IN MY LIFE...
HAS ANYONE MADE ME AS ANGRY AS SHANKS DID!!
THAT SCALAWAG...
...STOLE A GREAT TREASURE FROM ME!!!
!
I'LL NEVER FORGIVE HIM FOR THAT!!
YAR
HEY! THEY'RE FIGHTING AGAIN!
HAR HAR HAR! GO TO IT!! FIGHT IT OUT!
HAR

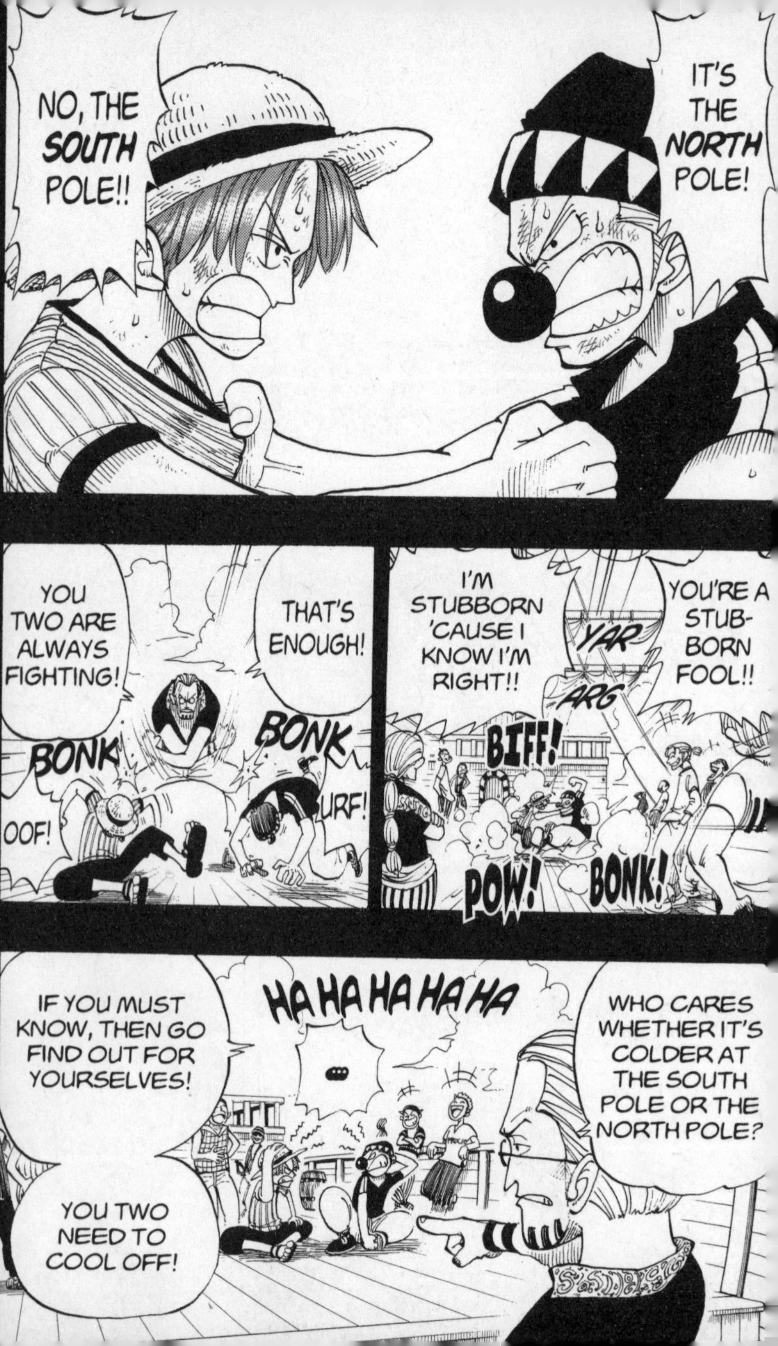
IT'S THE NORTH POLE!
NO, THE SOUTH POLE!!
YOU'RE A STUB-BORN FOOL!!
YAR
ARG
I'M STUBBORN 'CAUSE I KNOW I'M RIGHT!!
BIFF!
POW!
BONK!
THAT'S ENOUGH!
YOU TWO ARE ALWAYS FIGHTING!
BONK
BONK
URF!
OOF!
WHO CARES WHETHER IT'S COLDER AT THE SOUTH POLE OR THE NORTH POLE?
HA HA HA HA HA HA
...
IF YOU MUST KNOW, THEN GO FIND OUT FOR YOURSELVES!
YOU TWO NEED TO COOL OFF!

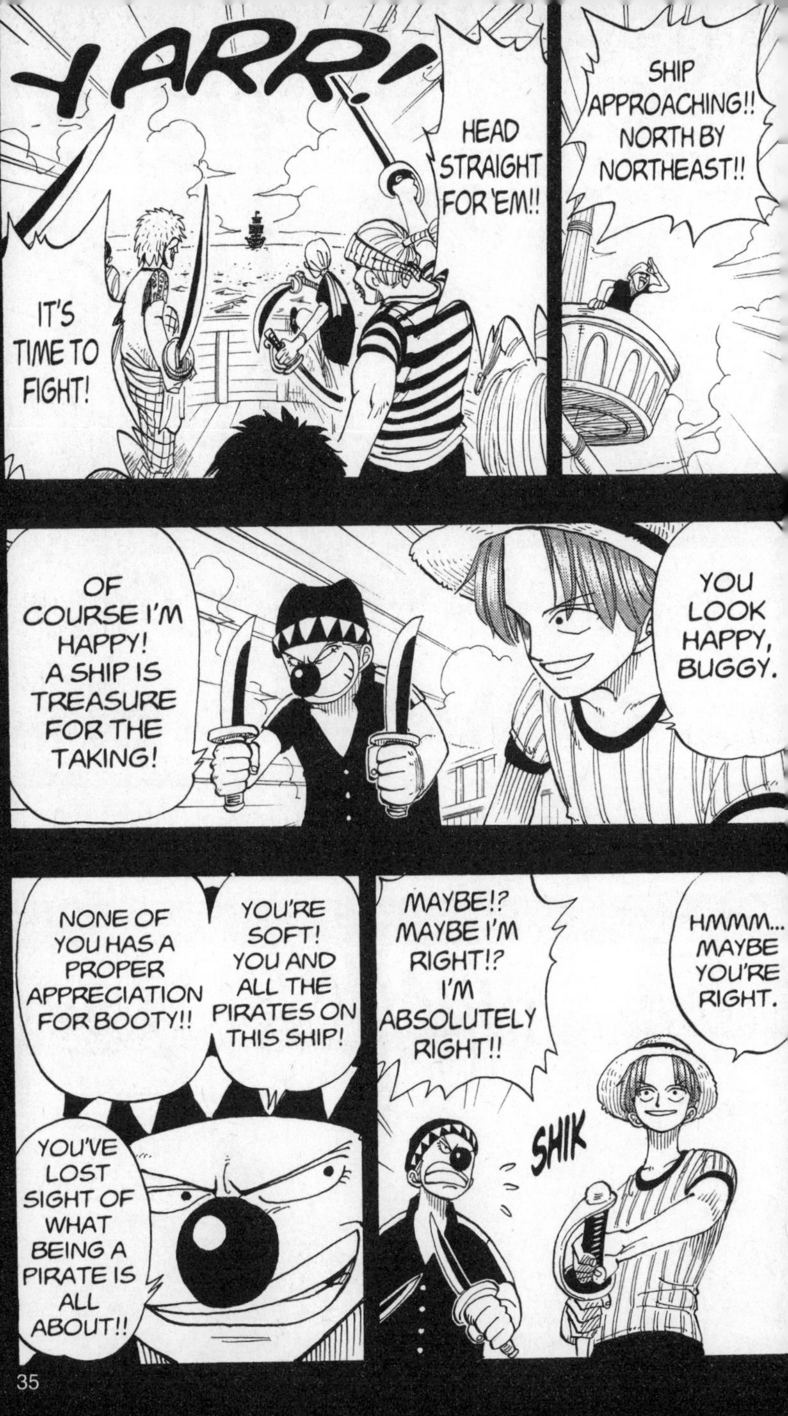
SHIP APPROACHING!! NORTH BY NORTHEAST!!
HEAD STRAIGHT FOR 'EM!!
YARR!
IT'S TIME TO FIGHT!
YOU LOOK HAPPY, BUGGY.
OF COURSE I'M HAPPY! A SHIP IS TREASURE FOR THE TAKING!
HMMM... MAYBE YOU'RE RIGHT.
MAYBE!? MAYBE I'M RIGHT!? I'M ABSOLUTELY RIGHT!!
SHIK
YOU'RE SOFT! YOU AND ALL THE PIRATES ON THIS SHIP!
NONE OF YOU HAS A PROPER APPRECIATION FOR BOOTY!!
YOU'VE LOST SIGHT OF WHAT BEING A PIRATE IS ALL ABOUT!!

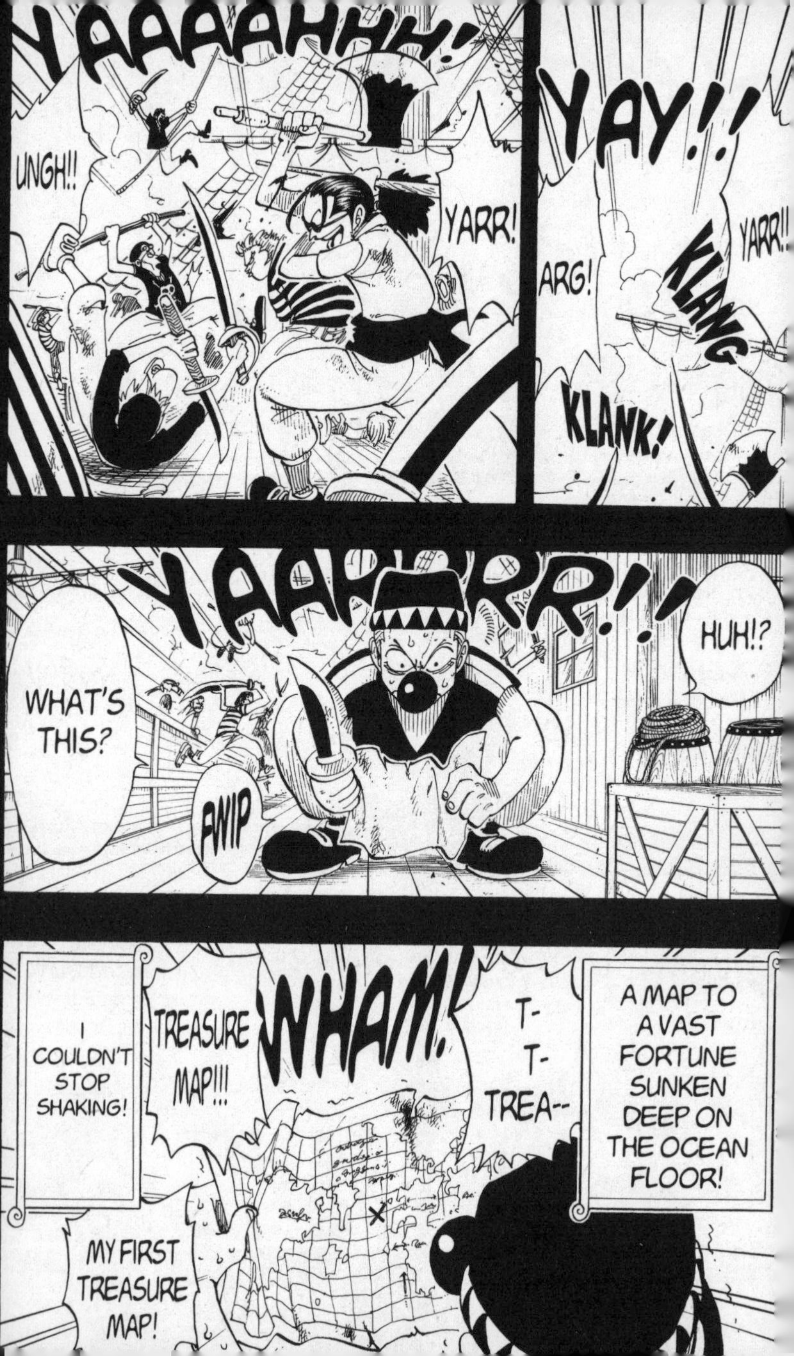
YAY!!
YARR!!
KLANG
ARG!
KLANK!
YAAAAHHH!
YARR!
UNGH!!
YAA RR!!
HUH!?
WHAT'S THIS?
FWIP
A MAP TO A VAST FORTUNE SUNKEN DEEP ON THE OCEAN FLOOR!
T- T- TREA--
WHAM!
TREASURE MAP!!!
I COULDN'T STOP SHAKING!
MY FIRST TREASURE MAP!

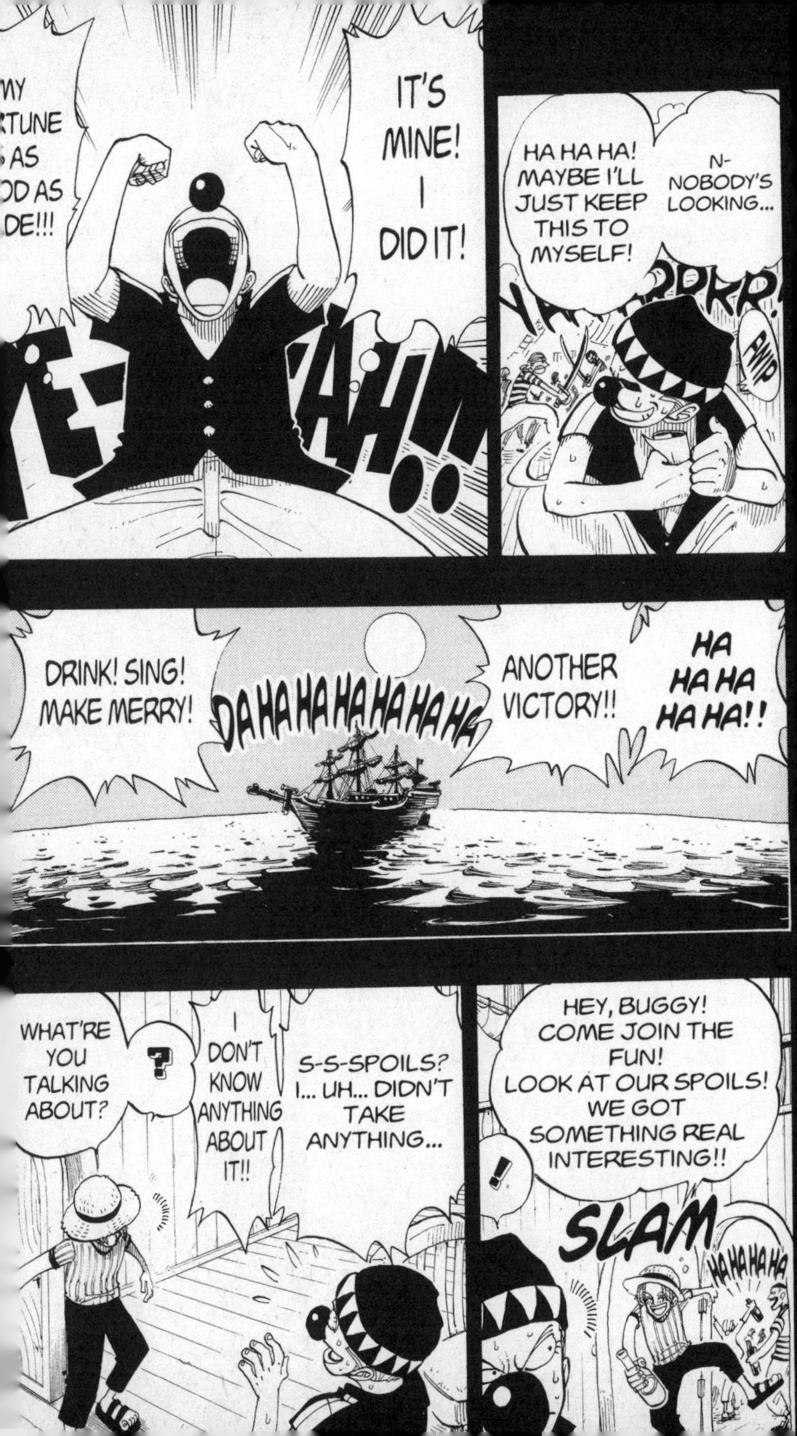
N- NOBODY'S LOOKING...
HA HA HA! MAYBE I'LL JUST KEEP THIS TO MYSELF!
AWP
IT'S MINE! I DID IT!
HA HA HA HA HA!!
ANOTHER VICTORY!!
DA HA HA HA HA HA HA HA
DRINK! SING! MAKE MERRY!
HEY, BUGGY! COME JOIN THE FUN! LOOK AT OUR SPOILS! WE GOT SOMETHING REAL INTERESTING!!
!
SLAM
HA HA HA HA
S-S-SPOILS? I... UH... DIDN'T TAKE ANYTHING...
I DON'T KNOW ANYTHING ABOUT IT!!
?
WHAT'RE YOU TALKING ABOUT?

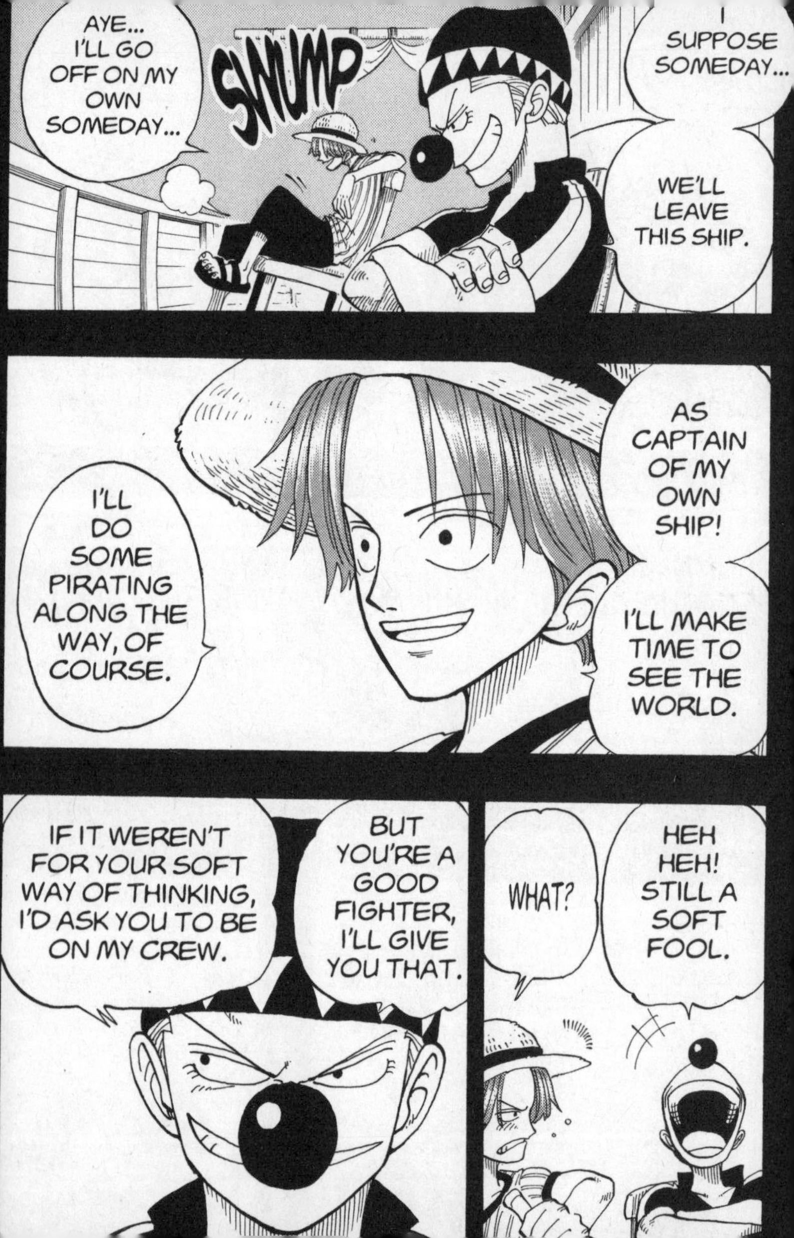
I SUPPOSE SOMEDAY...
WE'LL LEAVE THIS SHIP.
SHUMP
AYE... I'LL GO OFF ON MY OWN SOMEDAY...
AS CAPTAIN OF MY OWN SHIP!
I'LL MAKE TIME TO SEE THE WORLD.
I'LL DO SOME PIRATING ALONG THE WAY, OF COURSE.
HEH HEH! STILL A SOFT FOOL.
WHAT?
BUT YOU'RE A GOOD FIGHTER, I'LL GIVE YOU THAT.
IF IT WEREN'T FOR YOUR SOFT WAY OF THINKING, I'D ASK YOU TO BE ON MY CREW.

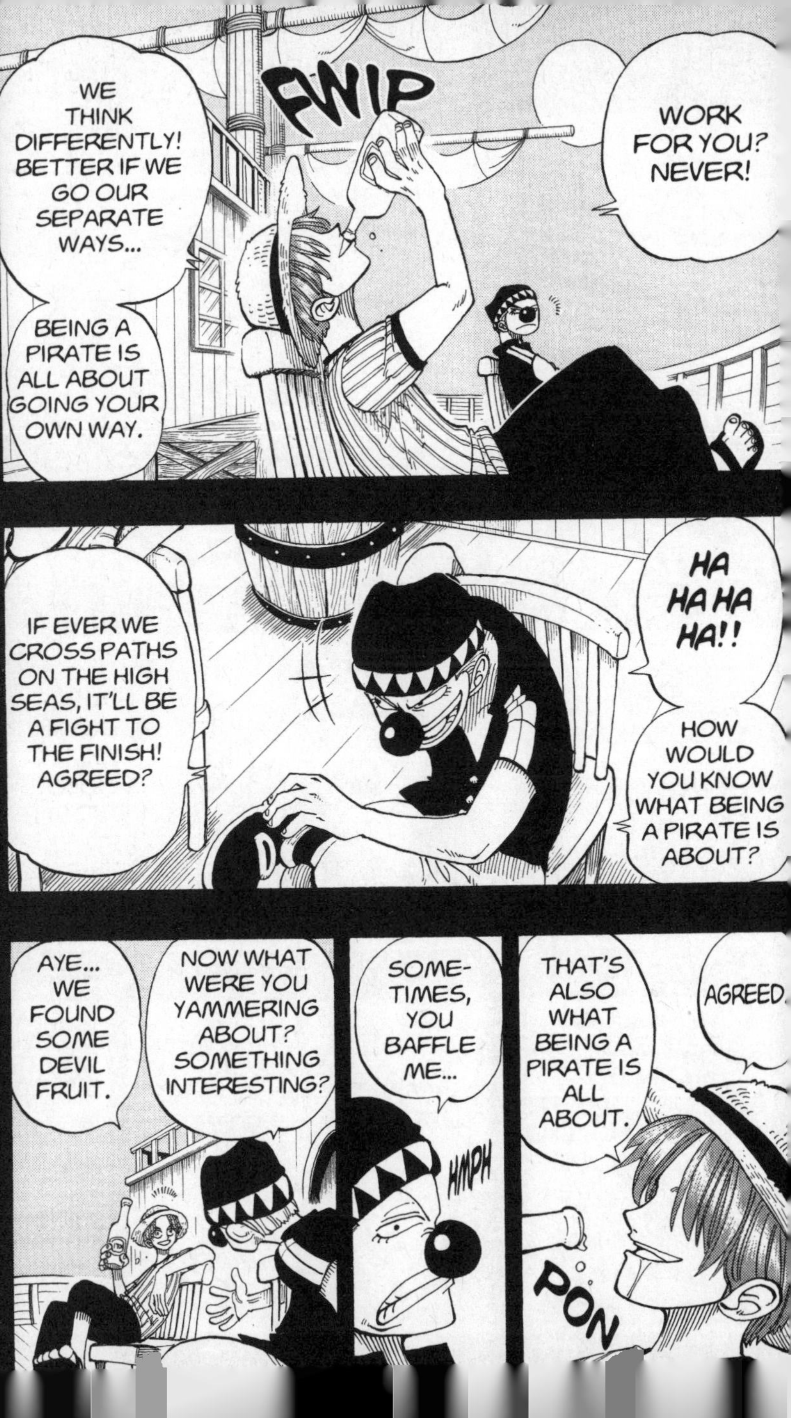
WORK FOR YOU? NEVER!
FWIP
WE THINK DIFFERENTLY! BETTER IF WE GO OUR SEPARATE WAYS...
BEING A PIRATE IS ALL ABOUT GOING YOUR OWN WAY.
HA HA HA HA!!
HOW WOULD YOU KNOW WHAT BEING A PIRATE IS ABOUT?
IF EVER WE CROSS PATHS ON THE HIGH SEAS, IT'LL BE A FIGHT TO THE FINISH! AGREED?
AGREED.
THAT'S ALSO WHAT BEING A PIRATE IS ALL ABOUT.
PON
SOME-TIMES, YOU BAFFLE ME...
HMPH
NOW WHAT WERE YOU YAMMERING ABOUT? SOMETHING INTERESTING?
AYE... WE FOUND SOME DEVIL FRUIT.

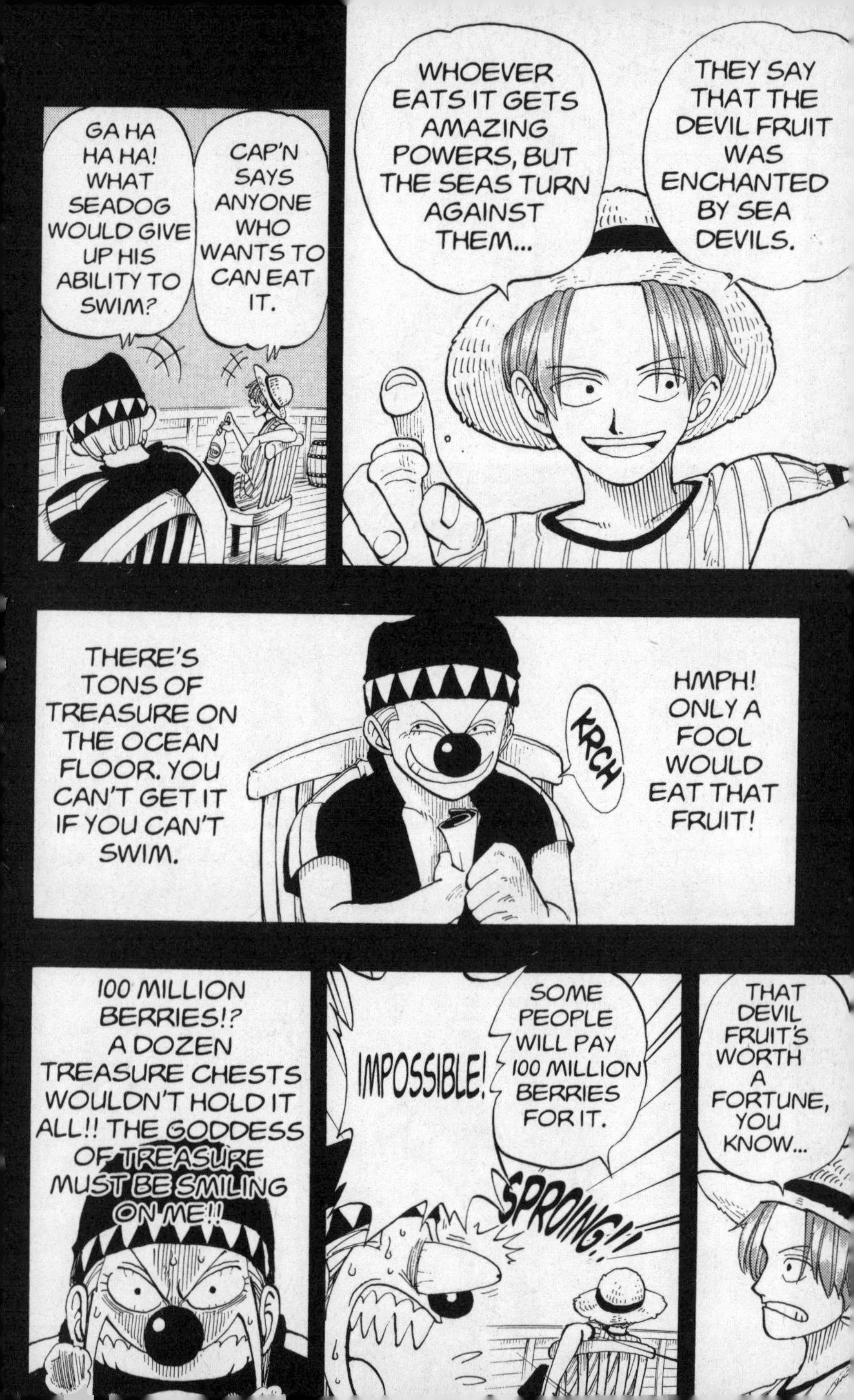
THEY SAY THAT THE DEVIL FRUIT WAS ENCHANTED BY SEA DEVILS.
WHOEVER EATS IT GETS AMAZING POWERS, BUT THE SEAS TURN AGAINST THEM...
CAP'N SAYS ANYONE WHO WANTS TO CAN EAT IT.
GA HA HA HA! WHAT SEADOG WOULD GIVE UP HIS ABILITY TO SWIM?
HMPH! ONLY A FOOL WOULD EAT THAT FRUIT!
KRCH
THERE'S TONS OF TREASURE ON THE OCEAN FLOOR. YOU CAN'T GET IT IF YOU CAN'T SWIM.
THAT DEVIL FRUIT'S WORTH A FORTUNE, YOU KNOW...
SOME PEOPLE WILL PAY 100 MILLION BERRIES FOR IT.
IMPOSSIBLE!
SPROING!!
100 MILLION BERRIES!? A DOZEN TREASURE CHESTS WOULDN'T HOLD IT ALL!! THE GODDESS OF TREASURE MUST BE SMILING ON ME!!

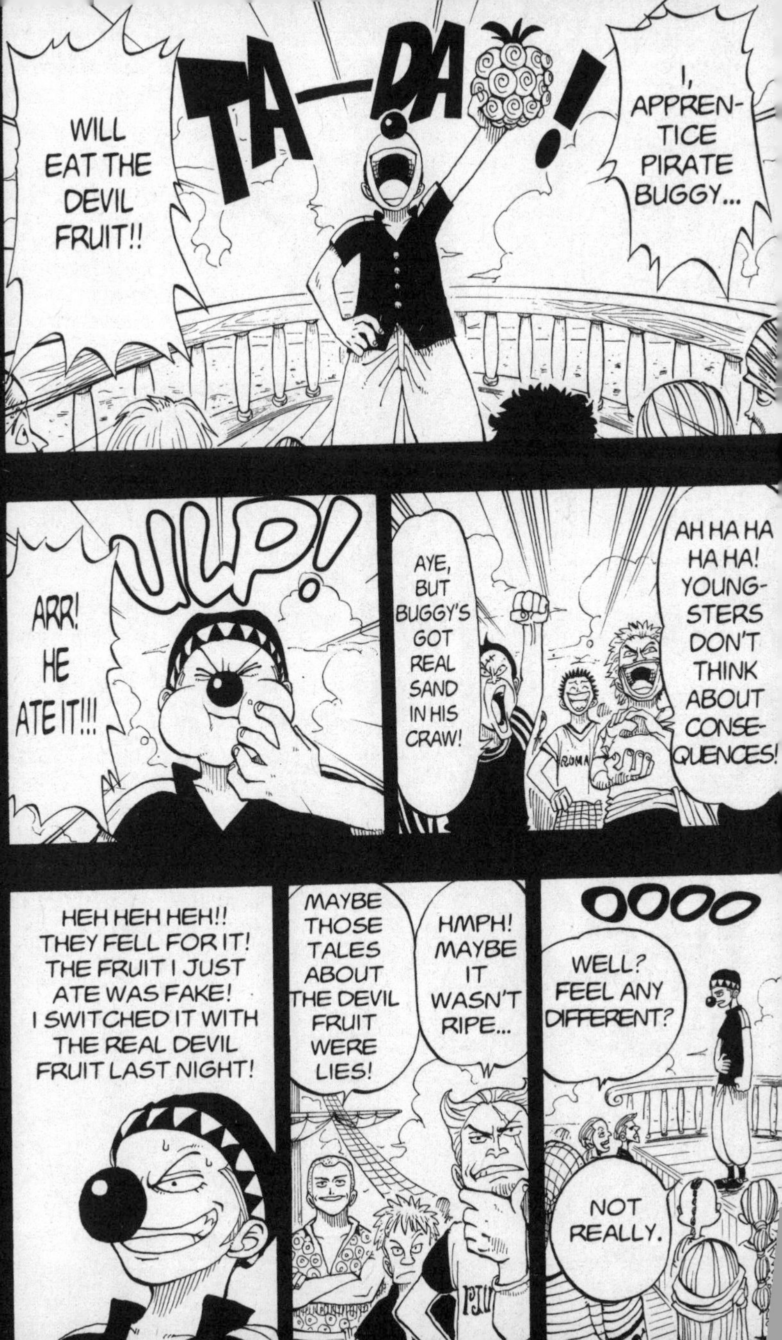
I, APPRENTICE PIRATE BUGGY...
TA-DA!
WILL EAT THE DEVIL FRUIT!!
AH HA HA HA HA! YOUNGSTERS DON'T THINK ABOUT CONSEQUENCES!
AYE, BUT BUGGY'S GOT REAL SAND IN HIS CRAW!
ULP!
ARR! HE ATE IT!!!
OOOO
WELL? FEEL ANY DIFFERENT?
NOT REALLY.
HMPH! MAYBE IT WASN'T RIPE...
MAYBE THOSE TALES ABOUT THE DEVIL FRUIT WERE LIES!
HEH HEH HEH!! THEY FELL FOR IT! THE FRUIT I JUST ATE WAS FAKE! I SWITCHED IT WITH THE REAL DEVIL FRUIT LAST NIGHT!

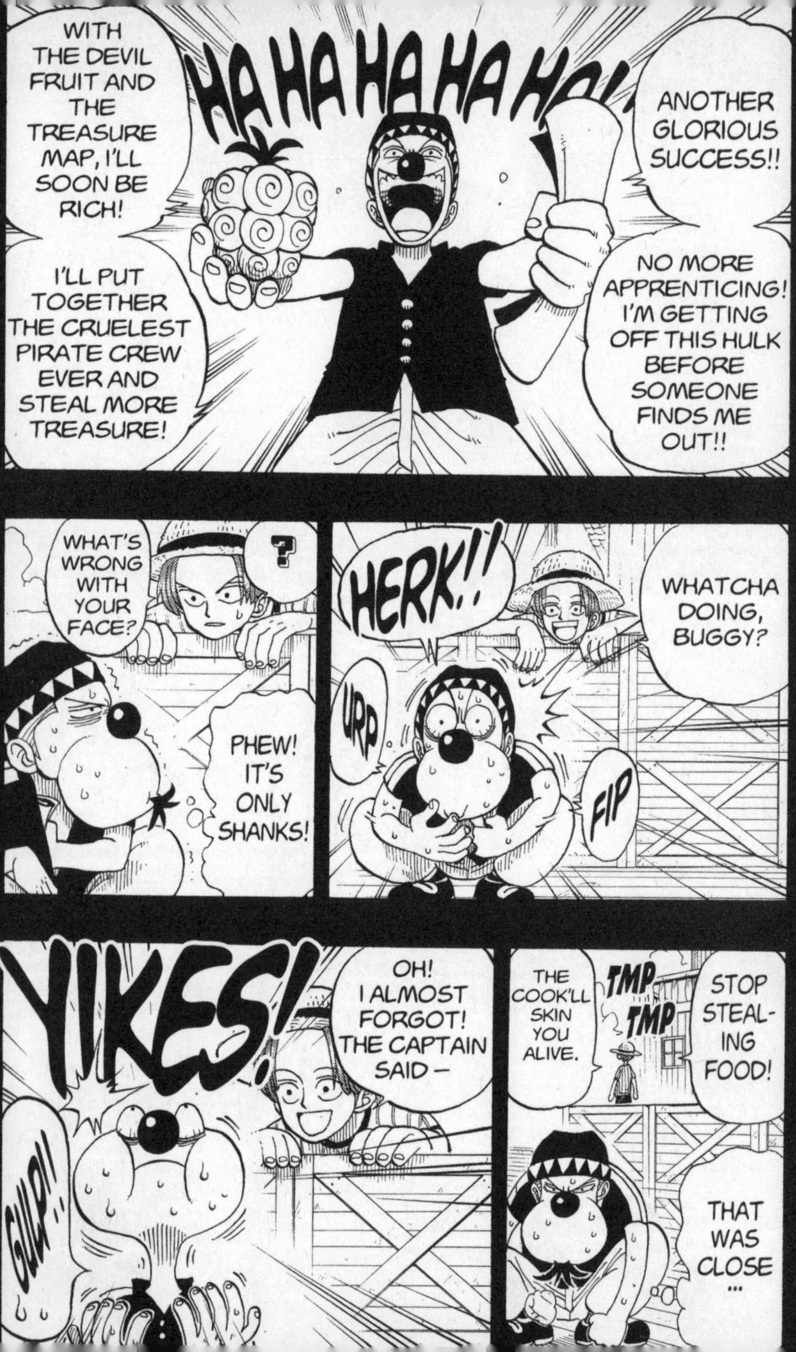
ANOTHER GLORIOUS SUCCESS!!
HA HA HA HA HA HA!!
NO MORE APPRENTICING! I'M GETTING OFF THIS HULK BEFORE SOMEONE FINDS ME OUT!!
WITH THE DEVIL FRUIT AND THE TREASURE MAP, I'LL SOON BE RICH!
I'LL PUT TOGETHER THE CRUELEST PIRATE CREW EVER AND STEAL MORE TREASURE!
WHATCHA DOING, BUGGY?
HERK!!
FIP
URP
?
WHAT'S WRONG WITH YOUR FACE?
PHEW! IT'S ONLY SHANKS!
STOP STEAL-ING FOOD!
TMP TMP
THE COOK'LL SKIN YOU ALIVE.
THAT WAS CLOSE...
OH! I ALMOST FORGOT! THE CAPTAIN SAID –
YIKES!
GULP!!

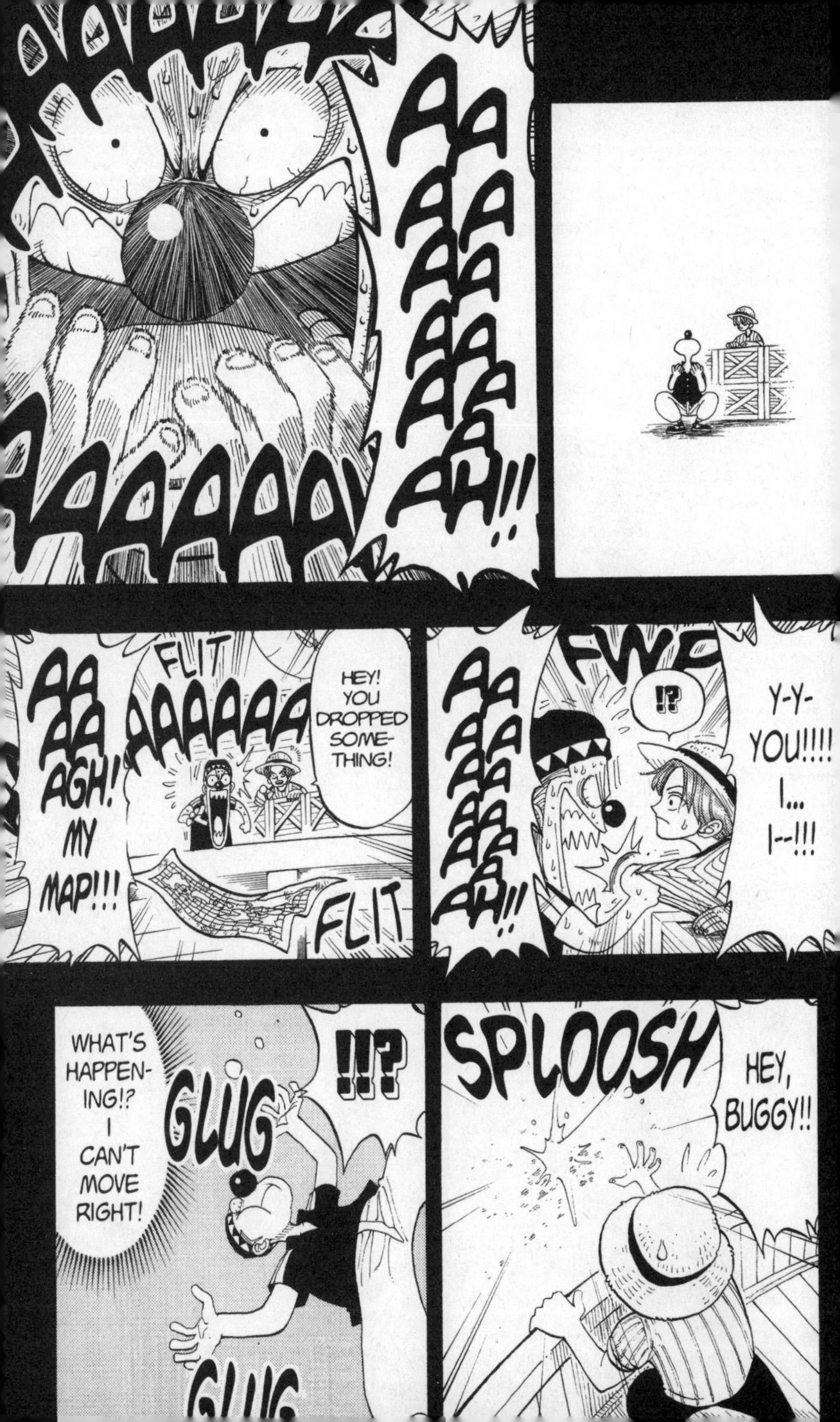
AAAAAAAAAAAAAAAAAAAH!!
AAAAAA
Y-Y-YOU!!!! I... I--!!!
!?
AAAAAAAAAAAAH!!
HEY! YOU DROPPED SOME-THING!
FLIT
AAAAAAAAAAGH! MY MAP!!!
FLIT
HEY, BUGGY!!
SPLOOSH
!!?
GLUG
WHAT'S HAPPEN-ING!? I CAN'T MOVE RIGHT!

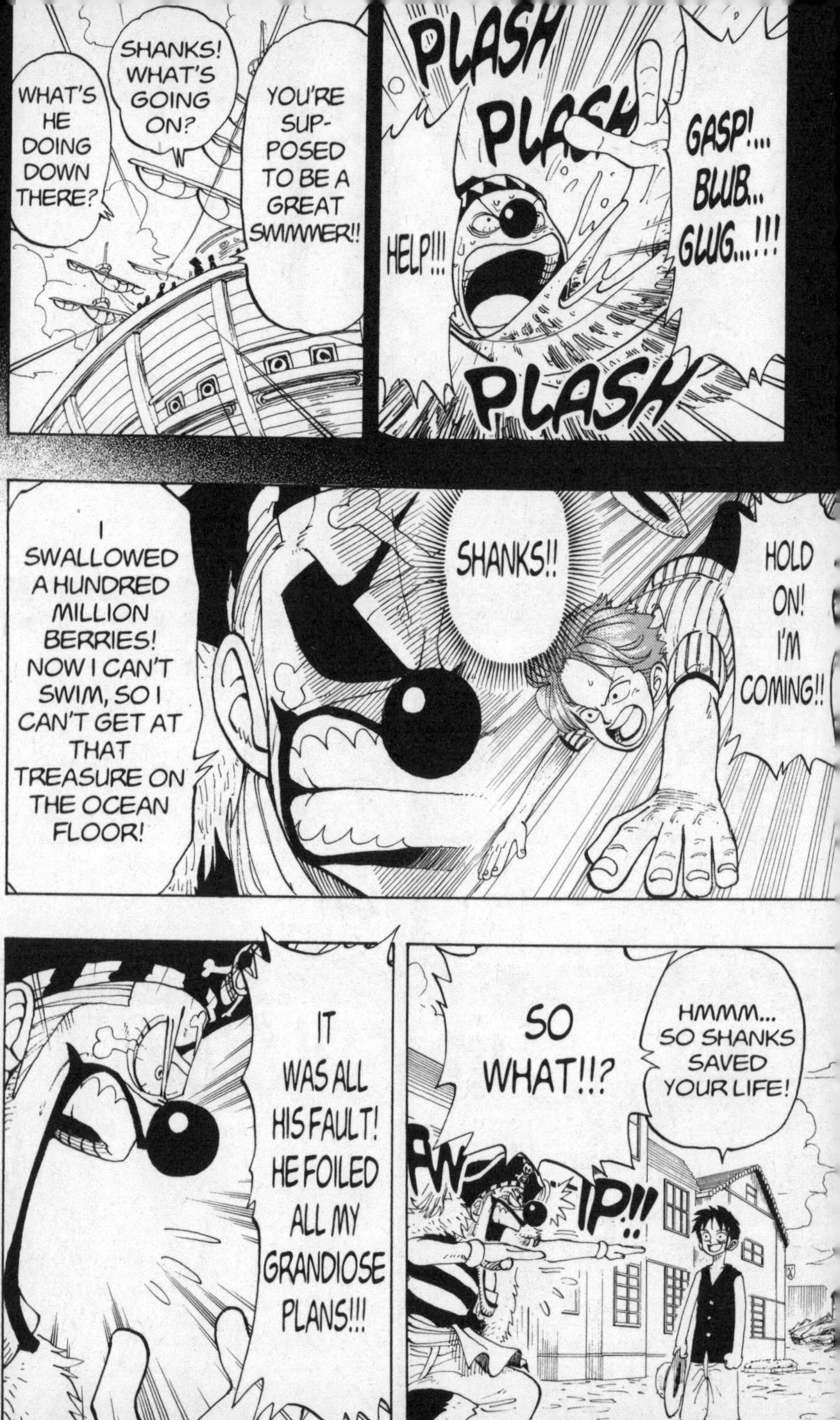
PLASH
PLASH
GASP!... BLUB.. GLUG...!!!
HELP!!!
PLASH
SHANKS! WHAT'S GOING ON?
YOU'RE SUP-POSED TO BE A GREAT SWIMMER!!
WHAT'S HE DOING DOWN THERE?
HOLD ON! I'M COMING!!
SHANKS!!
I SWALLOWED A HUNDRED MILLION BERRIES! NOW I CAN'T SWIM, SO I CAN'T GET AT THAT TREASURE ON THE OCEAN FLOOR!
HMMM... SO SHANKS SAVED YOUR LIFE!
SO WHAT!!?
IT WAS ALL HIS FAULT! HE FOILED ALL MY GRANDIOSE PLANS!!!

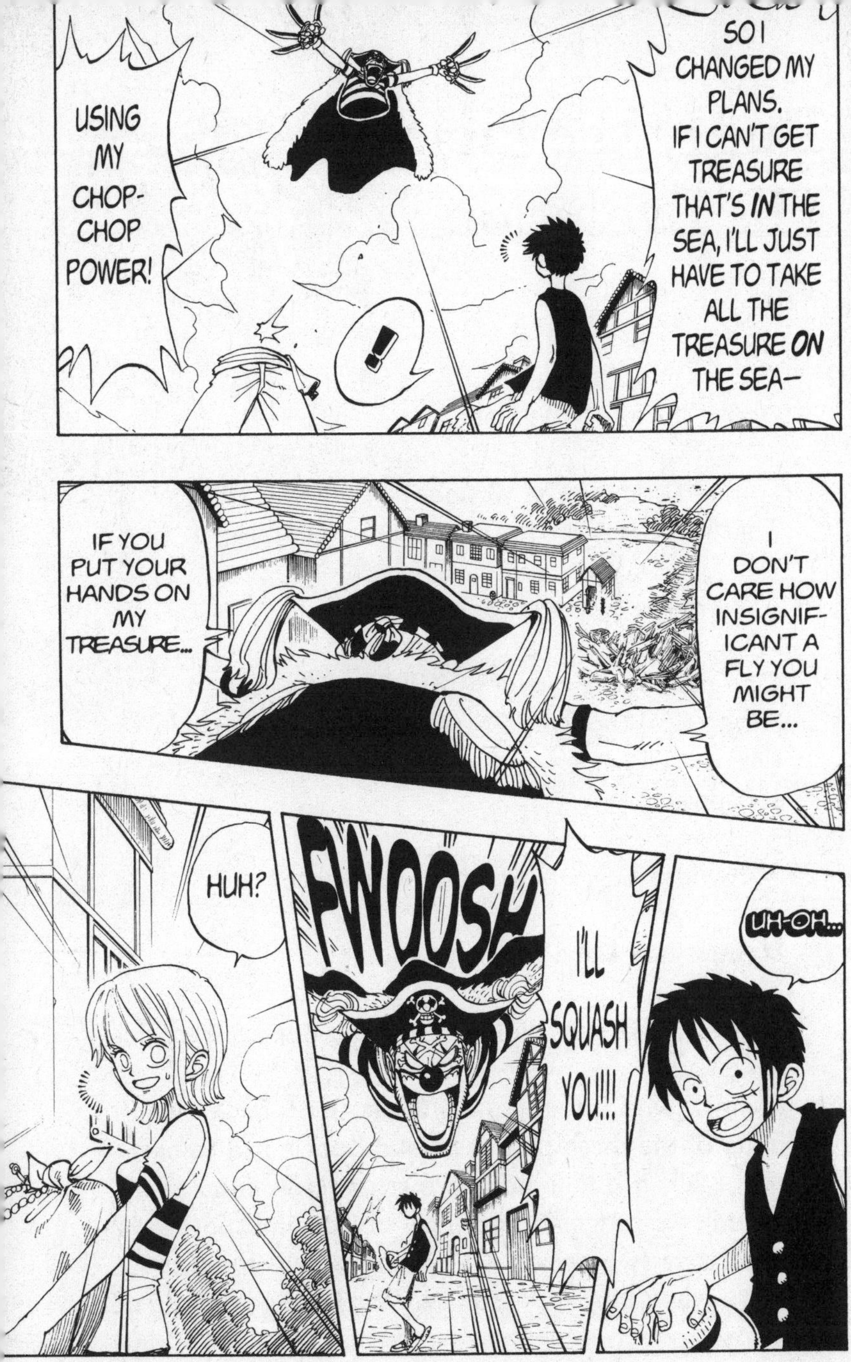
SO I CHANGED MY PLANS. IF I CAN'T GET TREASURE THAT'S IN THE SEA, I'LL JUST HAVE TO TAKE ALL THE TREASURE ON THE SEA–
!
USING MY CHOP-CHOP POWER!
I DON'T CARE HOW INSIGNIF-ICANT A FLY YOU MIGHT BE...
IF YOU PUT YOUR HANDS ON MY TREASURE...
UH-OH...
I'LL SQUASH YOU!!!
FWOOSH
HUH?

Buggy the Pirate
His Evolution
Part 1

Die gloriously!

✤ About "Boogie" and Gang…

Some of you may be wondering who this "Boogie" is.
That was my original name for Captain Buggy.

✤ Why did he become "Buggy"?

One day I saw a movie with a character named
"Boogie." I thought, "Darn, Boogie's already taken.
Oh well, I'll name him Buggy!" (Total thinking time: 0.2
seconds.)

✤ Why does Buggy have a big round nose?

So he'll look like a clown, of course.

✤ Who's the guy on the far left of the Boogie sketch?

Hmm… who is that guy on the far left? Back then,
none of the three pirates behind Boogie had names.
All I really had in mind was that the crew should
include a strongman, an animal trainer, and some kind
of strange swordsman. The sketch shows them at a
stage when they were still very far from completion.

Chapter 20:

THE WAY OF THE THIEF

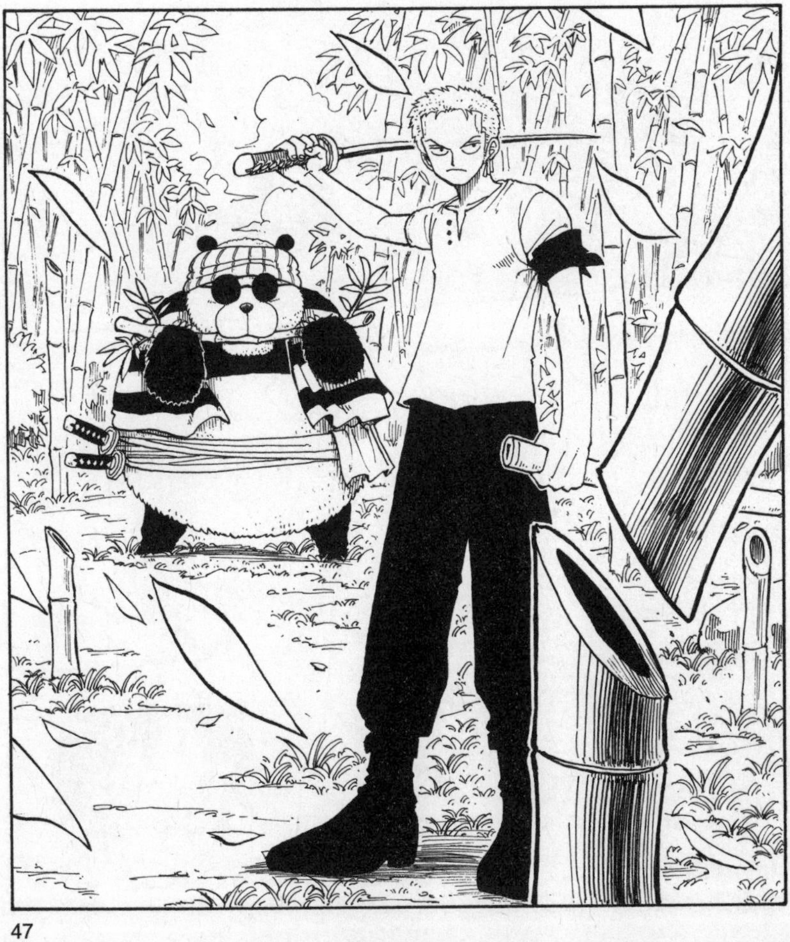

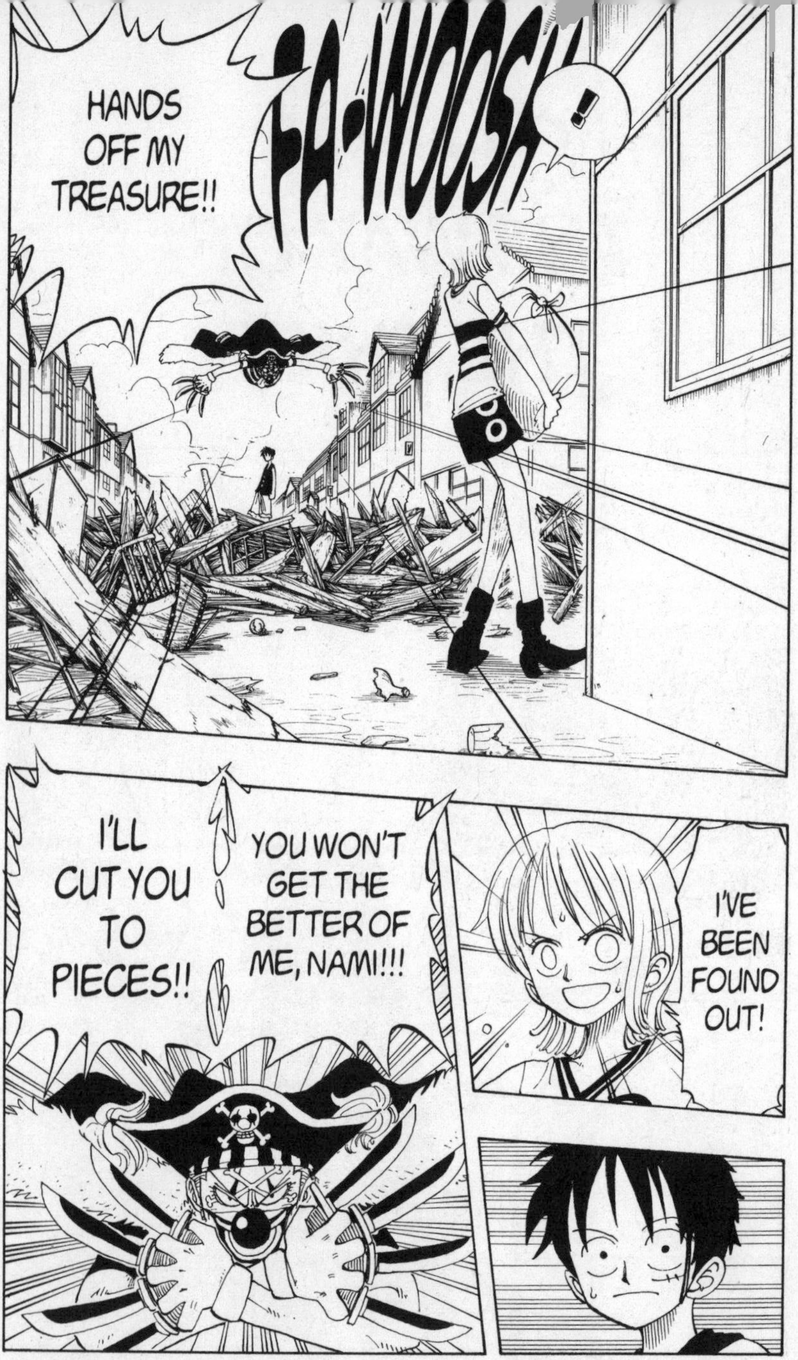
!
FA-WOOSH
HANDS OFF MY TREASURE!!
I'VE BEEN FOUND OUT!
YOU WON'T GET THE BETTER OF ME, NAMI!!!
I'LL CUT YOU TO PIECES!!

READ THIS WAY

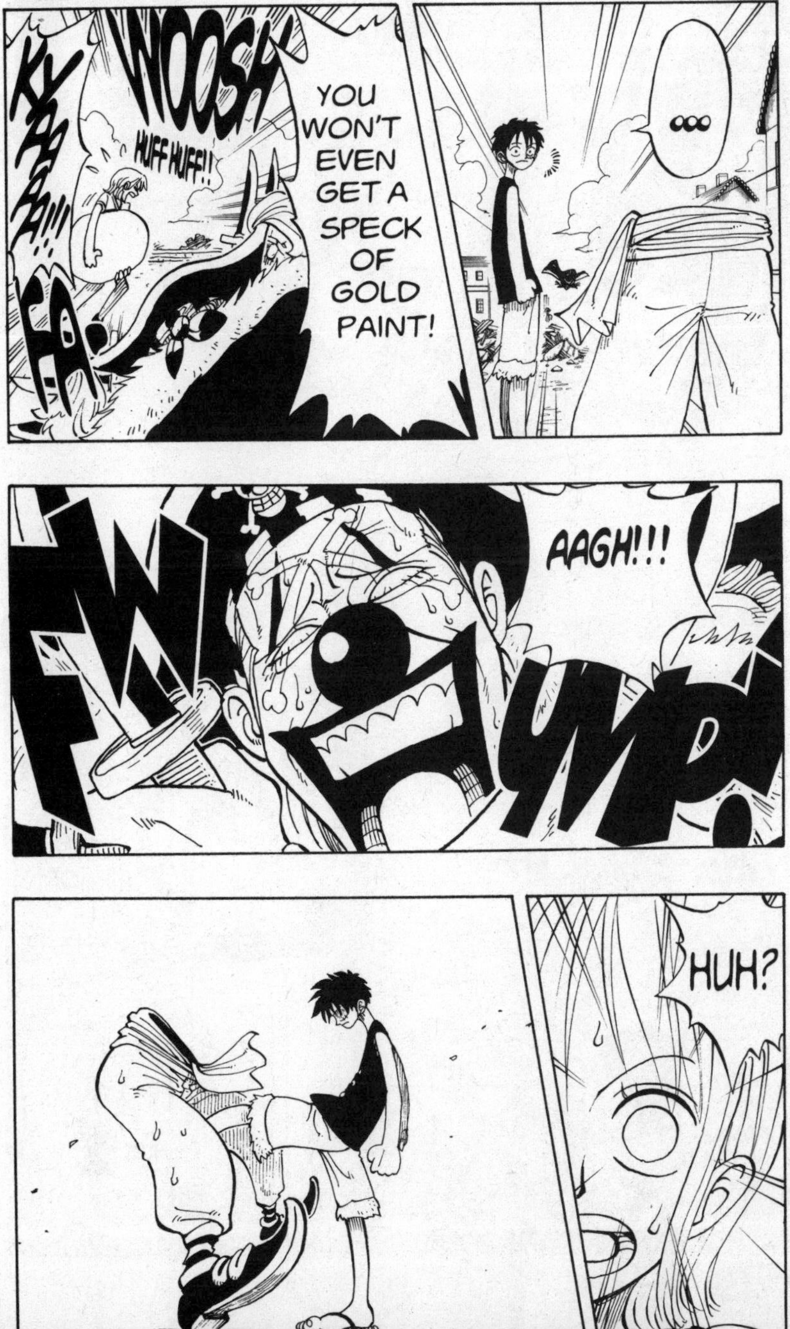
...
YOU WON'T EVEN GET A SPECK OF GOLD PAINT!
WOOSH
HUFF HUFF!!
AAGH!!!
HUH?

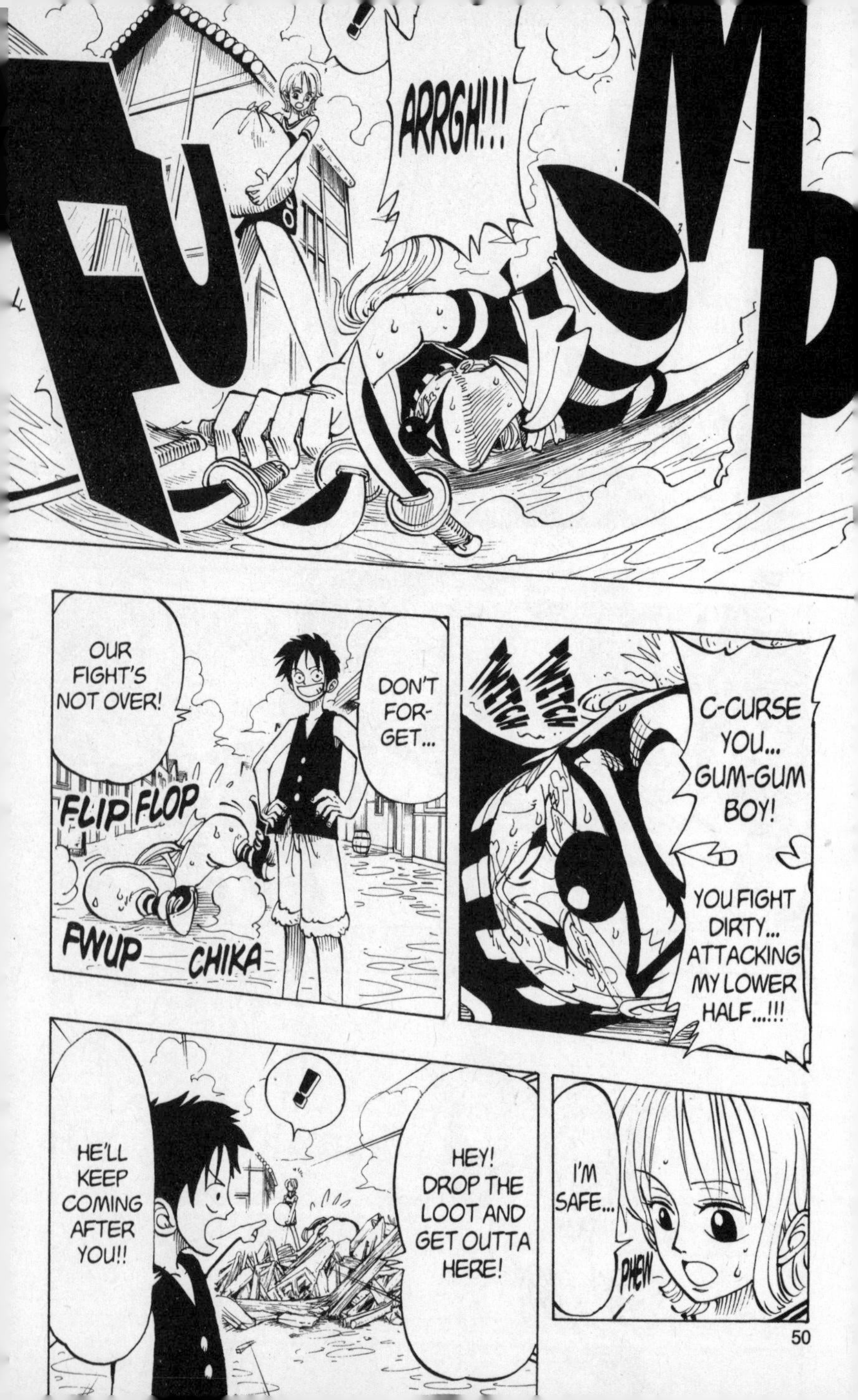

FUMP
ARRGH!!!
TWITCH TWITCH
C-CURSE YOU... GUM-GUM BOY!
YOU FIGHT DIRTY... ATTACKING MY LOWER HALF...!!!
DON'T FOR-GET...
OUR FIGHT'S NOT OVER!
FLIP FLOP
FWUP
CHIKA
I'M SAFE...
PHEW
!
HEY! DROP THE LOOT AND GET OUTTA HERE!
HE'LL KEEP COMING AFTER YOU!!

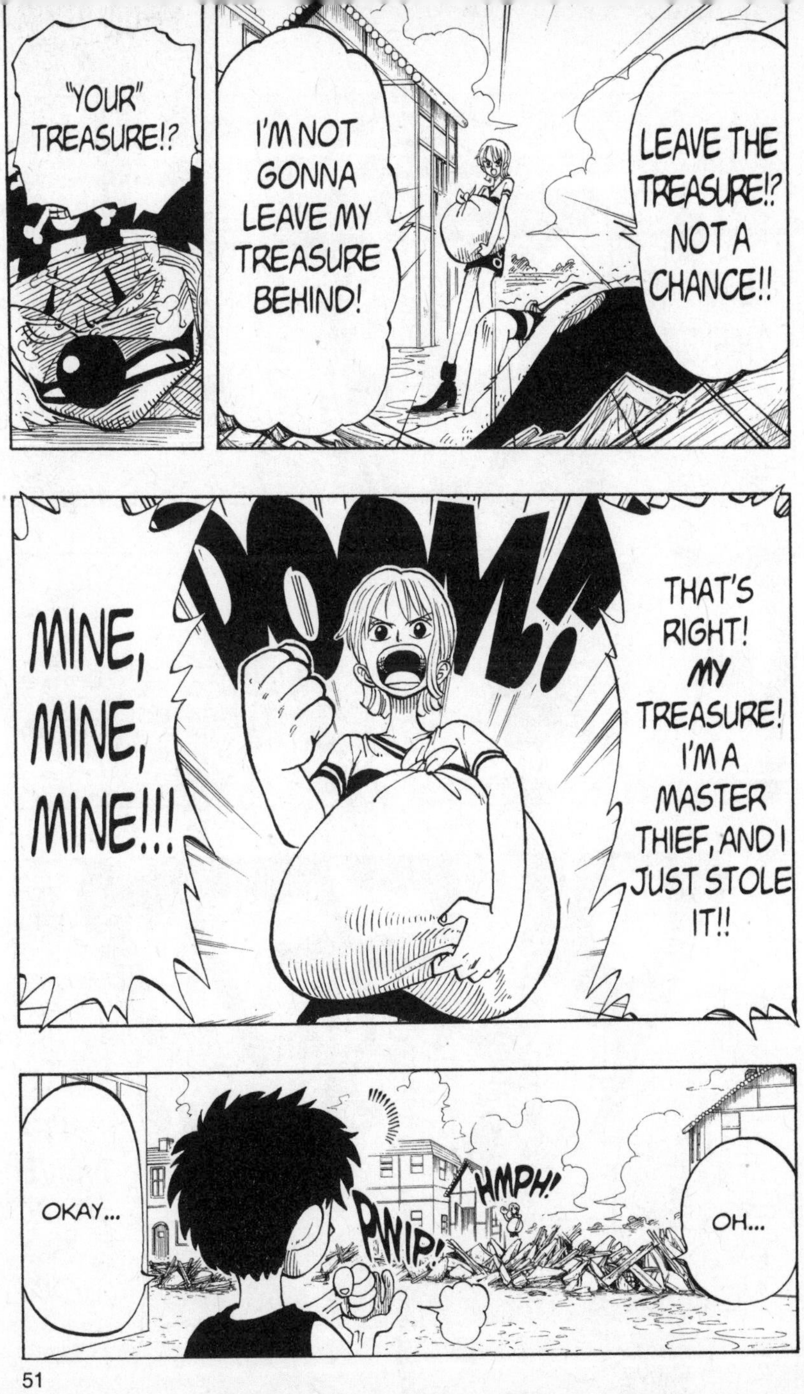
LEAVE THE TREASURE!? NOT A CHANCE!!
I'M NOT GONNA LEAVE MY TREASURE BEHIND!
"YOUR" TREASURE!?
BOOM!!
THAT'S RIGHT! MY TREASURE! I'M A MASTER THIEF, AND I JUST STOLE IT!!
MINE, MINE, MINE!!!
OH...
HMPH!
PWIP!
OKAY...

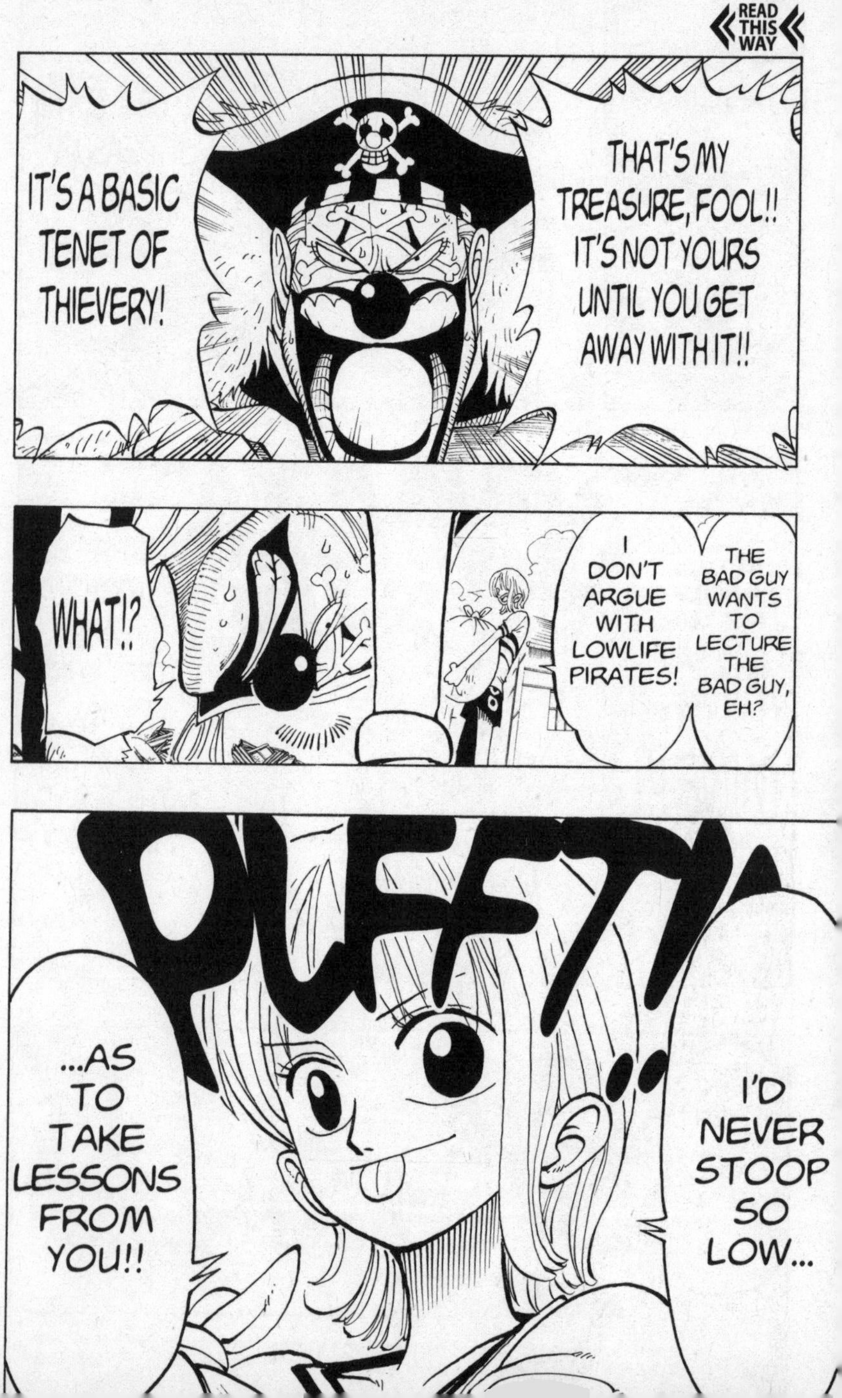
READ THIS WAY
THAT'S MY TREASURE, FOOL!! IT'S NOT YOURS UNTIL YOU GET AWAY WITH IT!!
IT'S A BASIC TENET OF THIEVERY!
THE BAD GUY WANTS TO LECTURE THE BAD GUY, EH?
I DON'T ARGUE WITH LOWLIFE PIRATES!
WHAT!?
PLFFT!
I'D NEVER STOOP SO LOW...
...AS TO TAKE LESSONS FROM YOU!!

READ THIS WAY

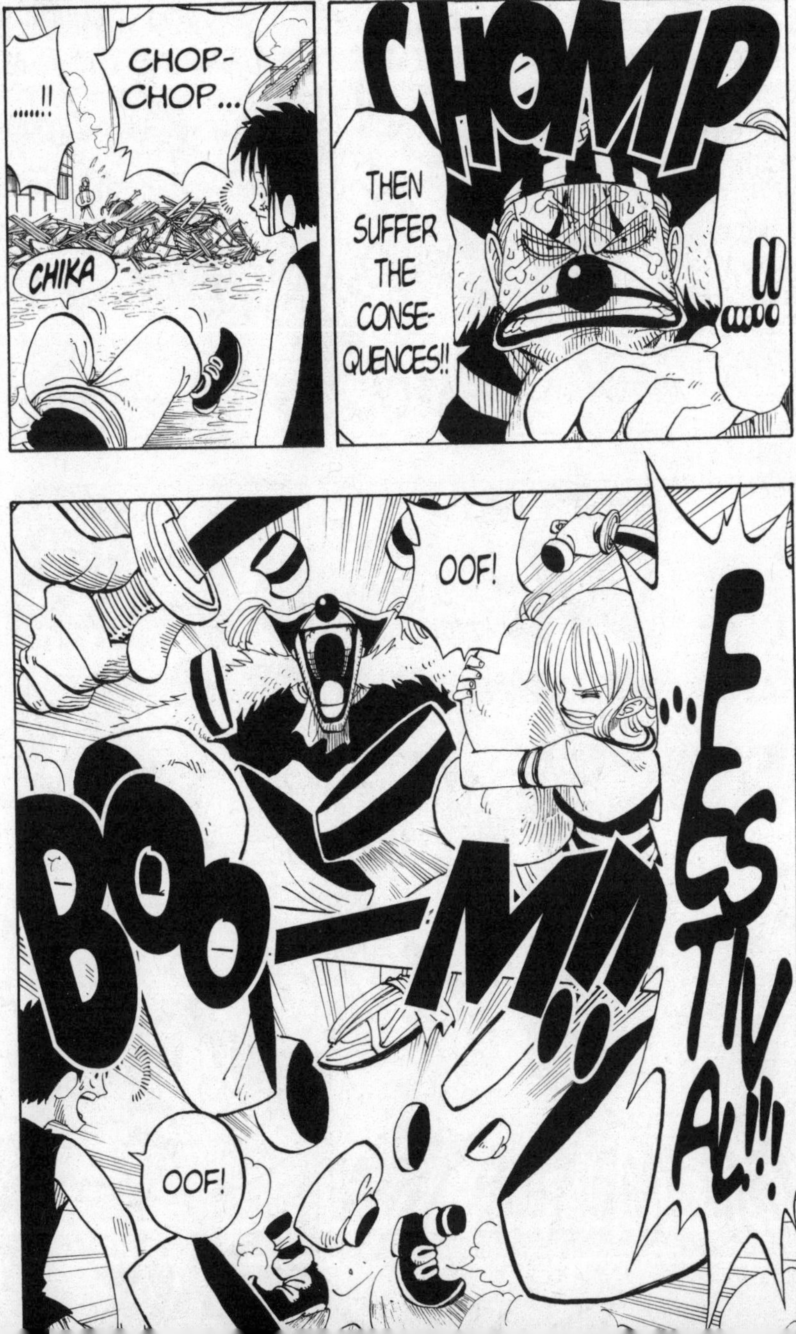
CHOMP
THEN SUFFER THE CONSE-QUENCES!!
......!!
CHOP-CHOP...
......!!
CHIKA
OOF!
...FESTIVAL!!!
BOOM!!
OOF!

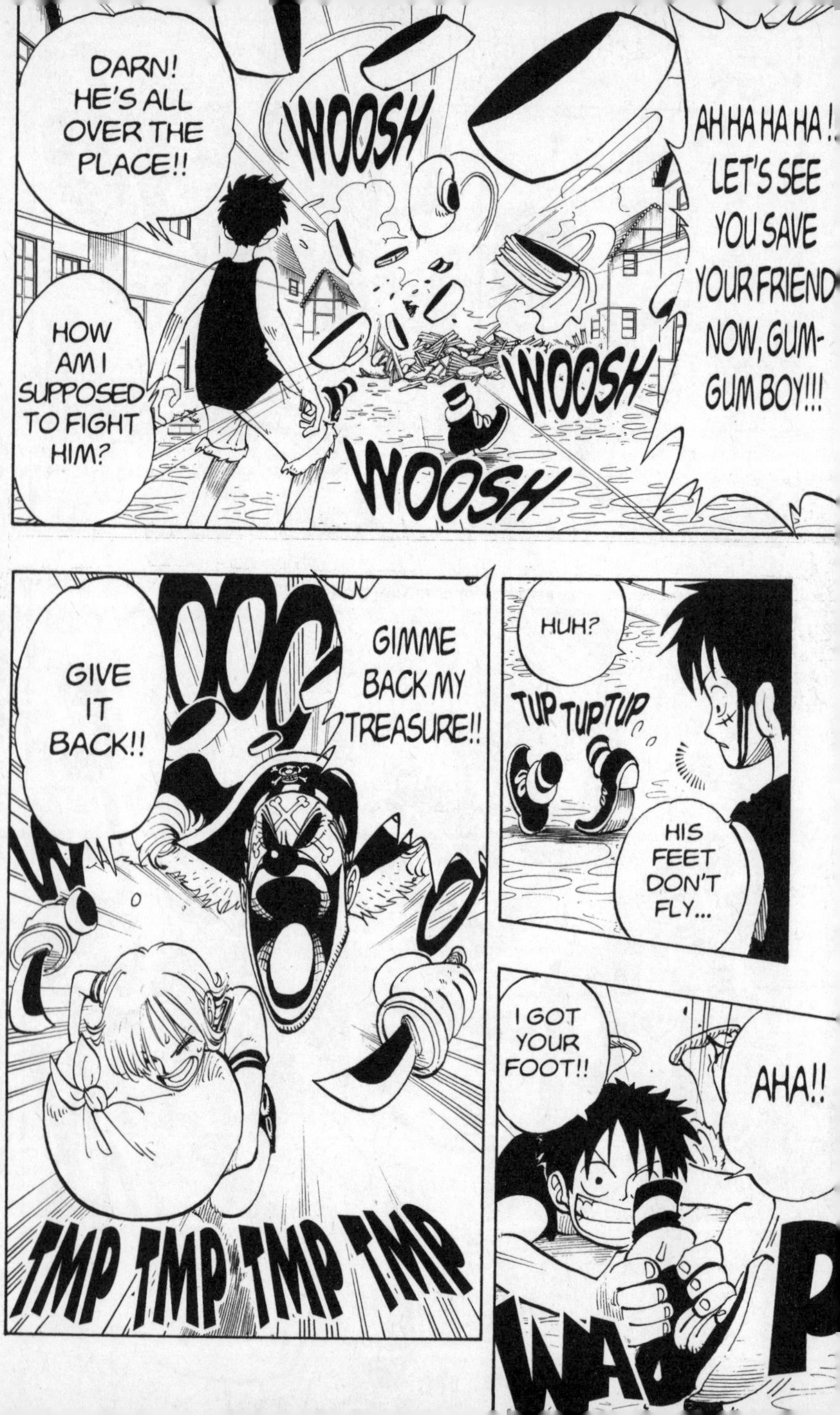

AH HA HA HA!! LET'S SEE YOU SAVE YOUR FRIEND NOW, GUM-GUM BOY!!!
WOOSH
WOOSH
WOOSH
DARN! HE'S ALL OVER THE PLACE!!
HOW AM I SUPPOSED TO FIGHT HIM?
HUH?
TUP TUP TUP
HIS FEET DON'T FLY...
AHA!!
I GOT YOUR FOOT!!
WAP
GIMME BACK MY TREASURE!!
GIVE IT BACK!!
TMP TMP TMP TMP

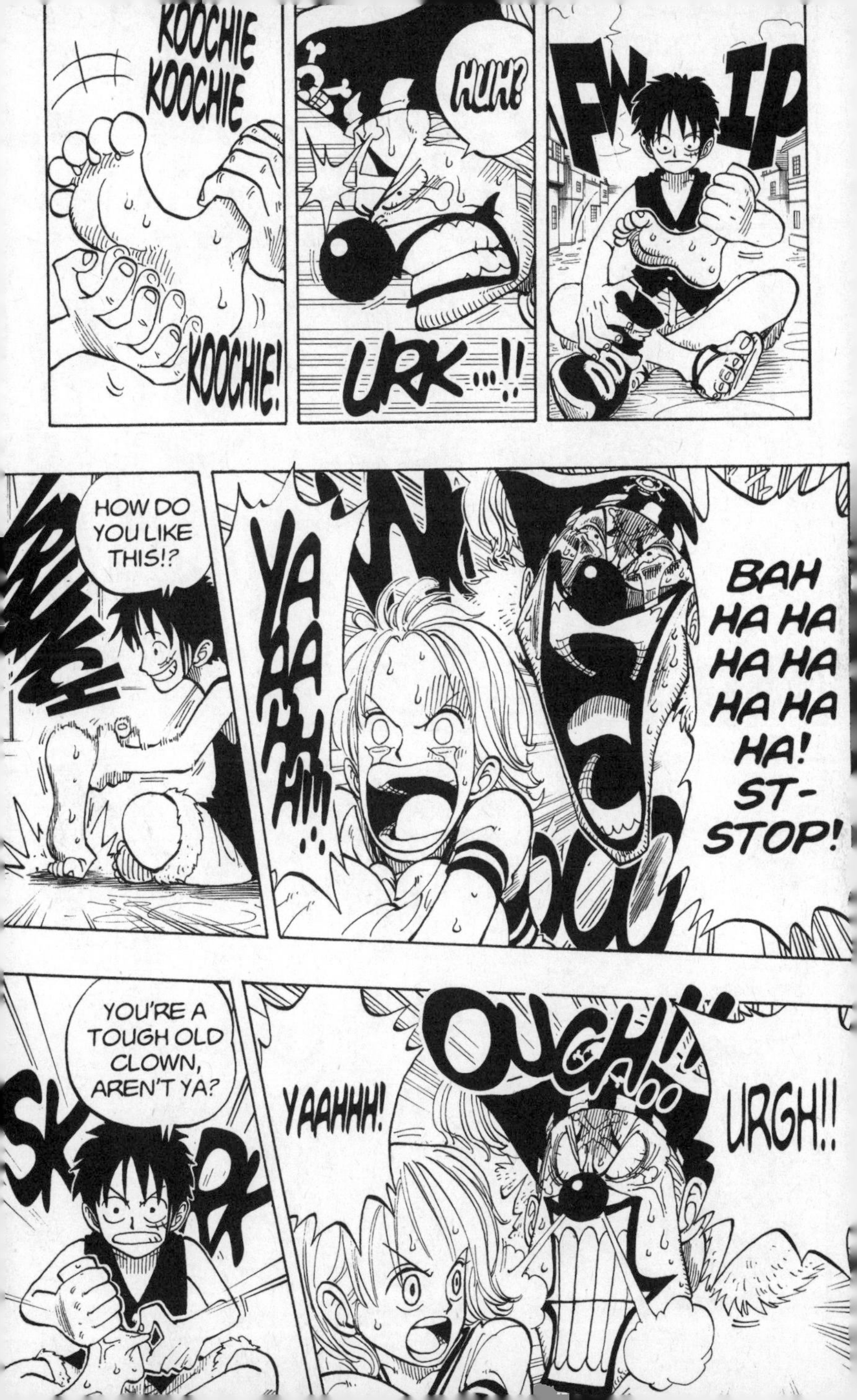
FWIP
HUH?
URK...!!
KOOCHIE KOOCHIE
KOOCHIE!
BAH HA HA HA HA HA HA HA! ST-STOP!
YAAAHH!!...
HOW DO YOU LIKE THIS!?
OUCH!!
URGH!!
YAAHHH!
YOU'RE A TOUGH OLD CLOWN, AREN'T YA?

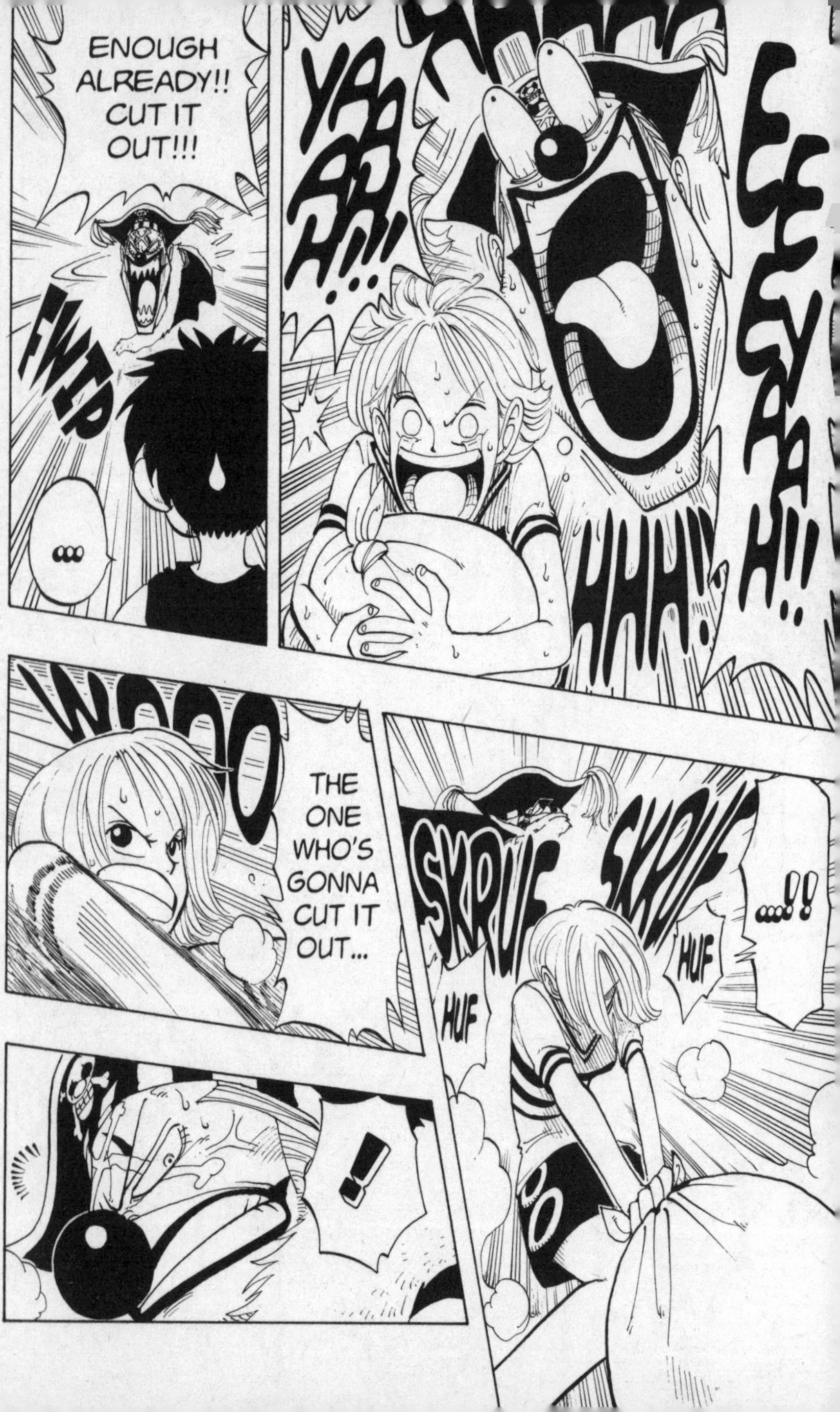
EEEYAAAH!!
HHHH!!
YAAAH!!...
ENOUGH ALREADY!! CUT IT OUT!!!
FWIP
...
SKRUF
SKRUF
...!!
HUF
HUF
WOOO
THE ONE WHO'S GONNA CUT IT OUT...
!

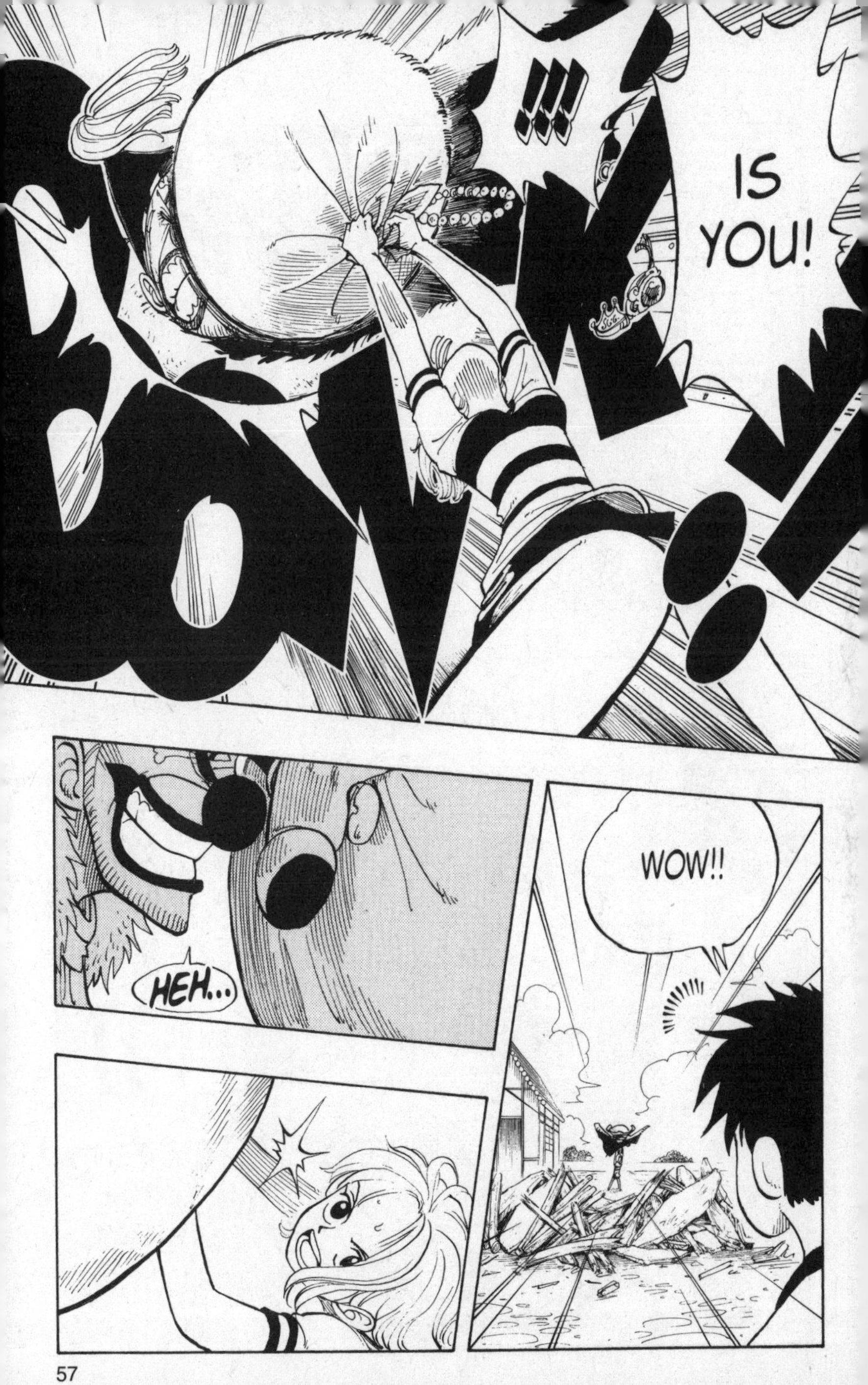
IS YOU!
WOW!!
HEH...

FOR RETURNING MY TREASURE!!

THANK YOU...

TUG

LET GO...!!!

TUG

!

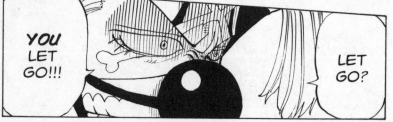

YOU LET GO!!!

LET GO?

58

READ THIS WAY

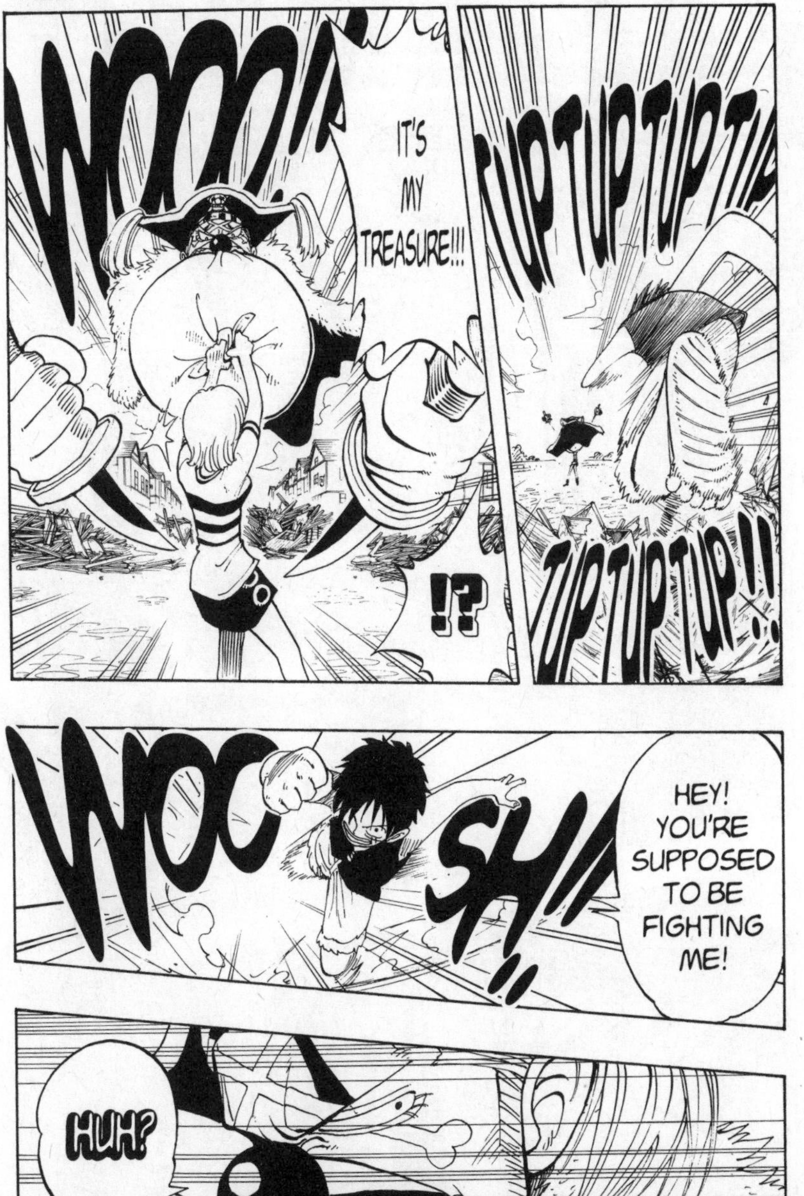
TUP TUP TUP TU
TUP TUP TUP!!
IT'S MY TREASURE!!!
WOOO!
!?
HEY! YOU'RE SUPPOSED TO BE FIGHTING ME!
WOOSH!!
HUH?

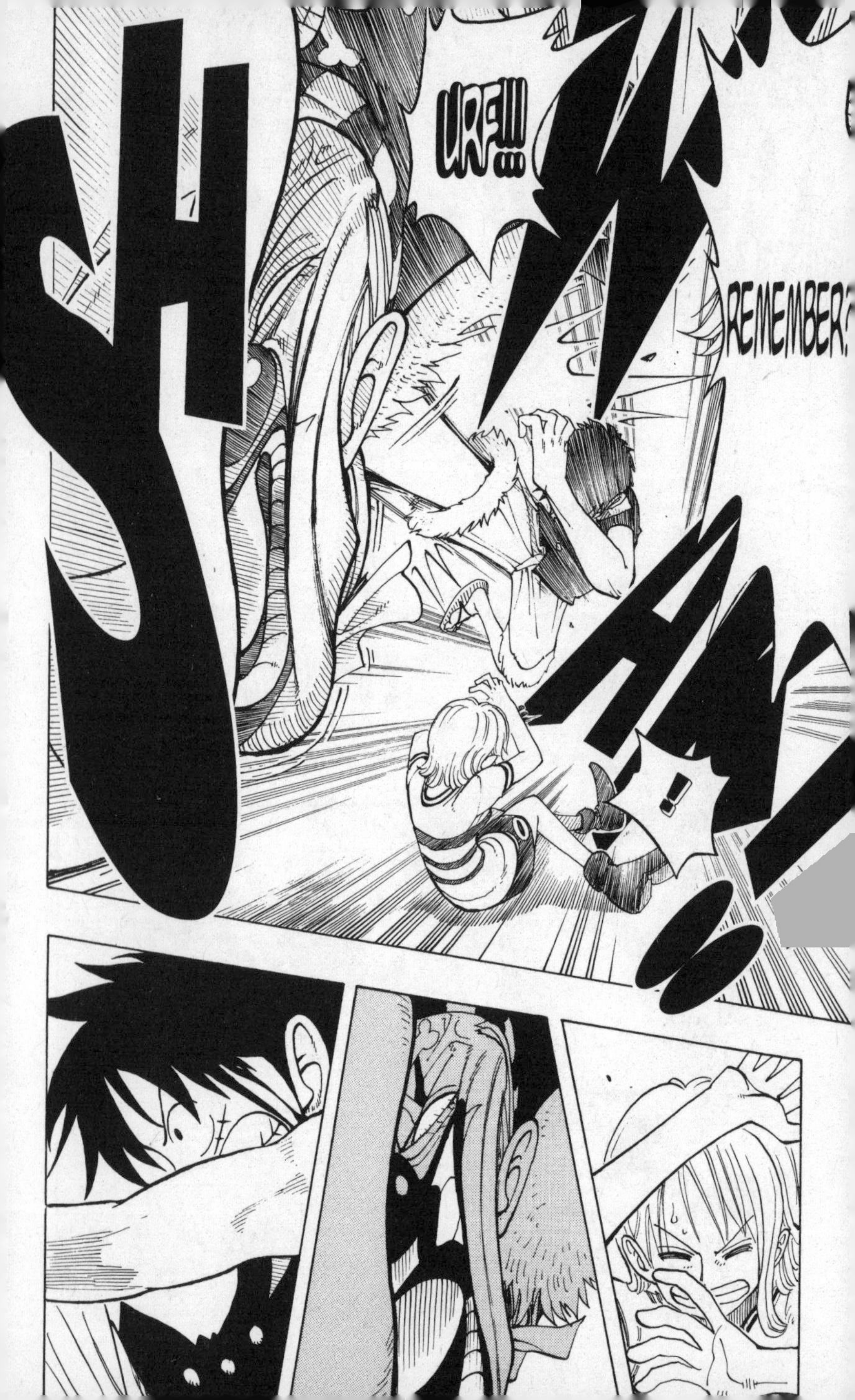
URF!!!
REMEMBER?
!

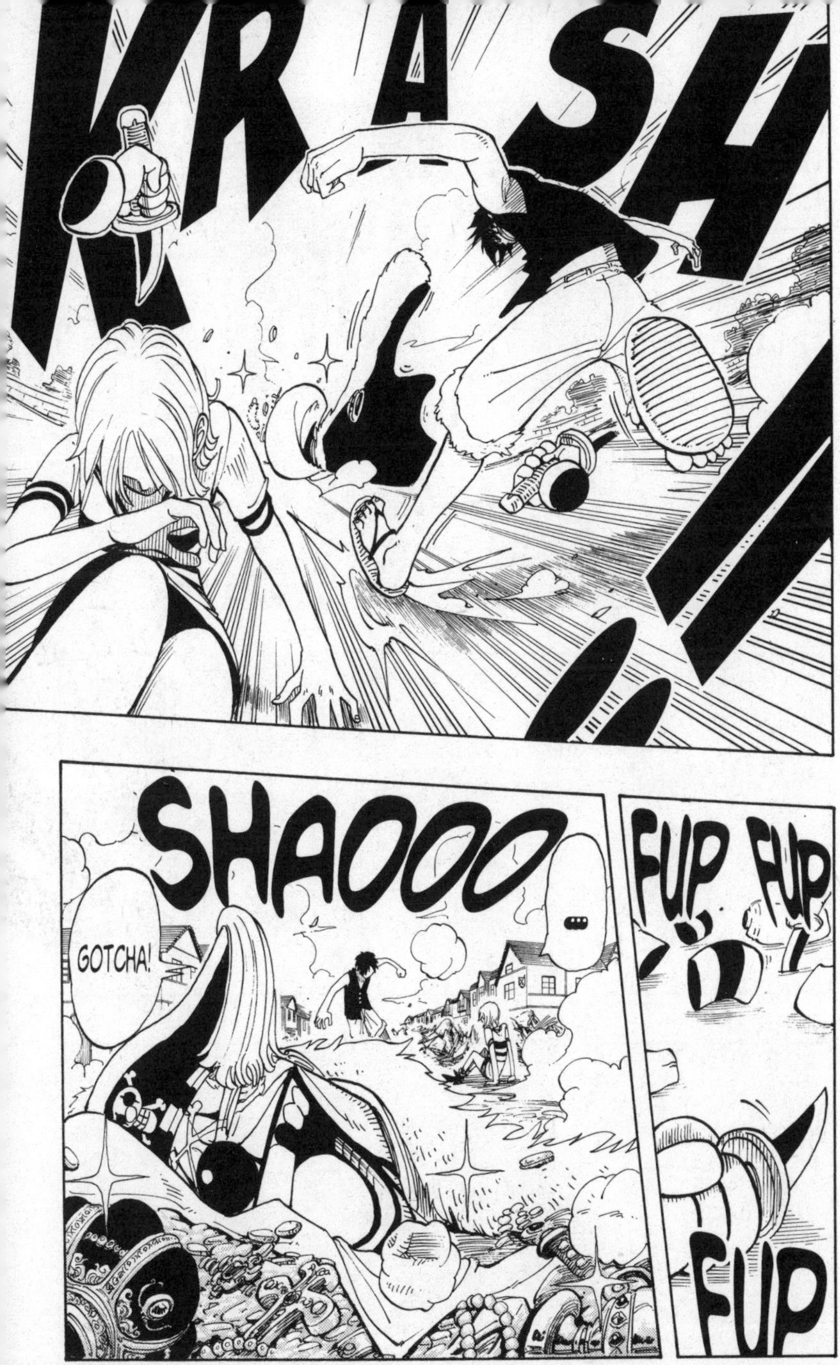
KRASH
FUP FUP
FUP
SHAOOO
...
GOTCHA!

READ THIS WAY

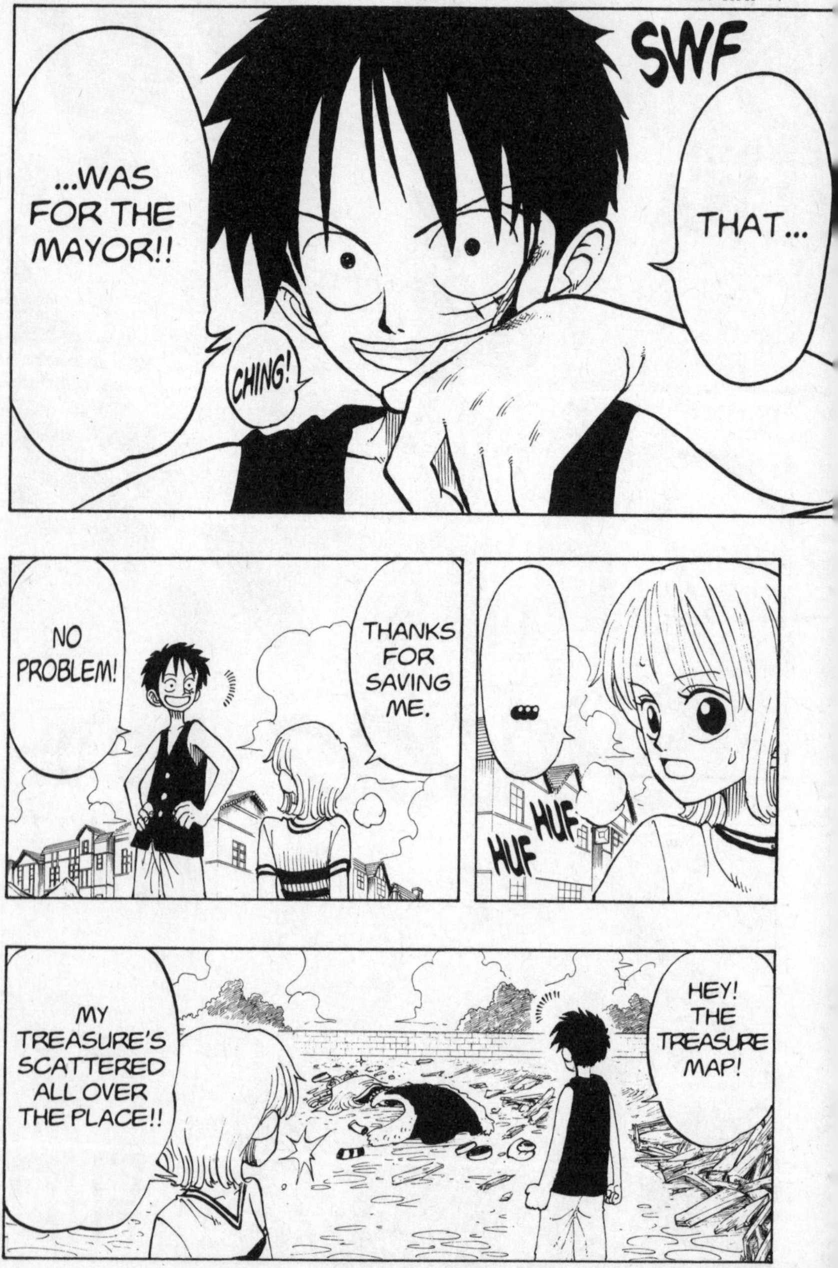

SWF
THAT...
CHING!
...WAS FOR THE MAYOR!!
...
HUF HUF
THANKS FOR SAVING ME.
NO PROBLEM!
HEY! THE TREASURE MAP!
MY TREASURE'S SCATTERED ALL OVER THE PLACE!!

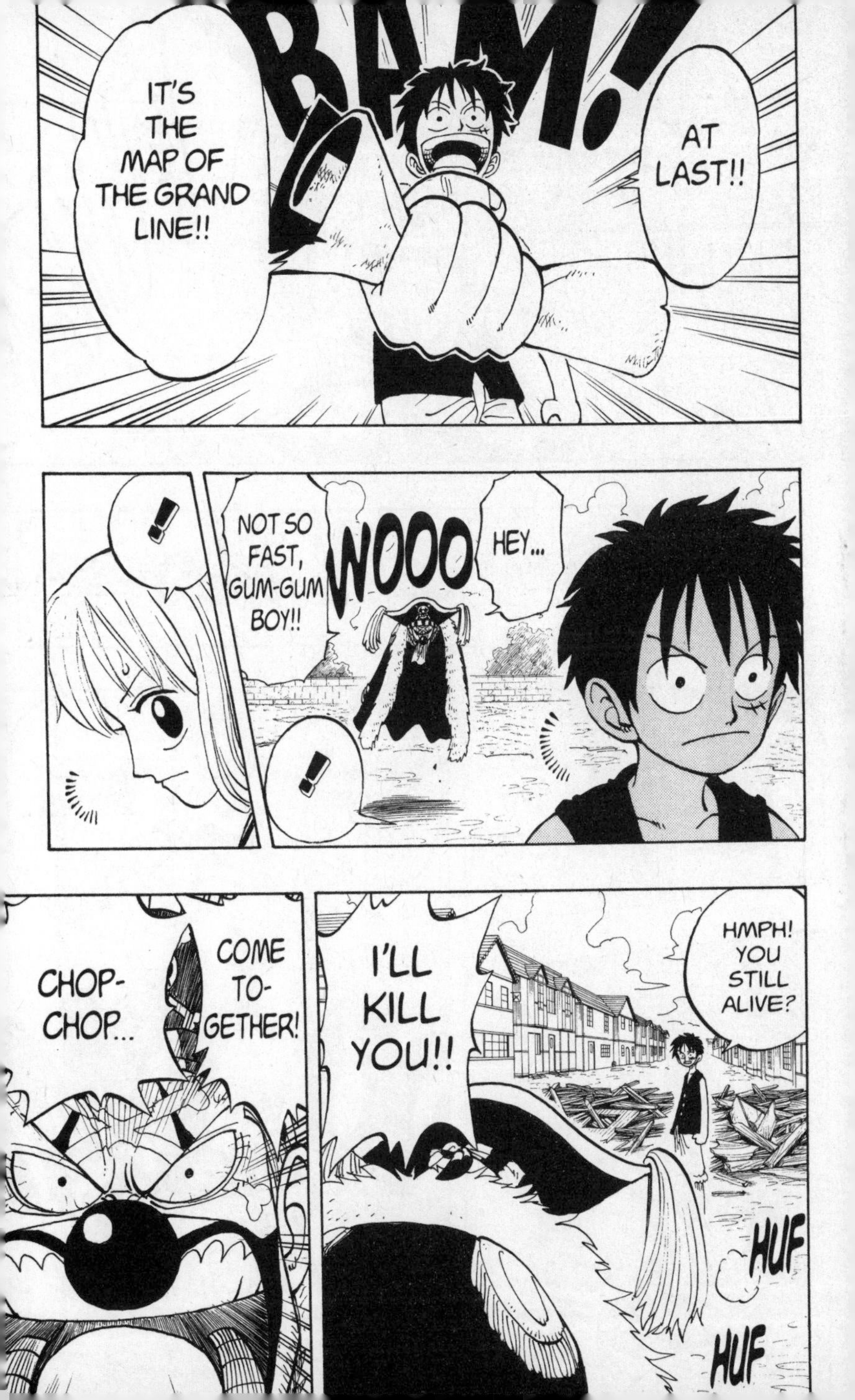
AT LAST!!
BAM!
IT'S THE MAP OF THE GRAND LINE!!
HEY...
WOOO
NOT SO FAST, GUM-GUM BOY!!
!
!
HMPH! YOU STILL ALIVE?
I'LL KILL YOU!!
HUF
HUF
COME TO-GETHER!
CHOP-CHOP...

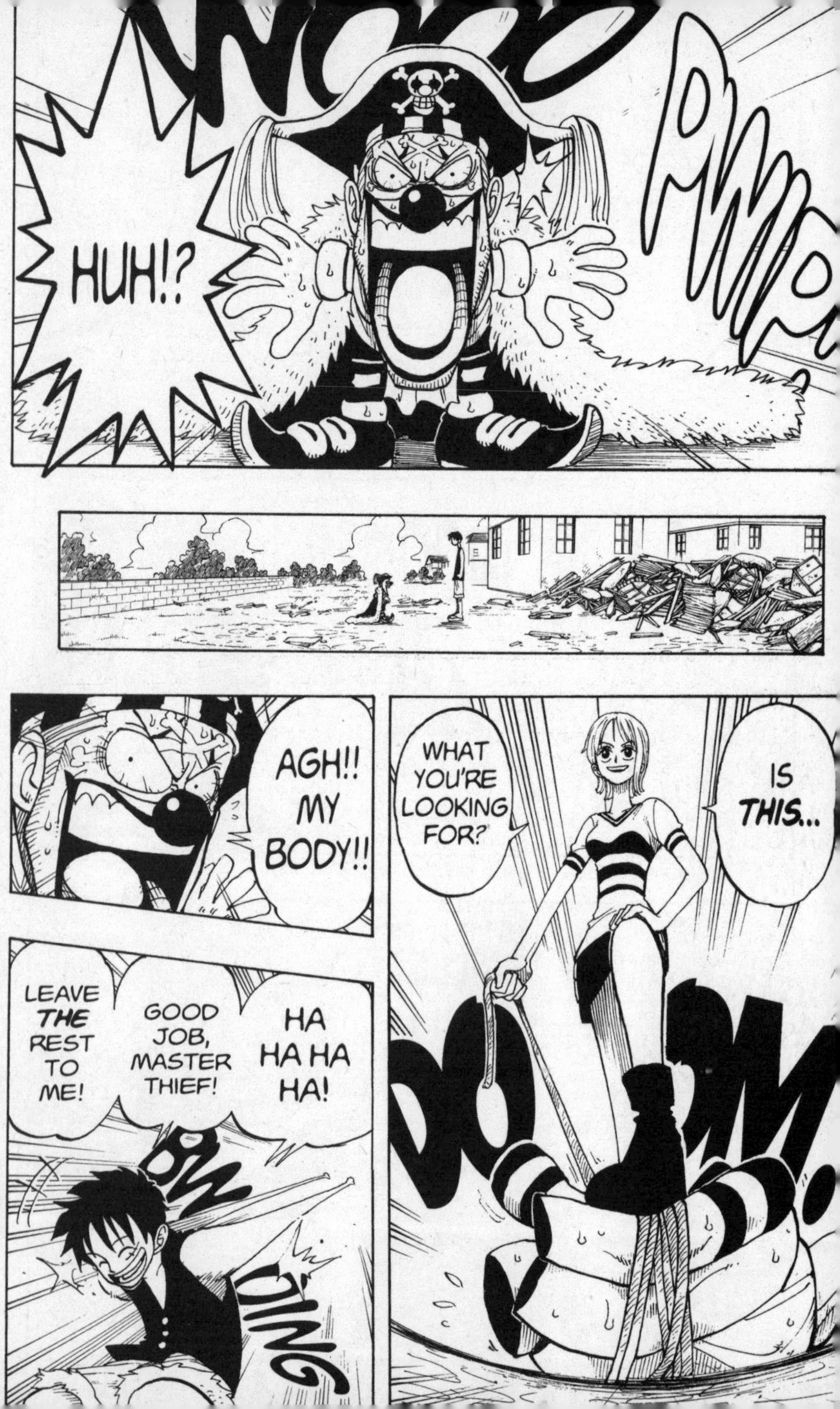
HUH!?
IS THIS...
WHAT YOU'RE LOOKING FOR?
AGH!! MY BODY!!
HA HA HA HA!
GOOD JOB, MASTER THIEF!
LEAVE THE REST TO ME!

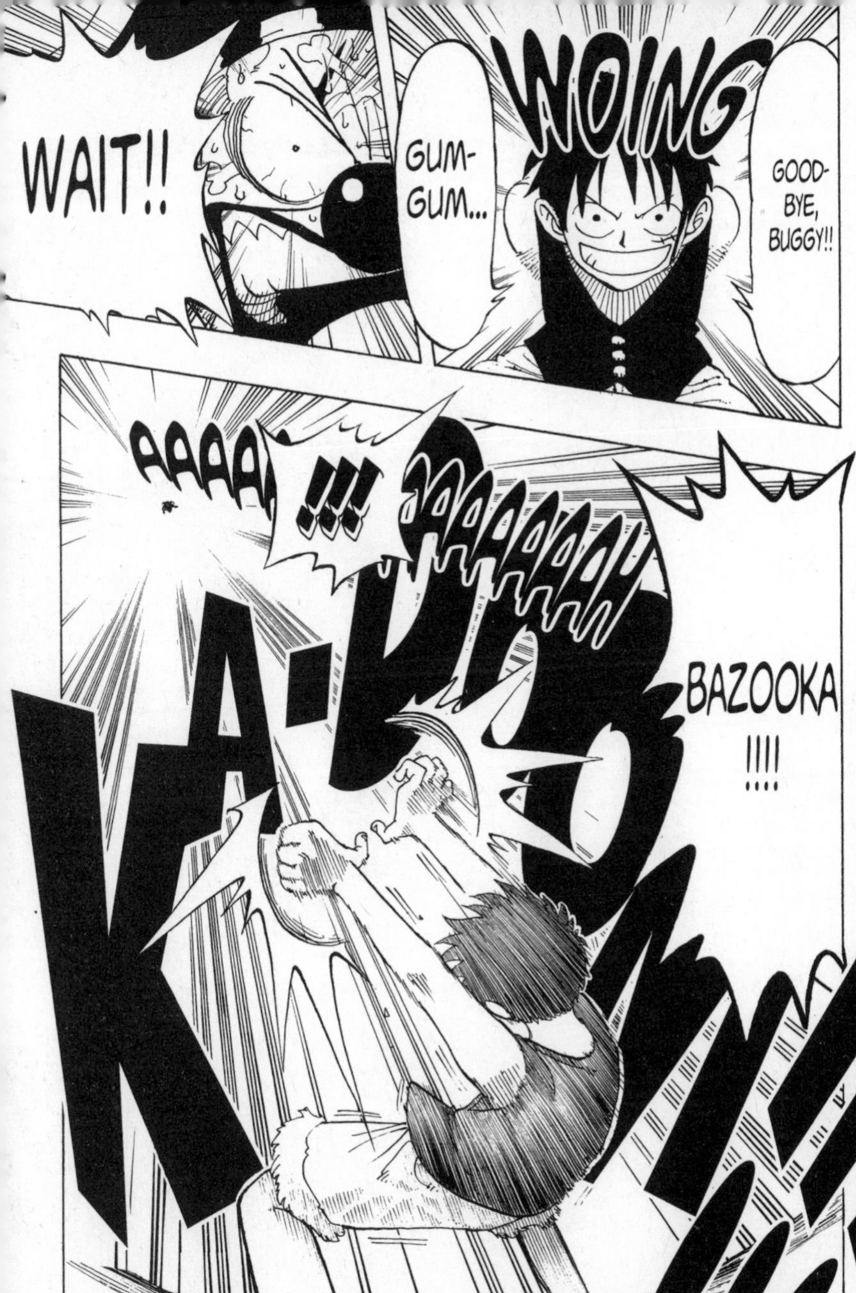
GOOD-BYE, BUGGY!!
WOING
GUM-GUM...
WAIT!!
BAZOOKA!!!!
AAAAA!!!
AAAAAAAAAH

One Piece Storyboards #6

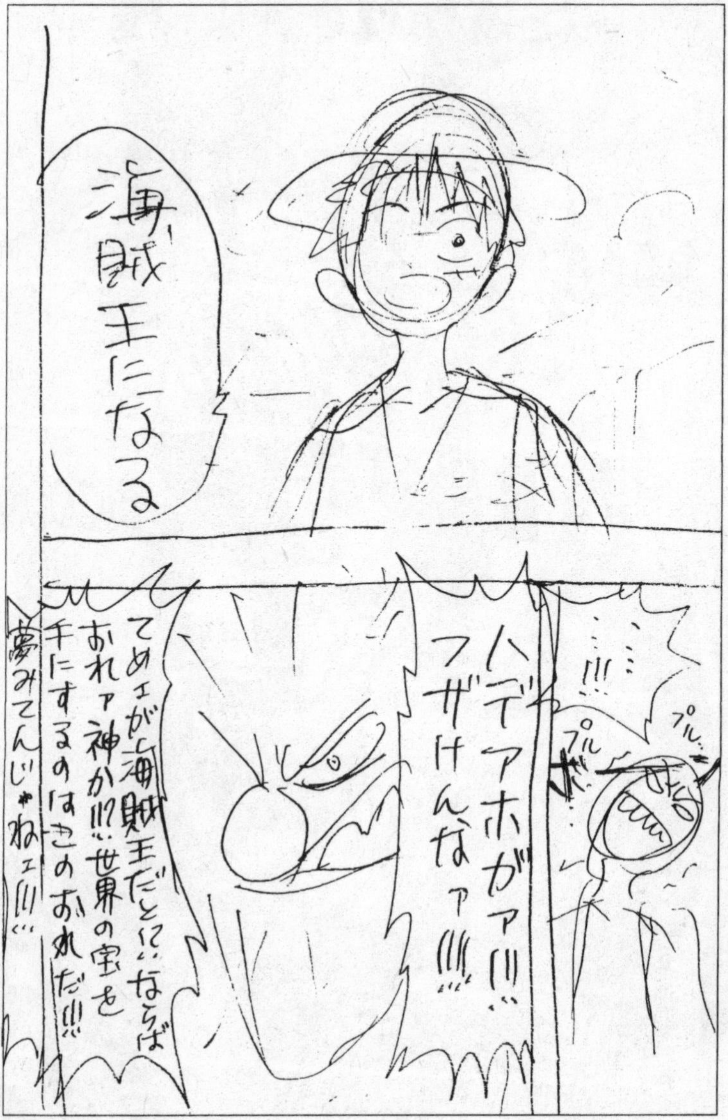
海賊王になる
…!!!
プル…
プル
ガ…
ハデアホがァ!!!
フザけんなァ!!!!
てめェが海賊王だと!?ならば
おれァ神か!!?世界の宝を
手にするのはこのおれだ!!!
夢みてんじゃねェ!!!

Chapter 21:

TOWNIES

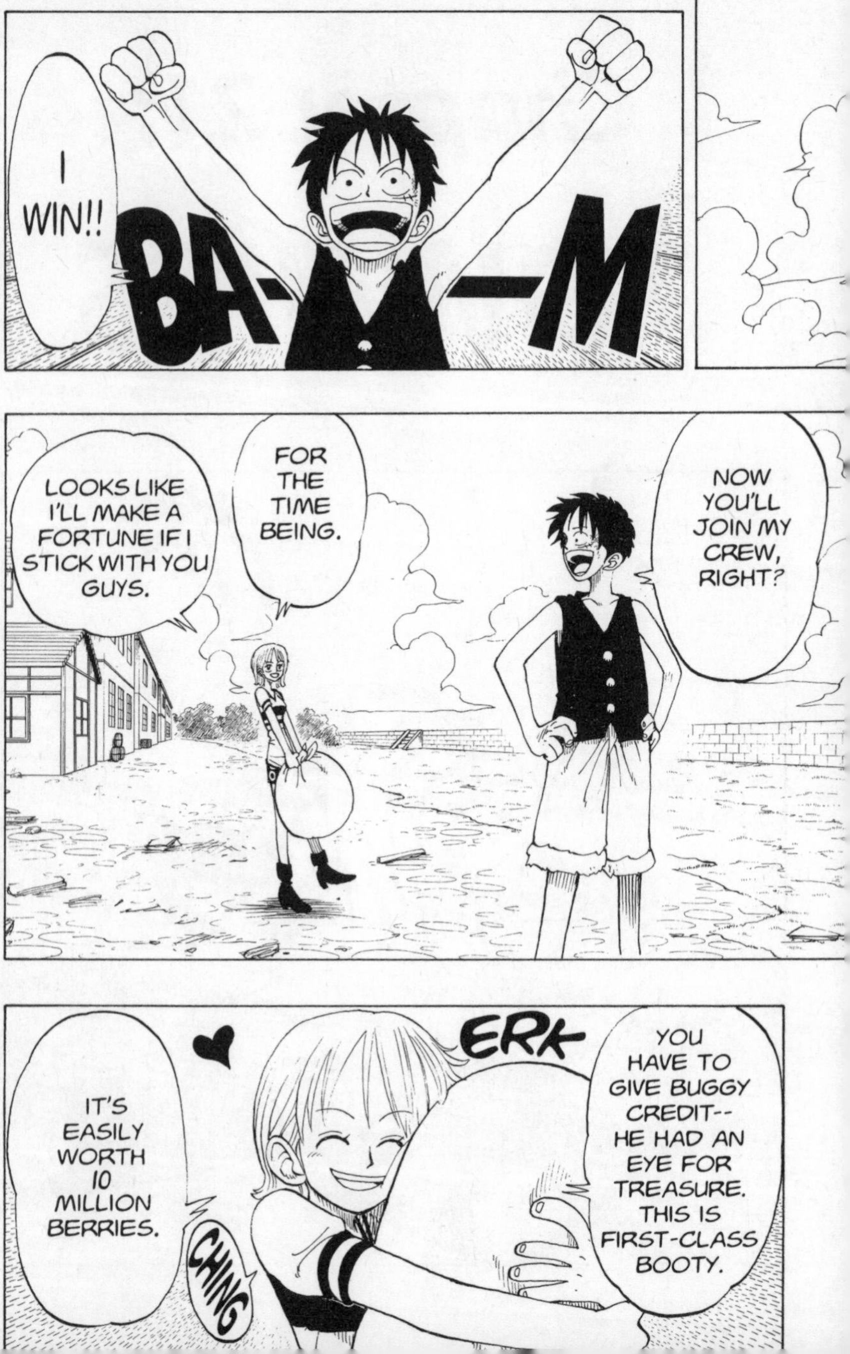
I WIN!!
BA--M
NOW YOU'LL JOIN MY CREW, RIGHT?
FOR THE TIME BEING.
LOOKS LIKE I'LL MAKE A FORTUNE IF I STICK WITH YOU GUYS.
ERK
YOU HAVE TO GIVE BUGGY CREDIT-- HE HAD AN EYE FOR TREASURE. THIS IS FIRST-CLASS BOOTY.
CHING
IT'S EASILY WORTH 10 MILLION BERRIES.

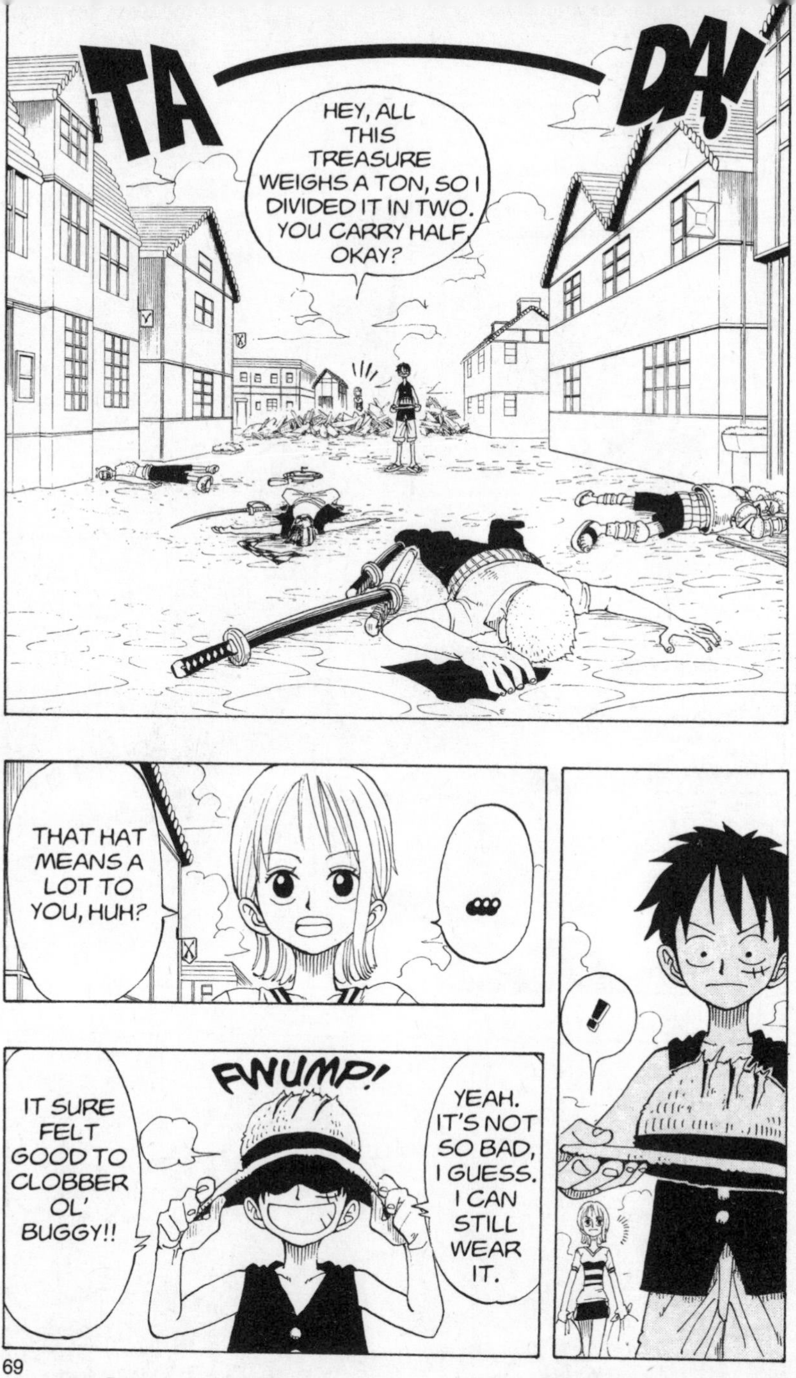
TA—DA!
HEY, ALL THIS TREASURE WEIGHS A TON, SO I DIVIDED IT IN TWO. YOU CARRY HALF, OKAY?
!
...
THAT HAT MEANS A LOT TO YOU, HUH?
FWUMP!
YEAH. IT'S NOT SO BAD, I GUESS. I CAN STILL WEAR IT.
IT SURE FELT GOOD TO CLOBBER OL' BUGGY!!

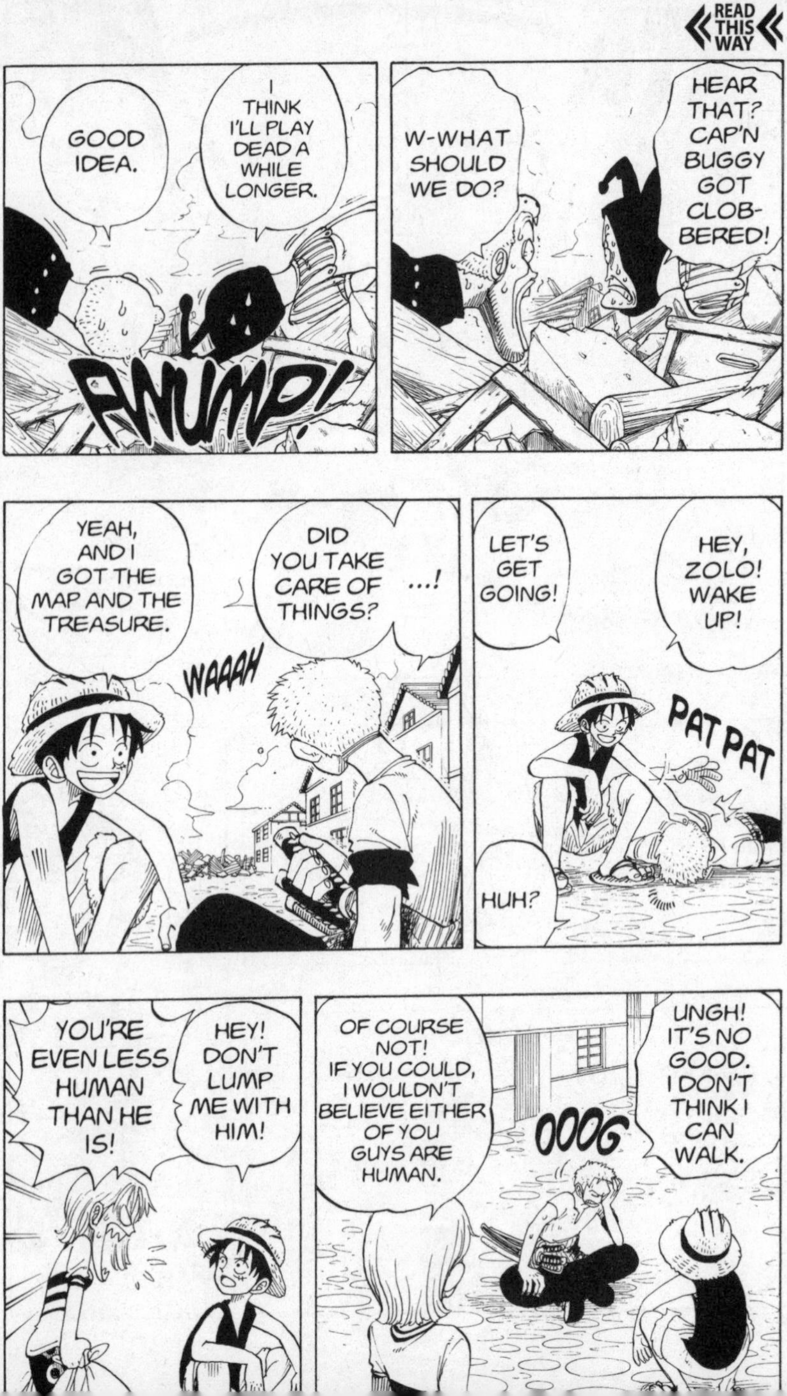
READ THIS WAY
HEAR THAT? CAP'N BUGGY GOT CLOB-BERED!
W-WHAT SHOULD WE DO?
I THINK I'LL PLAY DEAD A WHILE LONGER.
GOOD IDEA.
PHUMP!
HEY, ZOLO! WAKE UP!
LET'S GET GOING!
PAT PAT
HUH?
...!
DID YOU TAKE CARE OF THINGS?
YEAH, AND I GOT THE MAP AND THE TREASURE.
WAAAH
UNGH! IT'S NO GOOD. I DON'T THINK I CAN WALK.
OOOG
OF COURSE NOT! IF YOU COULD, I WOULDN'T BELIEVE EITHER OF YOU GUYS ARE HUMAN.
HEY! DON'T LUMP ME WITH HIM!
YOU'RE EVEN LESS HUMAN THAN HE IS!

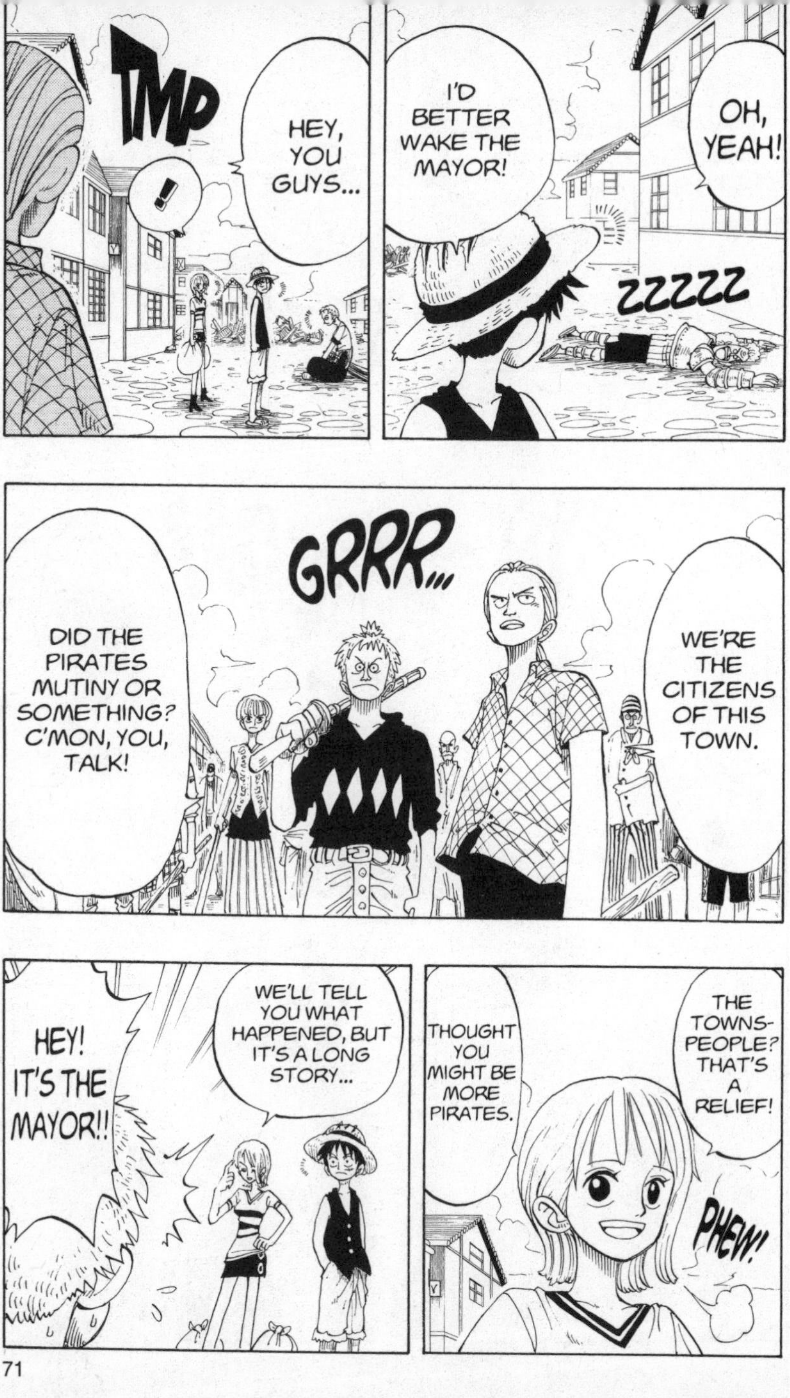
OH, YEAH!
I'D BETTER WAKE THE MAYOR!
ZZZZZ
HEY, YOU GUYS...
TMP
!
WE'RE THE CITIZENS OF THIS TOWN.
GRRR...
DID THE PIRATES MUTINY OR SOMETHING? C'MON, YOU, TALK!
THE TOWNS-PEOPLE? THAT'S A RELIEF!
THOUGHT YOU MIGHT BE MORE PIRATES.
PHEW!
WE'LL TELL YOU WHAT HAPPENED, BUT IT'S A LONG STORY...
HEY! IT'S THE MAYOR!!

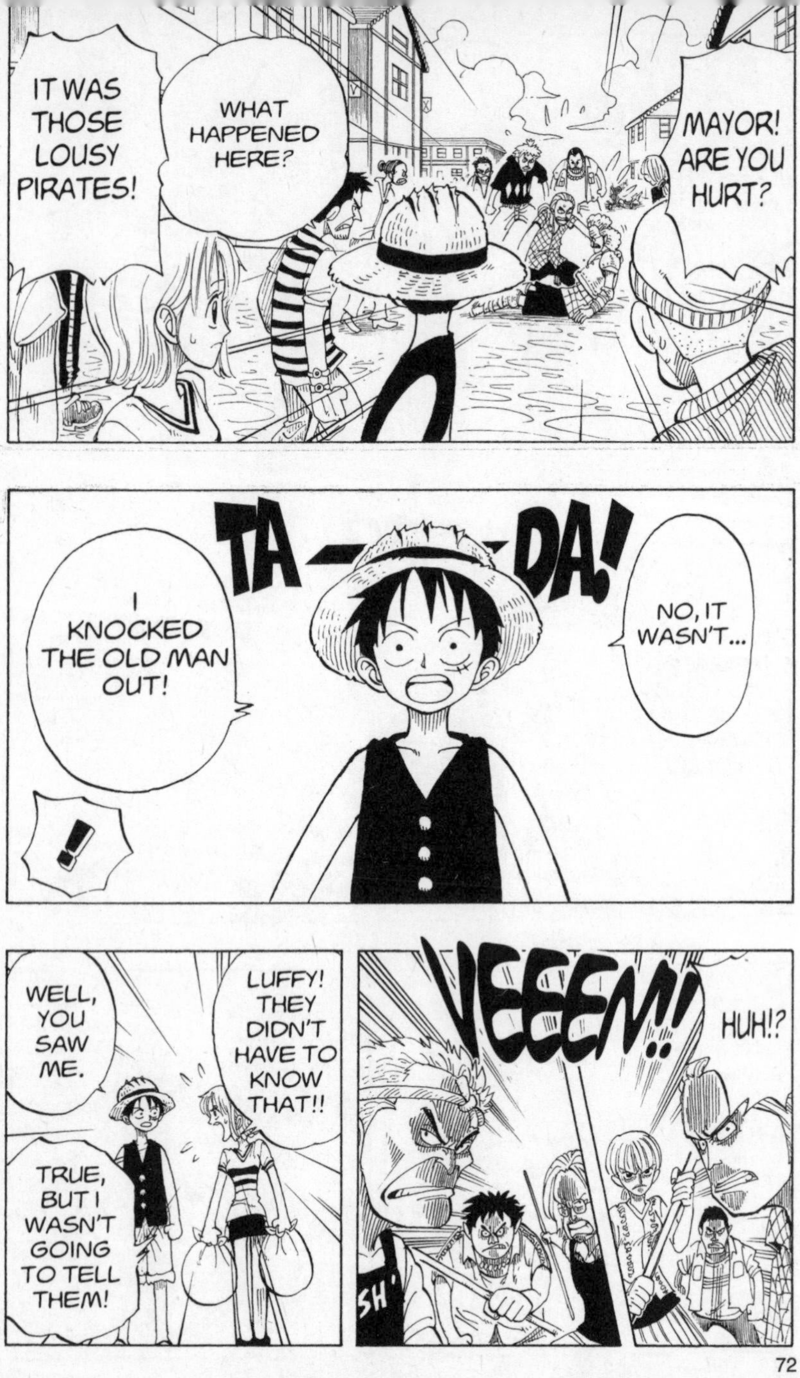
MAYOR! ARE YOU HURT?
WHAT HAPPENED HERE?
IT WAS THOSE LOUSY PIRATES!
NO, IT WASN'T...
TA--DA!
I KNOCKED THE OLD MAN OUT!
!
VEEEM!!
HUH!?
LUFFY! THEY DIDN'T HAVE TO KNOW THAT!!
WELL, YOU SAW ME.
TRUE, BUT I WASN'T GOING TO TELL THEM!

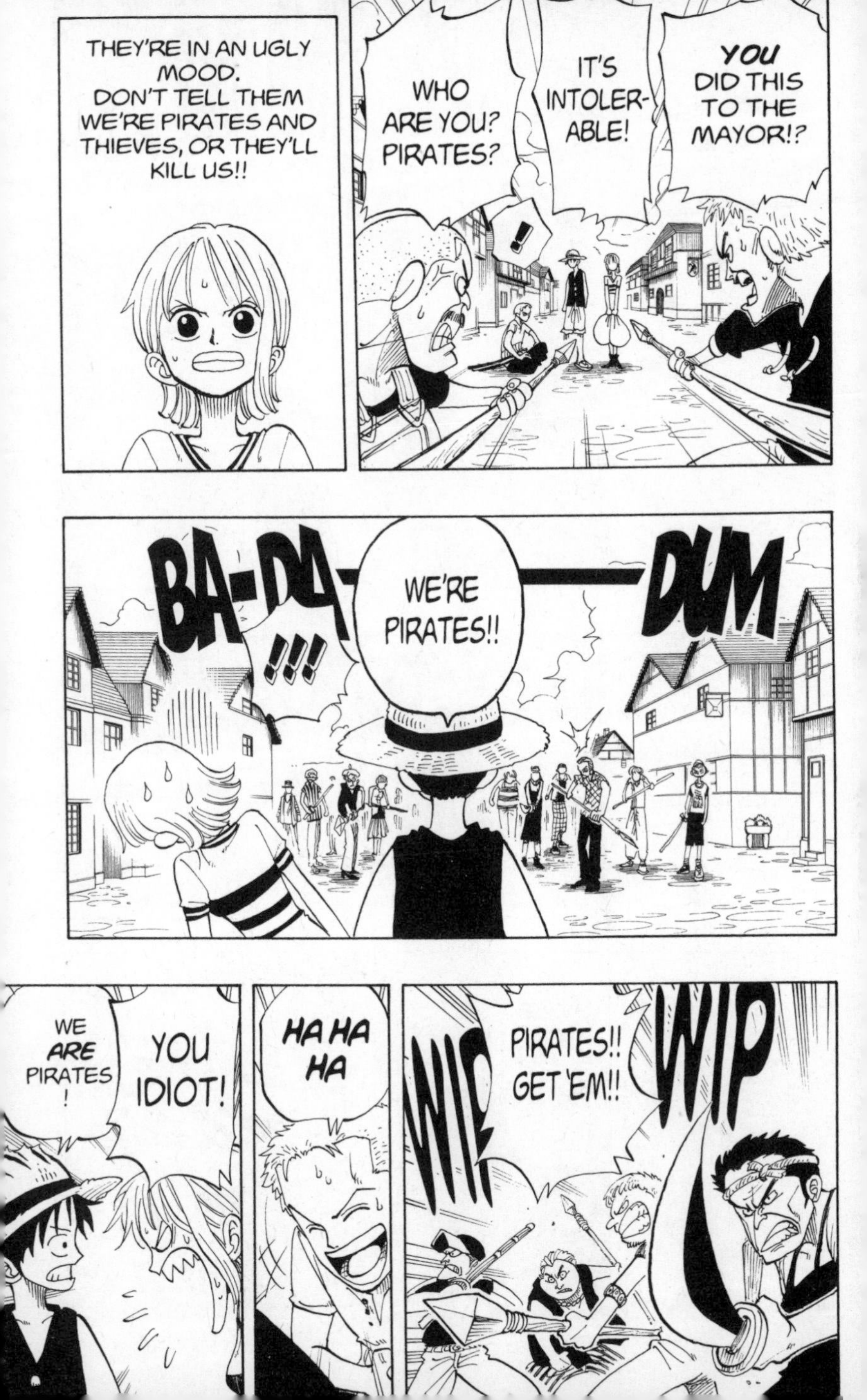
YOU DID THIS TO THE MAYOR!?
IT'S INTOLER-ABLE!
WHO ARE YOU? PIRATES?
!
THEY'RE IN AN UGLY MOOD. DON'T TELL THEM WE'RE PIRATES AND THIEVES, OR THEY'LL KILL US!!
BA-DA
WE'RE PIRATES!!
DUM
!!!
WIP
PIRATES!! GET 'EM!!
WIP
HA HA HA
YOU IDIOT!
WE ARE PIRATES!

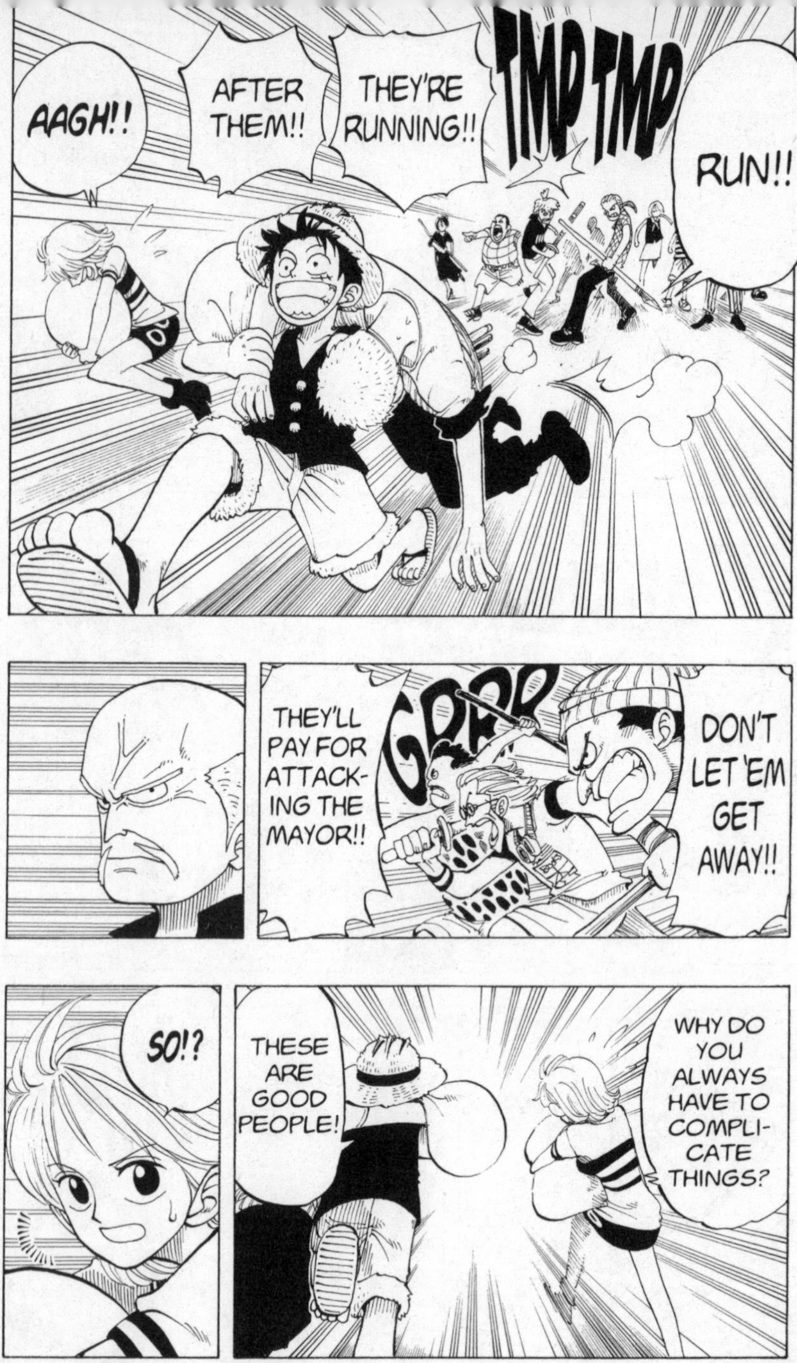
RUN!!
TMP TMP
THEY'RE RUNNING!!
AFTER THEM!!
AAGH!!
DON'T LET 'EM GET AWAY!!
GRRR
THEY'LL PAY FOR ATTACKING THE MAYOR!!
WHY DO YOU ALWAYS HAVE TO COMPLICATE THINGS?
THESE ARE GOOD PEOPLE!
SO!?

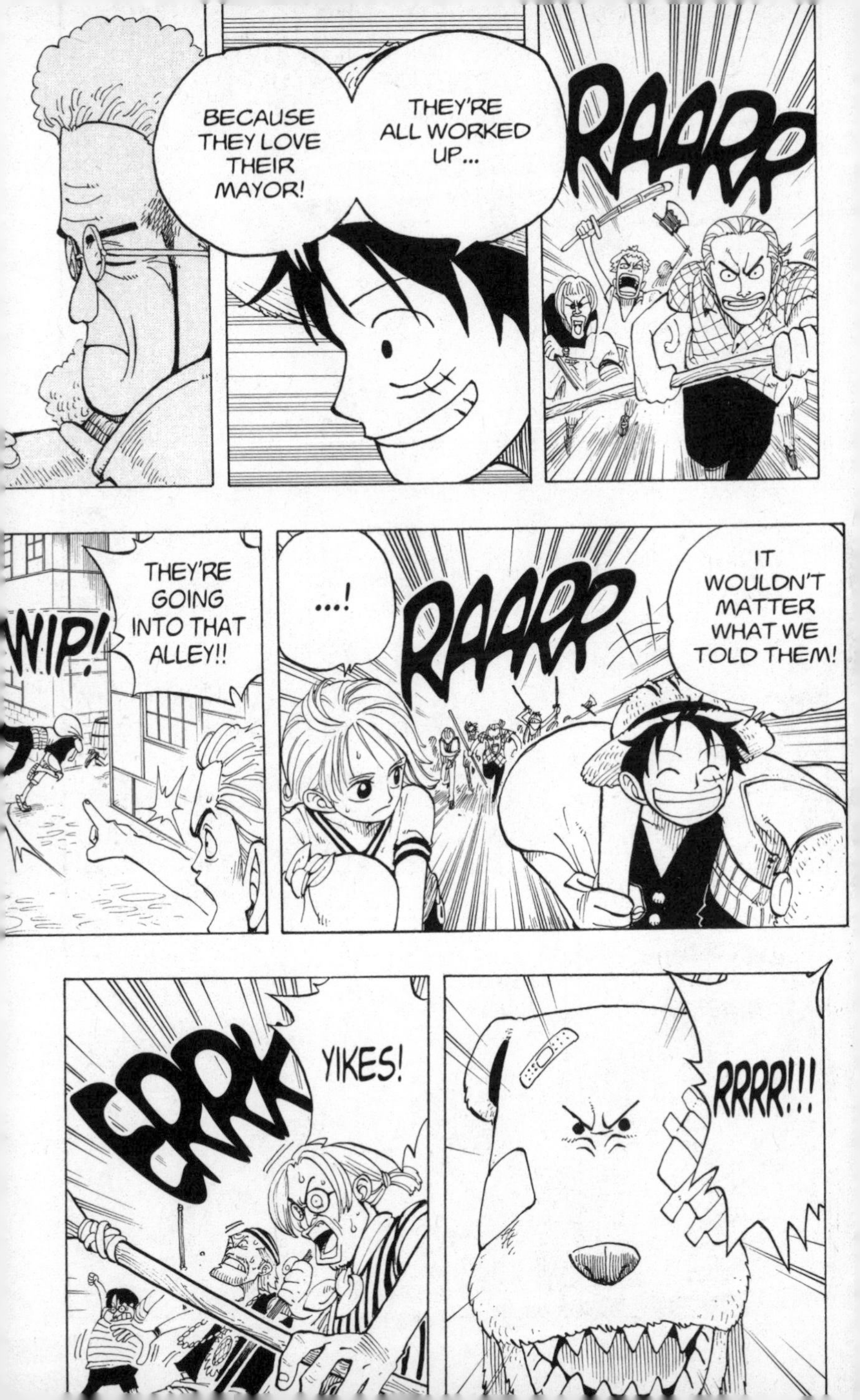
RAARR
THEY'RE ALL WORKED UP...
BECAUSE THEY LOVE THEIR MAYOR!
IT WOULDN'T MATTER WHAT WE TOLD THEM!
RAARR
...!
THEY'RE GOING INTO THAT ALLEY!!
WIP!
RRRR!!!
YIKES!
ERRK

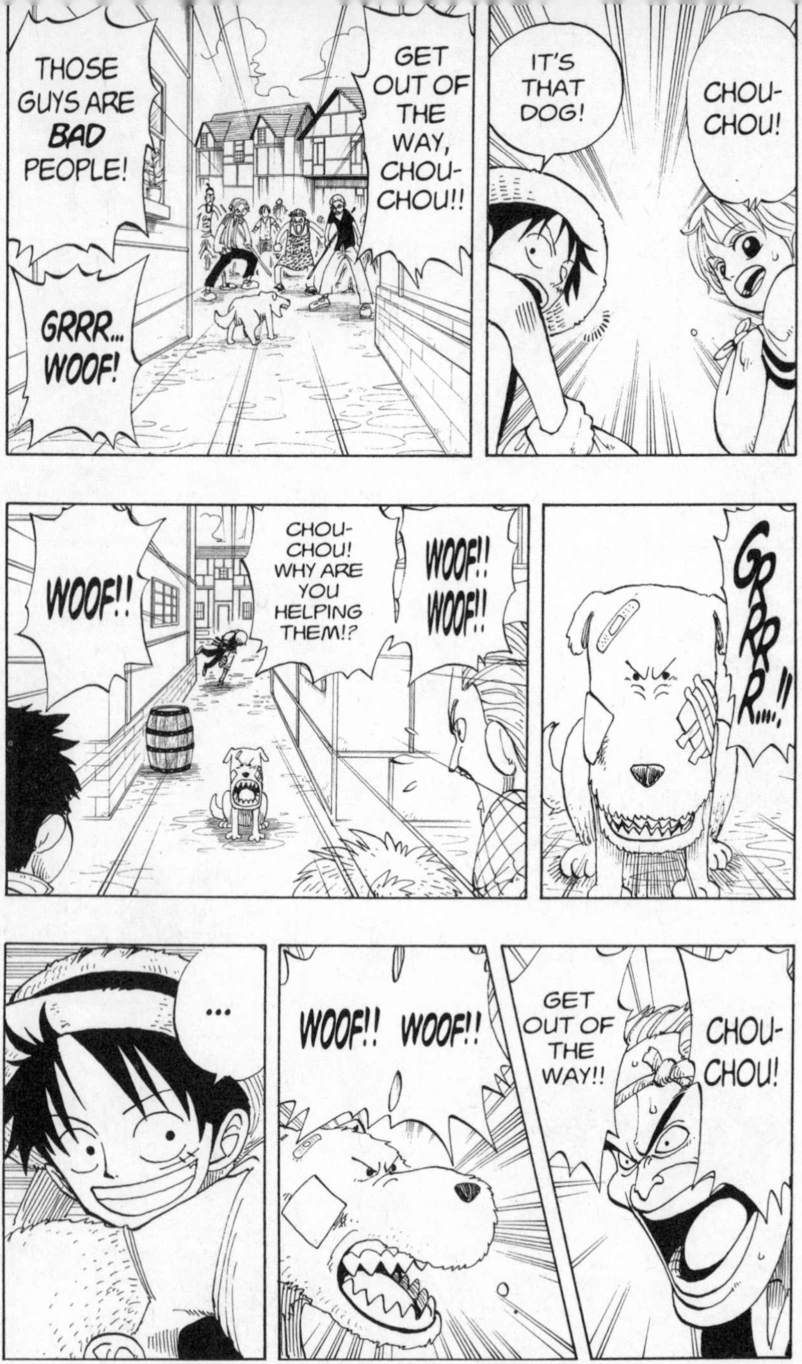
CHOU-CHOU!
IT'S THAT DOG!
GET OUT OF THE WAY, CHOU-CHOU!!
THOSE GUYS ARE BAD PEOPLE!
GRRR... WOOF!
GRRRR....!!
WOOF!! WOOF!!
CHOU-CHOU! WHY ARE YOU HELPING THEM!?
WOOF!!
CHOU-CHOU!
GET OUT OF THE WAY!!
WOOF!! WOOF!!
...

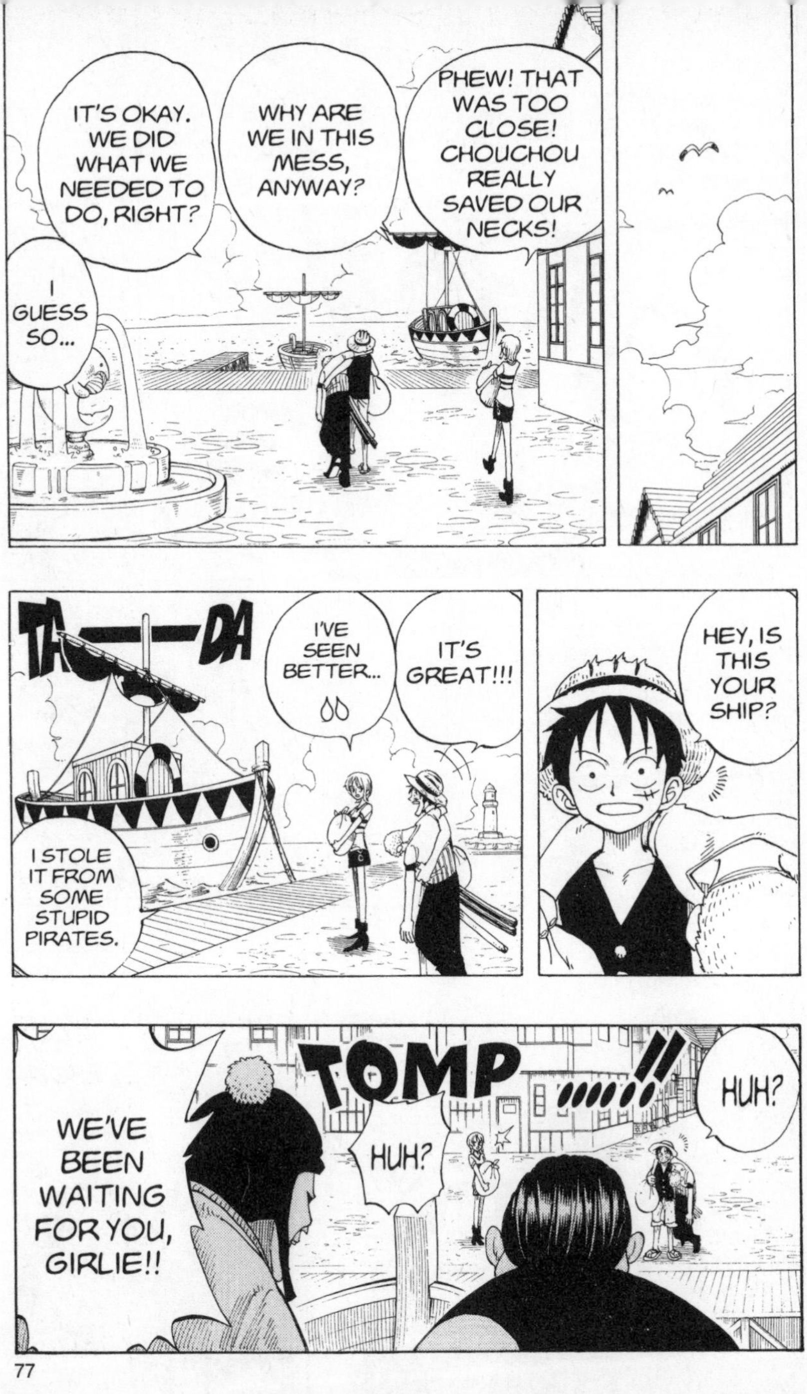
PHEW! THAT WAS TOO CLOSE! CHOUCHOU REALLY SAVED OUR NECKS!
WHY ARE WE IN THIS MESS, ANYWAY?
IT'S OKAY. WE DID WHAT WE NEEDED TO DO, RIGHT?
I GUESS SO...
HEY, IS THIS YOUR SHIP?
IT'S GREAT!!!
I'VE SEEN BETTER...
TA—DA
I STOLE IT FROM SOME STUPID PIRATES.
HUH?
TOMP!!
HUH?
WE'VE BEEN WAITING FOR YOU, GIRLIE!!

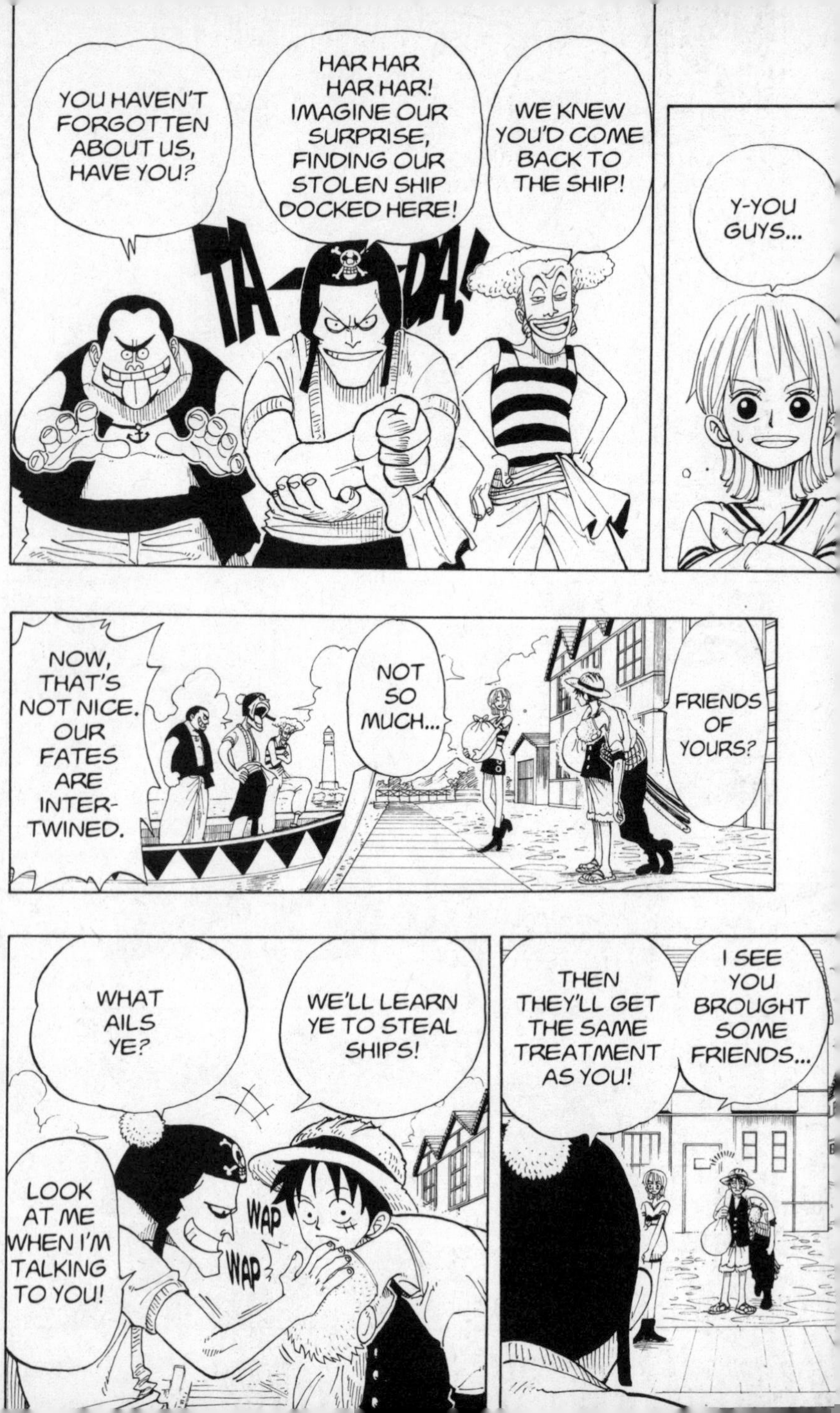
Y-YOU GUYS...
WE KNEW YOU'D COME BACK TO THE SHIP!
HAR HAR HAR HAR! IMAGINE OUR SURPRISE, FINDING OUR STOLEN SHIP DOCKED HERE!
YOU HAVEN'T FORGOTTEN ABOUT US, HAVE YOU?
TA-DA!
FRIENDS OF YOURS?
NOT SO MUCH...
NOW, THAT'S NOT NICE. OUR FATES ARE INTER-TWINED.
I SEE YOU BROUGHT SOME FRIENDS...
THEN THEY'LL GET THE SAME TREATMENT AS YOU!
WE'LL LEARN YE TO STEAL SHIPS!
WHAT AILS YE?
WAP
WAP
LOOK AT ME WHEN I'M TALKING TO YOU!

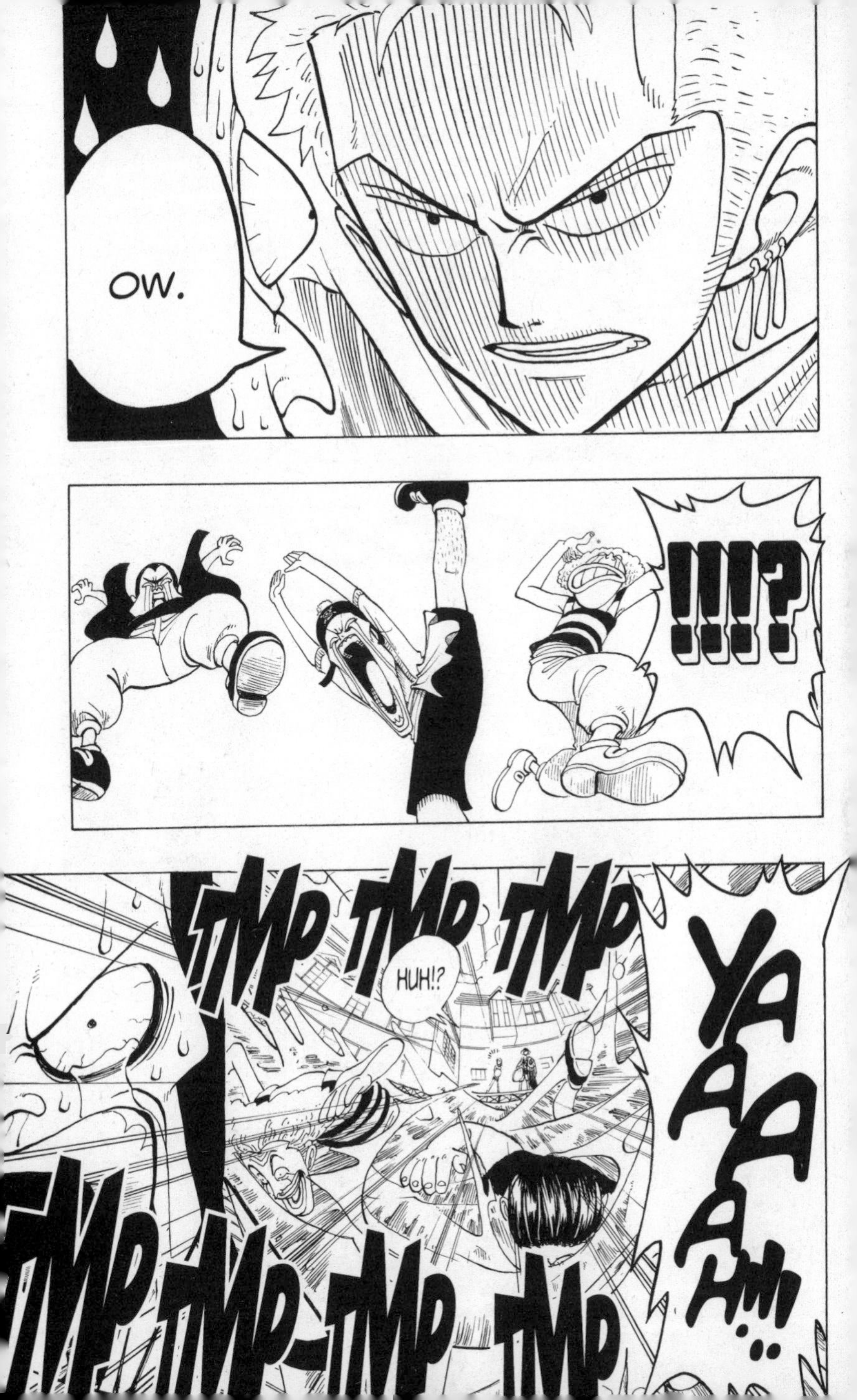
OW.
!!!?
YAAAAH!!
TMP TMP TMP
HUH!?
TMP TMP-TMP-TMP TMP

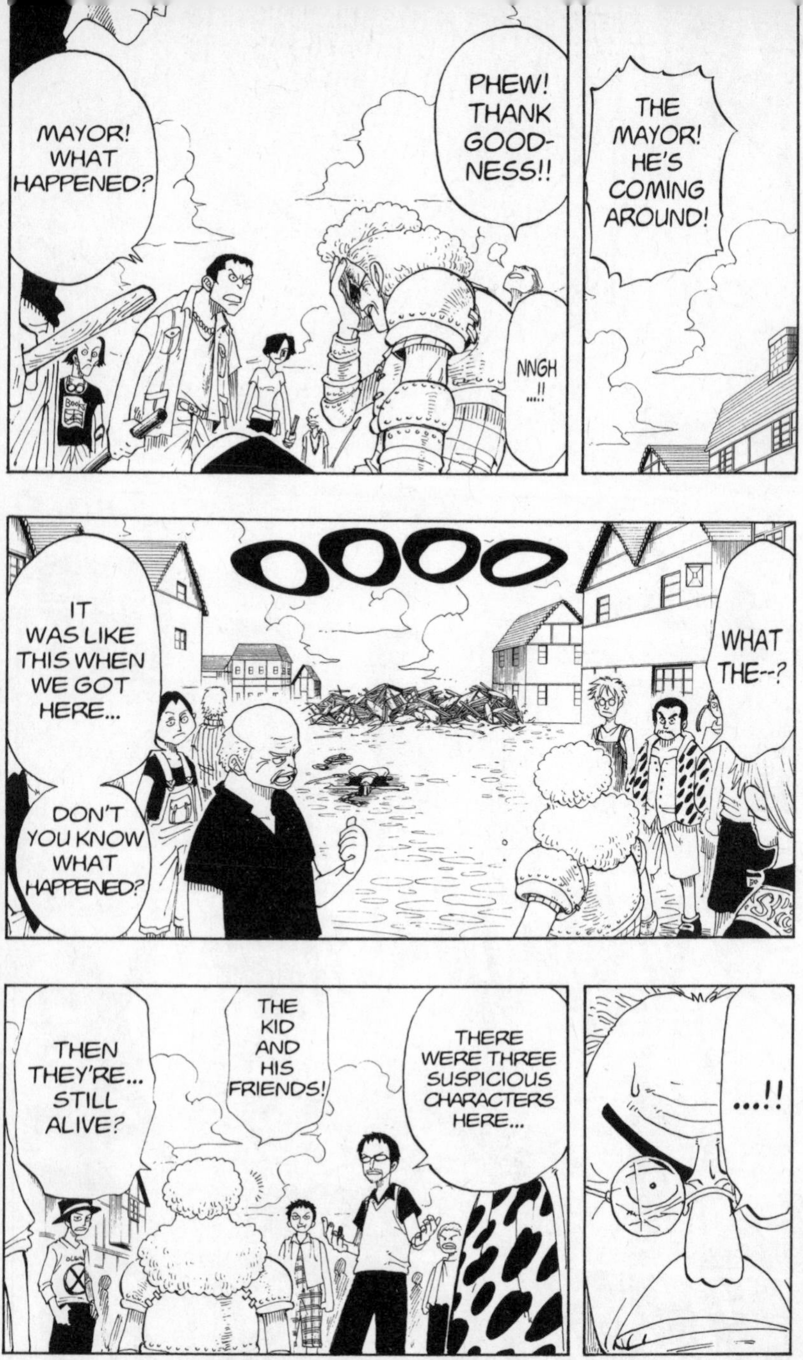
THE MAYOR! HE'S COMING AROUND!
PHEW! THANK GOOD-NESS!!
NNGH ..!!
MAYOR! WHAT HAPPENED?
OOOO
WHAT THE--?
IT WAS LIKE THIS WHEN WE GOT HERE...
DON'T YOU KNOW WHAT HAPPENED?
...!!
THERE WERE THREE SUSPICIOUS CHARACTERS HERE...
THE KID AND HIS FRIENDS!
THEN THEY'RE... STILL ALIVE?

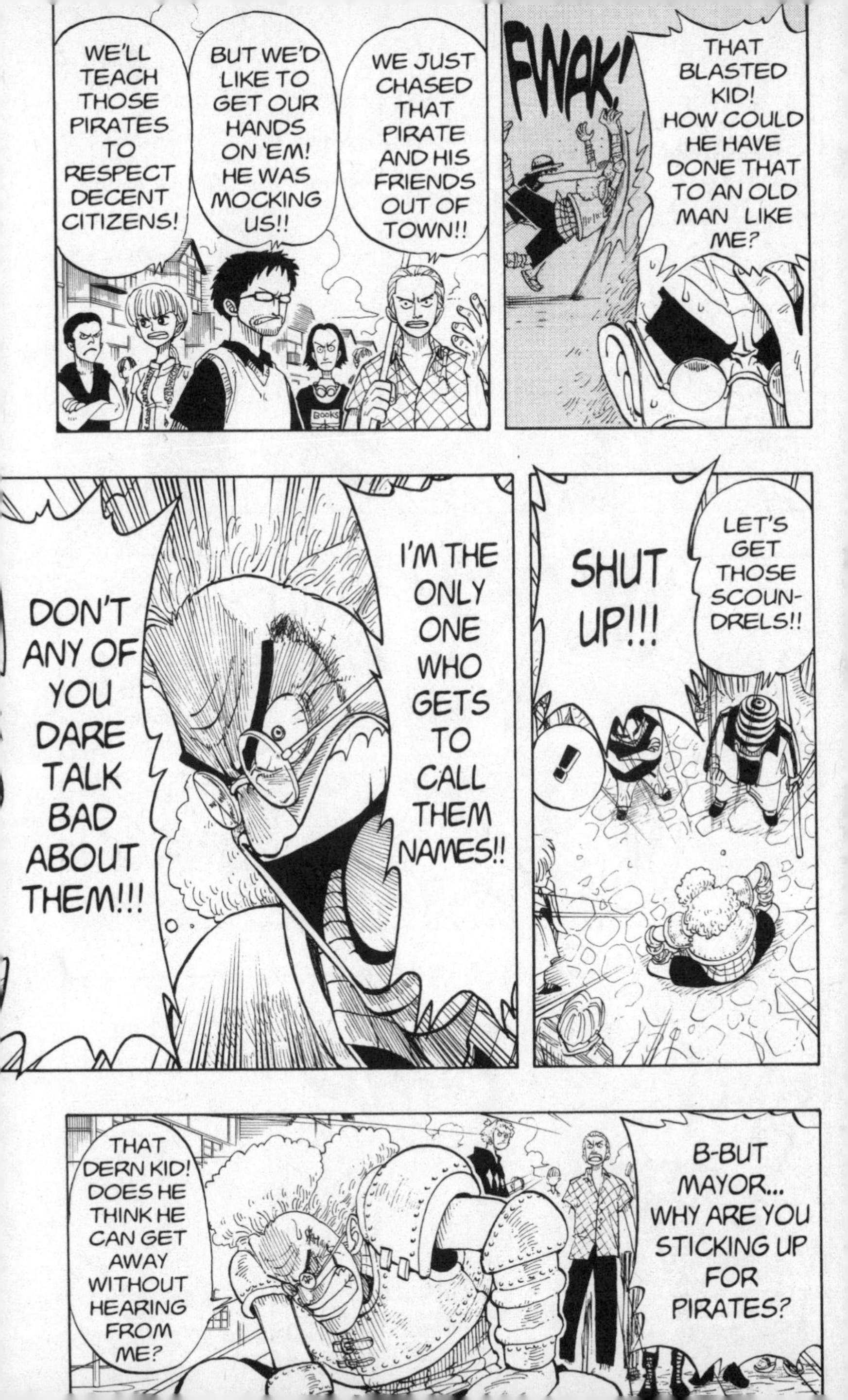
FWAK!
THAT BLASTED KID! HOW COULD HE HAVE DONE THAT TO AN OLD MAN LIKE ME?
WE JUST CHASED THAT PIRATE AND HIS FRIENDS OUT OF TOWN!!
BUT WE'D LIKE TO GET OUR HANDS ON 'EM! HE WAS MOCKING US!!
WE'LL TEACH THOSE PIRATES TO RESPECT DECENT CITIZENS!
LET'S GET THOSE SCOUN-DRELS!!
SHUT UP!!!
!
I'M THE ONLY ONE WHO GETS TO CALL THEM NAMES!!
DON'T ANY OF YOU DARE TALK BAD ABOUT THEM!!!
B-BUT MAYOR... WHY ARE YOU STICKING UP FOR PIRATES?
THAT DERN KID! DOES HE THINK HE CAN GET AWAY WITHOUT HEARING FROM ME?

READ THIS WAY

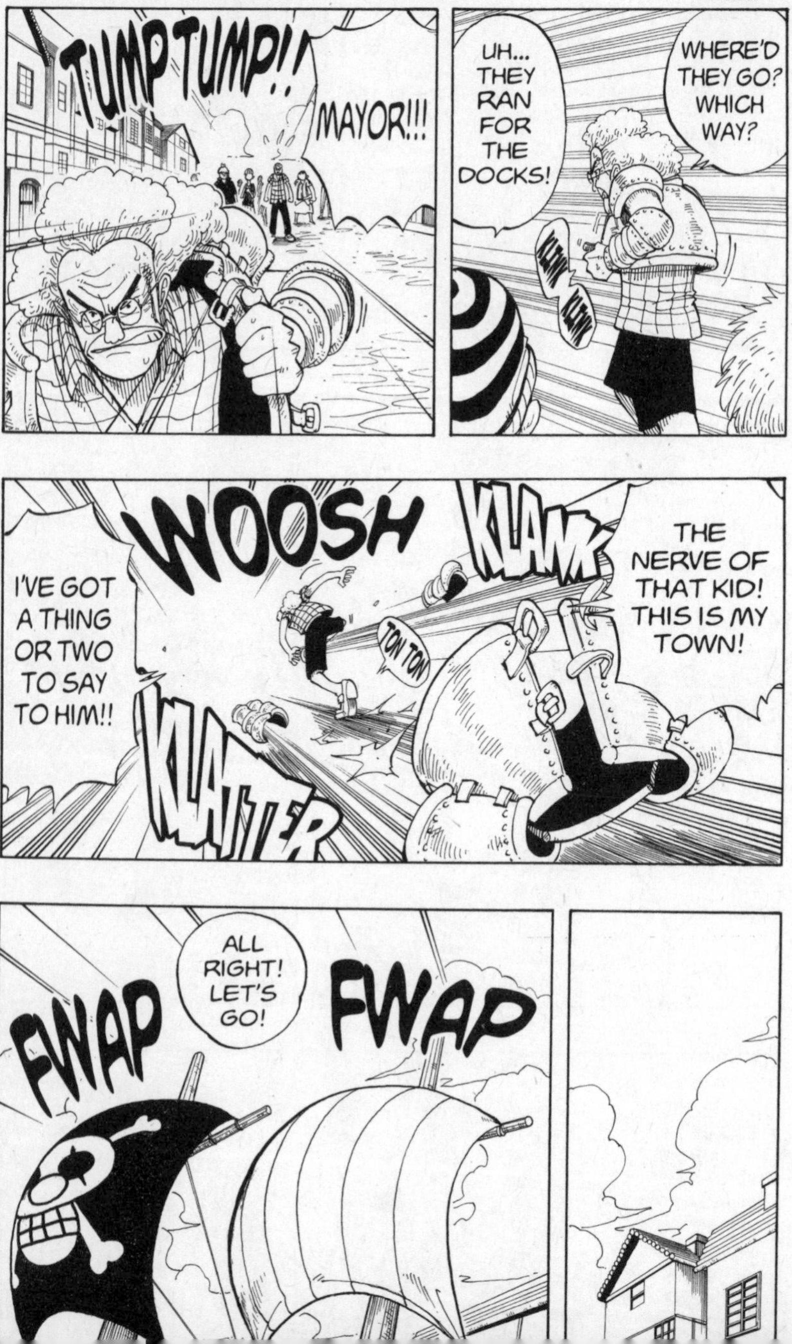
WHERE'D THEY GO? WHICH WAY?
UH... THEY RAN FOR THE DOCKS!
TUMP TUMP!!
MAYOR!!!
KLANK
THE NERVE OF THAT KID! THIS IS MY TOWN!
WOOSH
TON TON
I'VE GOT A THING OR TWO TO SAY TO HIM!!
KLATTER
FWAP
ALL RIGHT! LET'S GO!
FWAP

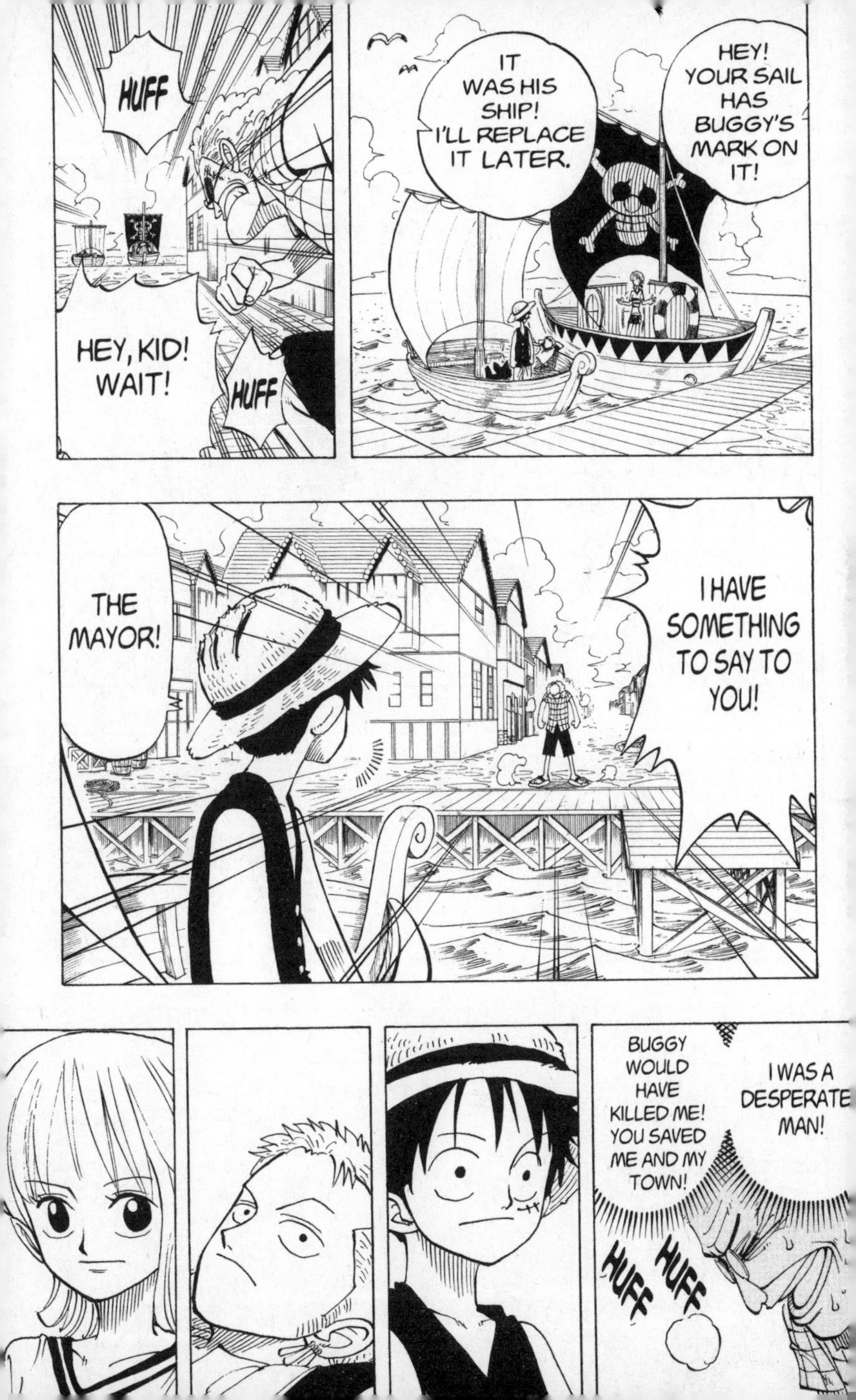
HEY! YOUR SAIL HAS BUGGY'S MARK ON IT!
IT WAS HIS SHIP! I'LL REPLACE IT LATER.
HUFF
HEY, KID! WAIT!
HUFF
I HAVE SOMETHING TO SAY TO YOU!
THE MAYOR!
I WAS A DESPERATE MAN!
BUGGY WOULD HAVE KILLED ME! YOU SAVED ME AND MY TOWN!
HUFF
HUFF

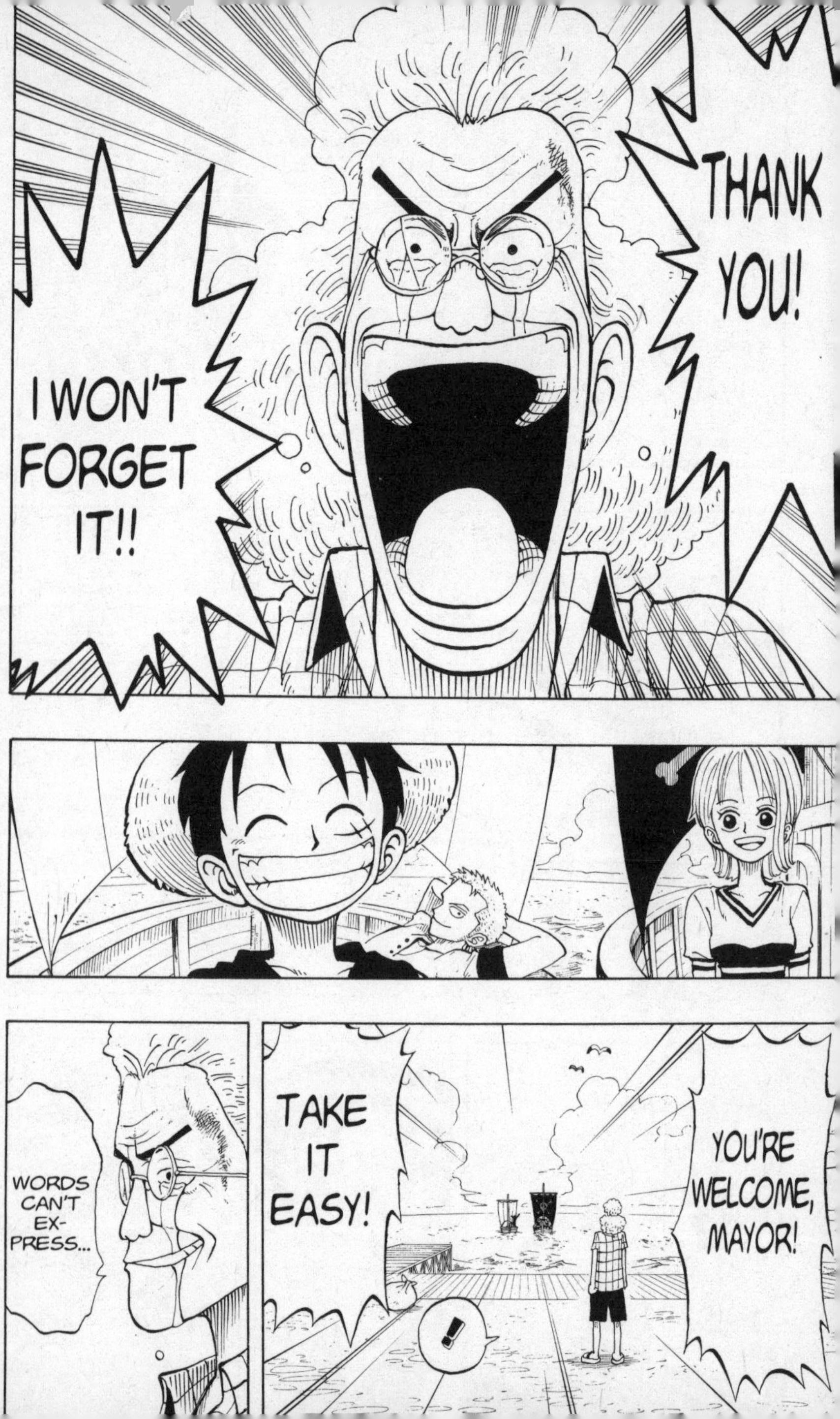
THANK YOU!
I WON'T FORGET IT!!
YOU'RE WELCOME, MAYOR!
TAKE IT EASY!
!
WORDS CAN'T EX-PRESS...

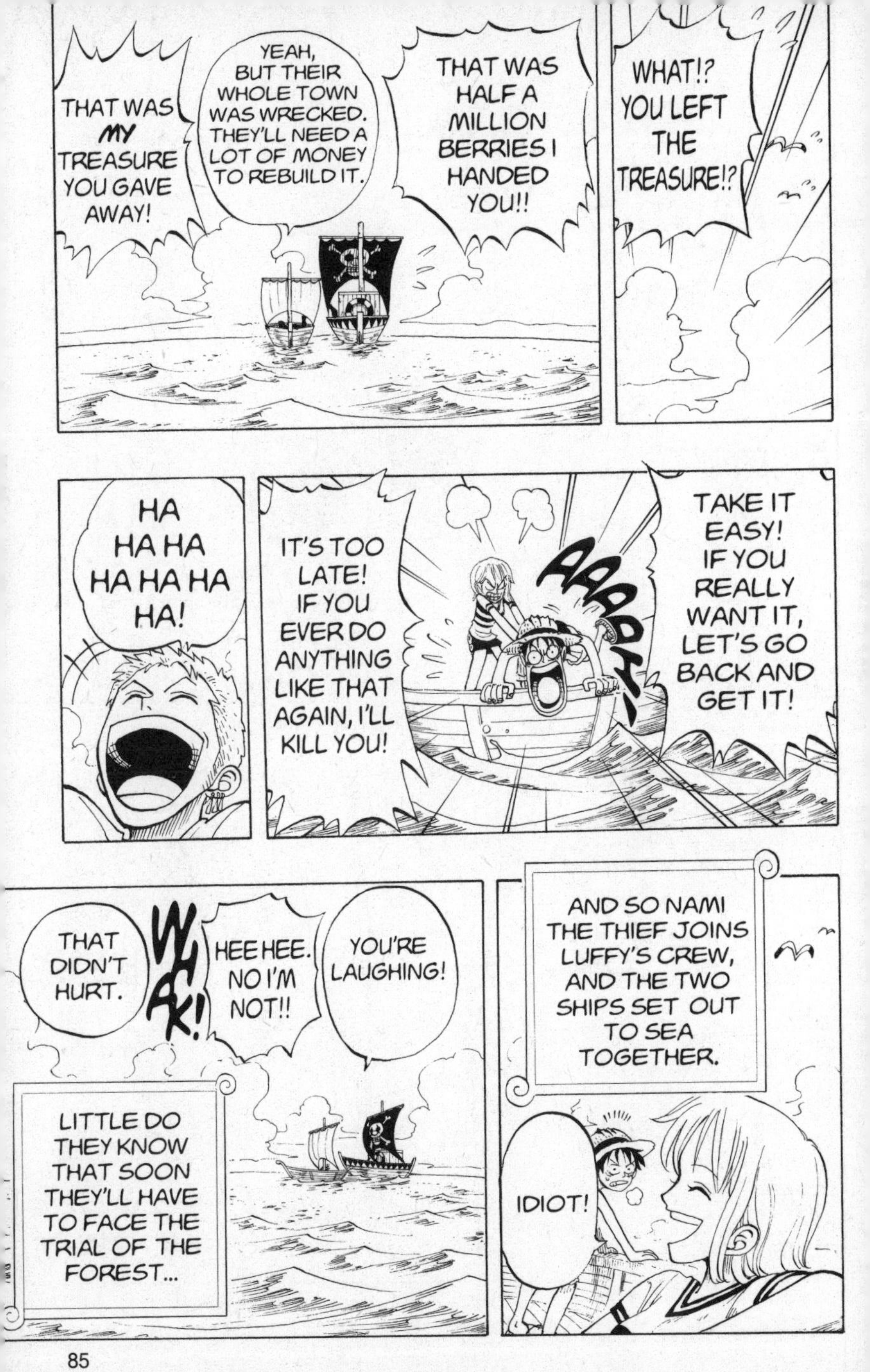
WHAT!? YOU LEFT THE TREASURE!?
THAT WAS HALF A MILLION BERRIES I HANDED YOU!!
YEAH, BUT THEIR WHOLE TOWN WAS WRECKED. THEY'LL NEED A LOT OF MONEY TO REBUILD IT.
THAT WAS MY TREASURE YOU GAVE AWAY!
TAKE IT EASY! IF YOU REALLY WANT IT, LET'S GO BACK AND GET IT!
AAAAH!
IT'S TOO LATE! IF YOU EVER DO ANYTHING LIKE THAT AGAIN, I'LL KILL YOU!
HA HA HA HA HA HA HA!
AND SO NAMI THE THIEF JOINS LUFFY'S CREW, AND THE TWO SHIPS SET OUT TO SEA TOGETHER.
IDIOT!
YOU'RE LAUGHING!
HEE HEE. NO I'M NOT!!
WHAK!
THAT DIDN'T HURT.
LITTLE DO THEY KNOW THAT SOON THEY'LL HAVE TO FACE THE TRIAL OF THE FOREST...

One Piece Storyboards #7

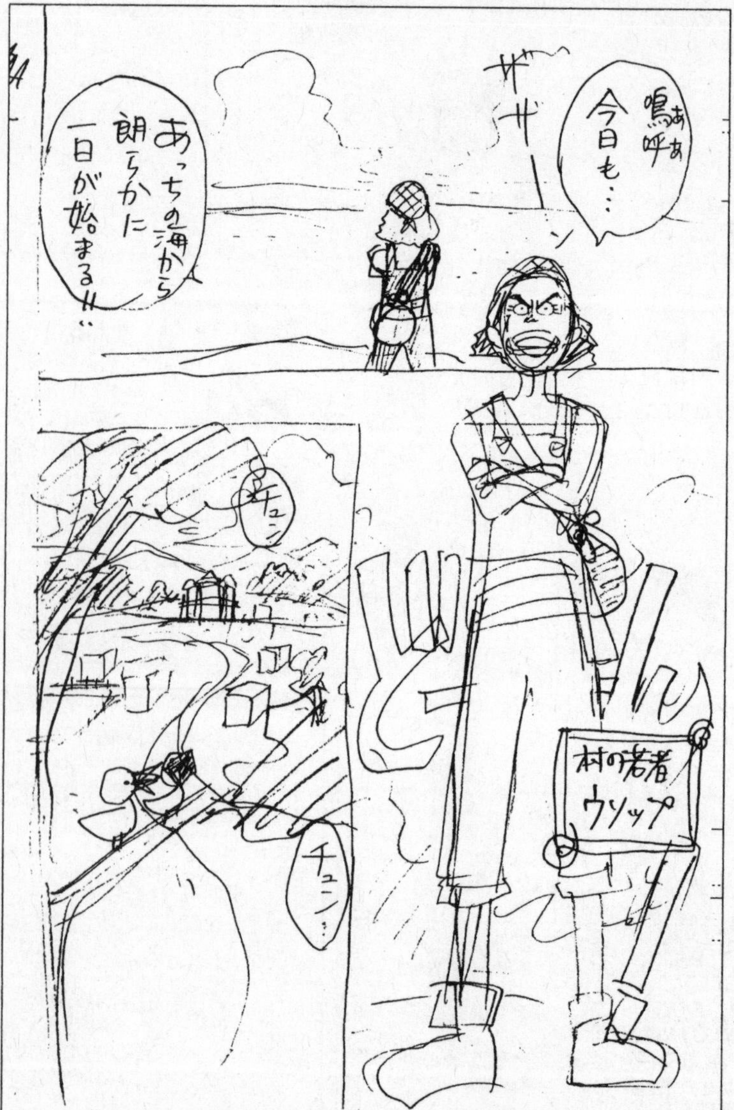
嗚呼 今日も‥
ザザーン
あっちの海から朗らかに一日が始まる!!‥
ドーン
村の若者
ウソップ
チュン
チュン‥

Chapter 22:
STRANGE CREATURES

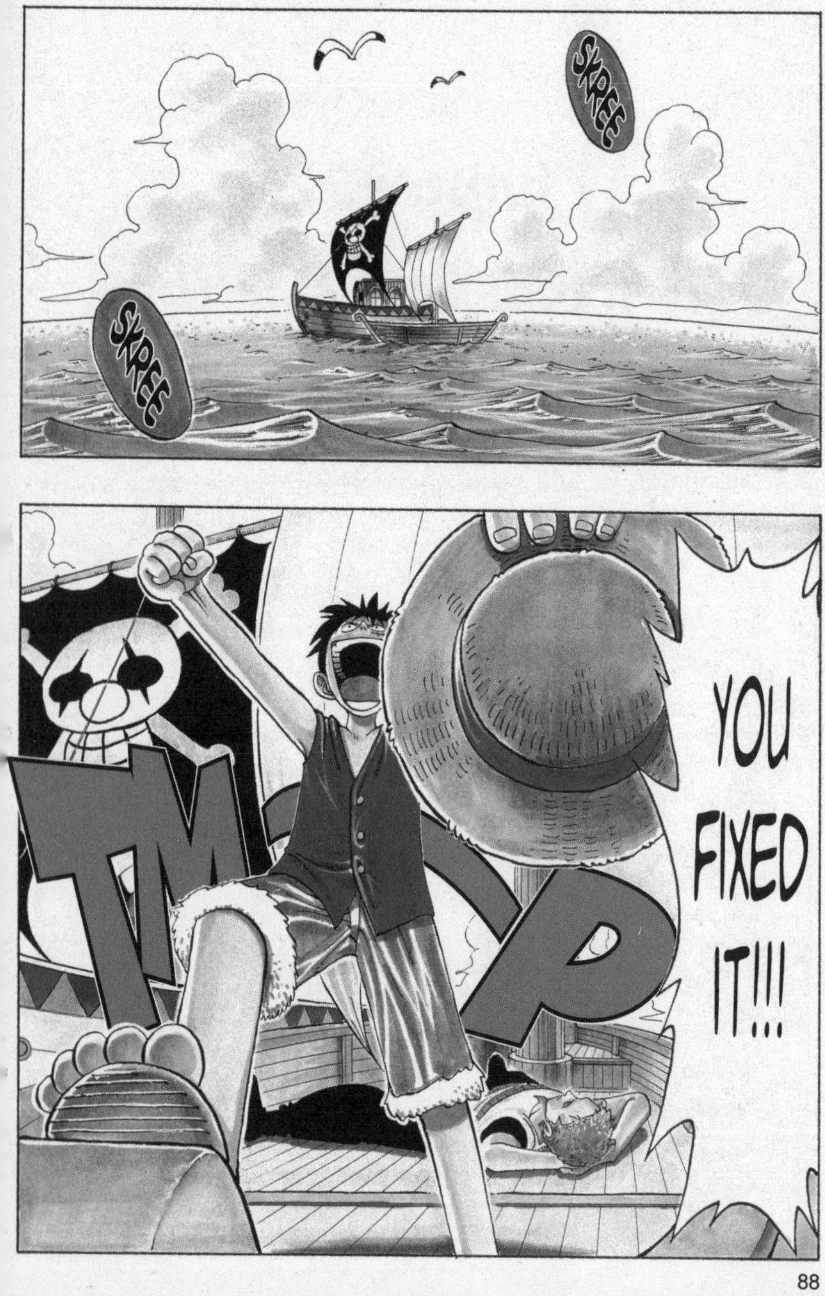
SKREE
SKREE
YOU FIXED IT!!!
TMP

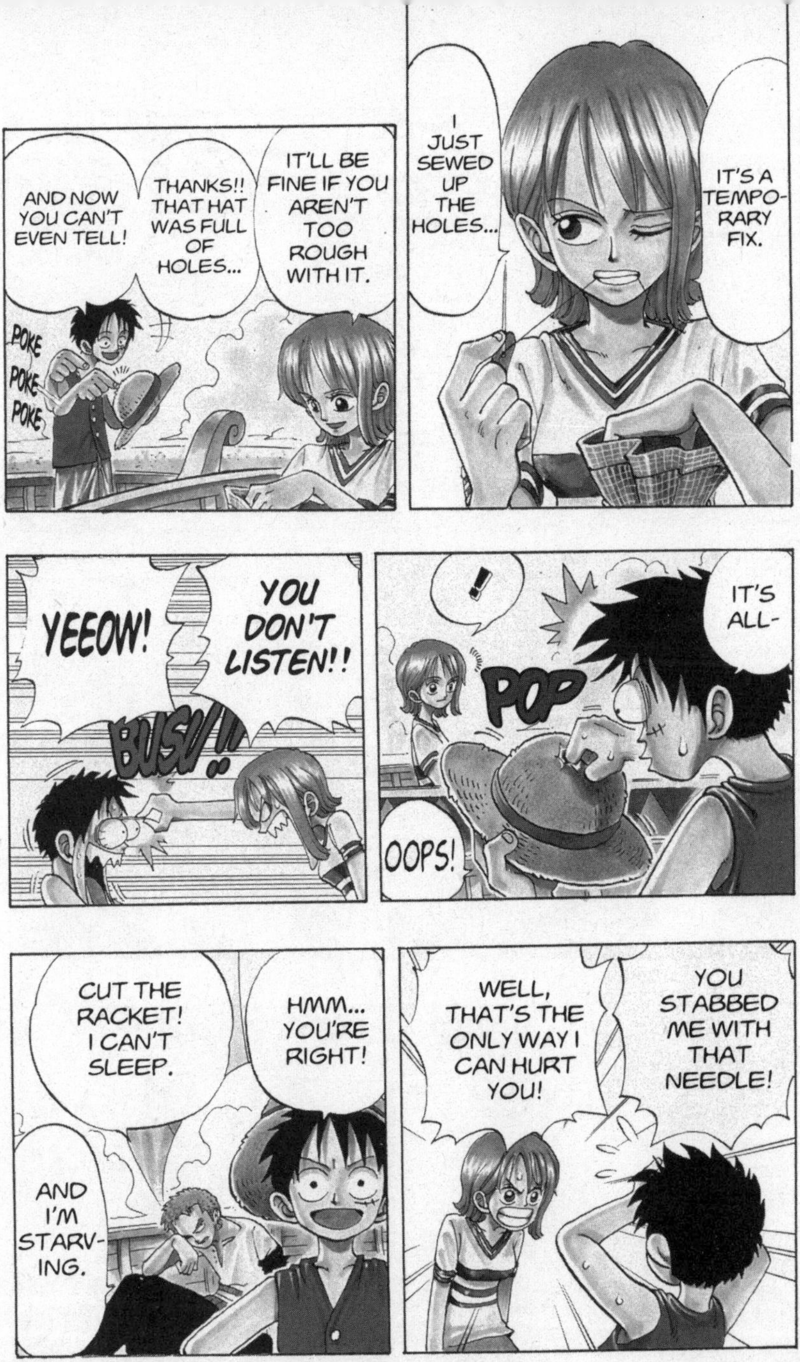
IT'S A TEMPORARY FIX.
I JUST SEWED UP THE HOLES...
IT'LL BE FINE IF YOU AREN'T TOO ROUGH WITH IT.
THANKS!! THAT HAT WAS FULL OF HOLES...
AND NOW YOU CAN'T EVEN TELL!
POKE
POKE
POKE
IT'S ALL-
!
POP
OOPS!
YOU DON'T LISTEN!!
YEEOW!
BUSU!!
YOU STABBED ME WITH THAT NEEDLE!
WELL, THAT'S THE ONLY WAY I CAN HURT YOU!
HMM... YOU'RE RIGHT!
CUT THE RACKET! I CAN'T SLEEP.
AND I'M STARVING.

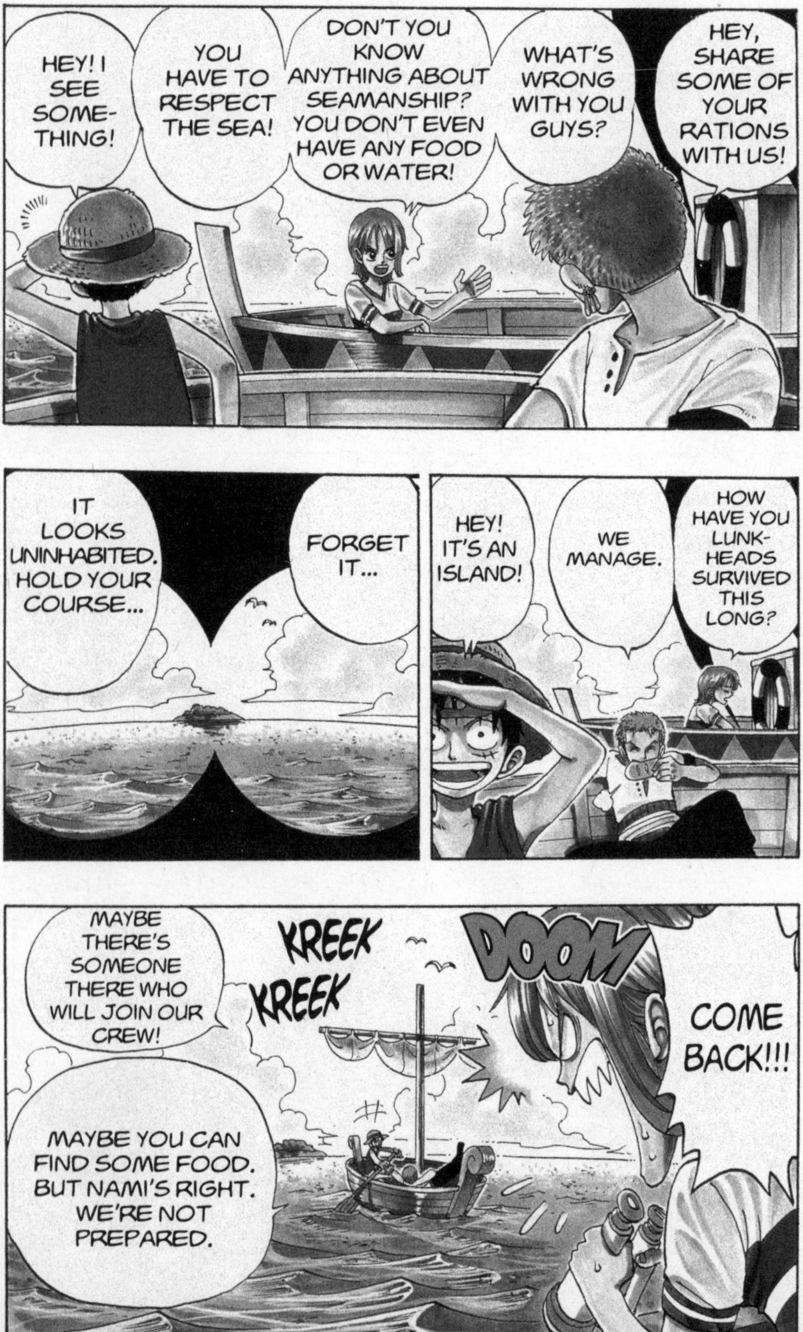
HEY, SHARE SOME OF YOUR RATIONS WITH US!
WHAT'S WRONG WITH YOU GUYS?
DON'T YOU KNOW ANYTHING ABOUT SEAMANSHIP? YOU DON'T EVEN HAVE ANY FOOD OR WATER!
YOU HAVE TO RESPECT THE SEA!
HEY! I SEE SOMETHING!
HOW HAVE YOU LUNKHEADS SURVIVED THIS LONG?
WE MANAGE.
HEY! IT'S AN ISLAND!
FORGET IT...
IT LOOKS UNINHABITED. HOLD YOUR COURSE...
DOOM
COME BACK!!!
KREEK
KREEK
MAYBE THERE'S SOMEONE THERE WHO WILL JOIN OUR CREW!
MAYBE YOU CAN FIND SOME FOOD. BUT NAMI'S RIGHT. WE'RE NOT PREPARED.

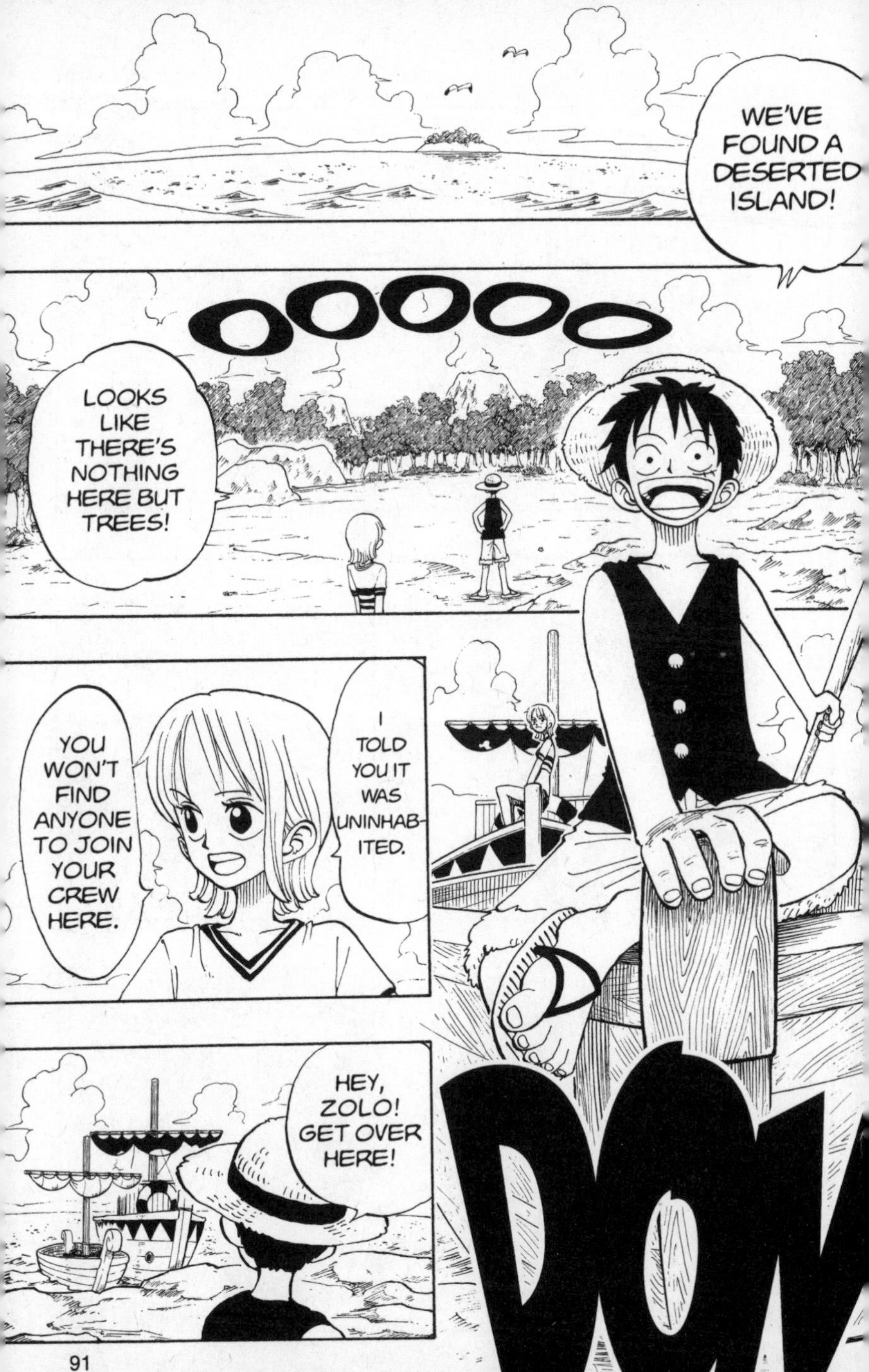

WE'VE FOUND A DESERTED ISLAND!
OOOOO
LOOKS LIKE THERE'S NOTHING HERE BUT TREES!
DON
I TOLD YOU IT WAS UNINHABITED.
YOU WON'T FIND ANYONE TO JOIN YOUR CREW HERE.
HEY, ZOLO! GET OVER HERE!

READ THIS WAY

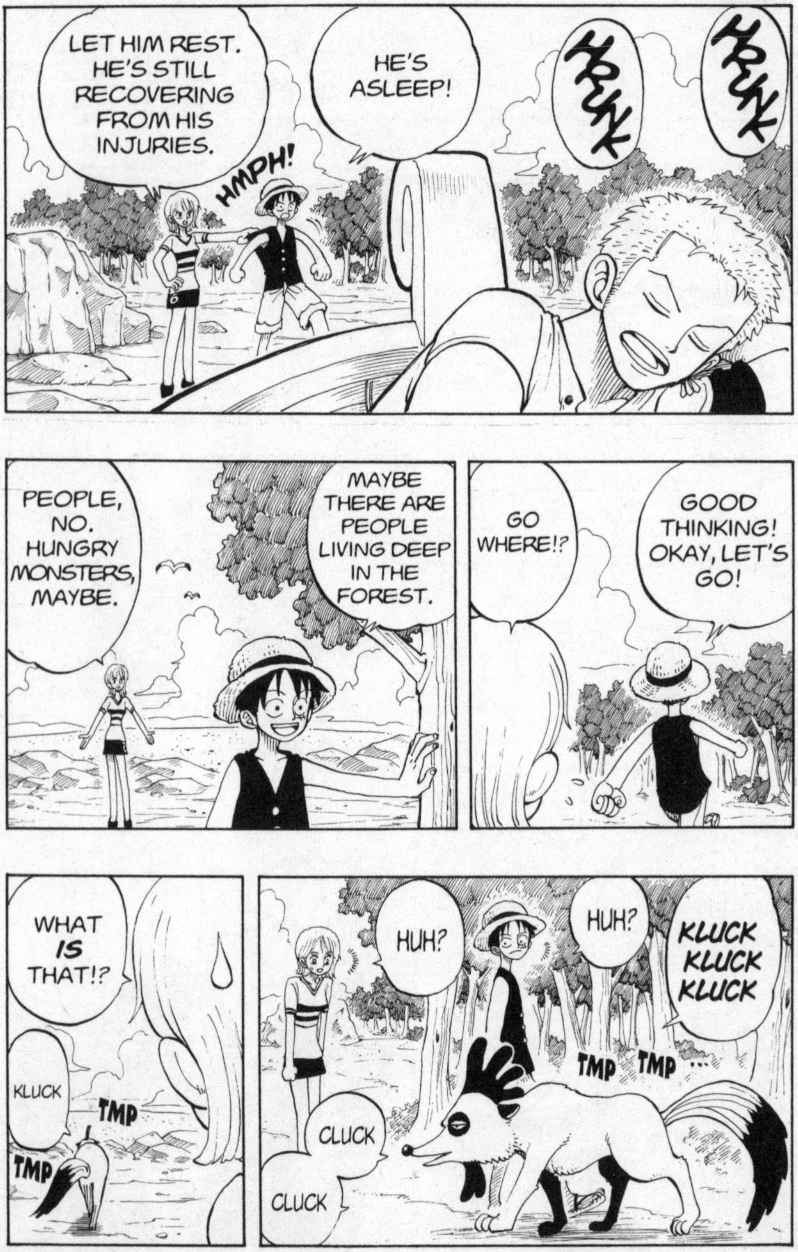
HONK
HONK
HE'S ASLEEP!
LET HIM REST. HE'S STILL RECOVERING FROM HIS INJURIES.
HMPH!
GOOD THINKING! OKAY, LET'S GO!
GO WHERE!?
MAYBE THERE ARE PEOPLE LIVING DEEP IN THE FOREST.
PEOPLE, NO. HUNGRY MONSTERS, MAYBE.
KLUCK KLUCK KLUCK
HUH?
HUH?
TMP TMP ...
CLUCK
CLUCK
WHAT IS THAT!?
KLUCK
TMP
TMP

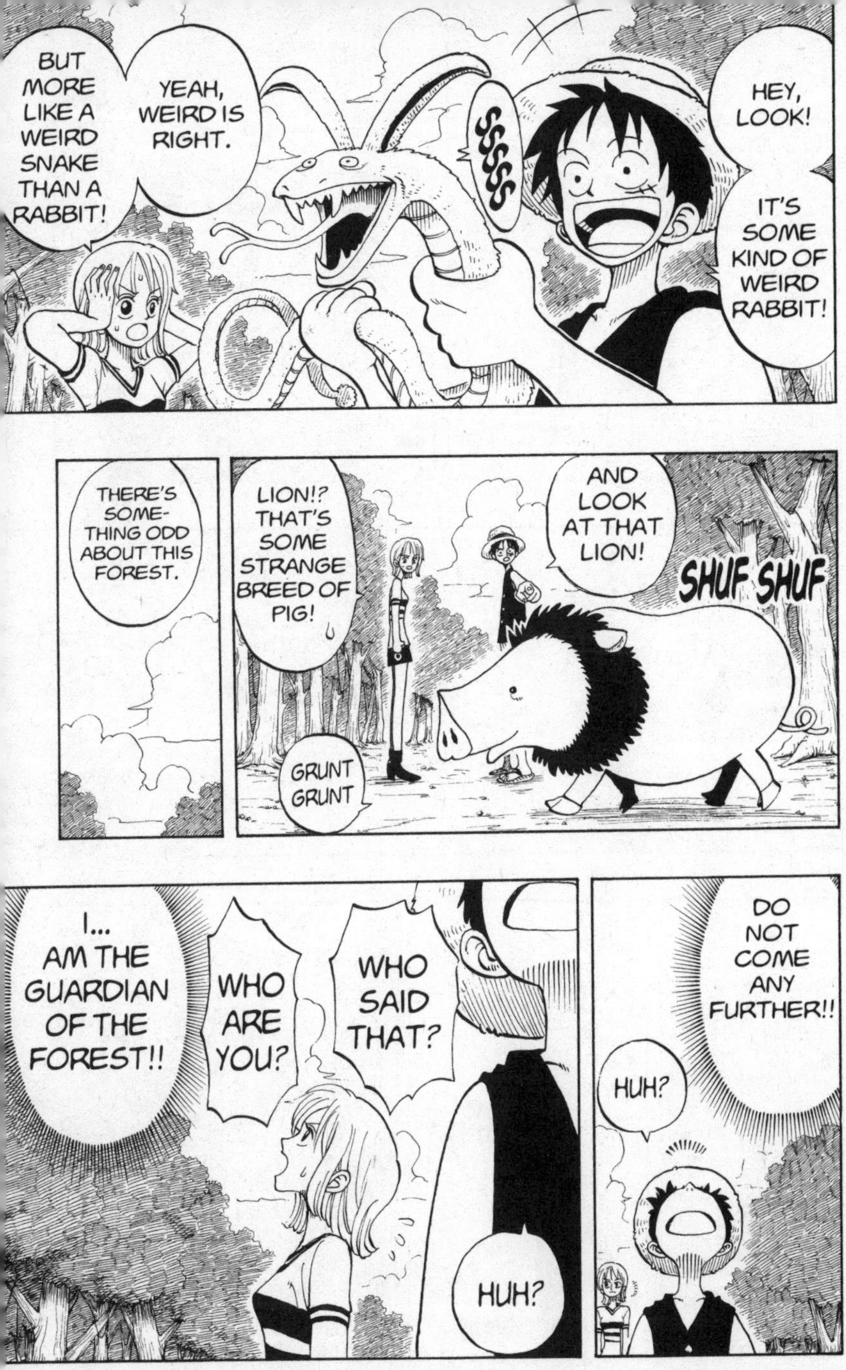
HEY, LOOK!
IT'S SOME KIND OF WEIRD RABBIT!
SSSSS
YEAH, WEIRD IS RIGHT.
BUT MORE LIKE A WEIRD SNAKE THAN A RABBIT!
AND LOOK AT THAT LION!
SHUF SHUF
LION!? THAT'S SOME STRANGE BREED OF PIG!
GRUNT GRUNT
THERE'S SOME-THING ODD ABOUT THIS FOREST.
DO NOT COME ANY FURTHER!!
HUH?
WHO SAID THAT?
HUH?
WHO ARE YOU?
I... AM THE GUARDIAN OF THE FOREST!!

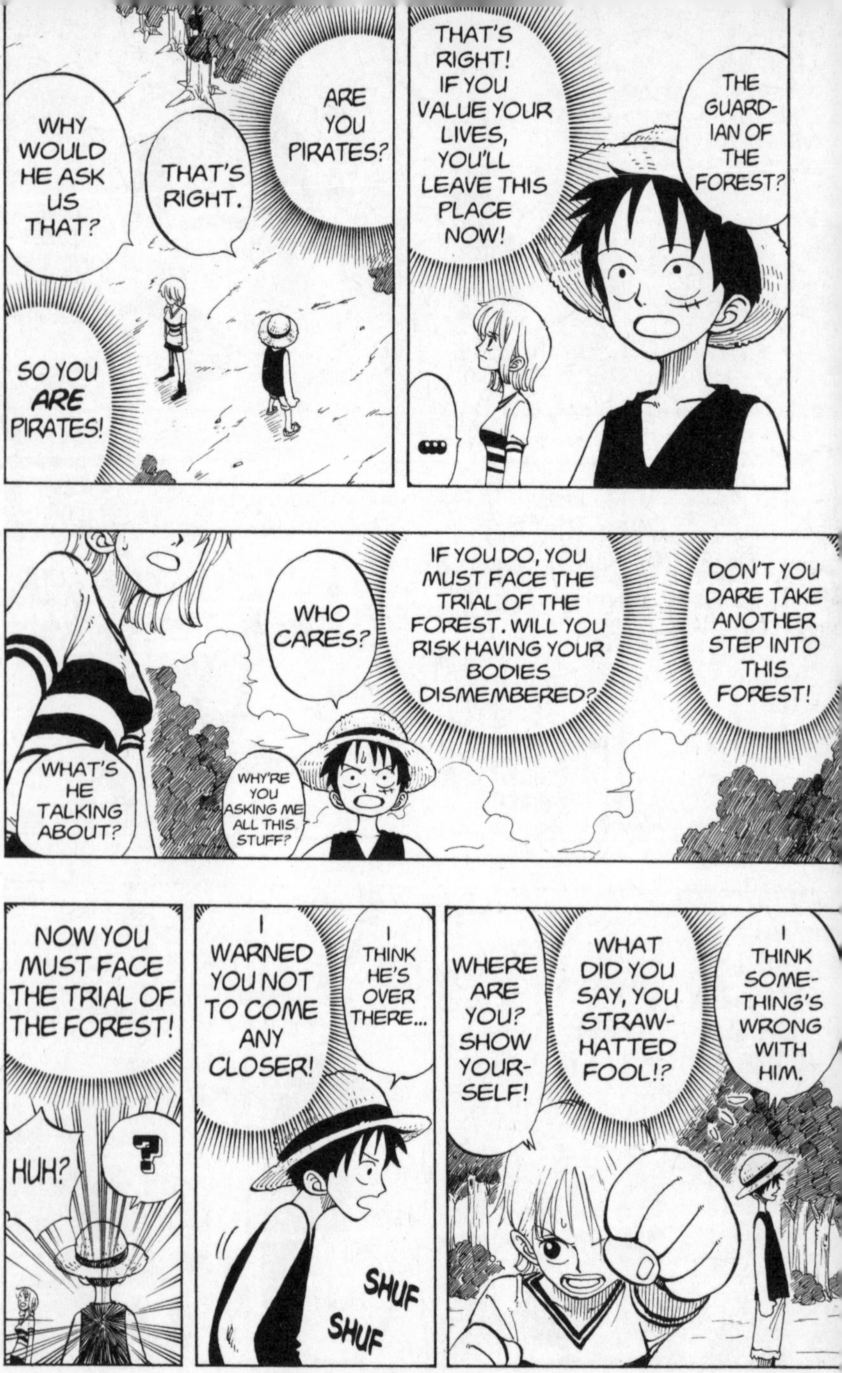
THE GUARDIAN OF THE FOREST?
THAT'S RIGHT! IF YOU VALUE YOUR LIVES, YOU'LL LEAVE THIS PLACE NOW!
...
ARE YOU PIRATES?
THAT'S RIGHT.
WHY WOULD HE ASK US THAT?
SO YOU ARE PIRATES!
DON'T YOU DARE TAKE ANOTHER STEP INTO THIS FOREST!
IF YOU DO, YOU MUST FACE THE TRIAL OF THE FOREST. WILL YOU RISK HAVING YOUR BODIES DISMEMBERED?
WHO CARES?
WHY'RE YOU ASKING ME ALL THIS STUFF?
WHAT'S HE TALKING ABOUT?
I THINK SOMETHING'S WRONG WITH HIM.
WHAT DID YOU SAY, YOU STRAW-HATTED FOOL!?
WHERE ARE YOU? SHOW YOURSELF!
I THINK HE'S OVER THERE...
I WARNED YOU NOT TO COME ANY CLOSER!
SHUF
SHUF
NOW YOU MUST FACE THE TRIAL OF THE FOREST!
?
HUH?

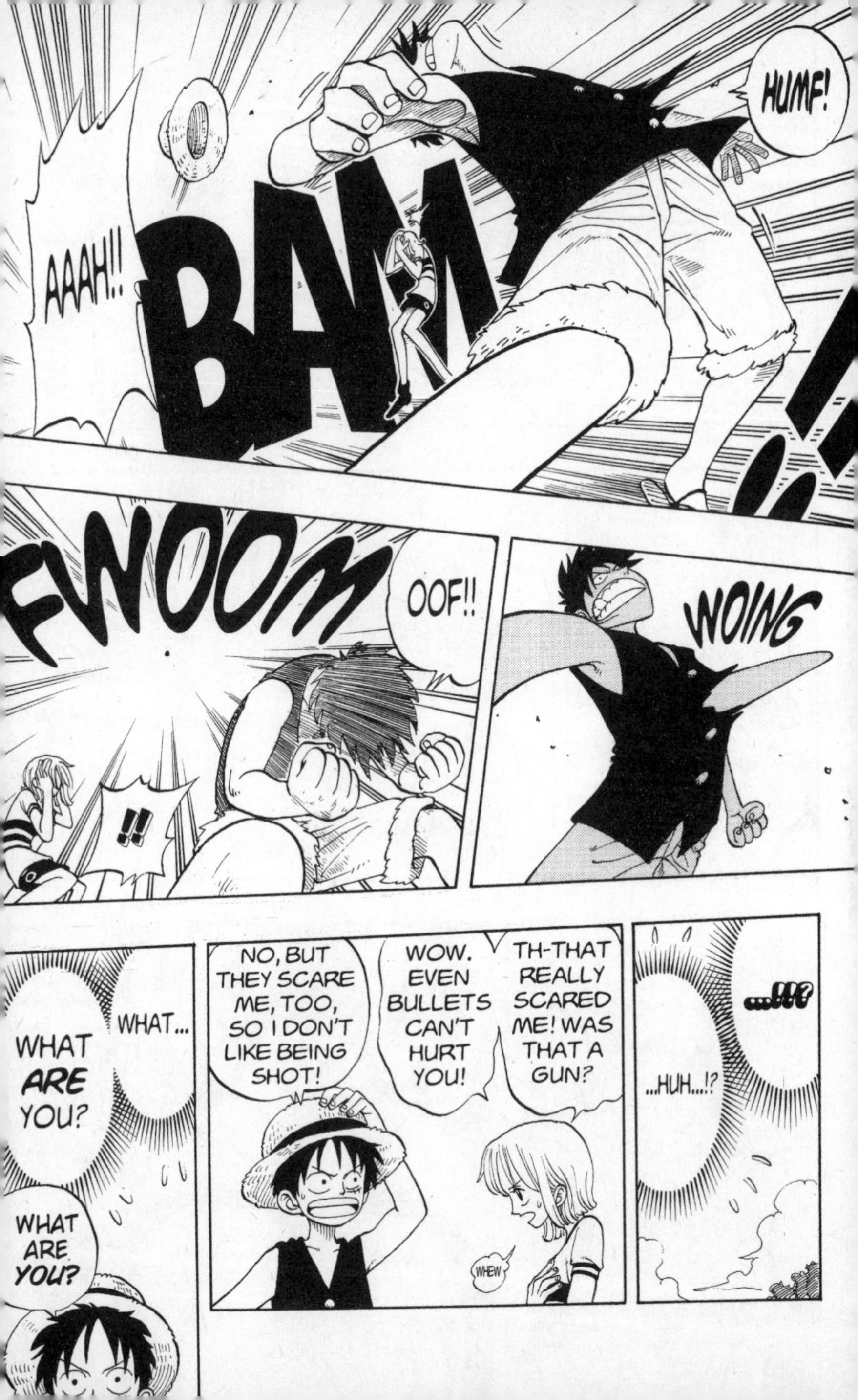
HUMF!
BAM
AAAH!!
WOING
OOF!!
FWOOM
!!
...!!?
...HUH...!?
TH-THAT REALLY SCARED ME! WAS THAT A GUN?
WOW. EVEN BULLETS CAN'T HURT YOU!
NO, BUT THEY SCARE ME, TOO, SO I DON'T LIKE BEING SHOT!
WHEW
WHAT...
WHAT *ARE* YOU?
WHAT ARE *YOU?*

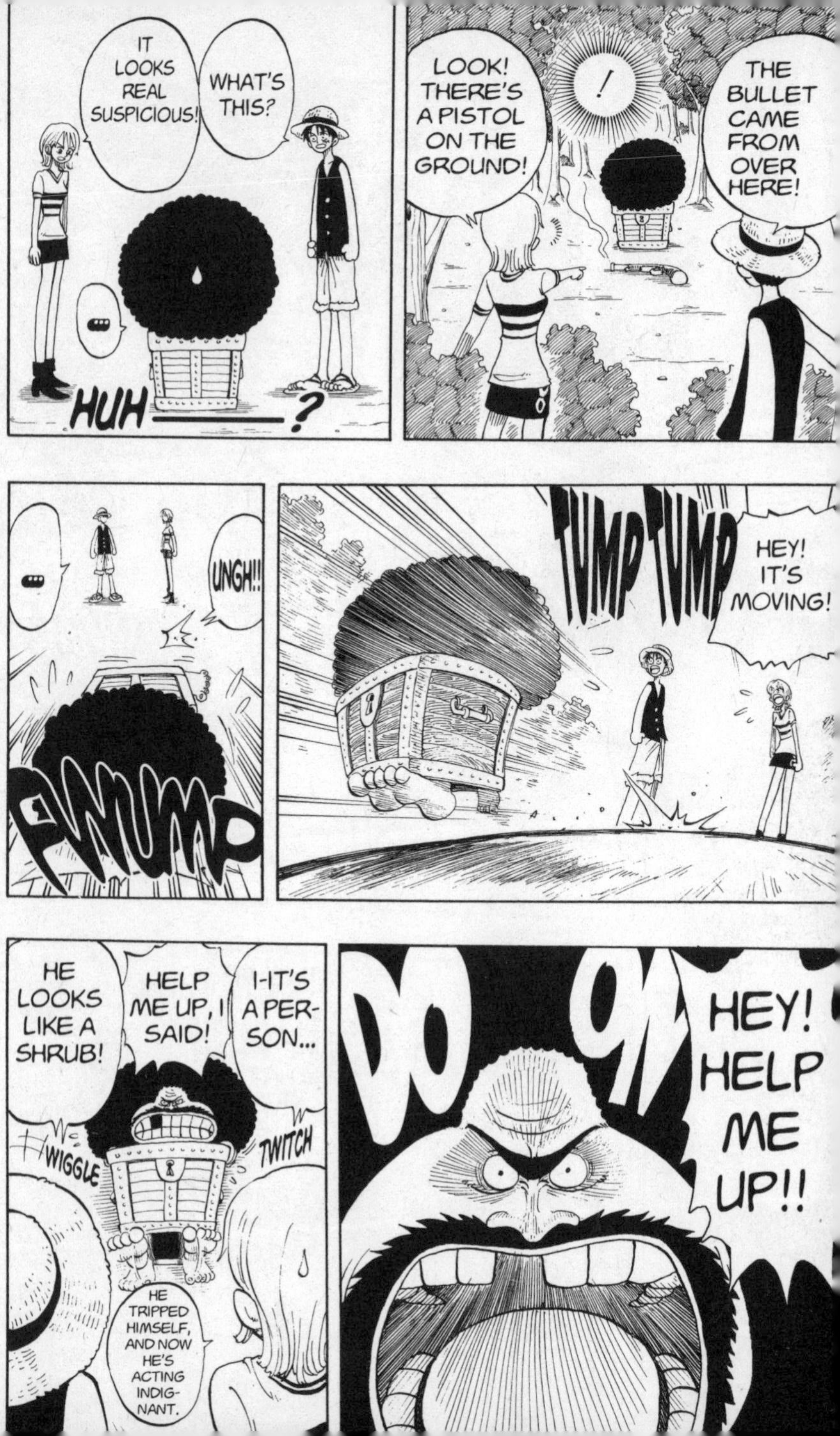
THE BULLET CAME FROM OVER HERE!
!
LOOK! THERE'S A PISTOL ON THE GROUND!
WHAT'S THIS?
IT LOOKS REAL SUSPICIOUS!
...
HUH——?
TUMP TUMP
HEY! IT'S MOVING!
UNGH!!
...
FWUMP
DO
HEY! HELP ME UP!!
I-IT'S A PERSON...
HELP ME UP, I SAID!
HE LOOKS LIKE A SHRUB!
TWITCH
WIGGLE
HE TRIPPED HIMSELF, AND NOW HE'S ACTING INDIGNANT.

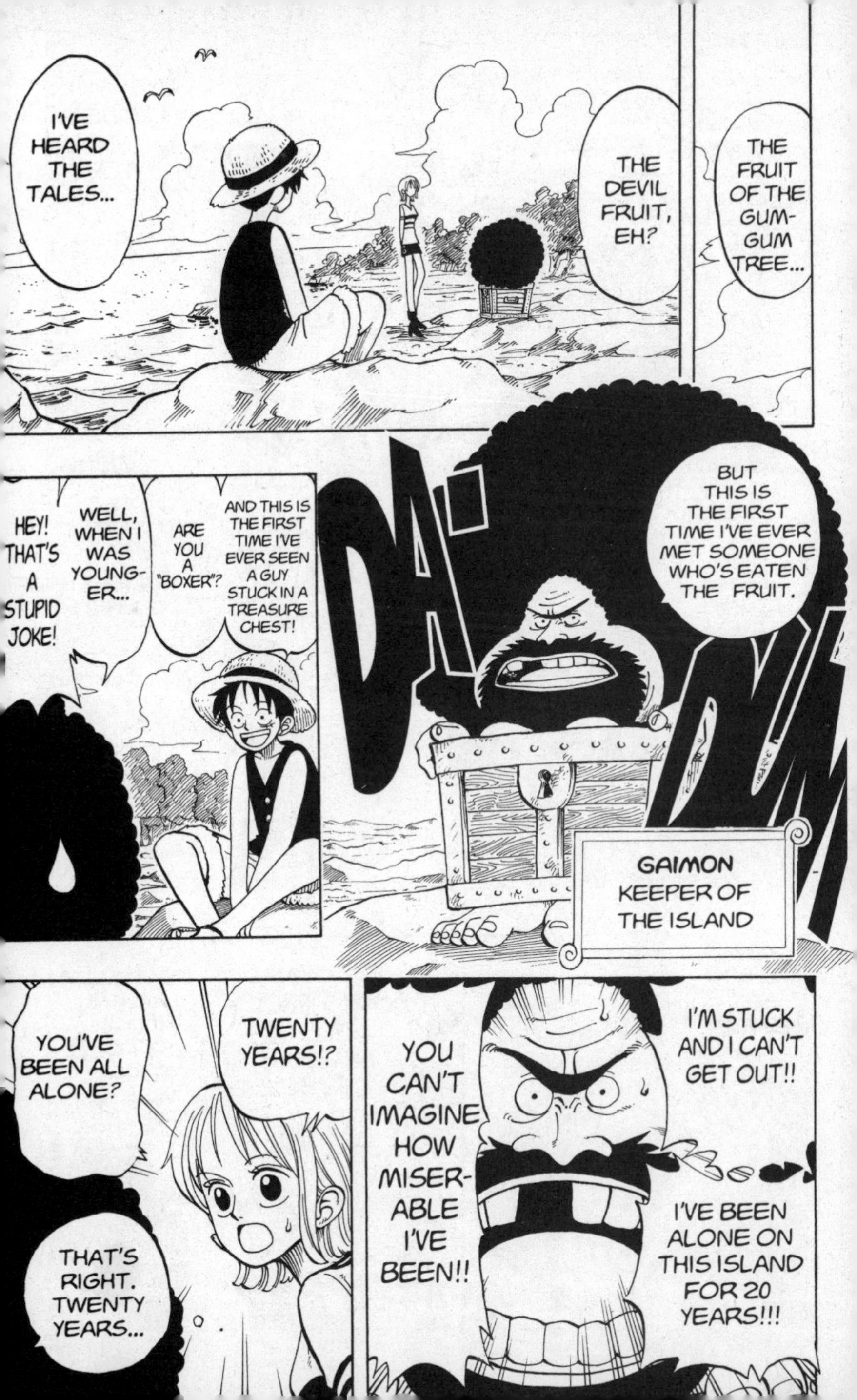
THE FRUIT OF THE GUM-GUM TREE...
THE DEVIL FRUIT, EH?
I'VE HEARD THE TALES...
BUT THIS IS THE FIRST TIME I'VE EVER MET SOMEONE WHO'S EATEN THE FRUIT.
GAIMON KEEPER OF THE ISLAND
AND THIS IS THE FIRST TIME I'VE EVER SEEN A GUY STUCK IN A TREASURE CHEST!
ARE YOU A "BOXER"?
WELL, WHEN I WAS YOUNGER...
HEY! THAT'S A STUPID JOKE!
I'M STUCK AND I CAN'T GET OUT!!
YOU CAN'T IMAGINE HOW MISERABLE I'VE BEEN!!
I'VE BEEN ALONE ON THIS ISLAND FOR 20 YEARS!!!
TWENTY YEARS!?
YOU'VE BEEN ALL ALONE?
THAT'S RIGHT. TWENTY YEARS...

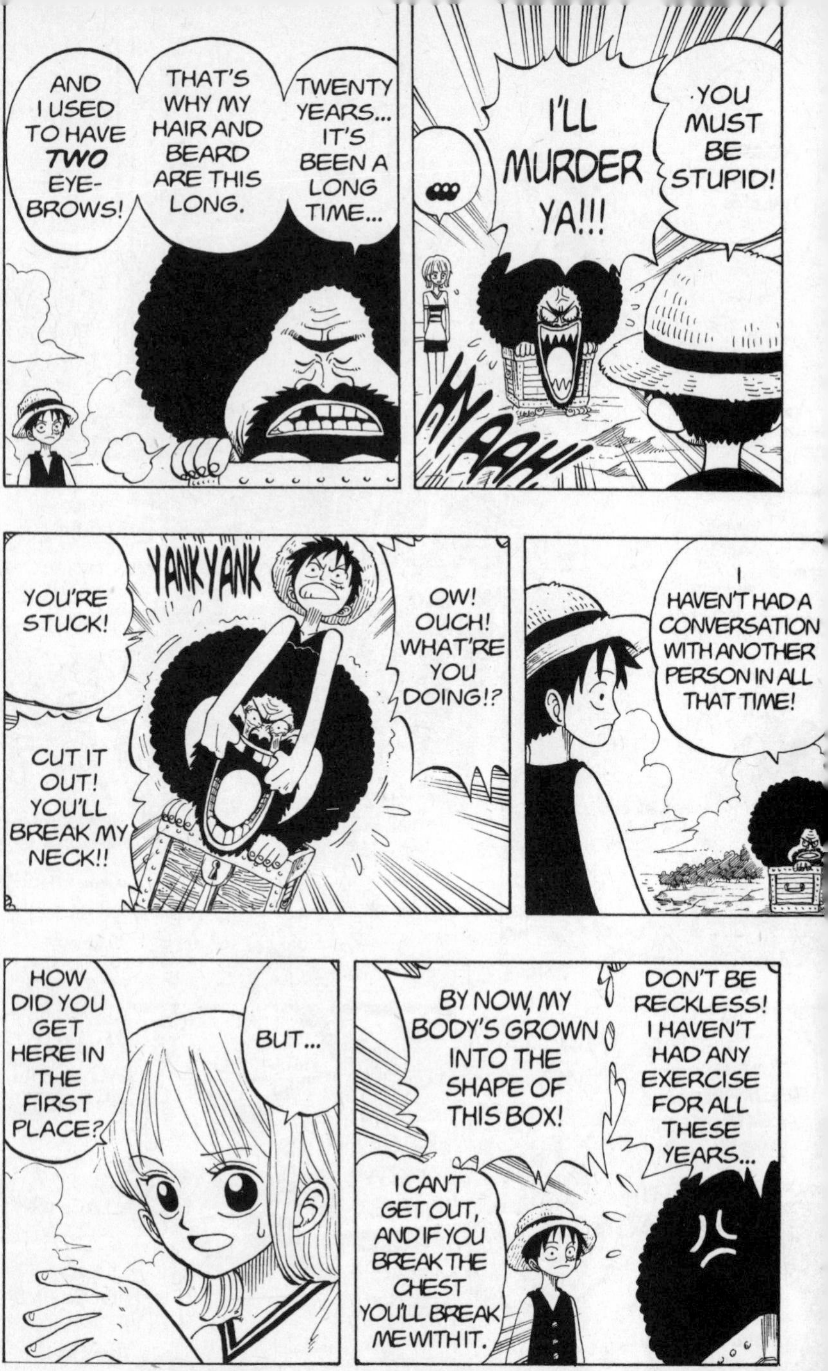
YOU MUST BE STUPID!
I'LL MURDER YA!!!
HYAAH!
TWENTY YEARS... IT'S BEEN A LONG TIME...
THAT'S WHY MY HAIR AND BEARD ARE THIS LONG.
AND I USED TO HAVE TWO EYEBROWS!
I HAVEN'T HAD A CONVERSATION WITH ANOTHER PERSON IN ALL THAT TIME!
OW! OUCH! WHAT'RE YOU DOING!?
YANK YANK
YOU'RE STUCK!
CUT IT OUT! YOU'LL BREAK MY NECK!!
DON'T BE RECKLESS! I HAVEN'T HAD ANY EXERCISE FOR ALL THESE YEARS...
BY NOW, MY BODY'S GROWN INTO THE SHAPE OF THIS BOX!
I CAN'T GET OUT, AND IF YOU BREAK THE CHEST YOU'LL BREAK ME WITH IT.
BUT...
HOW DID YOU GET HERE IN THE FIRST PLACE?

READ THIS WAY

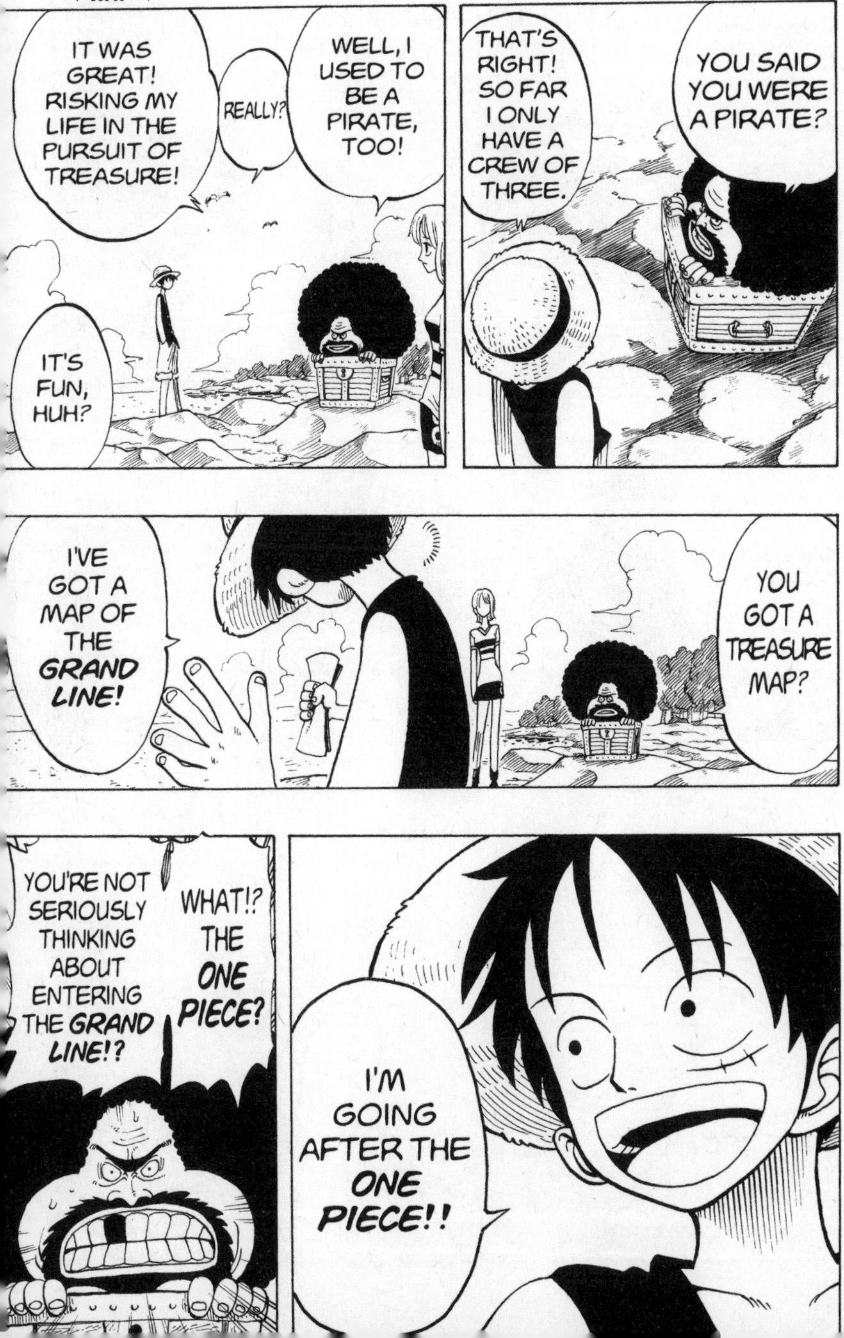
YOU SAID YOU WERE A PIRATE?
THAT'S RIGHT! SO FAR I ONLY HAVE A CREW OF THREE.
WELL, I USED TO BE A PIRATE, TOO!
REALLY?
IT WAS GREAT! RISKING MY LIFE IN THE PURSUIT OF TREASURE!
IT'S FUN, HUH?
YOU GOT A TREASURE MAP?
I'VE GOT A MAP OF THE GRAND LINE!
I'M GOING AFTER THE ONE PIECE!!
WHAT!? THE ONE PIECE?
YOU'RE NOT SERIOUSLY THINKING ABOUT ENTERING THE GRAND LINE!?

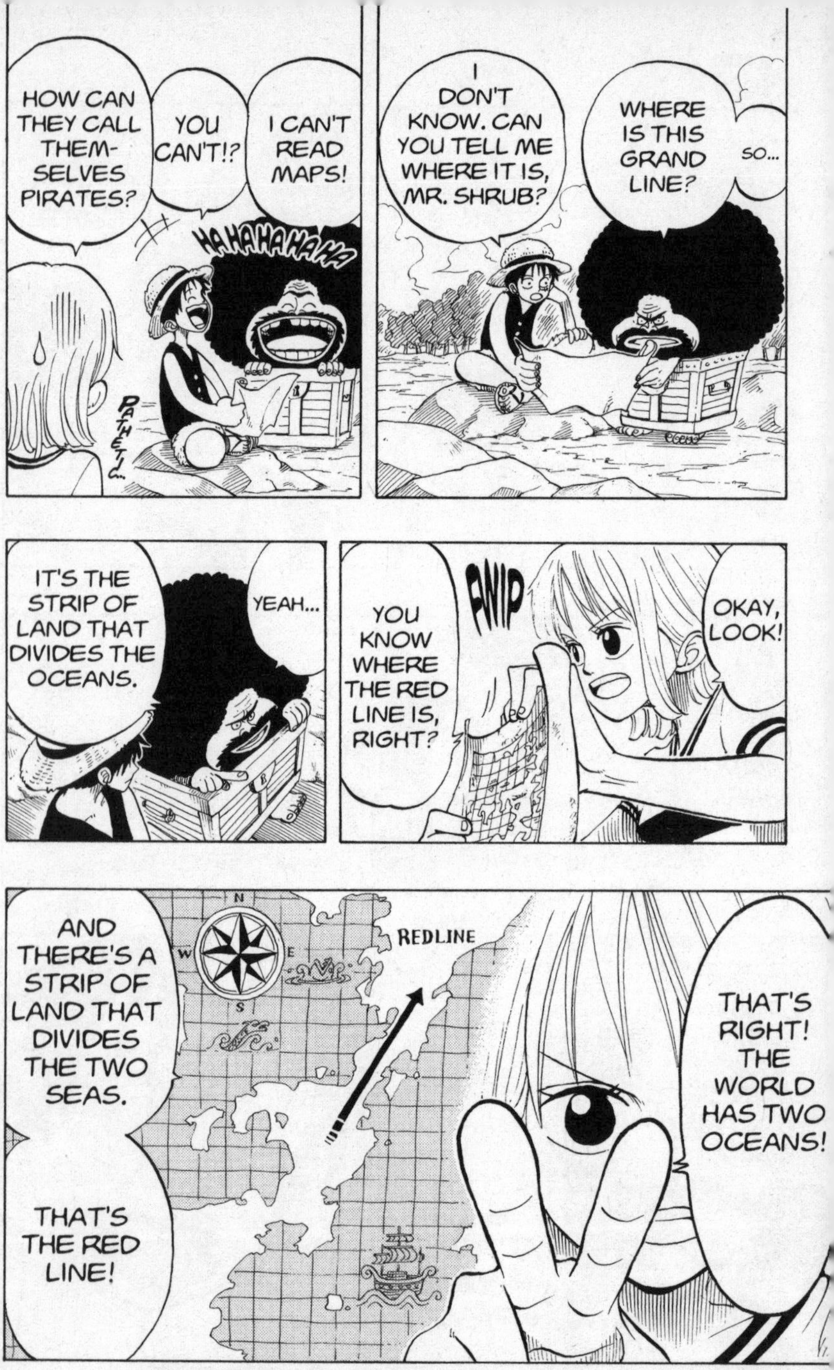
SO...
WHERE IS THIS GRAND LINE?
I DON'T KNOW. CAN YOU TELL ME WHERE IT IS, MR. SHRUB?
I CAN'T READ MAPS!
YOU CAN'T!?
HOW CAN THEY CALL THEM-SELVES PIRATES?
HAHAHAHAHA
PATHETIC...
OKAY, LOOK!
FWIP
YOU KNOW WHERE THE RED LINE IS, RIGHT?
YEAH...
IT'S THE STRIP OF LAND THAT DIVIDES THE OCEANS.
THAT'S RIGHT! THE WORLD HAS TWO OCEANS!
REDLINE
N
W
E
S
AND THERE'S A STRIP OF LAND THAT DIVIDES THE TWO SEAS.
THAT'S THE RED LINE!

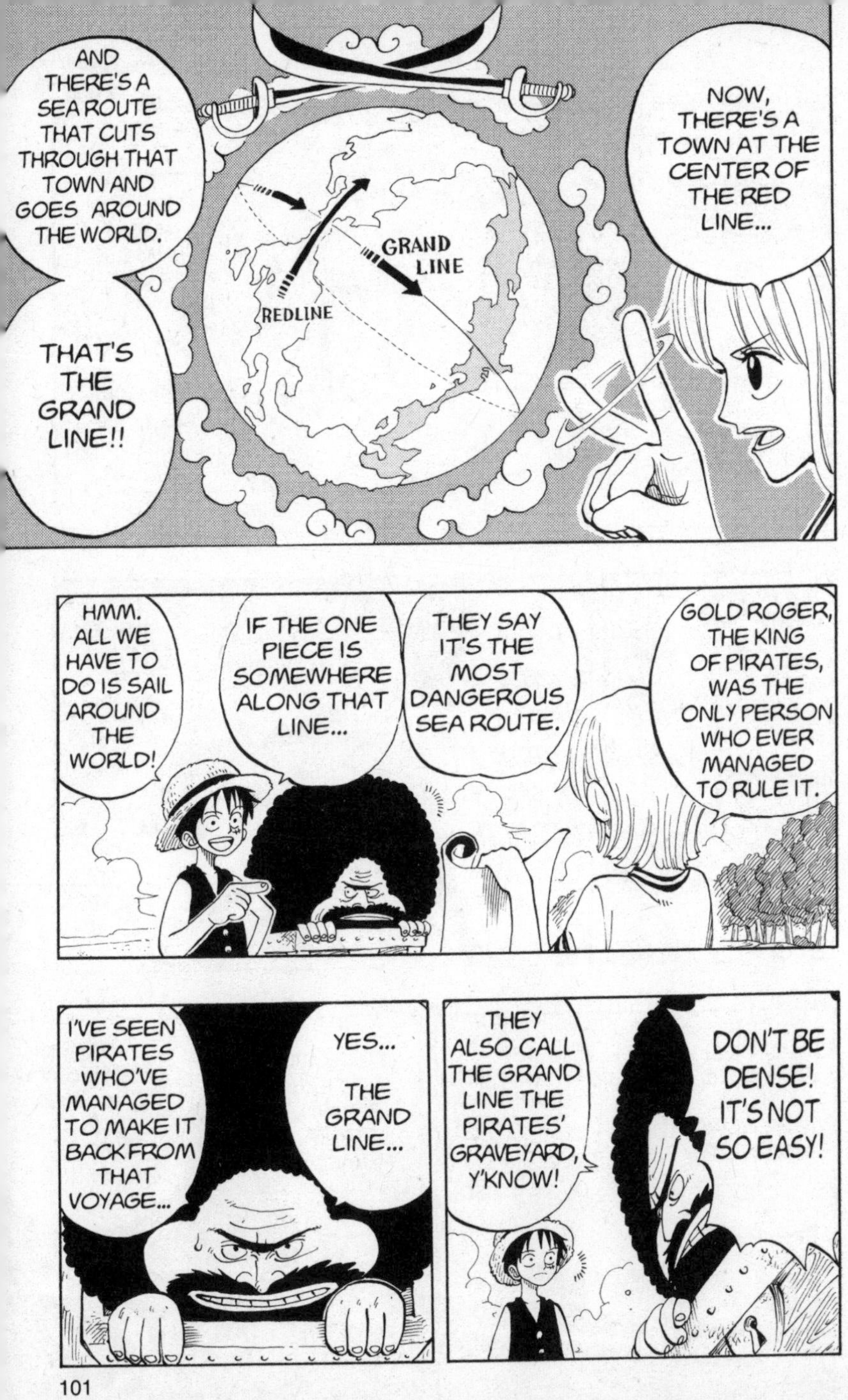
NOW, THERE'S A TOWN AT THE CENTER OF THE RED LINE...
GRAND LINE
REDLINE
AND THERE'S A SEA ROUTE THAT CUTS THROUGH THAT TOWN AND GOES AROUND THE WORLD.
THAT'S THE GRAND LINE!!
GOLD ROGER, THE KING OF PIRATES, WAS THE ONLY PERSON WHO EVER MANAGED TO RULE IT.
THEY SAY IT'S THE MOST DANGEROUS SEA ROUTE.
IF THE ONE PIECE IS SOMEWHERE ALONG THAT LINE...
HMM. ALL WE HAVE TO DO IS SAIL AROUND THE WORLD!
DON'T BE DENSE! IT'S NOT SO EASY!
THEY ALSO CALL THE GRAND LINE THE PIRATES' GRAVEYARD, Y'KNOW!
YES... THE GRAND LINE...
I'VE SEEN PIRATES WHO'VE MANAGED TO MAKE IT BACK FROM THAT VOYAGE...

READ THIS WAY

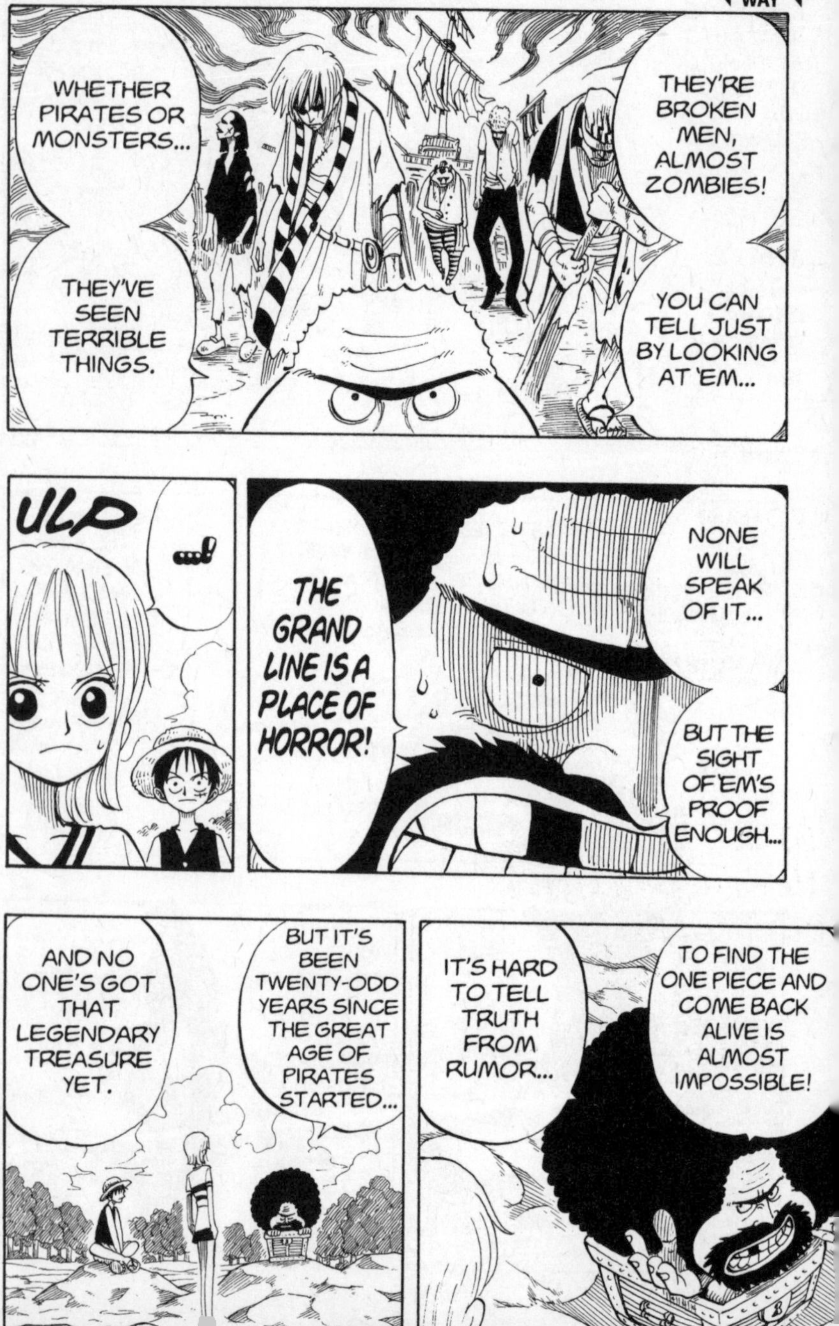
THEY'RE BROKEN MEN, ALMOST ZOMBIES!
YOU CAN TELL JUST BY LOOKING AT 'EM...
WHETHER PIRATES OR MONSTERS...
THEY'VE SEEN TERRIBLE THINGS.
NONE WILL SPEAK OF IT...
BUT THE SIGHT OF 'EM'S PROOF ENOUGH...
THE GRAND LINE IS A PLACE OF HORROR!
...!
ULP
TO FIND THE ONE PIECE AND COME BACK ALIVE IS ALMOST IMPOSSIBLE!
IT'S HARD TO TELL TRUTH FROM RUMOR...
BUT IT'S BEEN TWENTY-ODD YEARS SINCE THE GREAT AGE OF PIRATES STARTED...
AND NO ONE'S GOT THAT LEGENDARY TREASURE YET.

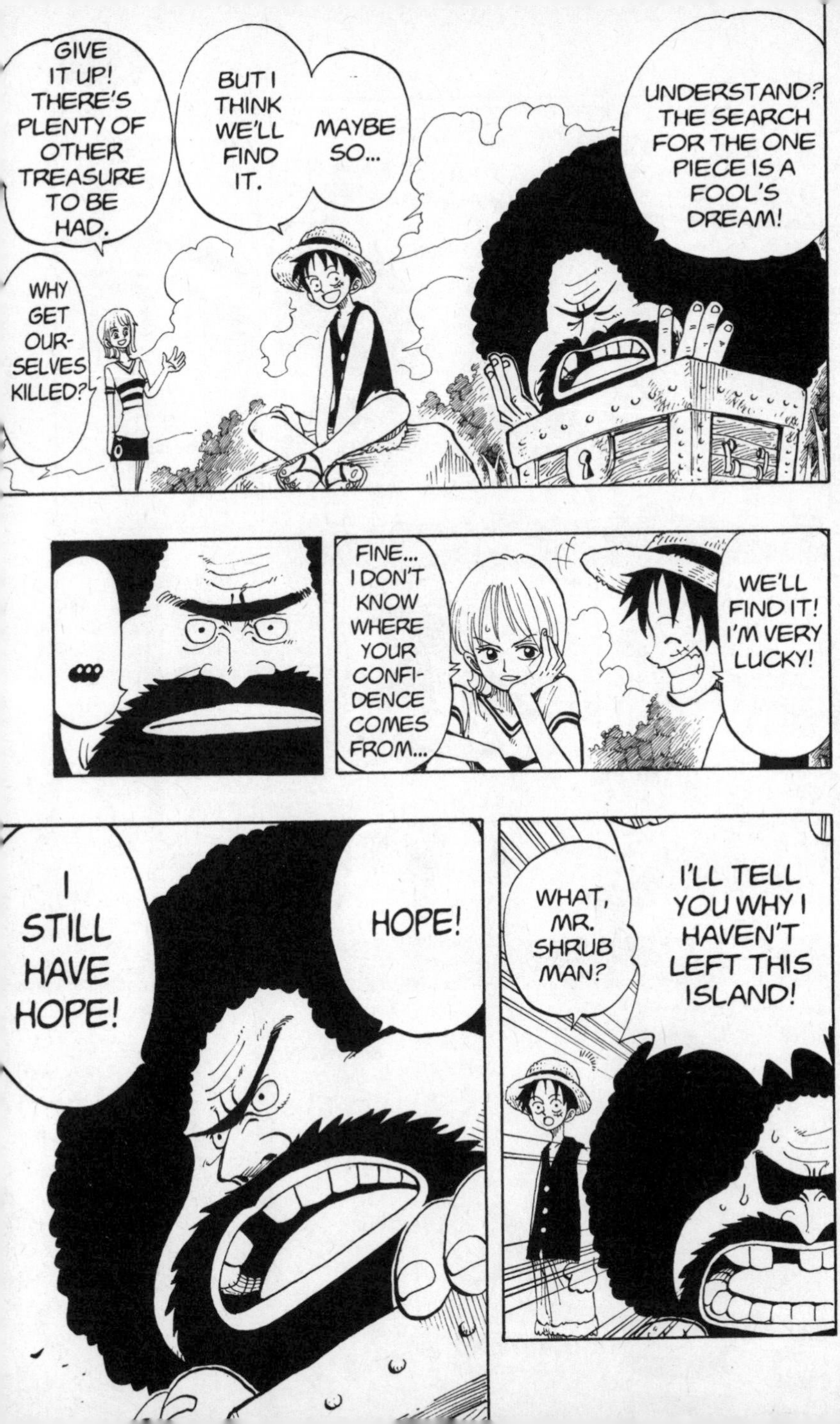
UNDERSTAND? THE SEARCH FOR THE ONE PIECE IS A FOOL'S DREAM!
MAYBE SO...
BUT I THINK WE'LL FIND IT.
GIVE IT UP! THERE'S PLENTY OF OTHER TREASURE TO BE HAD.
WHY GET OUR-SELVES KILLED?
WE'LL FIND IT! I'M VERY LUCKY!
FINE... I DON'T KNOW WHERE YOUR CONFI-DENCE COMES FROM...
...
I'LL TELL YOU WHY I HAVEN'T LEFT THIS ISLAND!
WHAT, MR. SHRUB MAN?
HOPE!
I STILL HAVE HOPE!

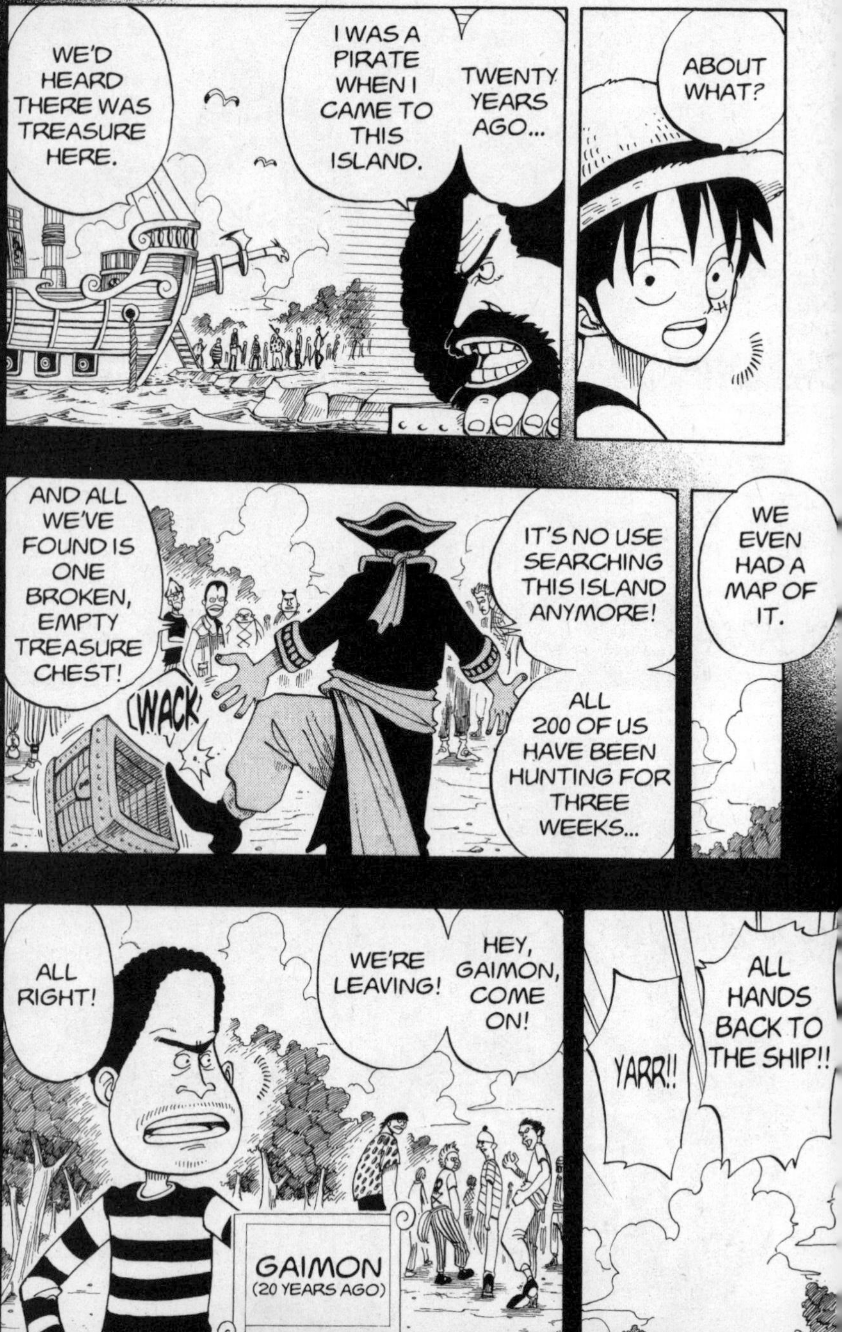
READ THIS WAY
ABOUT WHAT?
TWENTY YEARS AGO...
I WAS A PIRATE WHEN I CAME TO THIS ISLAND.
WE'D HEARD THERE WAS TREASURE HERE.
WE EVEN HAD A MAP OF IT.
IT'S NO USE SEARCHING THIS ISLAND ANYMORE!
ALL 200 OF US HAVE BEEN HUNTING FOR THREE WEEKS...
AND ALL WE'VE FOUND IS ONE BROKEN, EMPTY TREASURE CHEST!
WACK!
ALL HANDS BACK TO THE SHIP!!
YARR!!
HEY, GAIMON, COME ON!
WE'RE LEAVING!
ALL RIGHT!
GAIMON (20 YEARS AGO)

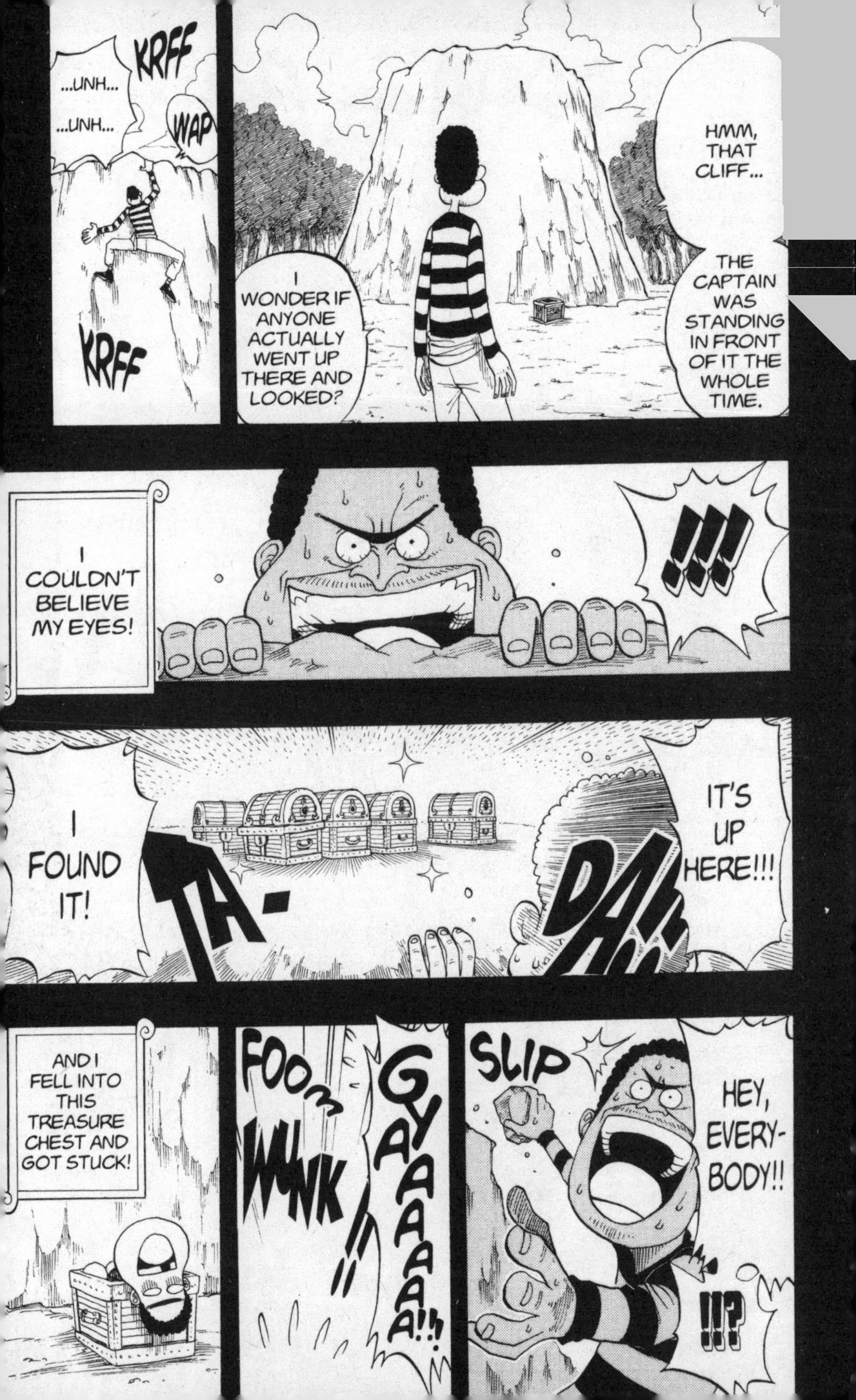
HMM, THAT CLIFF...
THE CAPTAIN WAS STANDING IN FRONT OF IT THE WHOLE TIME.
I WONDER IF ANYONE ACTUALLY WENT UP THERE AND LOOKED?
KRFF
...UNH...
...UNH...
WAP
KRFF
!!!
I COULDN'T BELIEVE MY EYES!
IT'S UP HERE!!!
TA-
DA
I FOUND IT!
SLIP
HEY, EVERY-BODY!!
!!?
FOOM
GYAAAAAAA!!
WUNK
!!
AND I FELL INTO THIS TREASURE CHEST AND GOT STUCK!

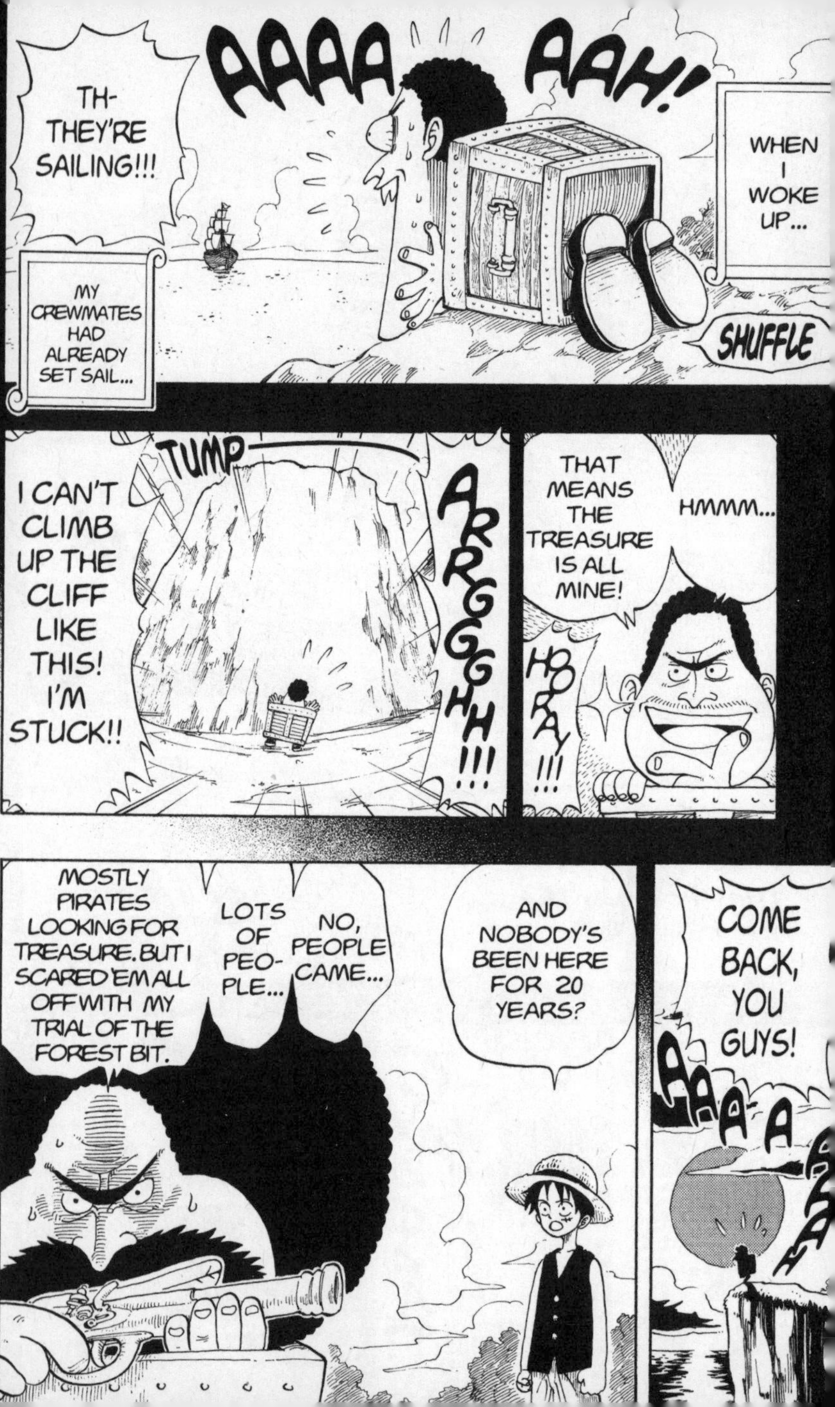
WHEN I WOKE UP...
AAAA AAH!
SHUFFLE
TH- THEY'RE SAILING!!!
MY CREWMATES HAD ALREADY SET SAIL...
HMMM...
THAT MEANS THE TREASURE IS ALL MINE!
HOORAY!!!
TUMP
ARRGGGHH!!!
I CAN'T CLIMB UP THE CLIFF LIKE THIS! I'M STUCK!!
COME BACK, YOU GUYS!
AAAA-A-A
AND NOBODY'S BEEN HERE FOR 20 YEARS?
NO, PEOPLE CAME...
LOTS OF PEO-PLE...
MOSTLY PIRATES LOOKING FOR TREASURE. BUT I SCARED 'EM ALL OFF WITH MY TRIAL OF THE FOREST BIT.

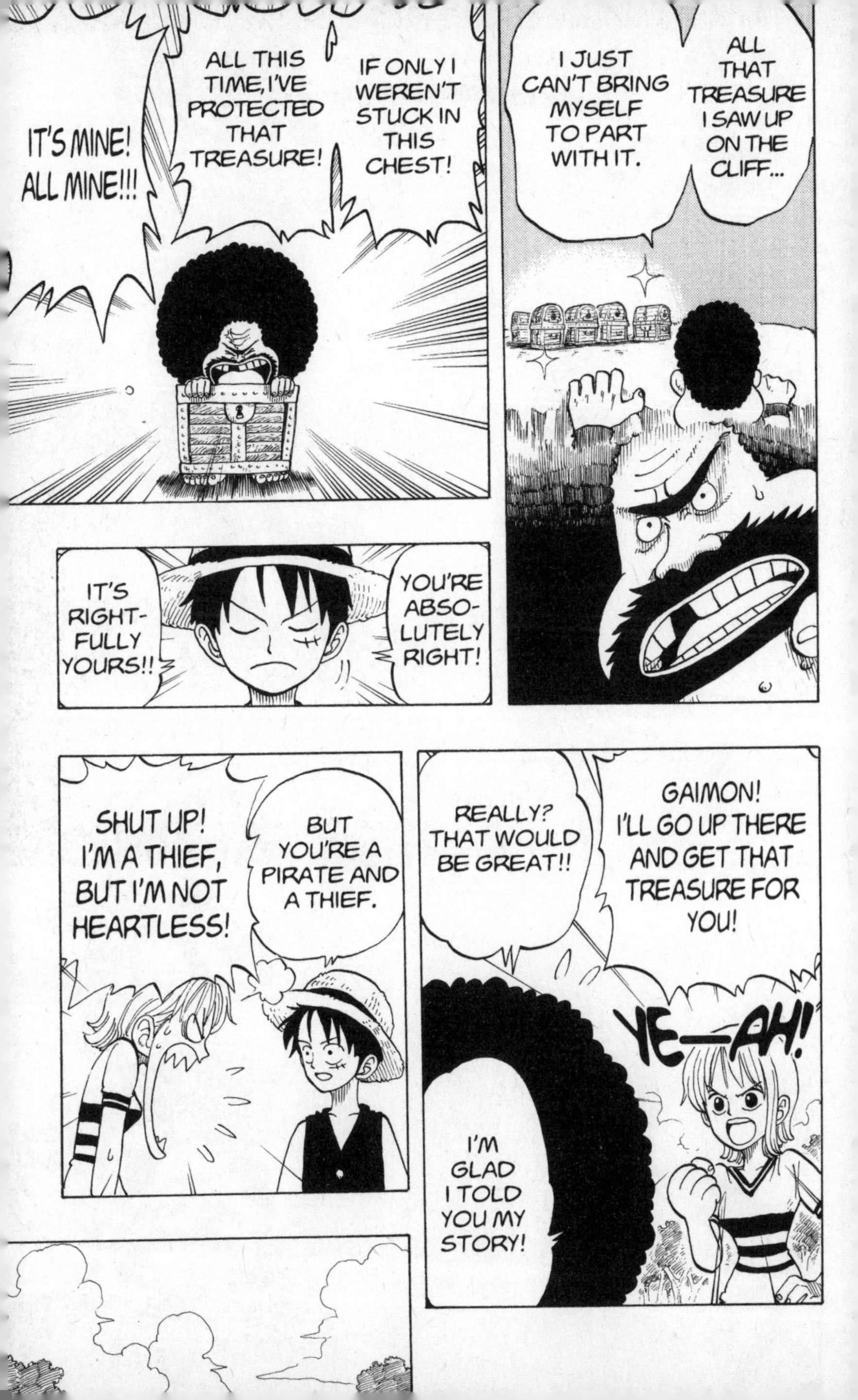
ALL THAT TREASURE I SAW UP ON THE CLIFF...
I JUST CAN'T BRING MYSELF TO PART WITH IT.
IF ONLY I WEREN'T STUCK IN THIS CHEST!
ALL THIS TIME, I'VE PROTECTED THAT TREASURE!
IT'S MINE! ALL MINE!!!
YOU'RE ABSO-LUTELY RIGHT!
IT'S RIGHT-FULLY YOURS!!
GAIMON! I'LL GO UP THERE AND GET THAT TREASURE FOR YOU!
REALLY? THAT WOULD BE GREAT!!
YE—AH!
I'M GLAD I TOLD YOU MY STORY!
BUT YOU'RE A PIRATE AND A THIEF.
SHUT UP! I'M A THIEF, BUT I'M NOT HEARTLESS!

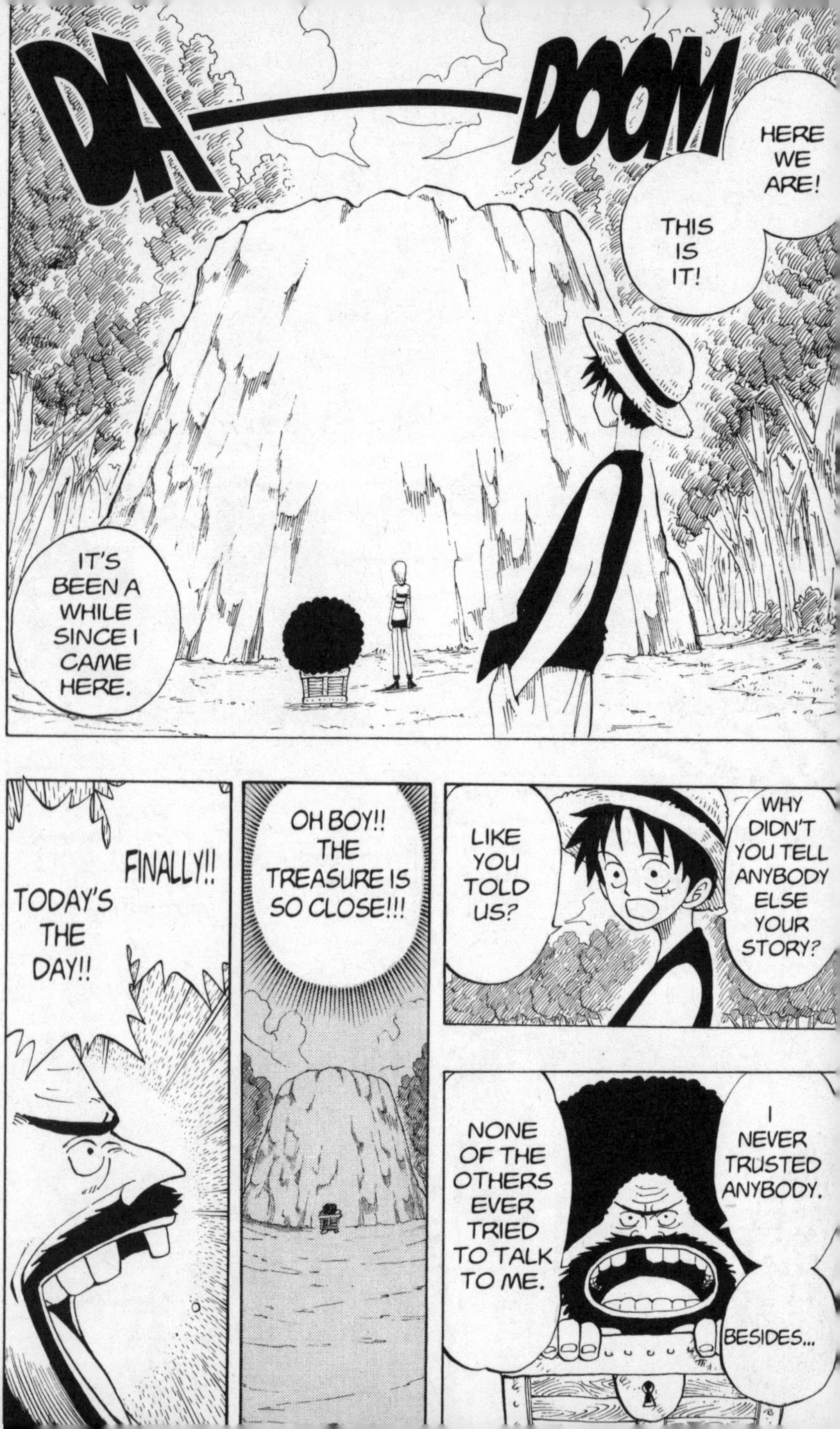
DA—DOOM
HERE WE ARE!
THIS IS IT!
IT'S BEEN A WHILE SINCE I CAME HERE.
WHY DIDN'T YOU TELL ANYBODY ELSE YOUR STORY?
LIKE YOU TOLD US?
I NEVER TRUSTED ANYBODY.
NONE OF THE OTHERS EVER TRIED TO TALK TO ME.
BESIDES...
OH BOY!! THE TREASURE IS SO CLOSE!!!
FINALLY!!
TODAY'S THE DAY!!

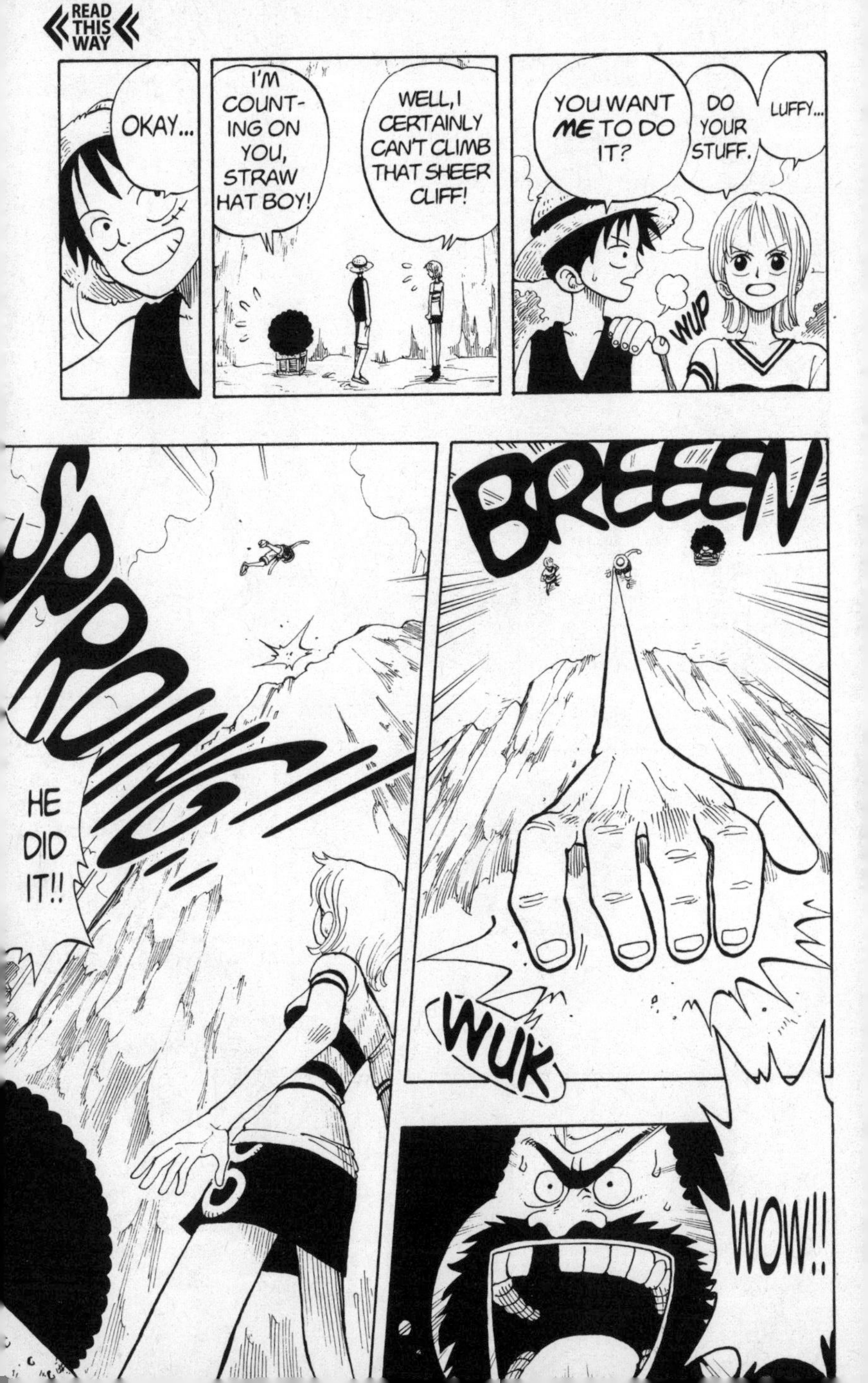
READ THIS WAY
LUFFY...
DO YOUR STUFF.
YOU WANT ME TO DO IT?
WUP
WELL, I CERTAINLY CAN'T CLIMB THAT SHEER CLIFF!
I'M COUNTING ON YOU, STRAW HAT BOY!
OKAY...
BREEEN
WUK
SPROING!!
HE DID IT!!
WOW!!

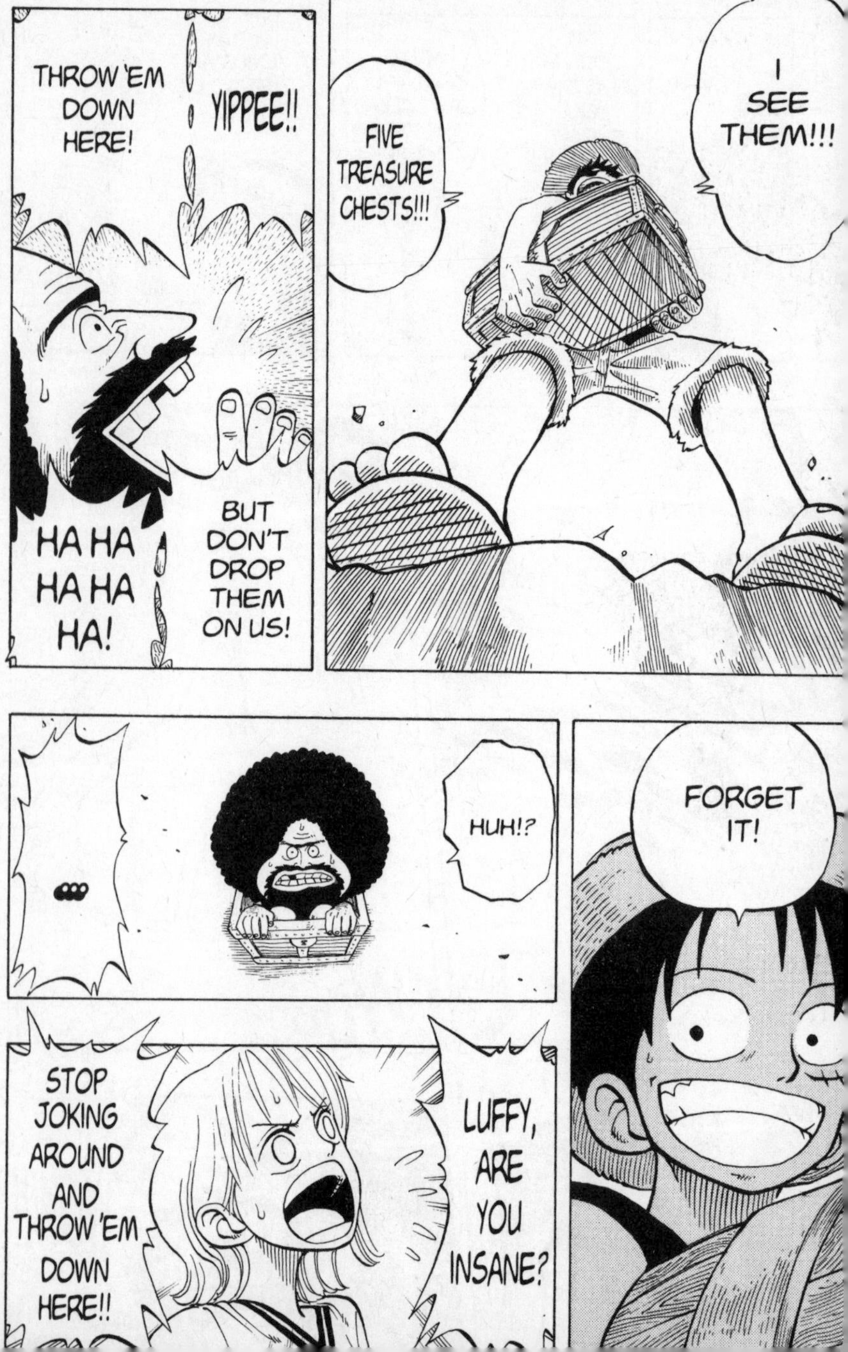
I SEE THEM!!!
FIVE TREASURE CHESTS!!!
YIPPEE!!
THROW 'EM DOWN HERE!
BUT DON'T DROP THEM ON US!
HA HA HA HA HA!
FORGET IT!
HUH!?
...
LUFFY, ARE YOU INSANE?
STOP JOKING AROUND AND THROW 'EM DOWN HERE!!

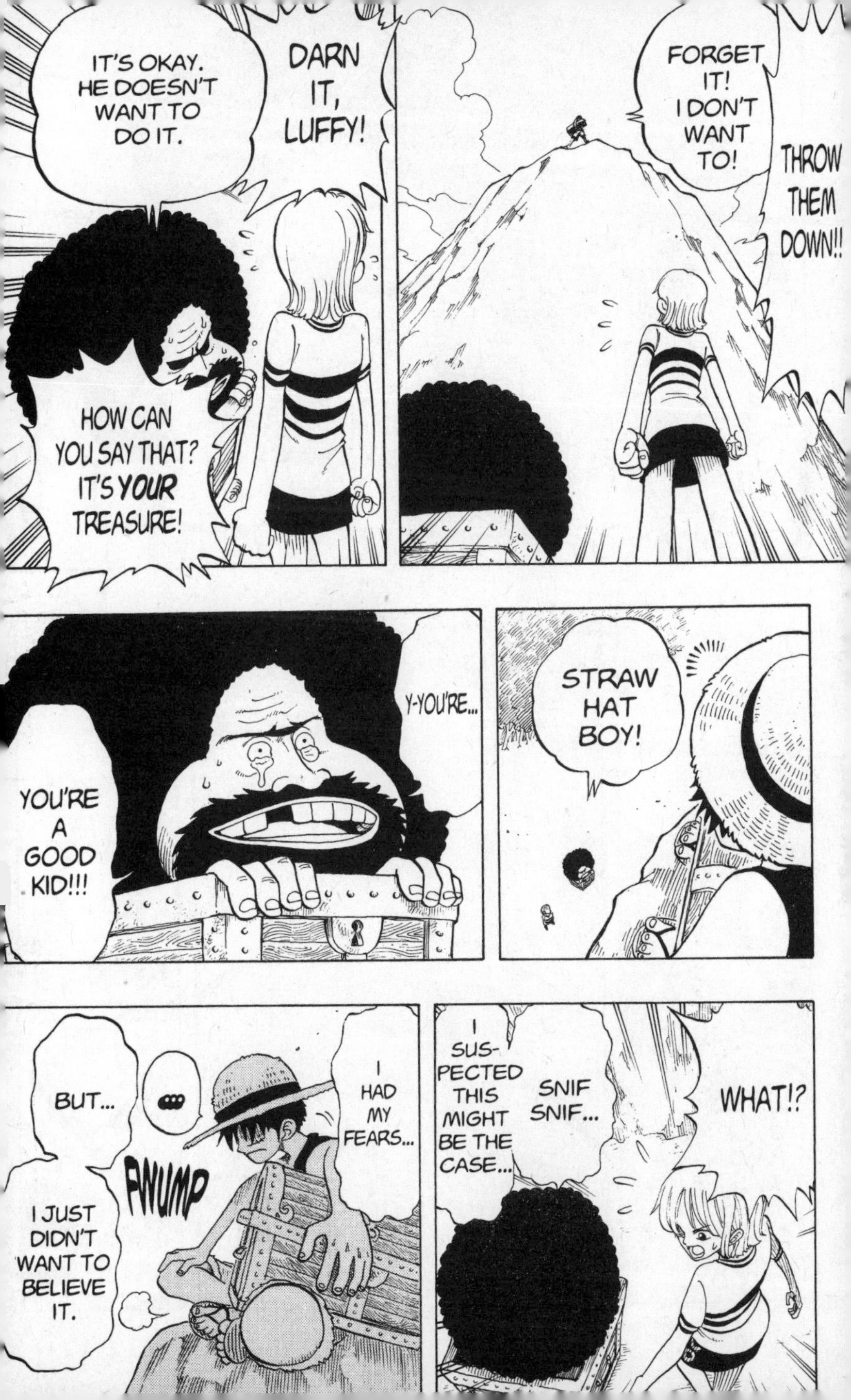
THROW THEM DOWN!!
FORGET IT! I DON'T WANT TO!
DARN IT, LUFFY!
IT'S OKAY. HE DOESN'T WANT TO DO IT.
HOW CAN YOU SAY THAT? IT'S **YOUR** TREASURE!
STRAW HAT BOY!
Y-YOU'RE...
YOU'RE A GOOD KID!!!
WHAT!?
SNIF SNIF...
I SUSPECTED THIS MIGHT BE THE CASE...
I HAD MY FEARS...
...
BUT...
FWUMP
I JUST DIDN'T WANT TO BELIEVE IT.

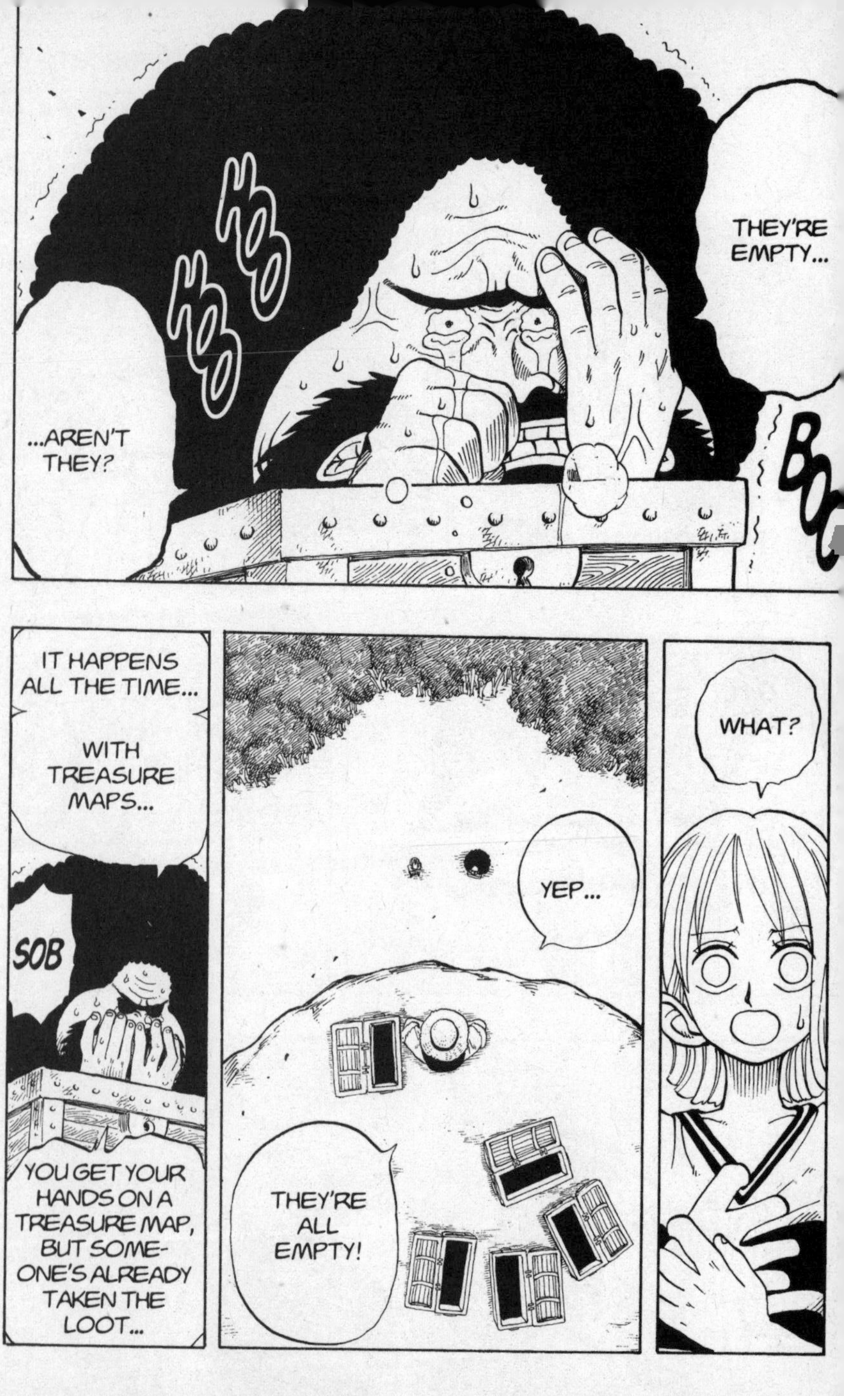
THEY'RE EMPTY...
...AREN'T THEY?
WHAT?
YEP...
THEY'RE ALL EMPTY!
IT HAPPENS ALL THE TIME...
WITH TREASURE MAPS...
SOB
YOU GET YOUR HANDS ON A TREASURE MAP, BUT SOME-ONE'S ALREADY TAKEN THE LOOT...

READ THIS WAY

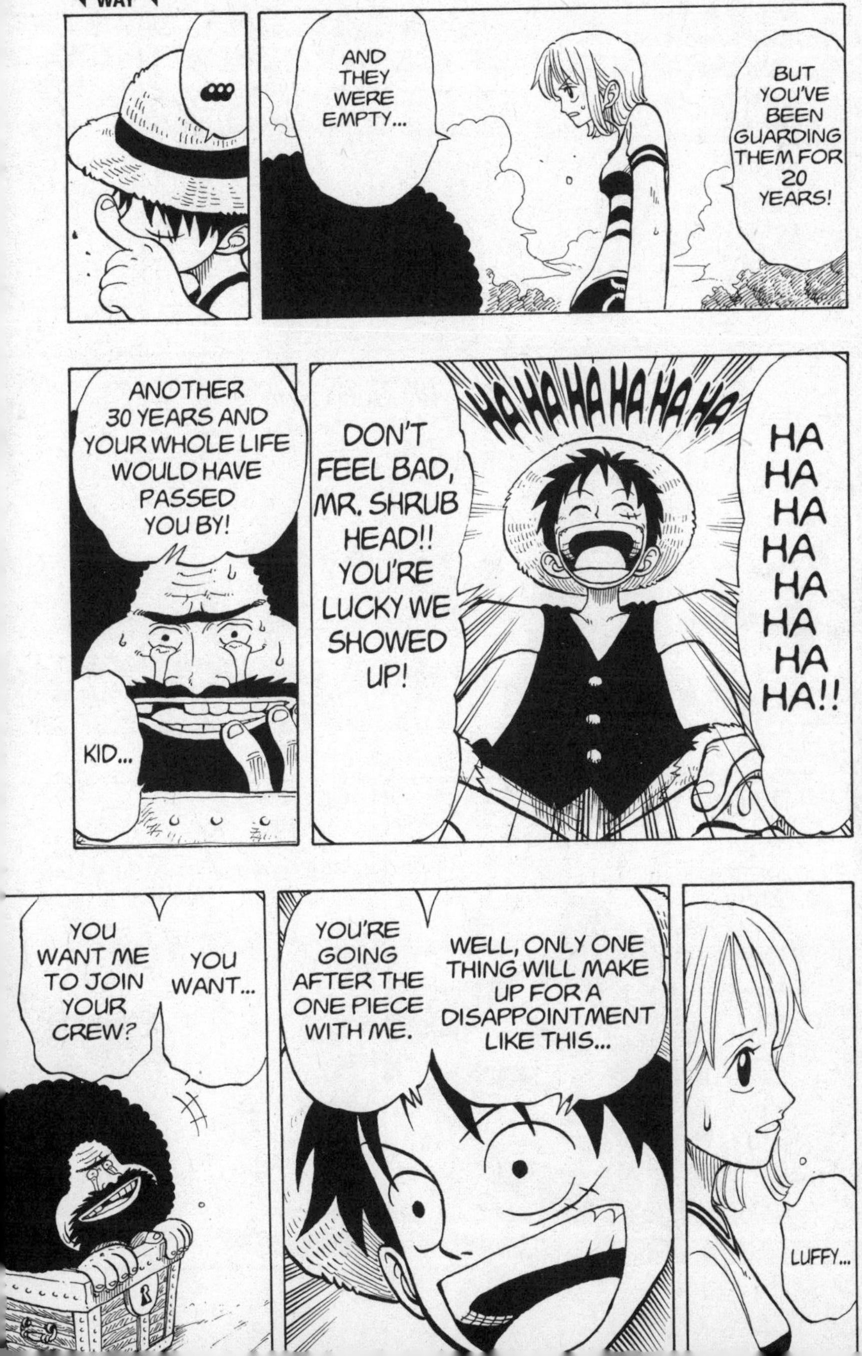
BUT YOU'VE BEEN GUARDING THEM FOR 20 YEARS!
AND THEY WERE EMPTY...
HA HA HA HA HA HA HA HA!!
HA HA HA HA HA HA HA
DON'T FEEL BAD, MR. SHRUB HEAD!! YOU'RE LUCKY WE SHOWED UP!
ANOTHER 30 YEARS AND YOUR WHOLE LIFE WOULD HAVE PASSED YOU BY!
KID...
LUFFY...
WELL, ONLY ONE THING WILL MAKE UP FOR A DISAPPOINTMENT LIKE THIS...
YOU'RE GOING AFTER THE ONE PIECE WITH ME.
YOU WANT...
YOU WANT ME TO JOIN YOUR CREW?

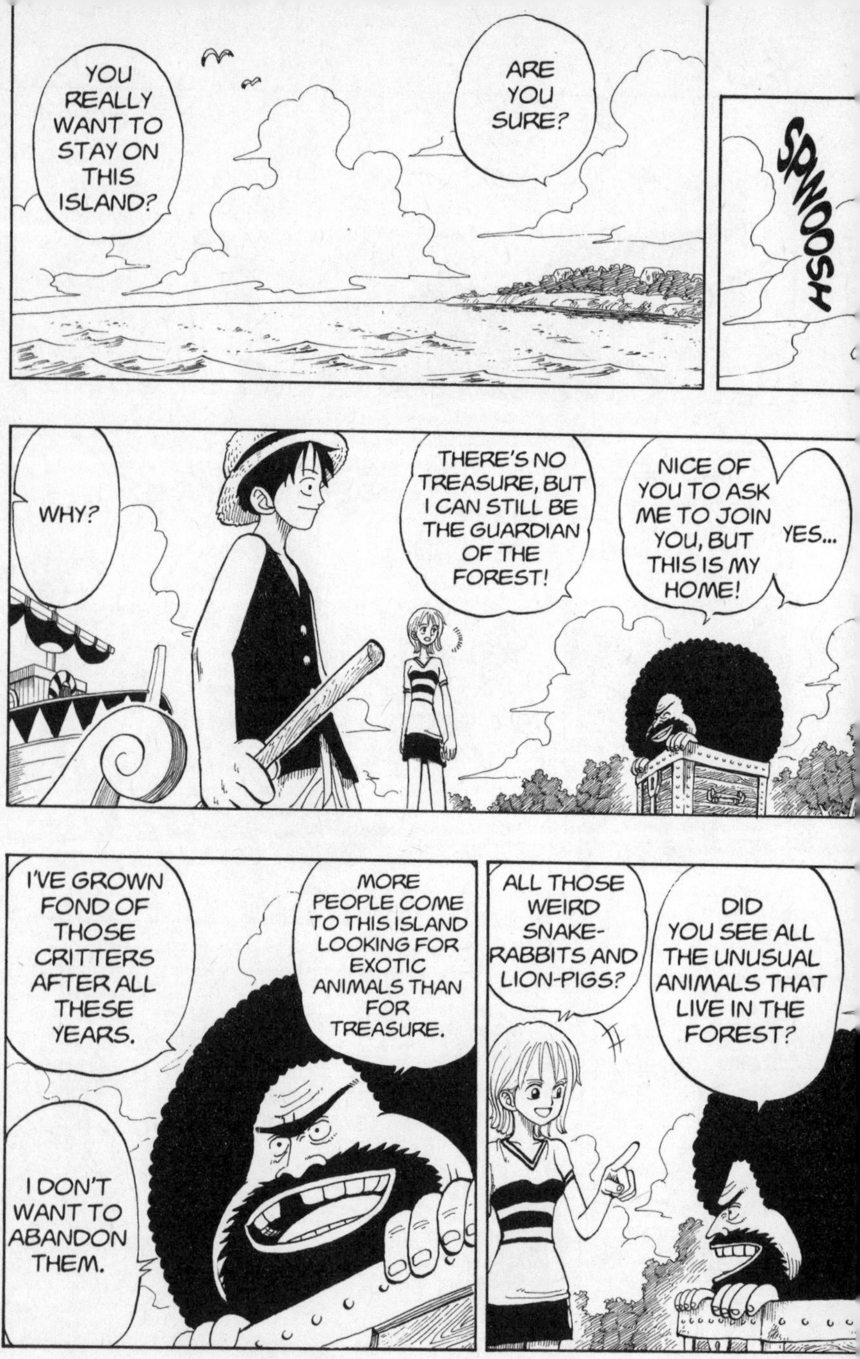
SPWOOSH
ARE YOU SURE?
YOU REALLY WANT TO STAY ON THIS ISLAND?
YES...
NICE OF YOU TO ASK ME TO JOIN YOU, BUT THIS IS MY HOME!
THERE'S NO TREASURE, BUT I CAN STILL BE THE GUARDIAN OF THE FOREST!
WHY?
DID YOU SEE ALL THE UNUSUAL ANIMALS THAT LIVE IN THE FOREST?
ALL THOSE WEIRD SNAKE-RABBITS AND LION-PIGS?
MORE PEOPLE COME TO THIS ISLAND LOOKING FOR EXOTIC ANIMALS THAN FOR TREASURE.
I'VE GROWN FOND OF THOSE CRITTERS AFTER ALL THESE YEARS.
I DON'T WANT TO ABANDON THEM.

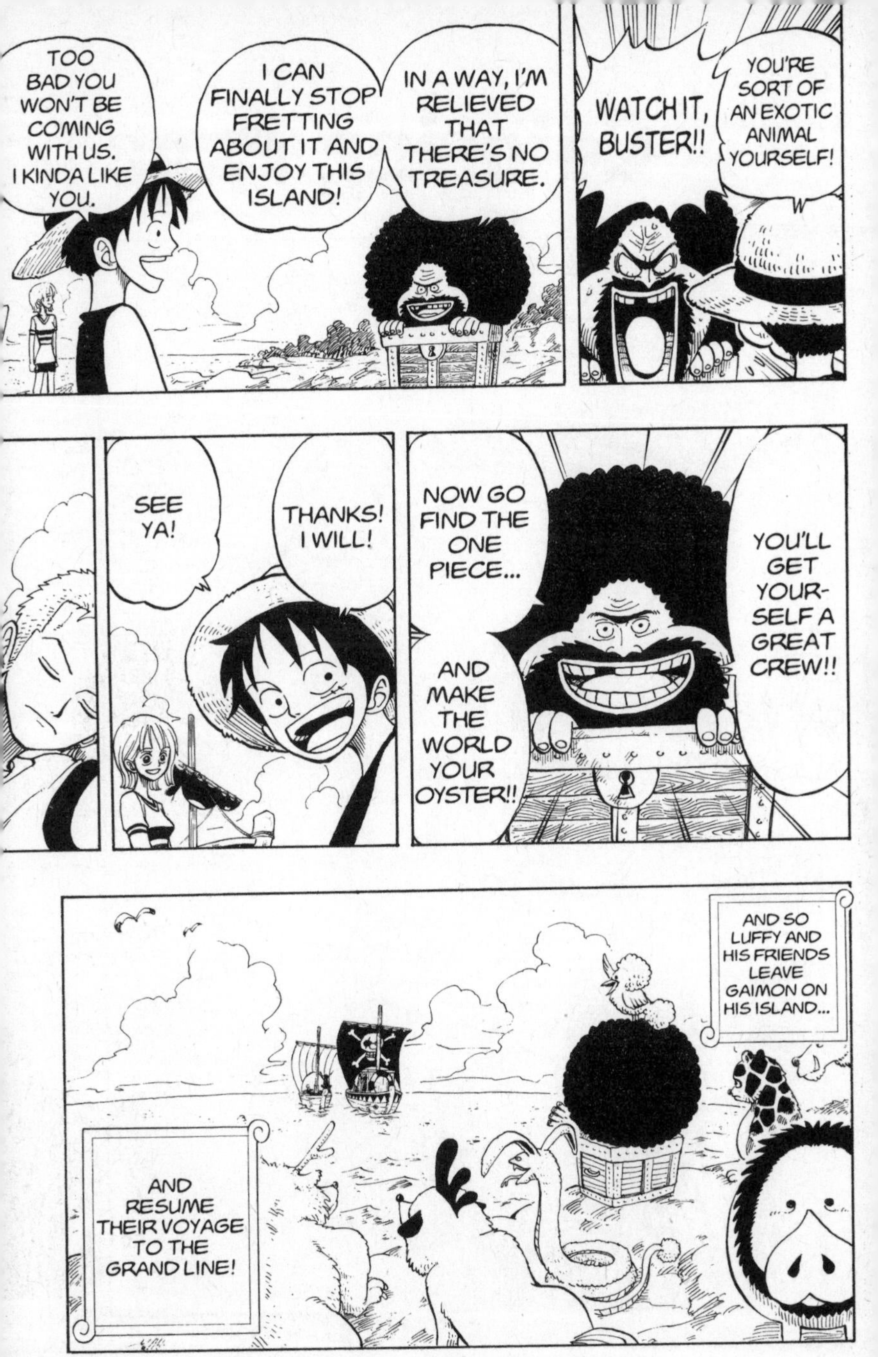
YOU'RE SORT OF AN EXOTIC ANIMAL YOURSELF!
WATCH IT, BUSTER!!
IN A WAY, I'M RELIEVED THAT THERE'S NO TREASURE.
I CAN FINALLY STOP FRETTING ABOUT IT AND ENJOY THIS ISLAND!
TOO BAD YOU WON'T BE COMING WITH US. I KINDA LIKE YOU.
YOU'LL GET YOURSELF A GREAT CREW!!
NOW GO FIND THE ONE PIECE...
AND MAKE THE WORLD YOUR OYSTER!!
THANKS! I WILL!
SEE YA!
AND SO LUFFY AND HIS FRIENDS LEAVE GAIMON ON HIS ISLAND...
AND RESUME THEIR VOYAGE TO THE GRAND LINE!

Coloring Page

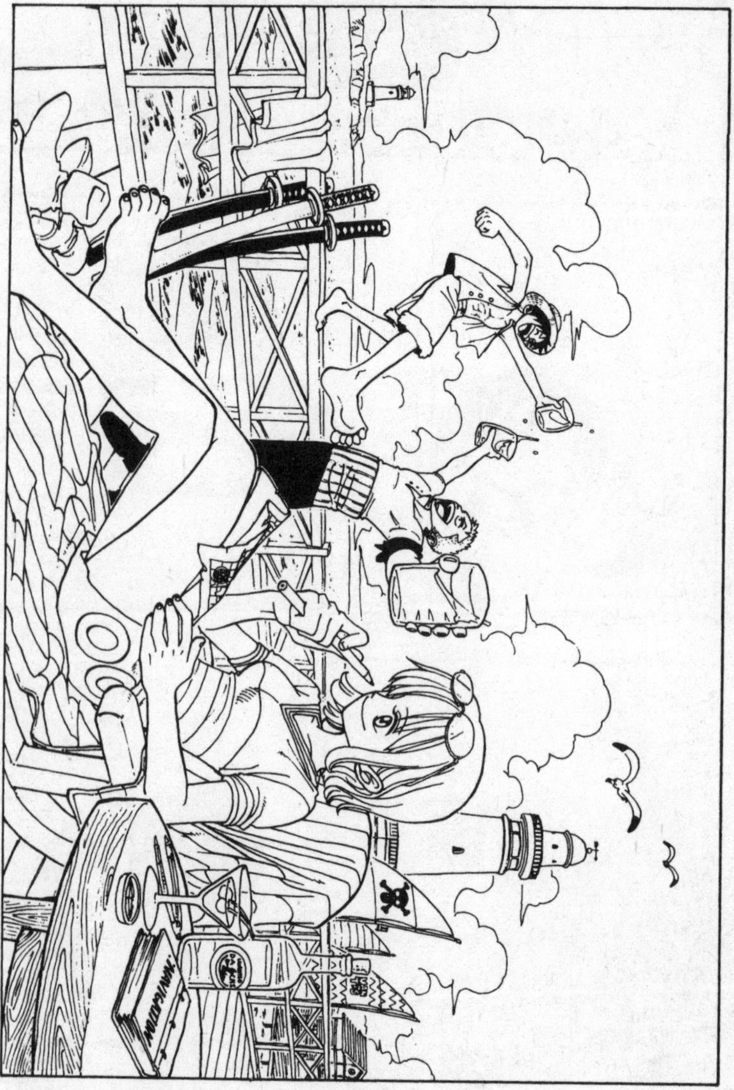
NAVIGATION

Chapter 23:
THE DREAD CAPTAIN USOPP

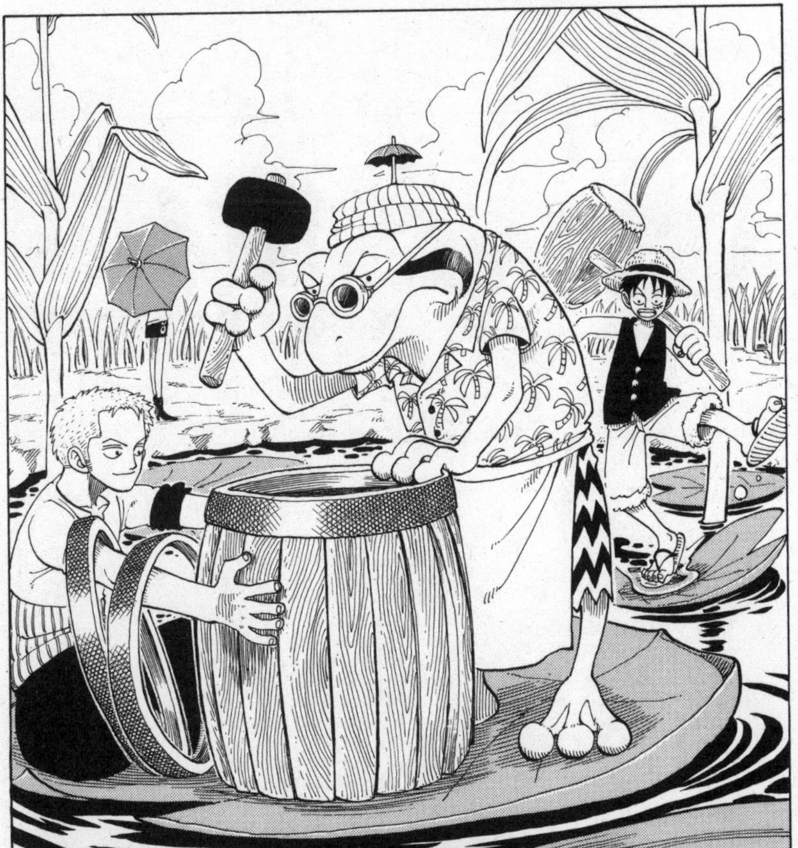

READ THIS WAY

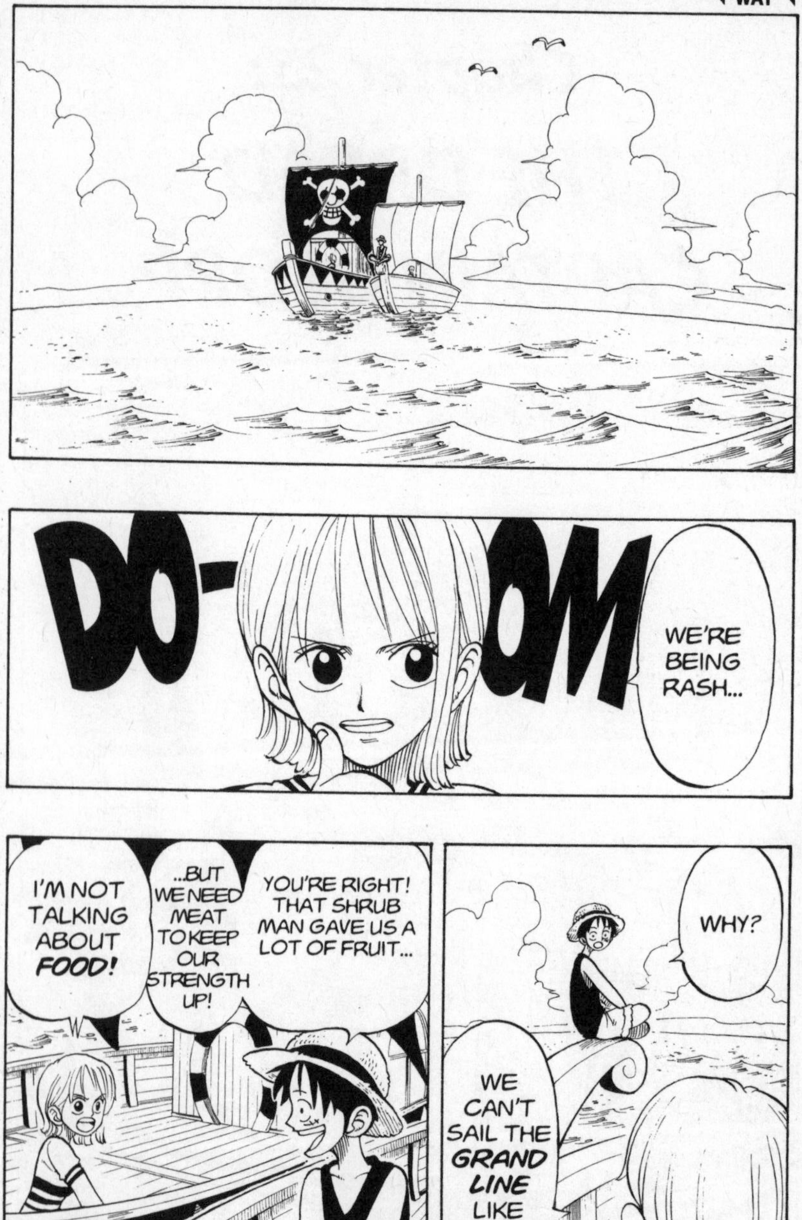

WE'RE BEING RASH...
DO-OM
WHY?
WE CAN'T SAIL THE GRAND LINE LIKE THIS!
YOU'RE RIGHT! THAT SHRUB MAN GAVE US A LOT OF FRUIT...
...BUT WE NEED MEAT TO KEEP OUR STRENGTH UP!
I'M NOT TALKING ABOUT FOOD!

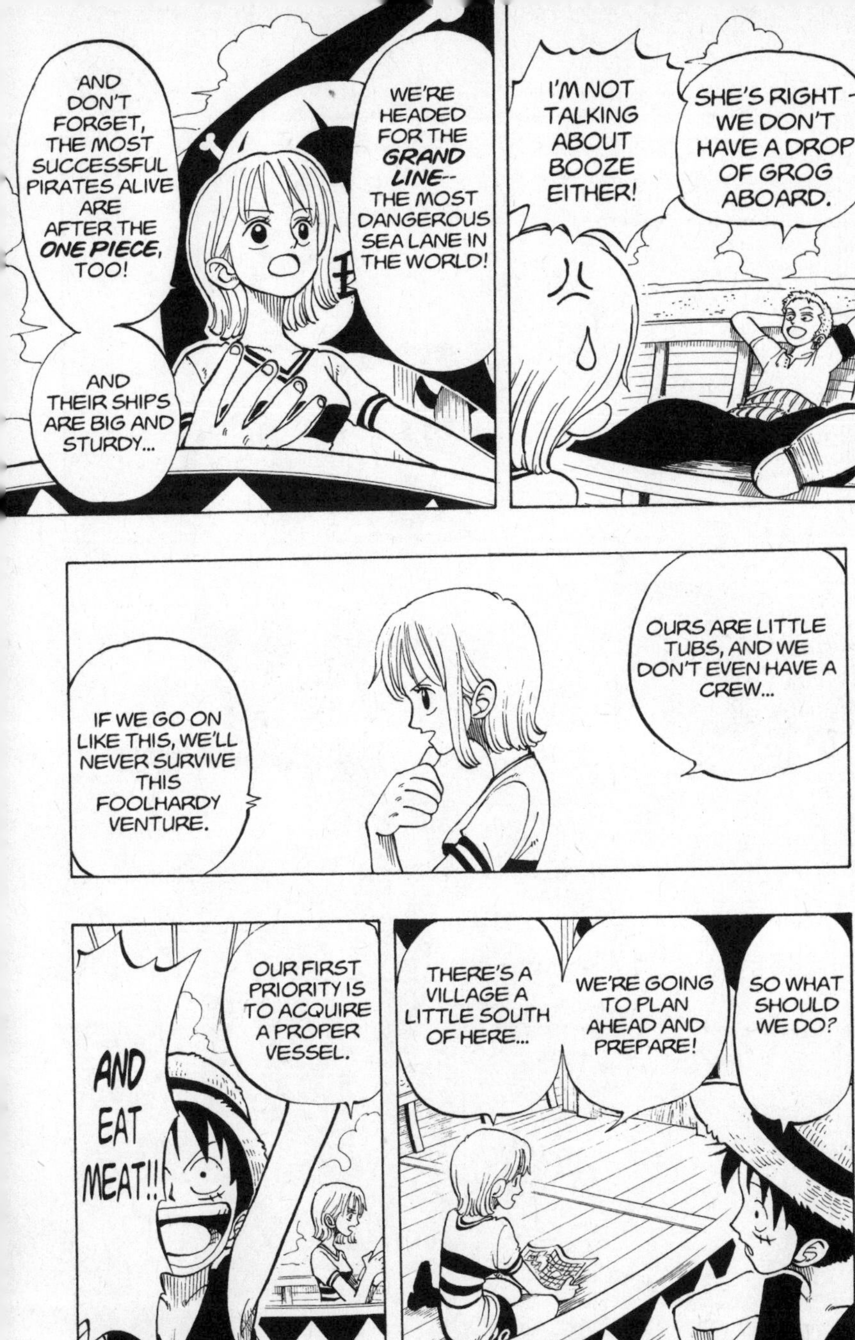
SHE'S RIGHT - WE DON'T HAVE A DROP OF GROG ABOARD.
I'M NOT TALKING ABOUT BOOZE EITHER!
WE'RE HEADED FOR THE GRAND LINE-- THE MOST DANGEROUS SEA LANE IN THE WORLD!
AND DON'T FORGET, THE MOST SUCCESSFUL PIRATES ALIVE ARE AFTER THE ONE PIECE, TOO!
AND THEIR SHIPS ARE BIG AND STURDY...
OURS ARE LITTLE TUBS, AND WE DON'T EVEN HAVE A CREW...
IF WE GO ON LIKE THIS, WE'LL NEVER SURVIVE THIS FOOLHARDY VENTURE.
SO WHAT SHOULD WE DO?
WE'RE GOING TO PLAN AHEAD AND PREPARE!
THERE'S A VILLAGE A LITTLE SOUTH OF HERE...
OUR FIRST PRIORITY IS TO ACQUIRE A PROPER VESSEL.
AND EAT MEAT!!

READ THIS WAY

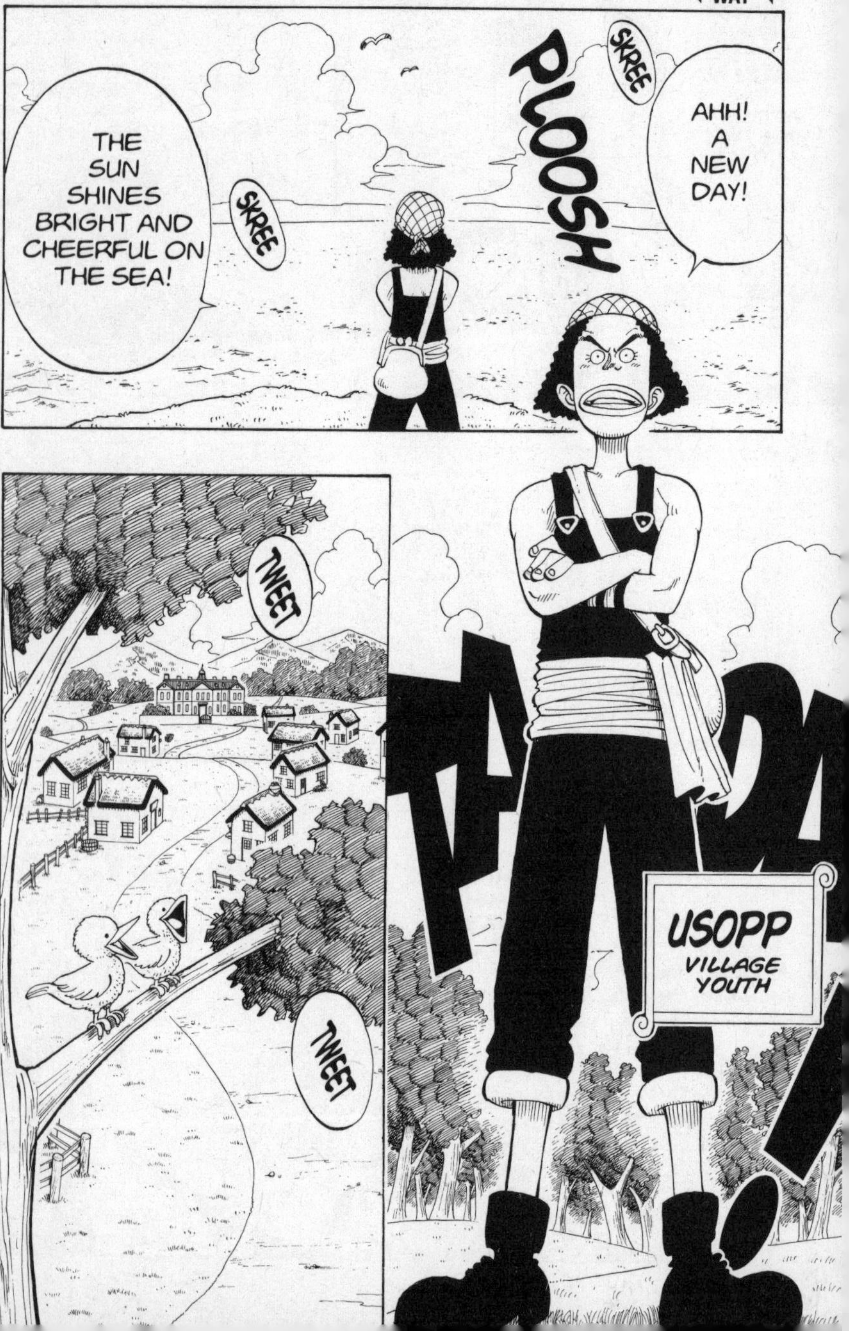
AHH! A NEW DAY!
SKREE
PLOOSH
SKREE
THE SUN SHINES BRIGHT AND CHEERFUL ON THE SEA!
USOPP
VILLAGE YOUTH
TWEET
TWEET

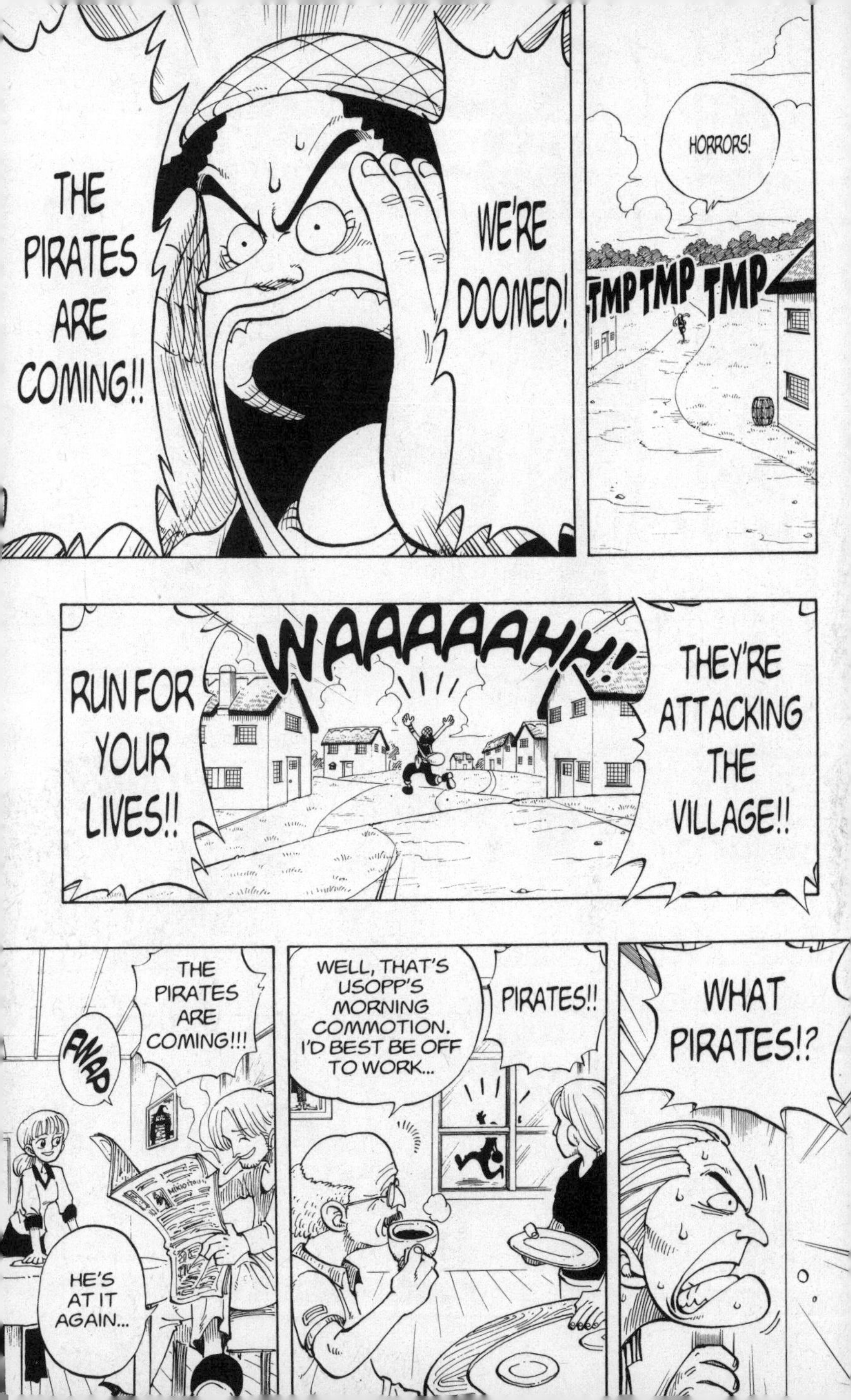
HORRORS!
TMP TMP TMP
WE'RE DOOMED!
THE PIRATES ARE COMING!!
THEY'RE ATTACKING THE VILLAGE!!
WAAAAAHH!
RUN FOR YOUR LIVES!!
WHAT PIRATES!?
PIRATES!!
WELL, THAT'S USOPP'S MORNING COMMOTION. I'D BEST BE OFF TO WORK...
THE PIRATES ARE COMING!!!
AWAP
HE'S AT IT AGAIN...

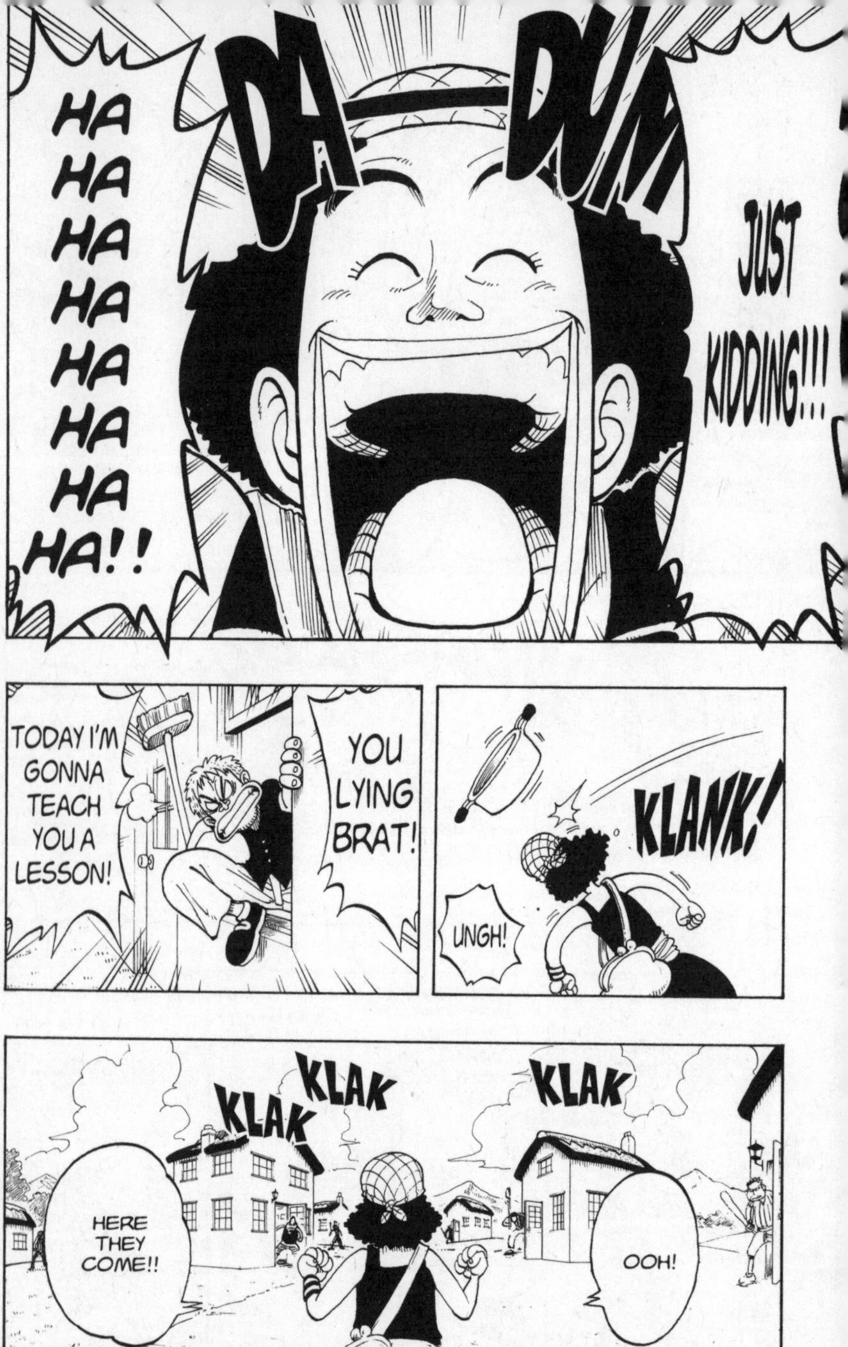
DA—DUM
JUST KIDDING!!!
HA HA HA HA HA HA HA HA!!
KLANK!
UNGH!
YOU LYING BRAT!
TODAY I'M GONNA TEACH YOU A LESSON!
KLAK
KLAK KLAK
OOH!
HERE THEY COME!!

READ THIS WAY

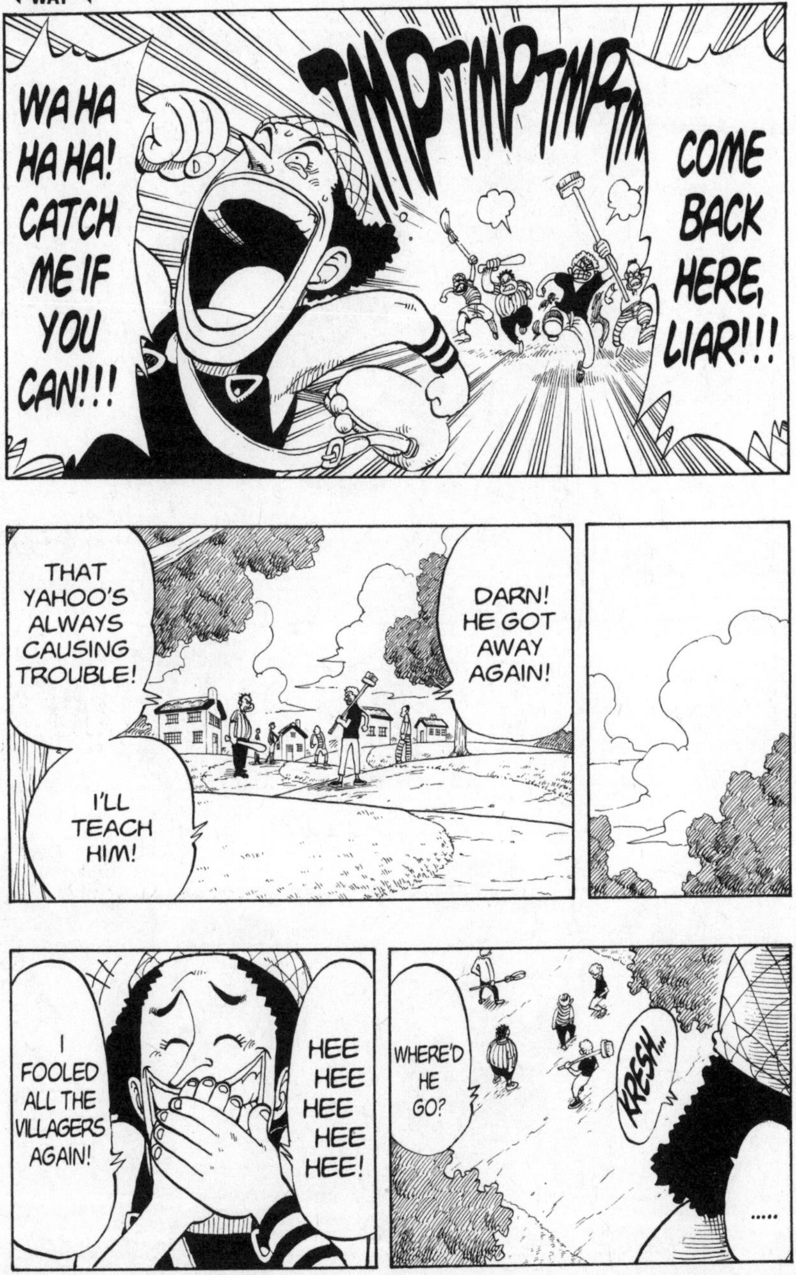
TMPTMPTMP
COME BACK HERE, LIAR!!!
WA HA HA HA! CATCH ME IF YOU CAN!!!
DARN! HE GOT AWAY AGAIN!
THAT YAHOO'S ALWAYS CAUSING TROUBLE!
I'LL TEACH HIM!
KRESH...
WHERE'D HE GO?
.....
HEE HEE HEE HEE HEE!
I FOOLED ALL THE VILLAGERS AGAIN!

READ THIS WAY

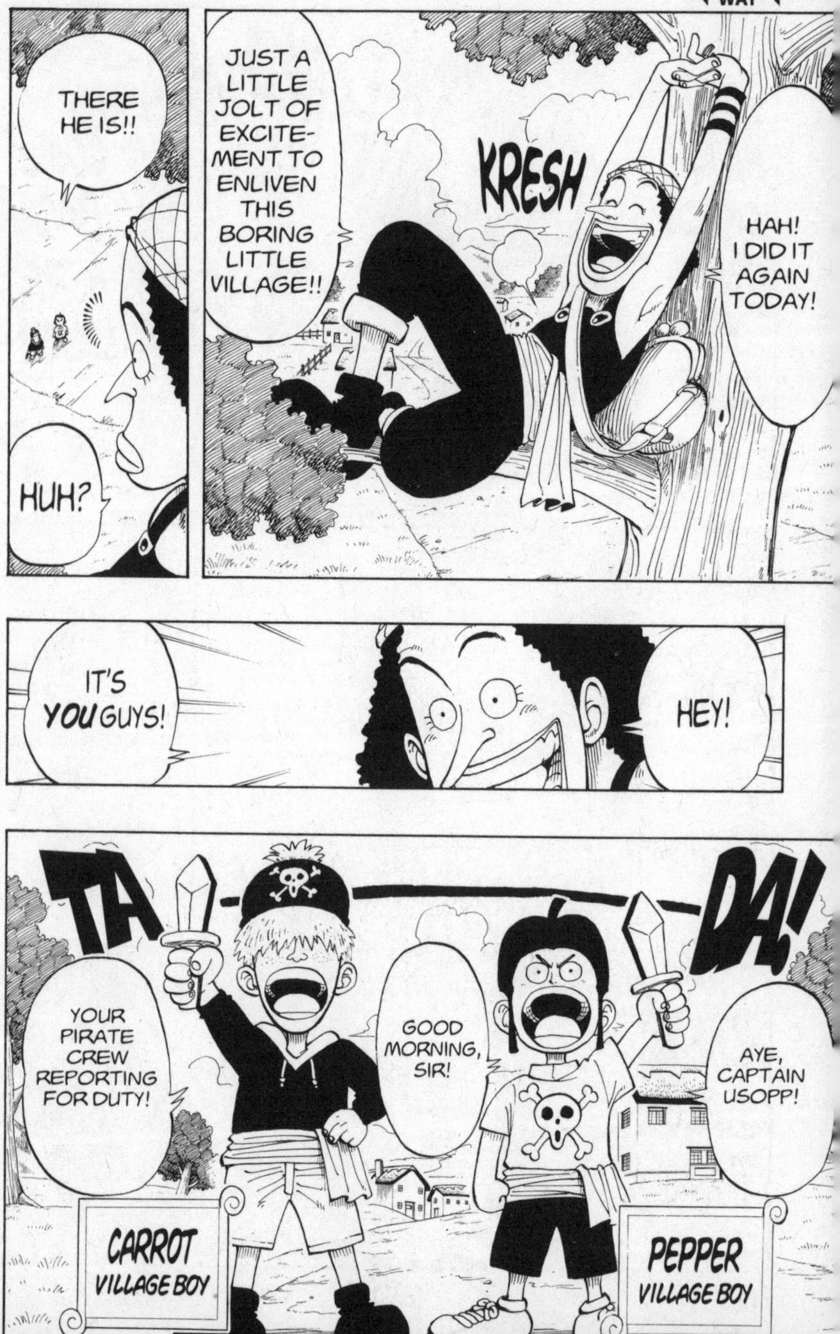
HAH! I DID IT AGAIN TODAY!
KRESH
JUST A LITTLE JOLT OF EXCITEMENT TO ENLIVEN THIS BORING LITTLE VILLAGE!!
THERE HE IS!!
HUH?
HEY!
IT'S YOU GUYS!
TA-DA!
AYE, CAPTAIN USOPP!
GOOD MORNING, SIR!
YOUR PIRATE CREW REPORTING FOR DUTY!
PEPPER VILLAGE BOY
CARROT VILLAGE BOY

READ THIS WAY

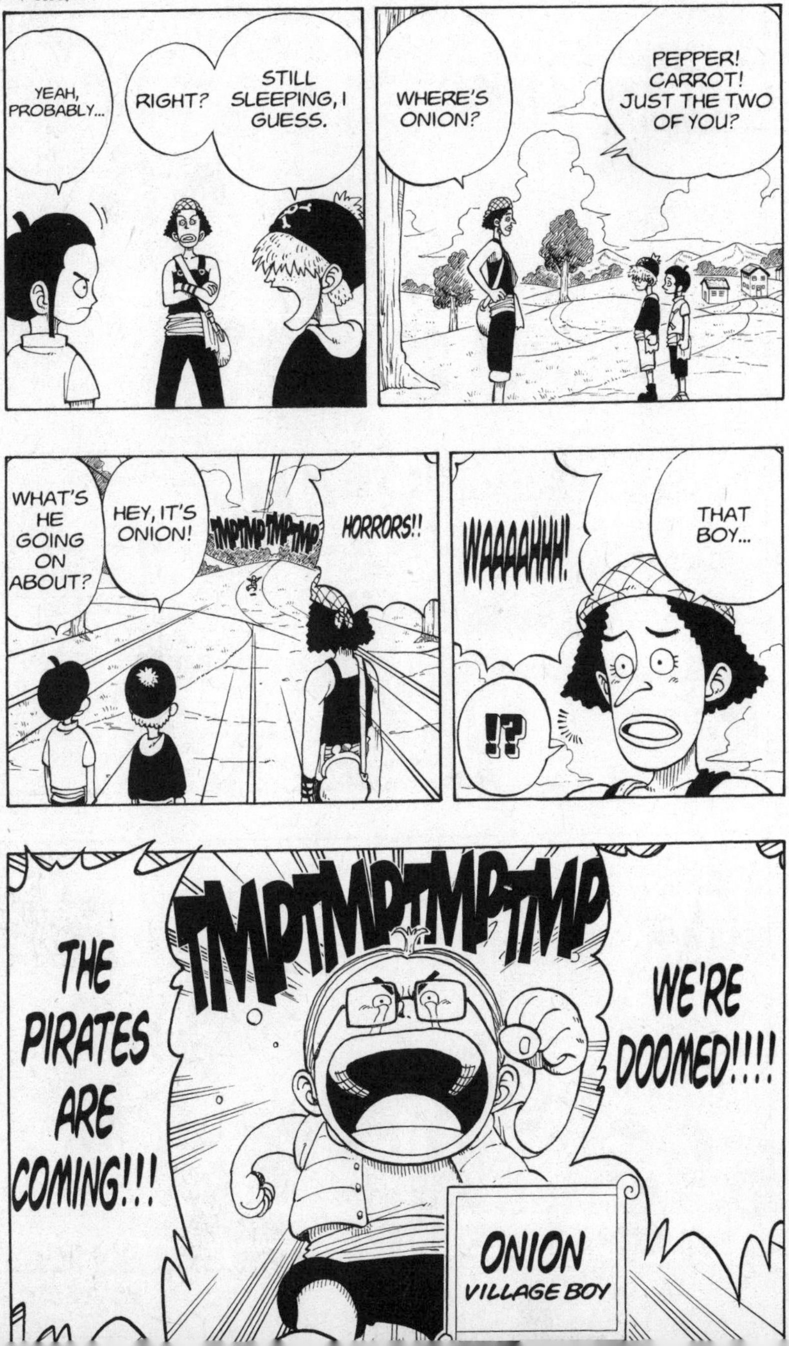
PEPPER! CARROT! JUST THE TWO OF YOU?
WHERE'S ONION?
STILL SLEEPING, I GUESS.
RIGHT?
YEAH, PROBABLY...
THAT BOY...
WAAAAAHH!
!?
HORRORS!!
TMPTMPTMPTMP
HEY, IT'S ONION!
WHAT'S HE GOING ON ABOUT?
WE'RE DOOMED!!!!
TMPTMPTMPTMP
THE PIRATES ARE COMING!!!
ONION
VILLAGE BOY

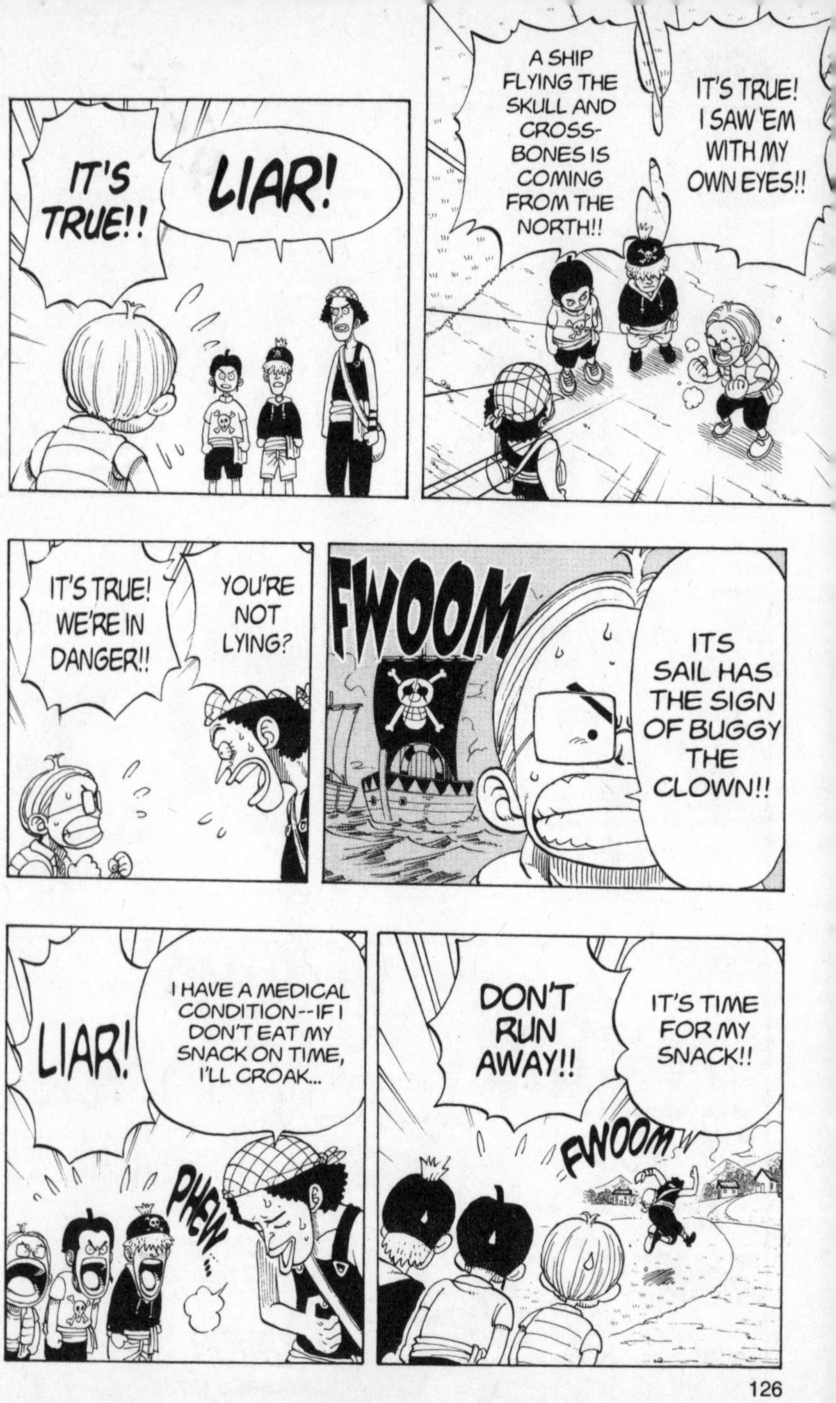
IT'S TRUE! I SAW 'EM WITH MY OWN EYES!!
A SHIP FLYING THE SKULL AND CROSS-BONES IS COMING FROM THE NORTH!!
LIAR!
IT'S TRUE!!
ITS SAIL HAS THE SIGN OF BUGGY THE CLOWN!!
FWOOM
YOU'RE NOT LYING?
IT'S TRUE! WE'RE IN DANGER!!
IT'S TIME FOR MY SNACK!!
DON'T RUN AWAY!!
FWOOM
I HAVE A MEDICAL CONDITION--IF I DON'T EAT MY SNACK ON TIME, I'LL CROAK...
LIAR!
PHEW...

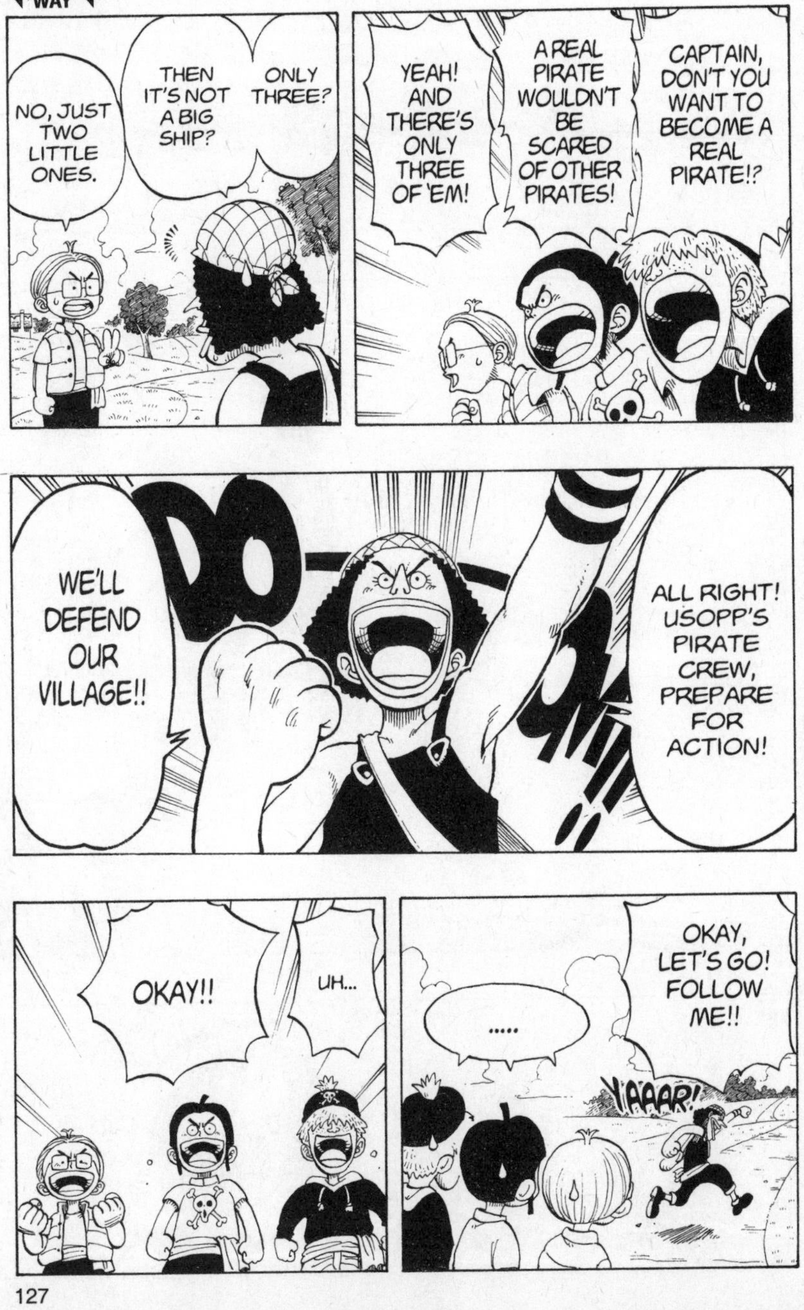
CAPTAIN, DON'T YOU WANT TO BECOME A REAL PIRATE!?
A REAL PIRATE WOULDN'T BE SCARED OF OTHER PIRATES!
YEAH! AND THERE'S ONLY THREE OF 'EM!
ONLY THREE?
THEN IT'S NOT A BIG SHIP?
NO, JUST TWO LITTLE ONES.
ALL RIGHT! USOPP'S PIRATE CREW, PREPARE FOR ACTION!
WE'LL DEFEND OUR VILLAGE!!
OKAY, LET'S GO! FOLLOW ME!!
YAAAR!
.....
UH...
OKAY!!

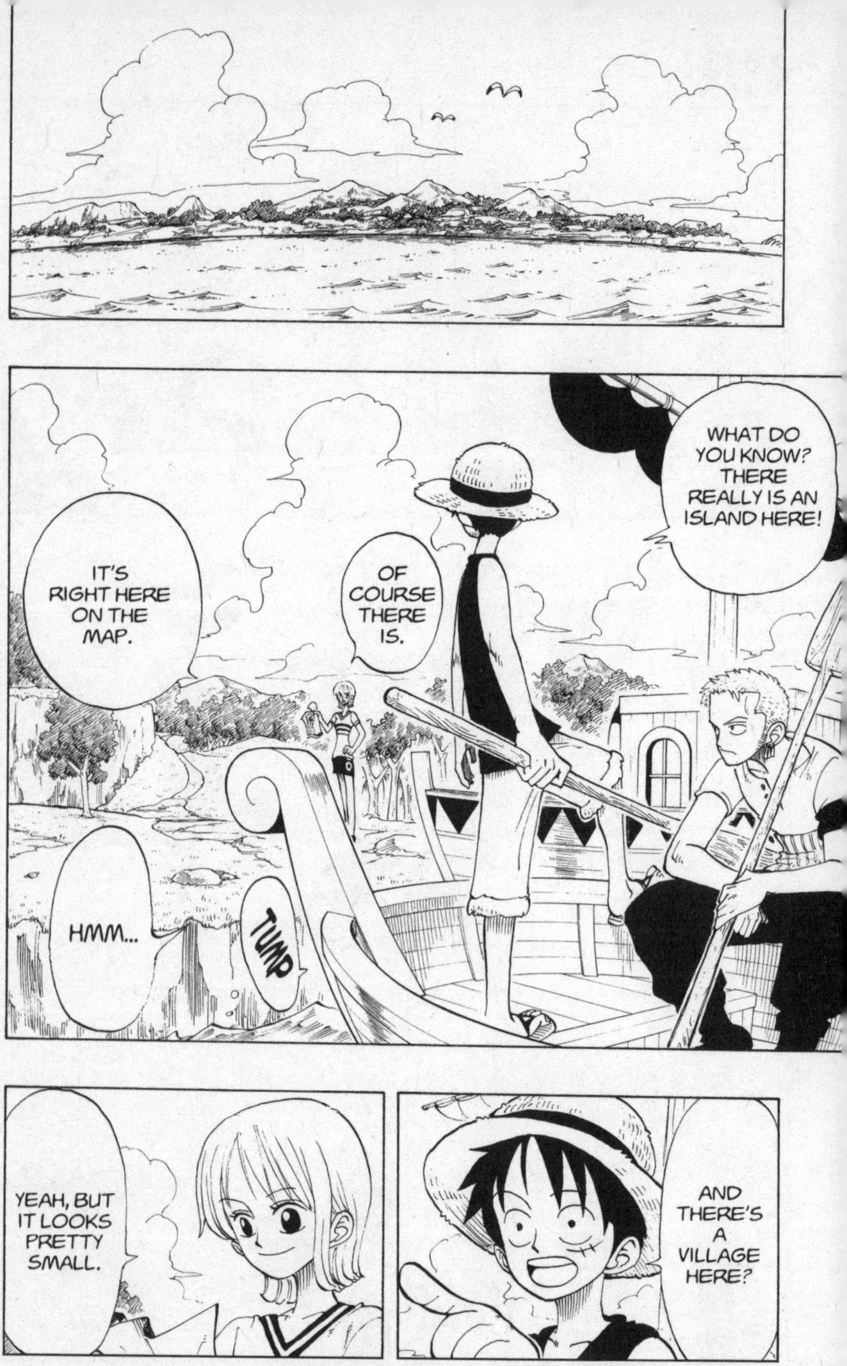
WHAT DO YOU KNOW? THERE REALLY IS AN ISLAND HERE!
OF COURSE THERE IS.
IT'S RIGHT HERE ON THE MAP.
TUMP
HMM...
AND THERE'S A VILLAGE HERE?
YEAH, BUT IT LOOKS PRETTY SMALL.

READ THIS WAY

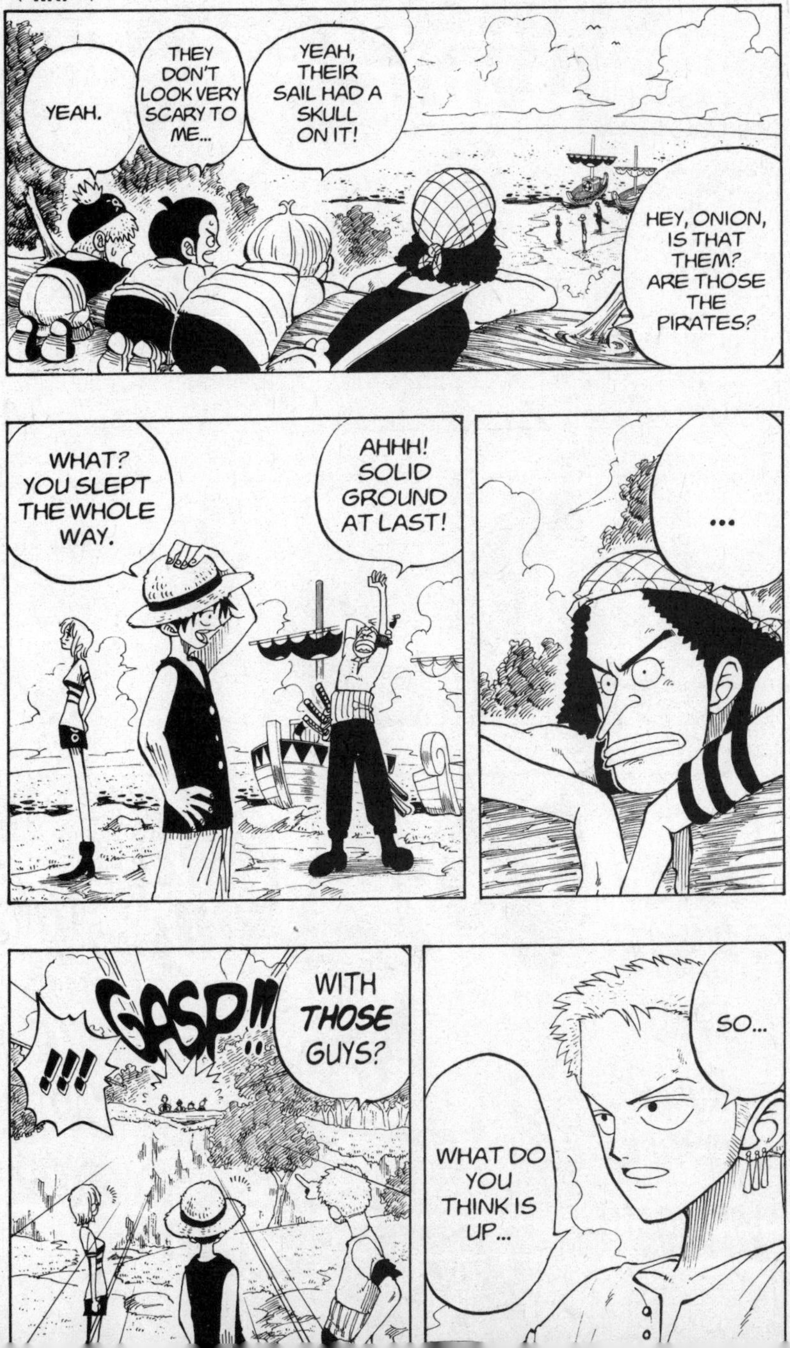
HEY, ONION, IS THAT THEM? ARE THOSE THE PIRATES?
YEAH, THEIR SAIL HAD A SKULL ON IT!
THEY DON'T LOOK VERY SCARY TO ME...
YEAH.
...
AHHH! SOLID GROUND AT LAST!
WHAT? YOU SLEPT THE WHOLE WAY.
SO...
WHAT DO YOU THINK IS UP...
WITH THOSE GUYS?
GASP!!
!!!

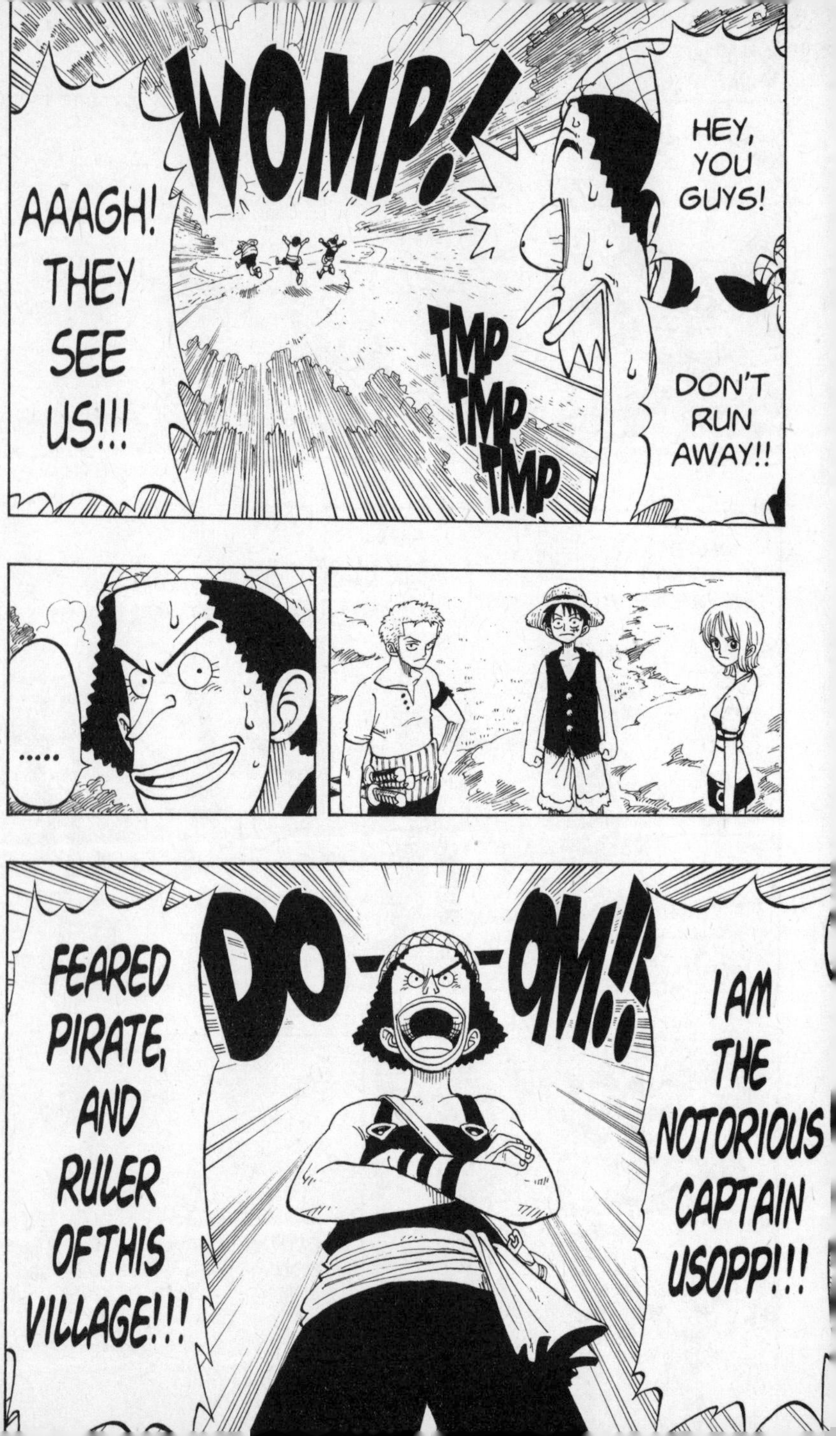
HEY, YOU GUYS!
DON'T RUN AWAY!!
WOMP!
AAAGH! THEY SEE US!!!
TMP TMP TMP
.....
I AM THE NOTORIOUS CAPTAIN USOPP!!!
DO-OM!!
FEARED PIRATE, AND RULER OF THIS VILLAGE!!!

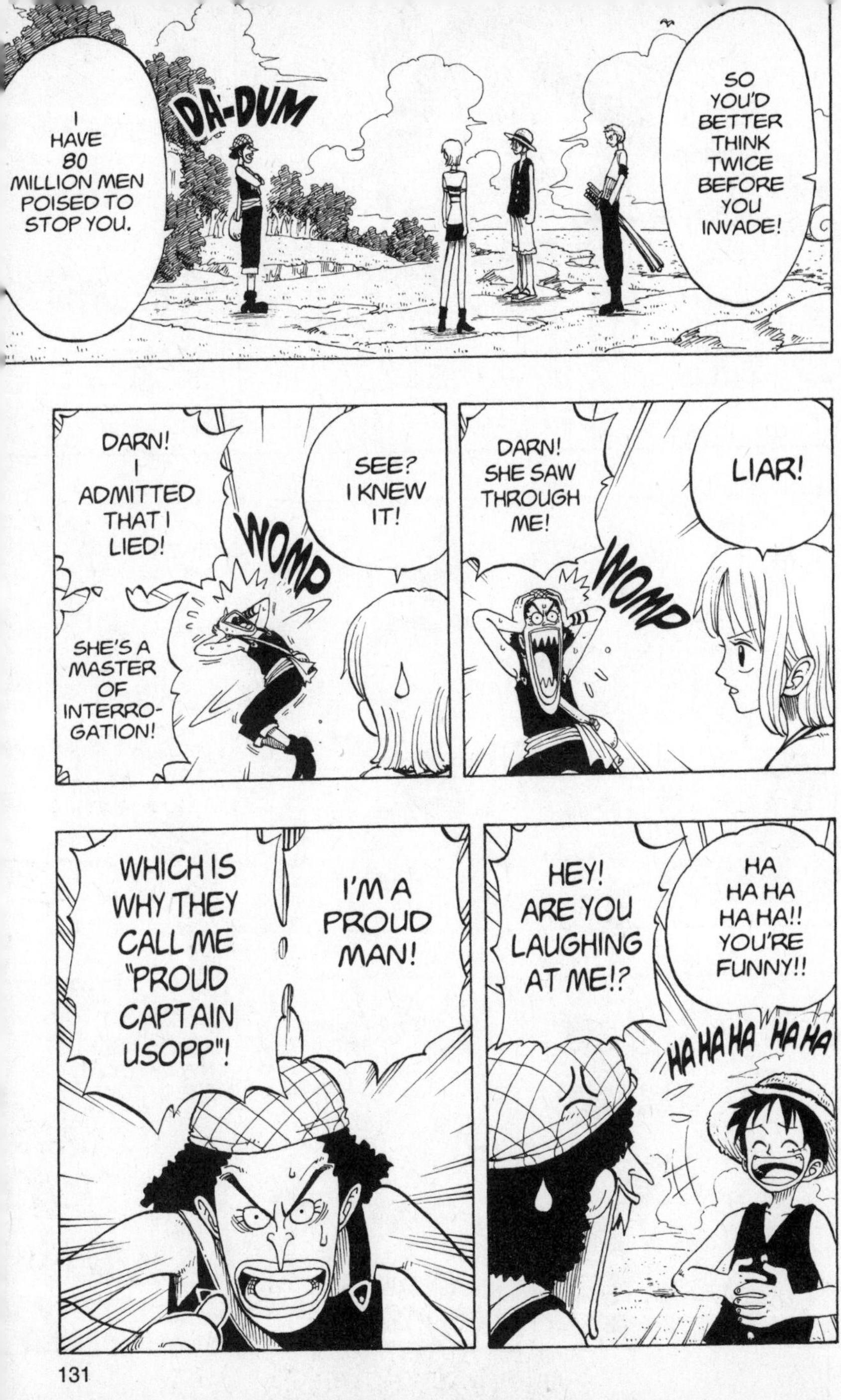
I HAVE 80 MILLION MEN POISED TO STOP YOU.
SO YOU'D BETTER THINK TWICE BEFORE YOU INVADE!
DA-DUM
LIAR!
DARN! SHE SAW THROUGH ME!
WOMP
SEE? I KNEW IT!
DARN! I ADMITTED THAT I LIED!
WOMP
SHE'S A MASTER OF INTERRO-GATION!
HA HA HA HA HA!! YOU'RE FUNNY!!
HEY! ARE YOU LAUGHING AT ME!?
HA HA HA HA HA
I'M A PROUD MAN!
WHICH IS WHY THEY CALL ME "PROUD CAPTAIN USOPP"!

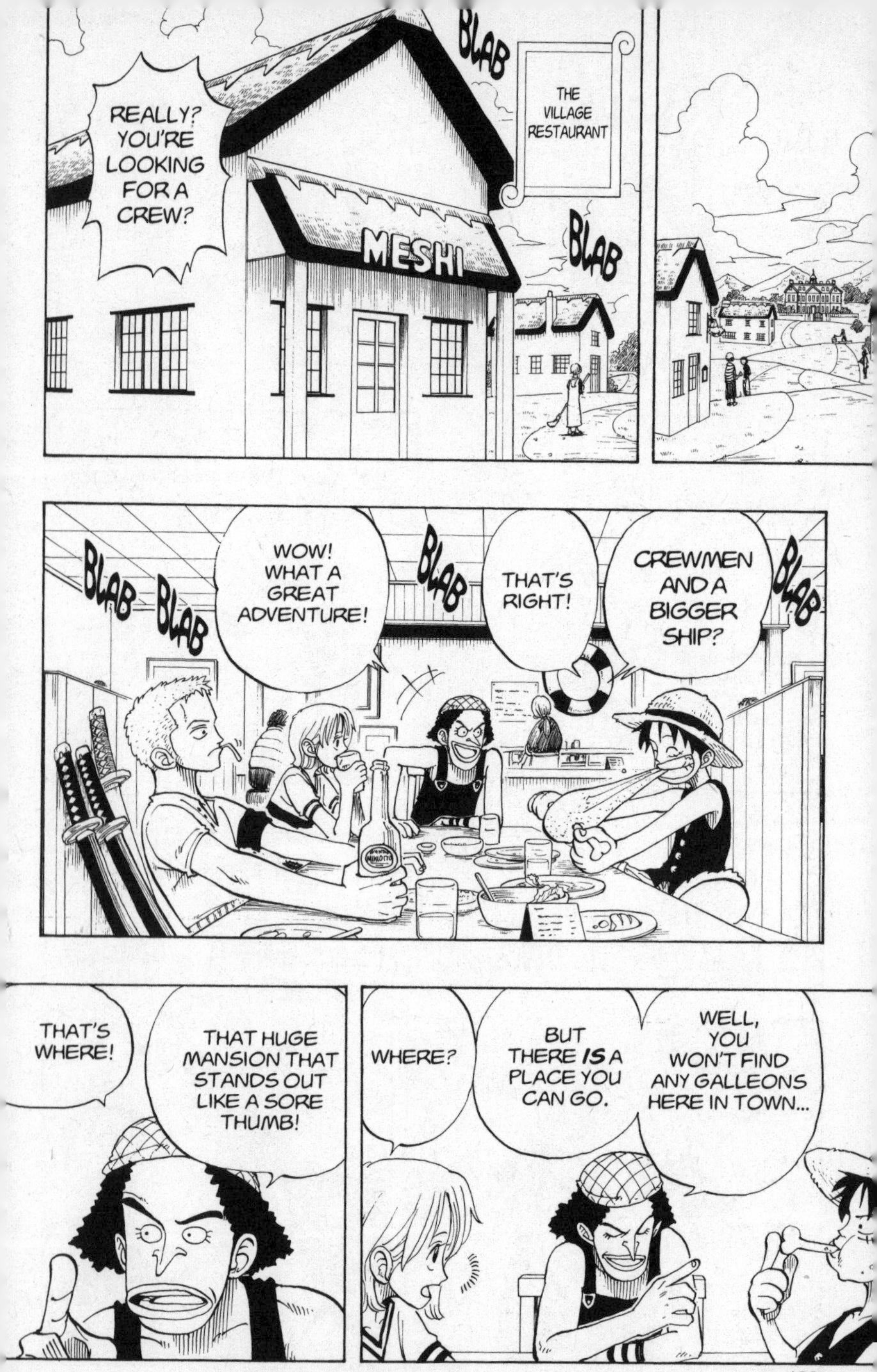
THE VILLAGE RESTAURANT
BLAB
REALLY? YOU'RE LOOKING FOR A CREW?
MESHI
BLAB
BLAB
CREWMEN AND A BIGGER SHIP?
THAT'S RIGHT!
BLAB
WOW! WHAT A GREAT ADVENTURE!
BLAB BLAB
WELL, YOU WON'T FIND ANY GALLEONS HERE IN TOWN...
BUT THERE *IS* A PLACE YOU CAN GO.
WHERE?
THAT HUGE MANSION THAT STANDS OUT LIKE A SORE THUMB!
THAT'S WHERE!

READ THIS WAY

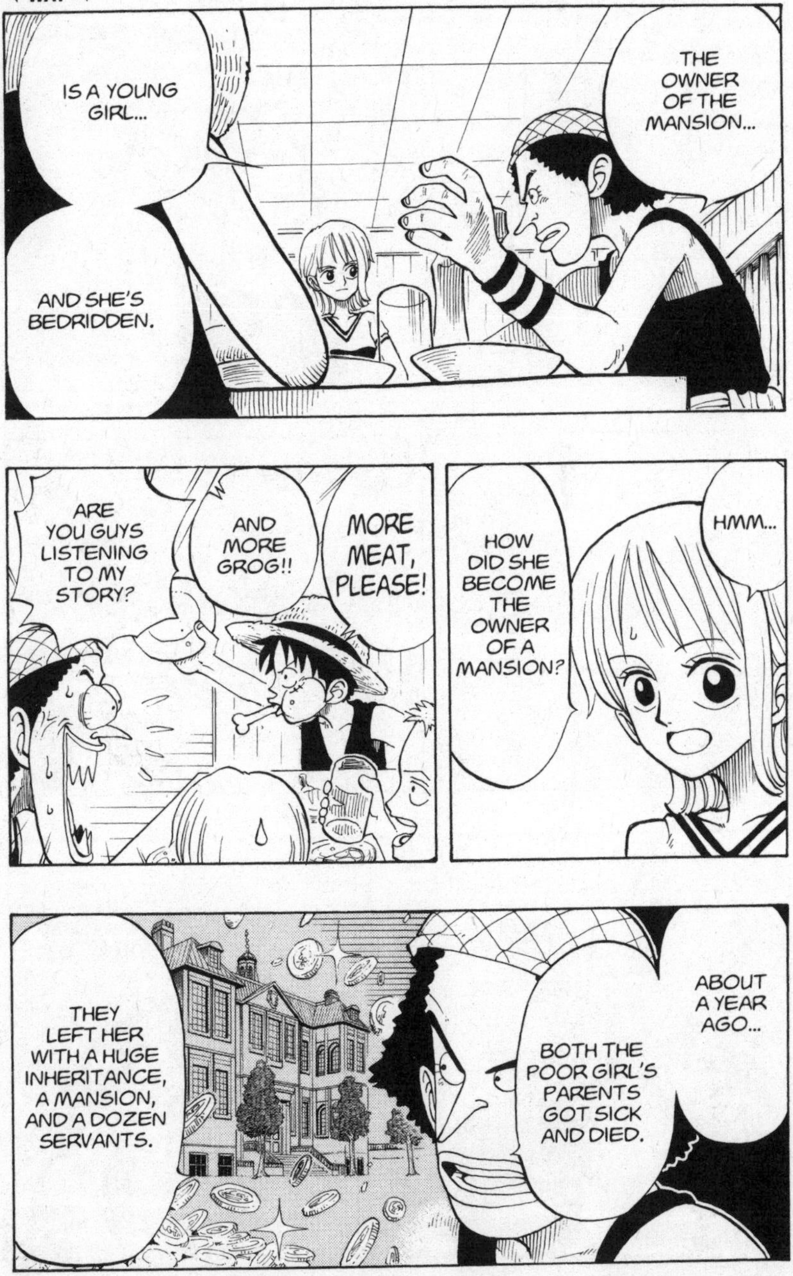
THE OWNER OF THE MANSION...
IS A YOUNG GIRL...
AND SHE'S BEDRIDDEN.
HMM...
HOW DID SHE BECOME THE OWNER OF A MANSION?
MORE MEAT, PLEASE!
AND MORE GROG!!
ARE YOU GUYS LISTENING TO MY STORY?
ABOUT A YEAR AGO...
BOTH THE POOR GIRL'S PARENTS GOT SICK AND DIED.
THEY LEFT HER WITH A HUGE INHERITANCE, A MANSION, AND A DOZEN SERVANTS.

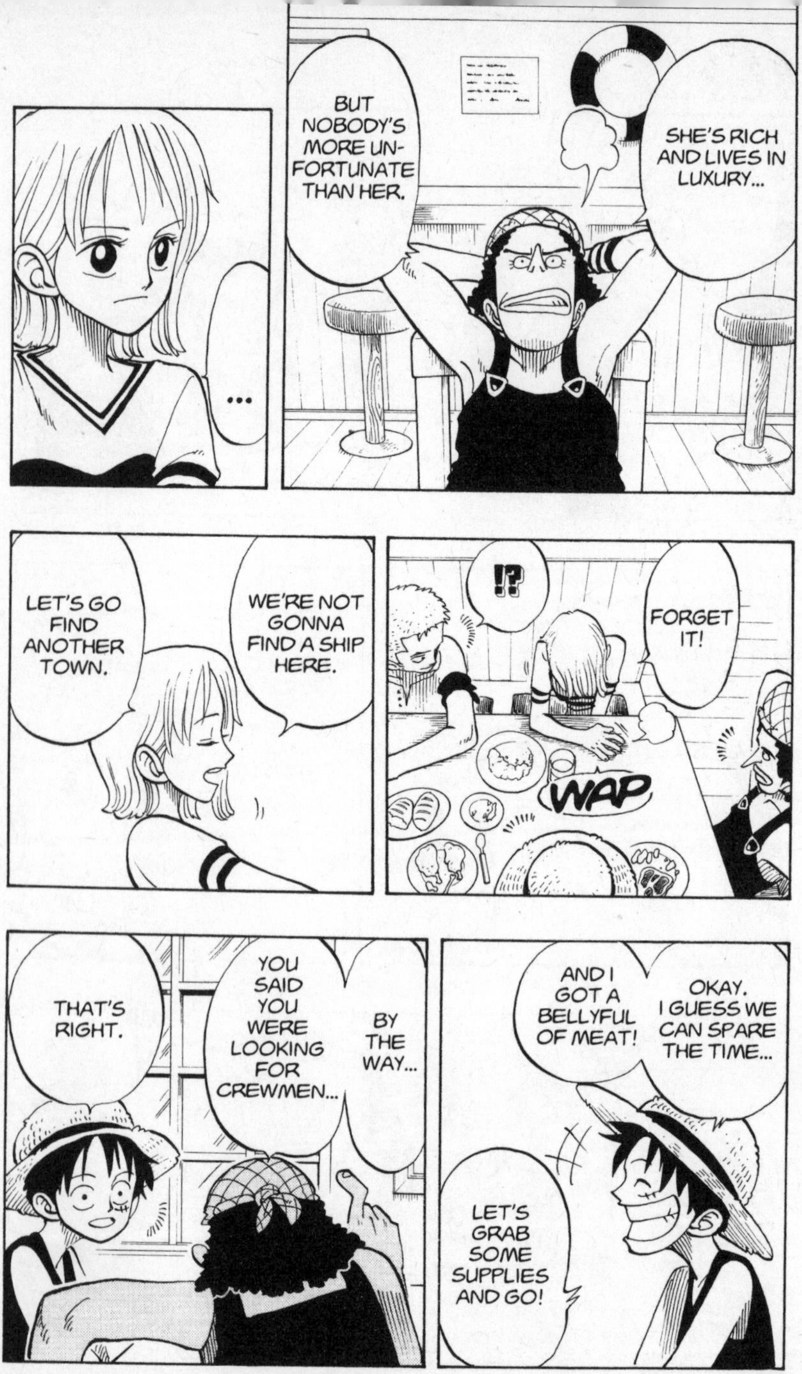
SHE'S RICH AND LIVES IN LUXURY...
BUT NOBODY'S MORE UN-FORTUNATE THAN HER.
...
FORGET IT!
!?
WAP
WE'RE NOT GONNA FIND A SHIP HERE.
LET'S GO FIND ANOTHER TOWN.
OKAY. I GUESS WE CAN SPARE THE TIME...
AND I GOT A BELLYFUL OF MEAT!
LET'S GRAB SOME SUPPLIES AND GO!
BY THE WAY...
YOU SAID YOU WERE LOOKING FOR CREWMEN...
THAT'S RIGHT.

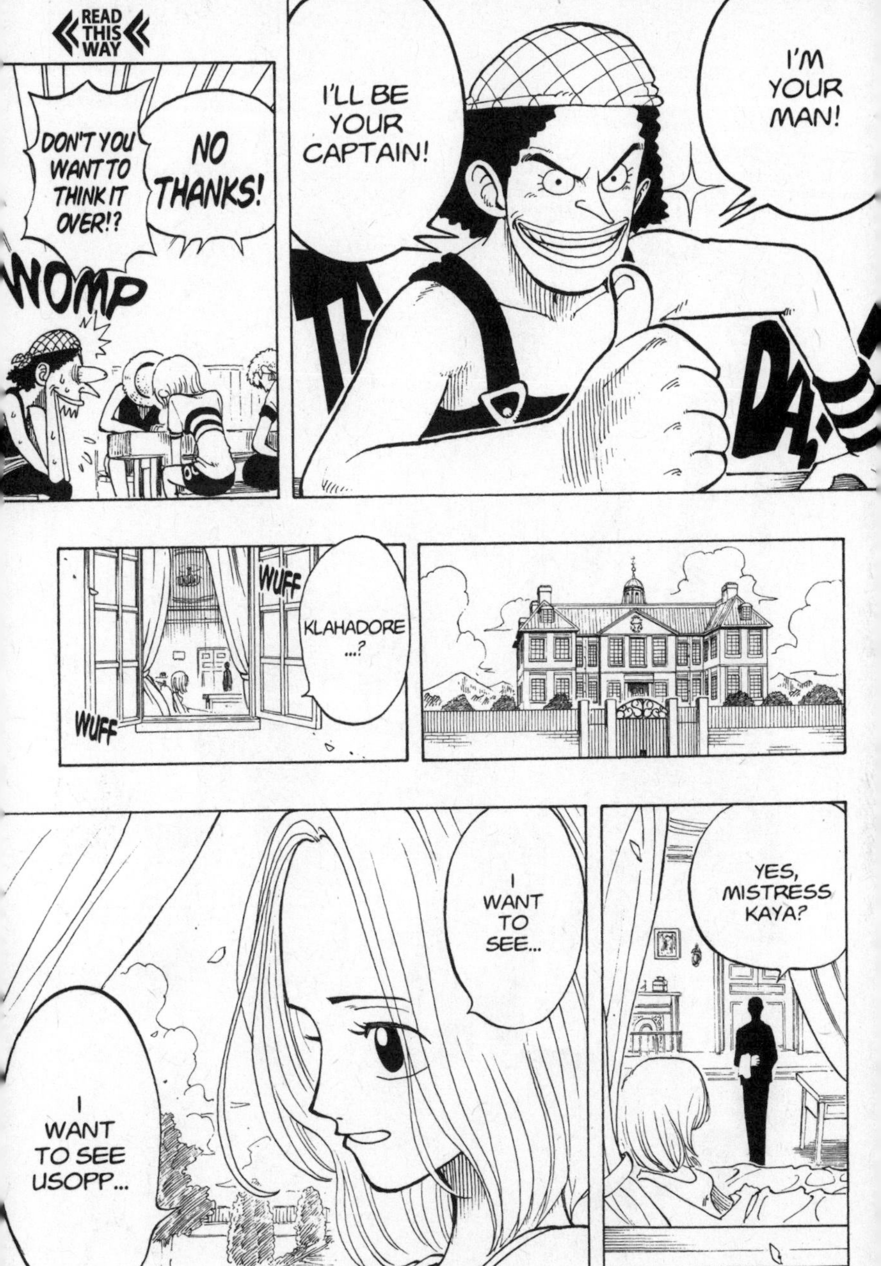
READ THIS WAY
I'M YOUR MAN!
DA
I'LL BE YOUR CAPTAIN!
TA
NO THANKS!
DON'T YOU WANT TO THINK IT OVER!?
WOMP
KLAHADORE ...?
WUFF
WUFF
YES, MISTRESS KAYA?
I WANT TO SEE...
I WANT TO SEE USOPP...

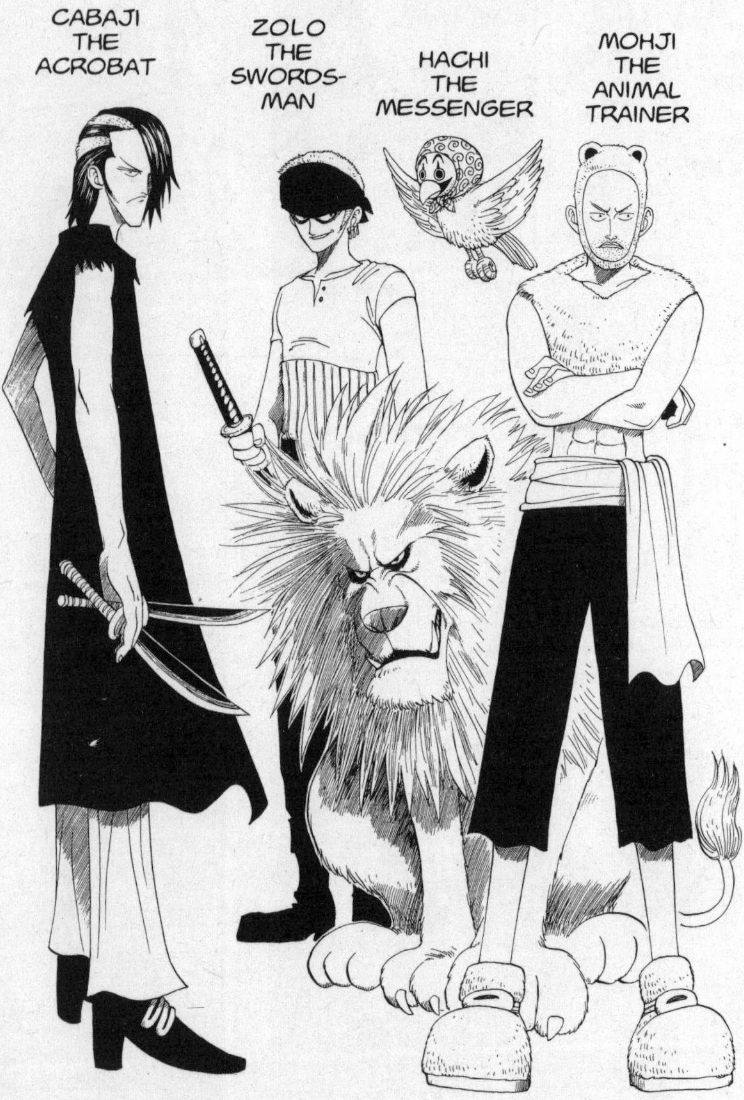
MOHJI
THE
ANIMAL
TRAINER
HACHI
THE
MESSENGER
ZOLO
THE
SWORDS-
MAN
CABAJI
THE
ACROBAT

Chapter 24:
THE LIE REJECTER

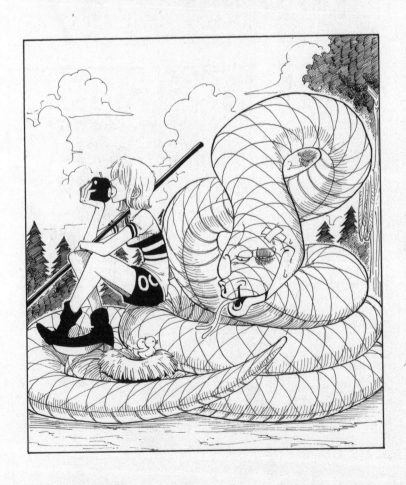

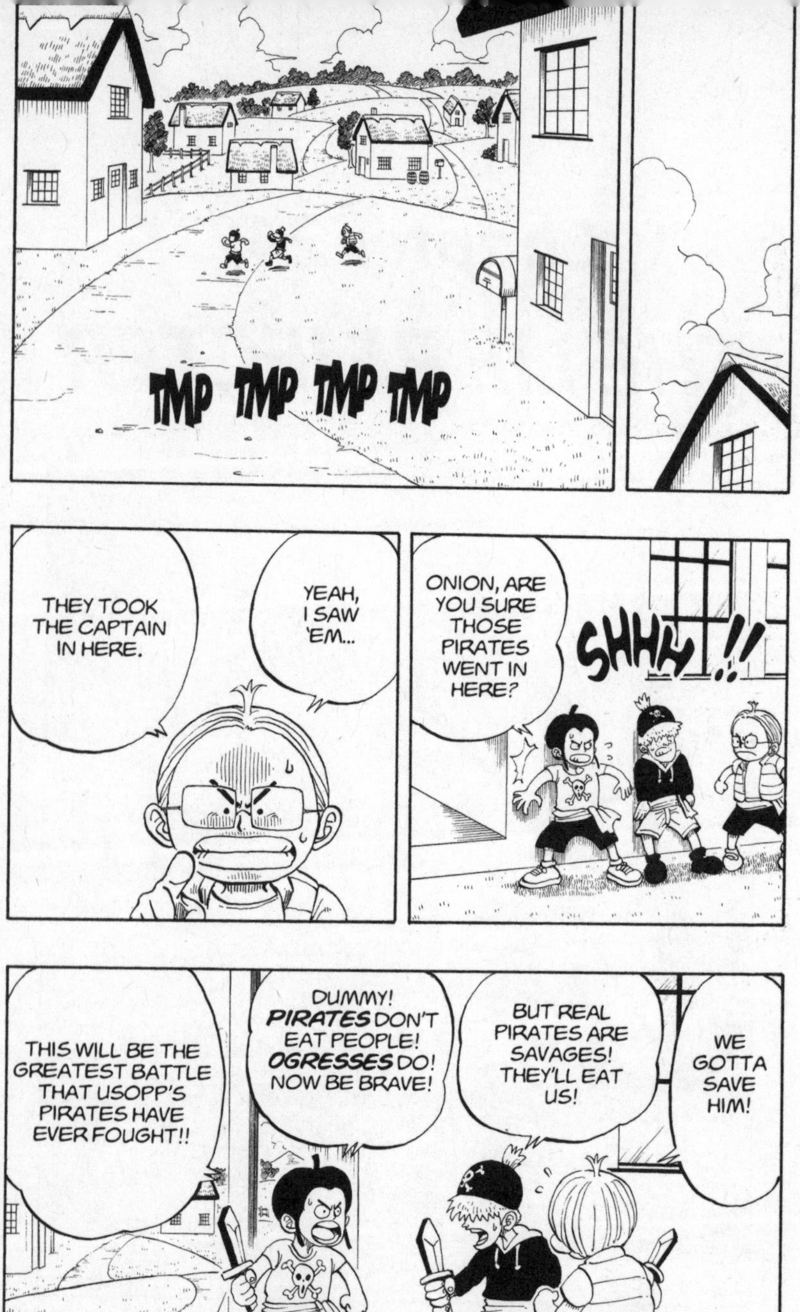
TMP TMP TMP TMP
ONION, ARE YOU SURE THOSE PIRATES WENT IN HERE?
SHHH!!
YEAH, I SAW 'EM...
THEY TOOK THE CAPTAIN IN HERE.
WE GOTTA SAVE HIM!
BUT REAL PIRATES ARE SAVAGES! THEY'LL EAT US!
DUMMY! PIRATES DON'T EAT PEOPLE! OGRESSES DO! NOW BE BRAVE!
THIS WILL BE THE GREATEST BATTLE THAT USOPP'S PIRATES HAVE EVER FOUGHT!!

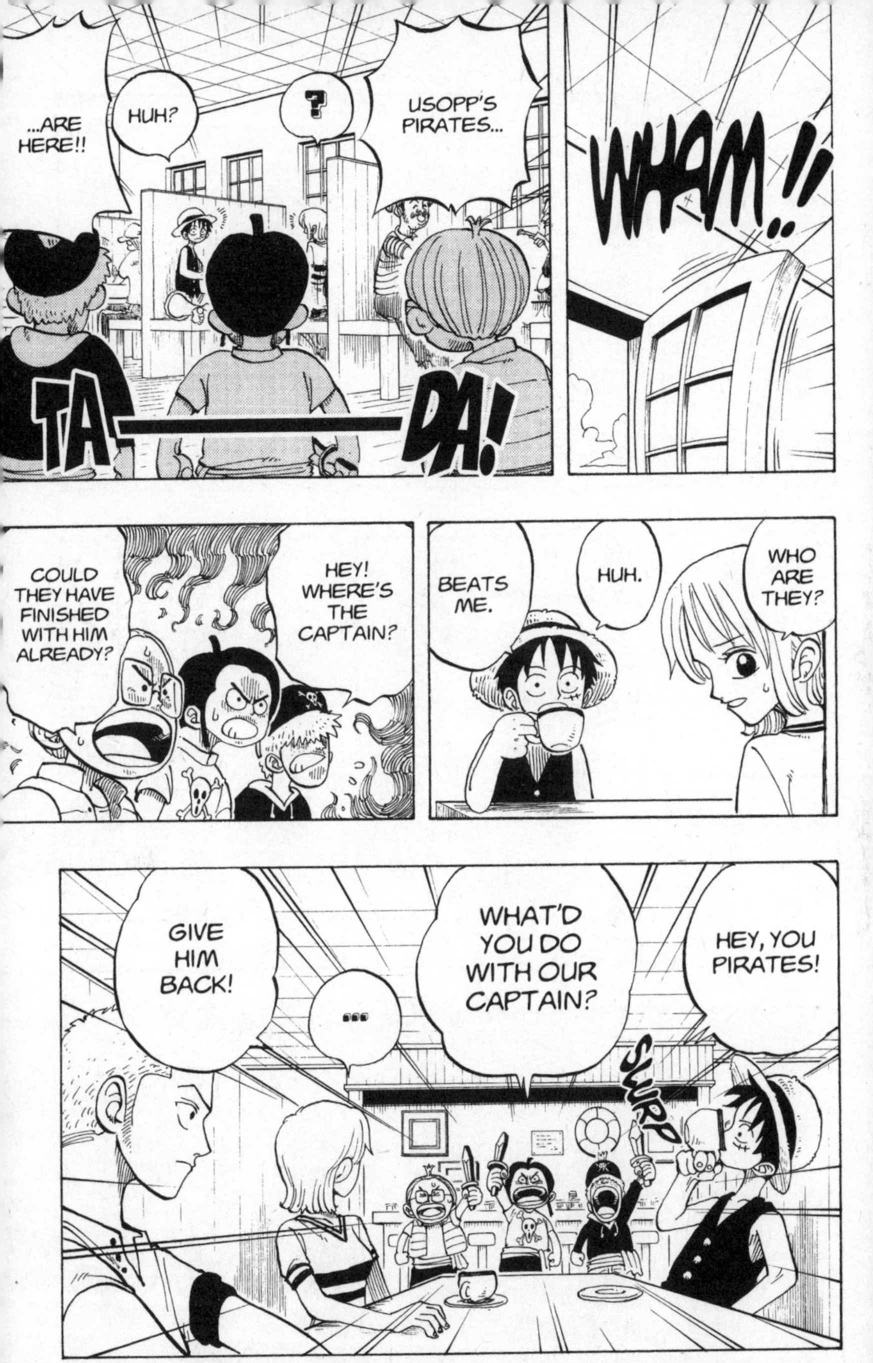
WHAM!!
USOPP'S PIRATES...
?
HUH?
...ARE HERE!!
TA-DA!
WHO ARE THEY?
HUH.
BEATS ME.
HEY! WHERE'S THE CAPTAIN?
COULD THEY HAVE FINISHED WITH HIM ALREADY?
HEY, YOU PIRATES!
SLURP
WHAT'D YOU DO WITH OUR CAPTAIN?
...
GIVE HIM BACK!

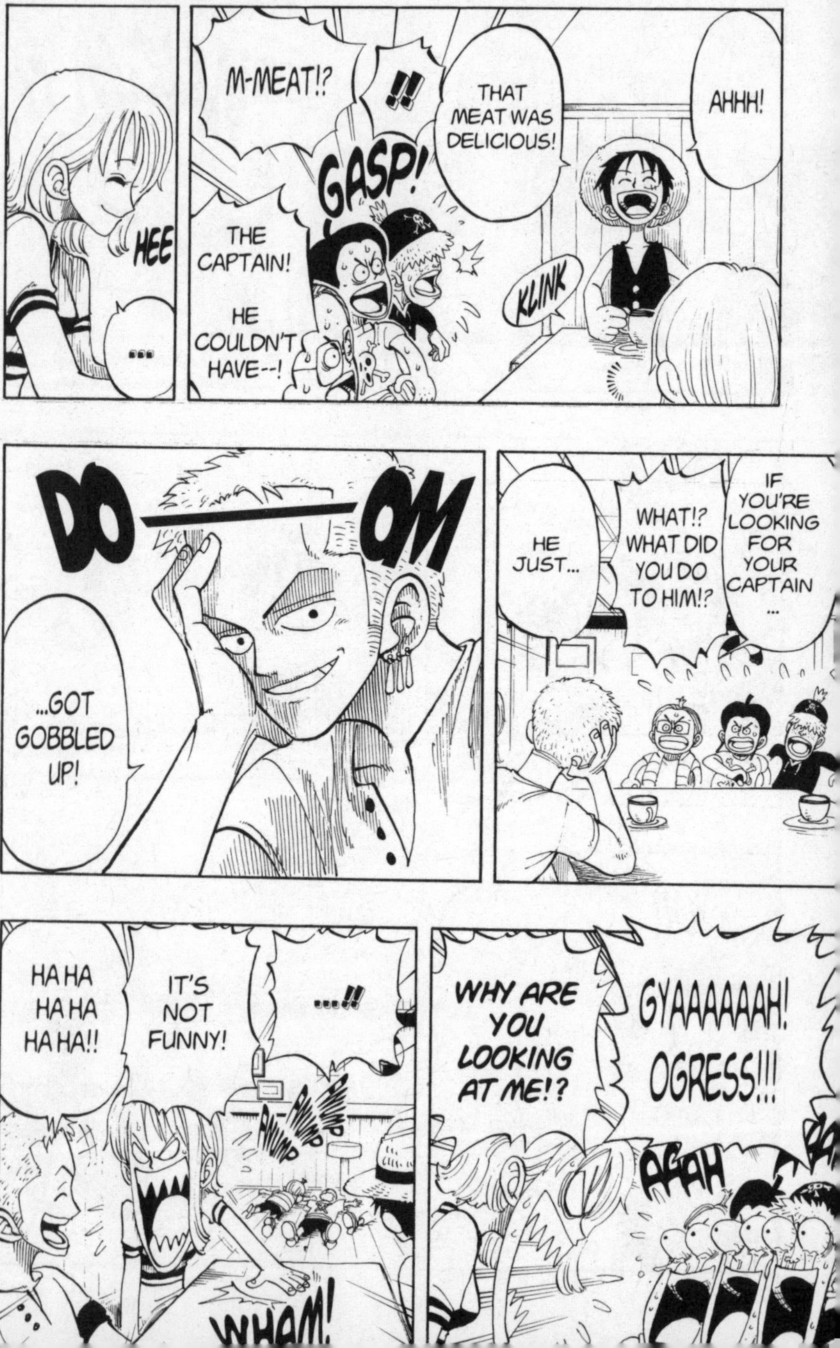
AHHH!
THAT MEAT WAS DELICIOUS!
!!
M-MEAT!?
GASP!
KLINK
THE CAPTAIN!
HE COULDN'T HAVE--!
HEE
...
IF YOU'RE LOOKING FOR YOUR CAPTAIN ...
WHAT!? WHAT DID YOU DO TO HIM!?
HE JUST...
DO——OM
...GOT GOBBLED UP!
GYAAAAAAH! OGRESS!!!
WHY ARE YOU LOOKING AT ME!?
AGAH
...!!
IT'S NOT FUNNY!
HA HA HA HA HA HA!!
WHAM!

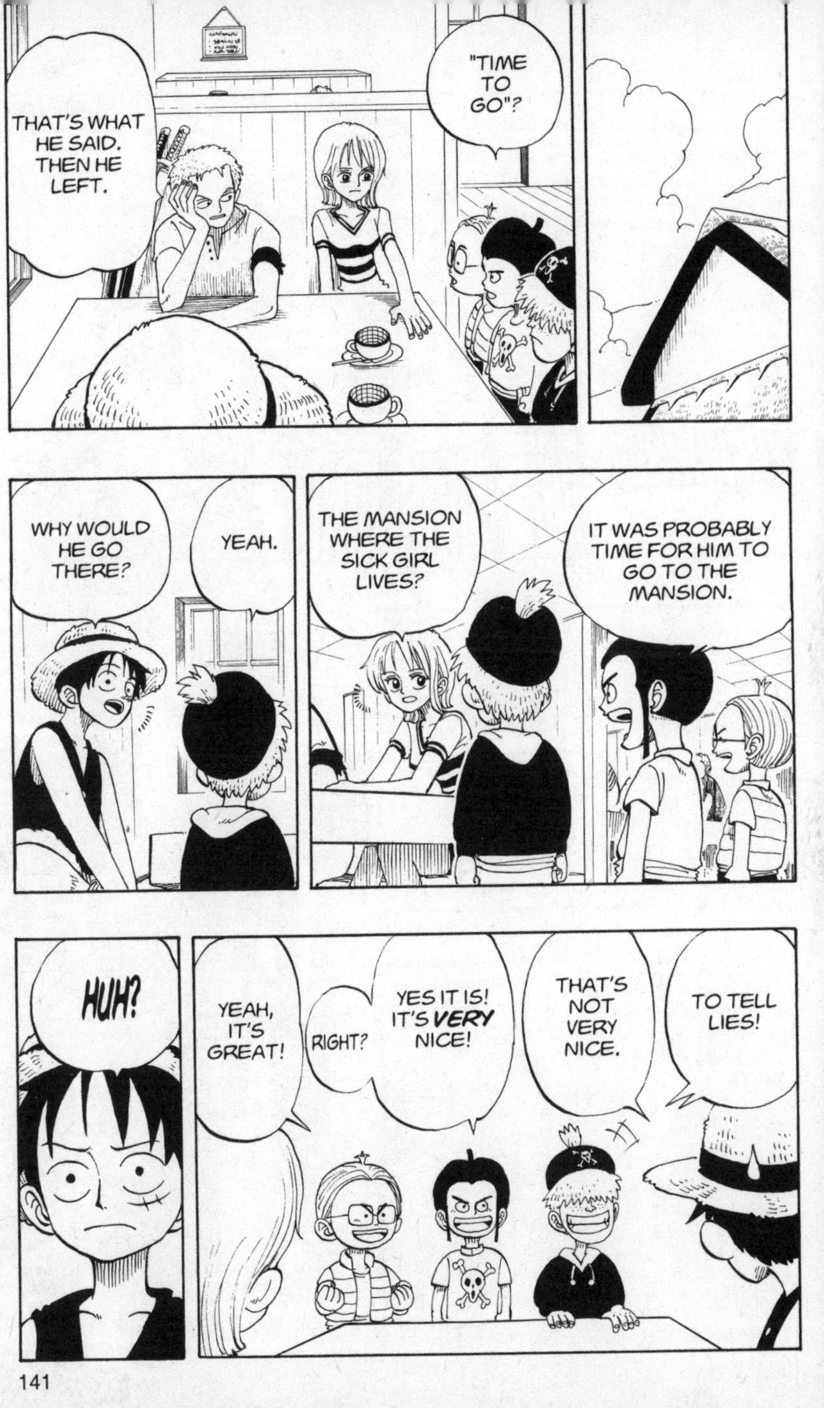
"TIME TO GO"?
THAT'S WHAT HE SAID. THEN HE LEFT.
IT WAS PROBABLY TIME FOR HIM TO GO TO THE MANSION.
THE MANSION WHERE THE SICK GIRL LIVES?
YEAH.
WHY WOULD HE GO THERE?
TO TELL LIES!
THAT'S NOT VERY NICE.
YES IT IS! IT'S *VERY* NICE!
RIGHT?
YEAH, IT'S GREAT!
HUH?

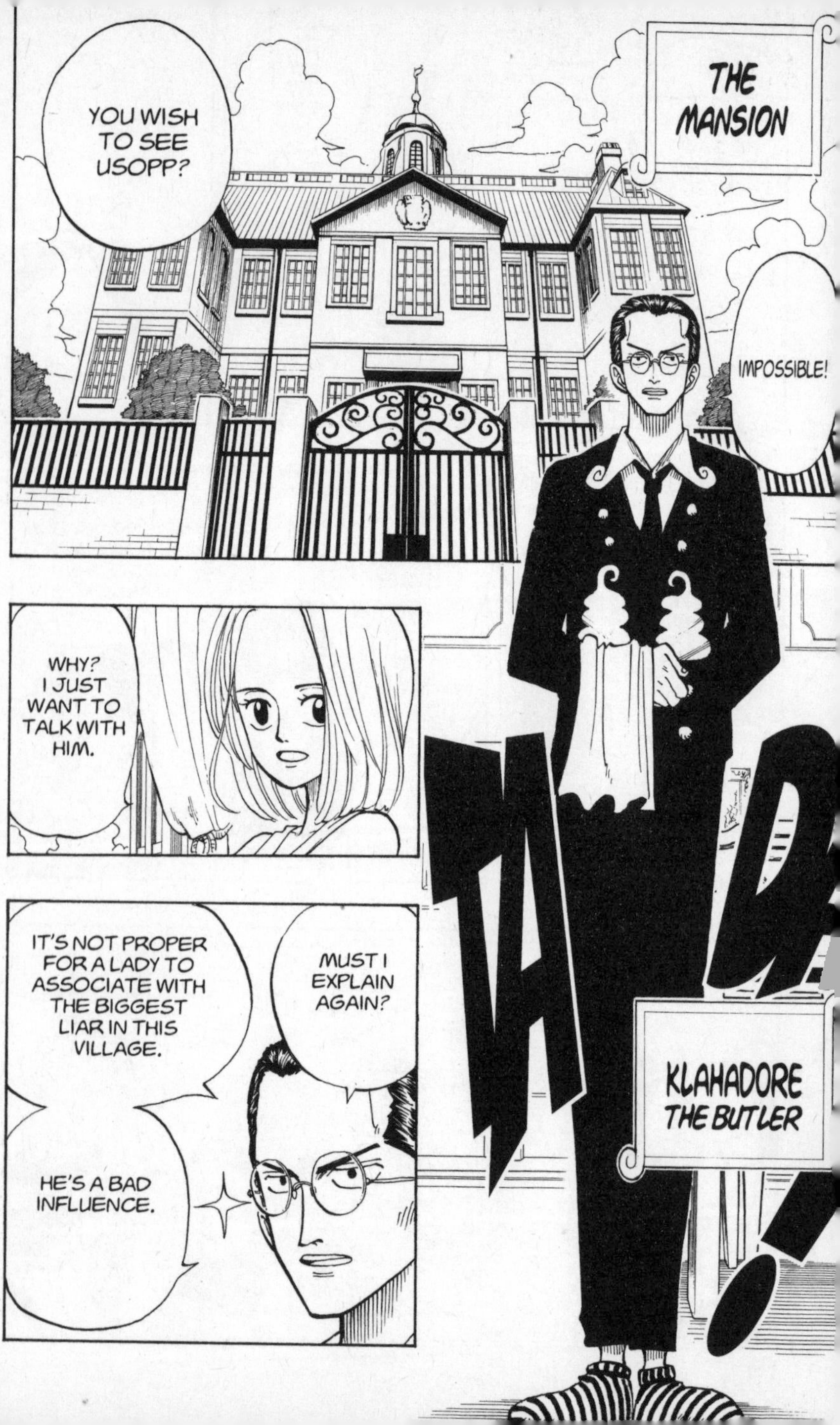
THE MANSION
YOU WISH TO SEE USOPP?
IMPOSSIBLE!
TA
KLAHADORE THE BUTLER
WHY? I JUST WANT TO TALK WITH HIM.
MUST I EXPLAIN AGAIN?
IT'S NOT PROPER FOR A LADY TO ASSOCIATE WITH THE BIGGEST LIAR IN THIS VILLAGE.
HE'S A BAD INFLUENCE.

READ THIS WAY

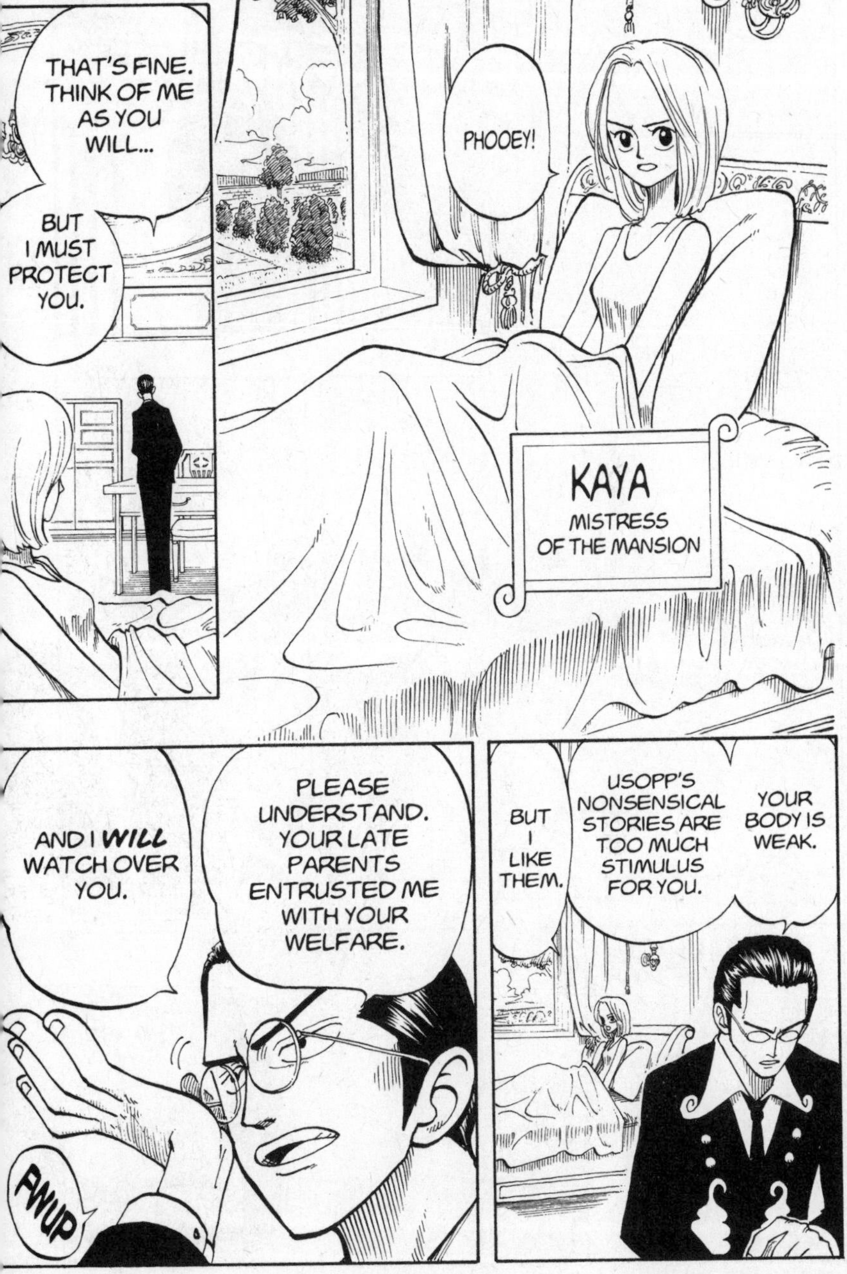
PHOOEY!
KAYA MISTRESS OF THE MANSION
THAT'S FINE. THINK OF ME AS YOU WILL...
BUT I MUST PROTECT YOU.
YOUR BODY IS WEAK.
USOPP'S NONSENSICAL STORIES ARE TOO MUCH STIMULUS FOR YOU.
BUT I LIKE THEM.
PLEASE UNDERSTAND. YOUR LATE PARENTS ENTRUSTED ME WITH YOUR WELFARE.
AND I **WILL** WATCH OVER YOU.
FWUP

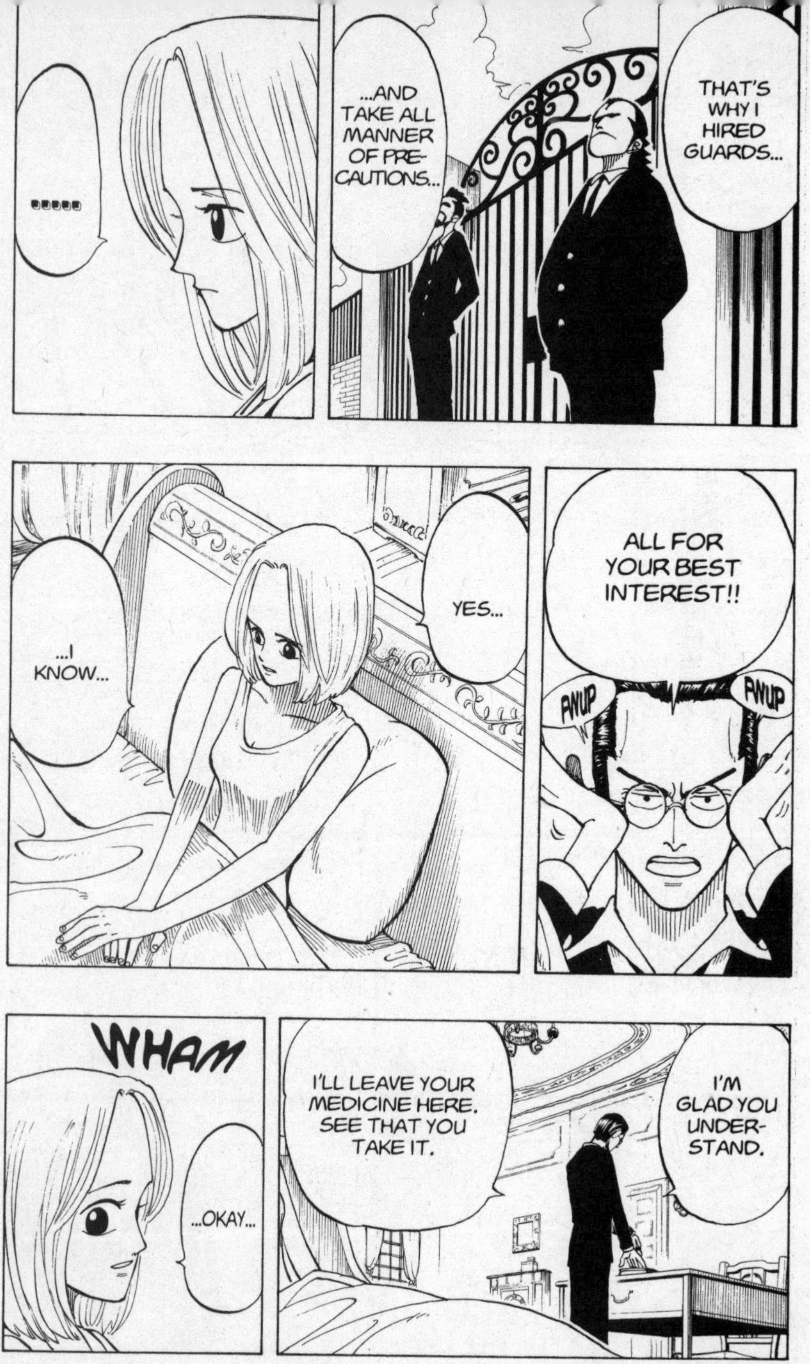
THAT'S WHY I HIRED GUARDS...
...AND TAKE ALL MANNER OF PRE-CAUTIONS...
.....
ALL FOR YOUR BEST INTEREST!!
FWUP
FWUP
YES...
...I KNOW...
I'M GLAD YOU UNDER-STAND.
I'LL LEAVE YOUR MEDICINE HERE. SEE THAT YOU TAKE IT.
WHAM
...OKAY...

READ THIS WAY

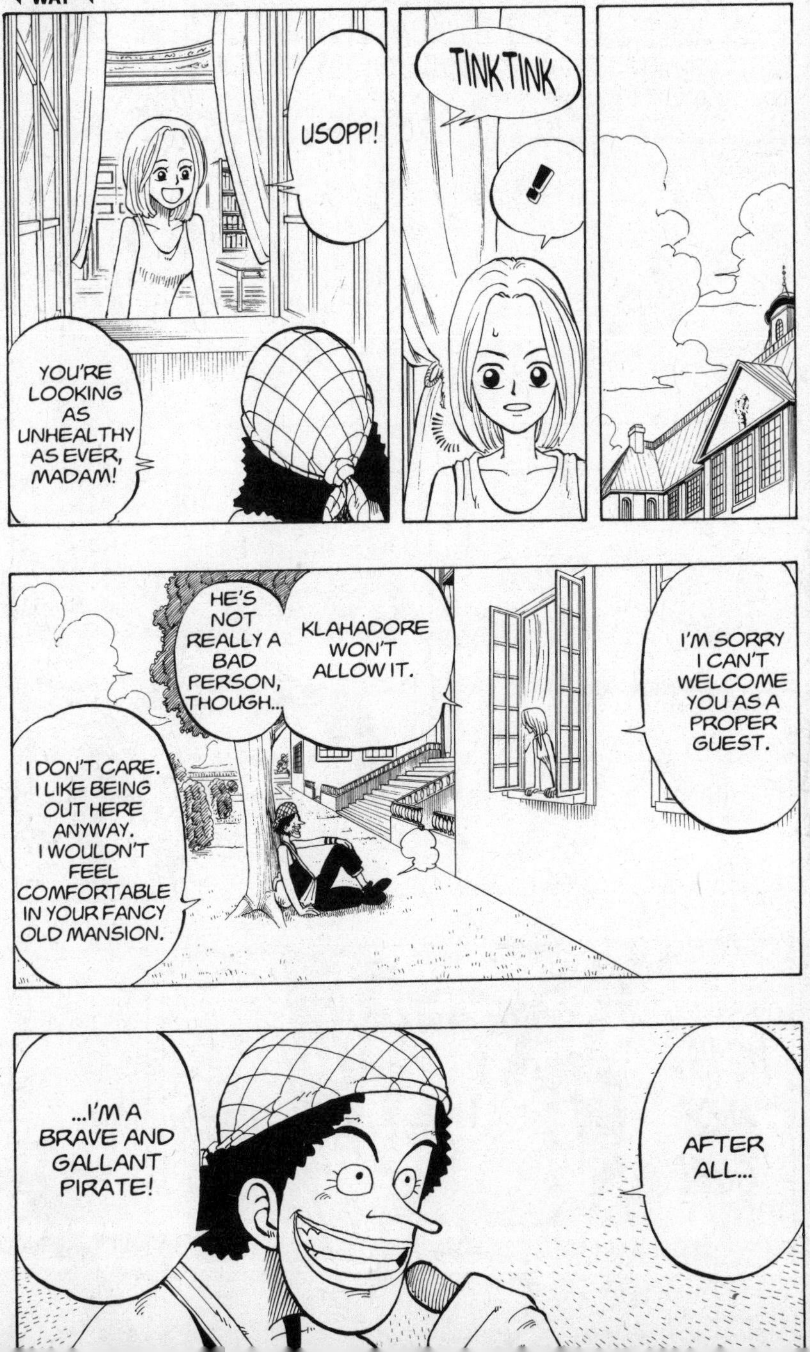
TINKTINK
!
USOPP!
YOU'RE LOOKING AS UNHEALTHY AS EVER, MADAM!
I'M SORRY I CAN'T WELCOME YOU AS A PROPER GUEST.
KLAHADORE WON'T ALLOW IT.
HE'S NOT REALLY A BAD PERSON, THOUGH...
I DON'T CARE. I LIKE BEING OUT HERE ANYWAY. I WOULDN'T FEEL COMFORTABLE IN YOUR FANCY OLD MANSION.
AFTER ALL...
...I'M A BRAVE AND GALLANT PIRATE!

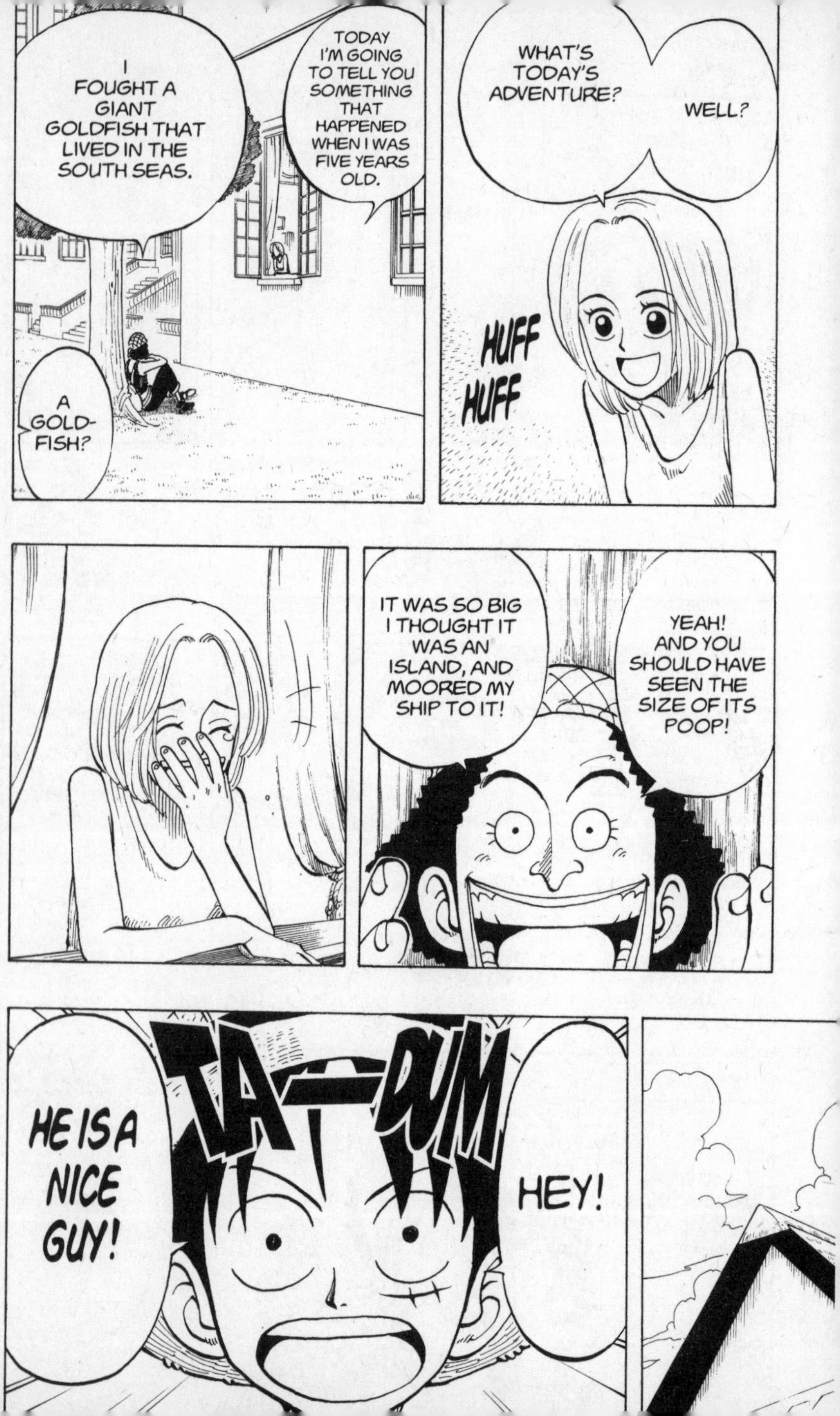
WHAT'S TODAY'S ADVENTURE?
WELL?
HUFF HUFF
TODAY I'M GOING TO TELL YOU SOMETHING THAT HAPPENED WHEN I WAS FIVE YEARS OLD.
I FOUGHT A GIANT GOLDFISH THAT LIVED IN THE SOUTH SEAS.
A GOLD-FISH?
IT WAS SO BIG I THOUGHT IT WAS AN ISLAND, AND MOORED MY SHIP TO IT!
YEAH! AND YOU SHOULD HAVE SEEN THE SIZE OF ITS POOP!
HEY!
TA-DUM
HE IS A NICE GUY!

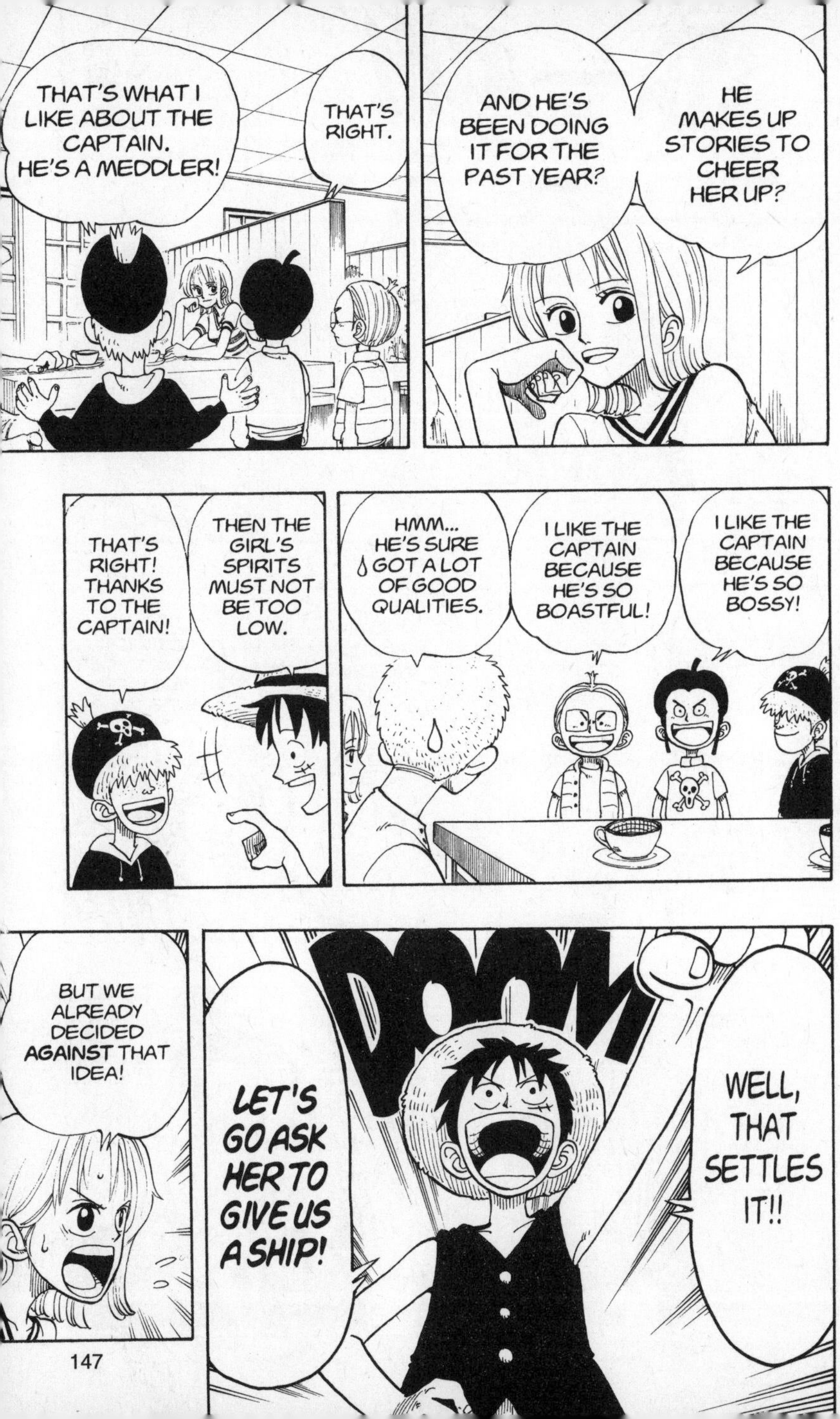
HE MAKES UP STORIES TO CHEER HER UP?
AND HE'S BEEN DOING IT FOR THE PAST YEAR?
THAT'S RIGHT.
THAT'S WHAT I LIKE ABOUT THE CAPTAIN. HE'S A MEDDLER!
I LIKE THE CAPTAIN BECAUSE HE'S SO BOSSY!
I LIKE THE CAPTAIN BECAUSE HE'S SO BOASTFUL!
HMM... HE'S SURE GOT A LOT OF GOOD QUALITIES.
THEN THE GIRL'S SPIRITS MUST NOT BE TOO LOW.
THAT'S RIGHT! THANKS TO THE CAPTAIN!
DOOM
WELL, THAT SETTLES IT!!
LET'S GO ASK HER TO GIVE US A SHIP!
BUT WE ALREADY DECIDED AGAINST THAT IDEA!

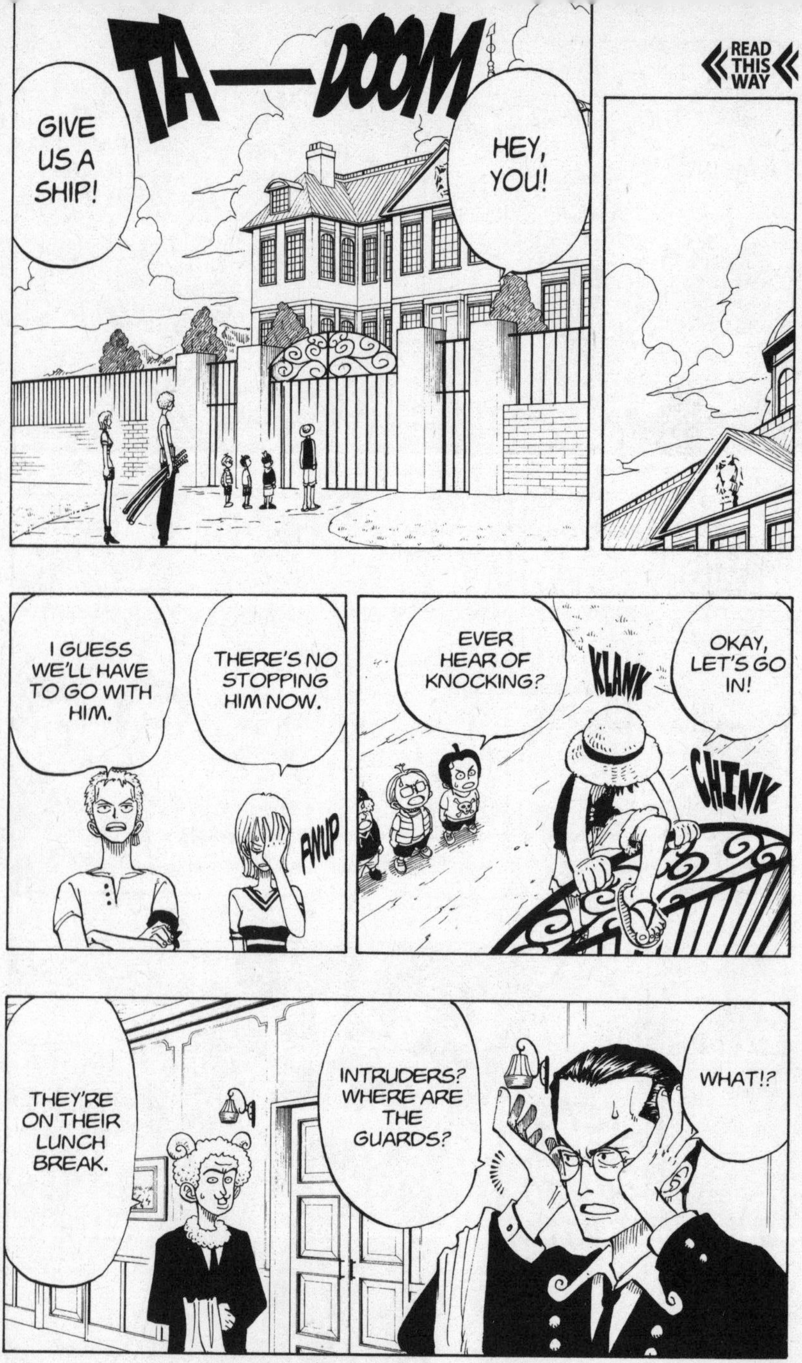
READ THIS WAY
TA—DOOM
HEY, YOU!
GIVE US A SHIP!
OKAY, LET'S GO IN!
KLANK
CHINK
EVER HEAR OF KNOCKING?
THERE'S NO STOPPING HIM NOW.
FWUP
I GUESS WE'LL HAVE TO GO WITH HIM.
WHAT!?
INTRUDERS? WHERE ARE THE GUARDS?
THEY'RE ON THEIR LUNCH BREAK.

READ THIS WAY

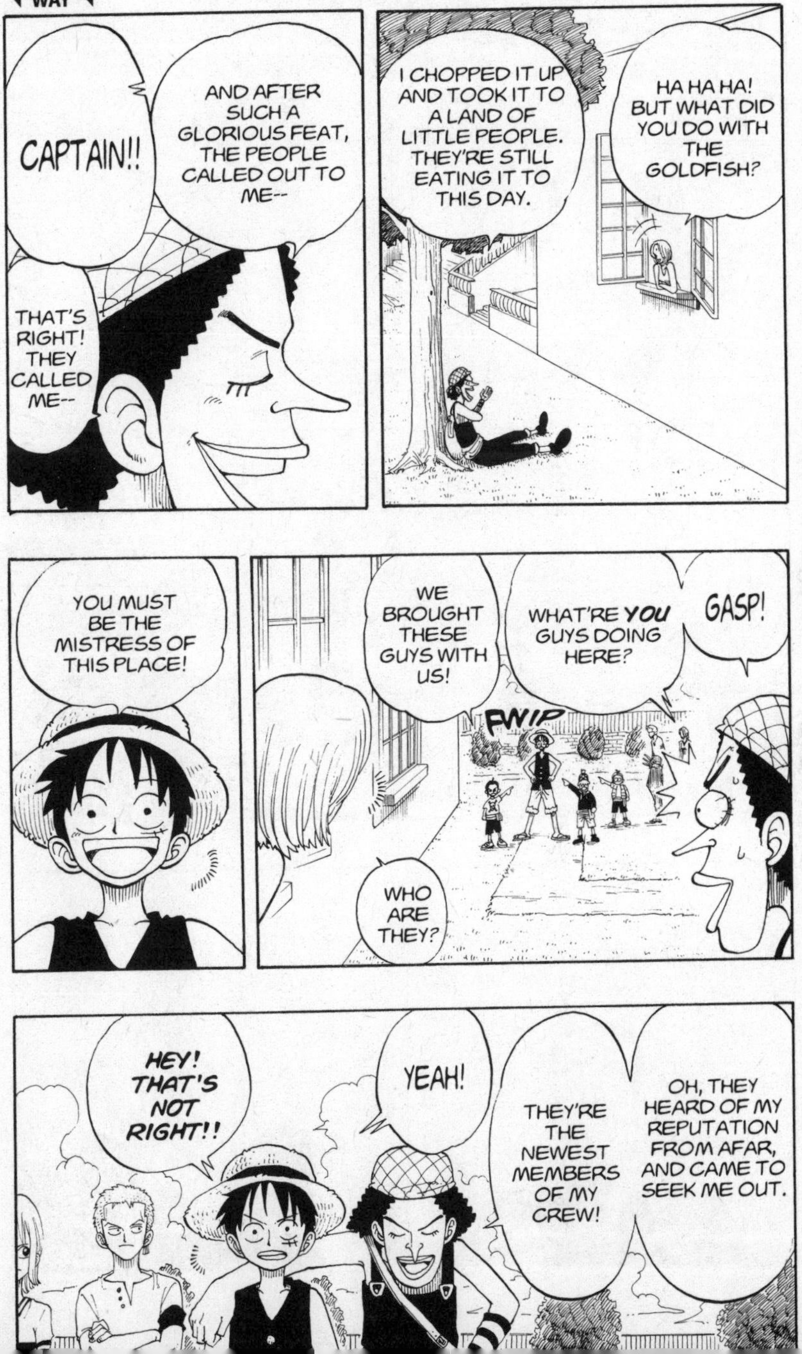
HA HA HA! BUT WHAT DID YOU DO WITH THE GOLDFISH?
I CHOPPED IT UP AND TOOK IT TO A LAND OF LITTLE PEOPLE. THEY'RE STILL EATING IT TO THIS DAY.
AND AFTER SUCH A GLORIOUS FEAT, THE PEOPLE CALLED OUT TO ME--
CAPTAIN!!
THAT'S RIGHT! THEY CALLED ME--
GASP!
WHAT'RE *YOU* GUYS DOING HERE?
WE BROUGHT THESE GUYS WITH US!
FWIP
WHO ARE THEY?
YOU MUST BE THE MISTRESS OF THIS PLACE!
OH, THEY HEARD OF MY REPUTATION FROM AFAR, AND CAME TO SEEK ME OUT.
THEY'RE THE NEWEST MEMBERS OF MY CREW!
YEAH!
HEY! THAT'S NOT RIGHT!!

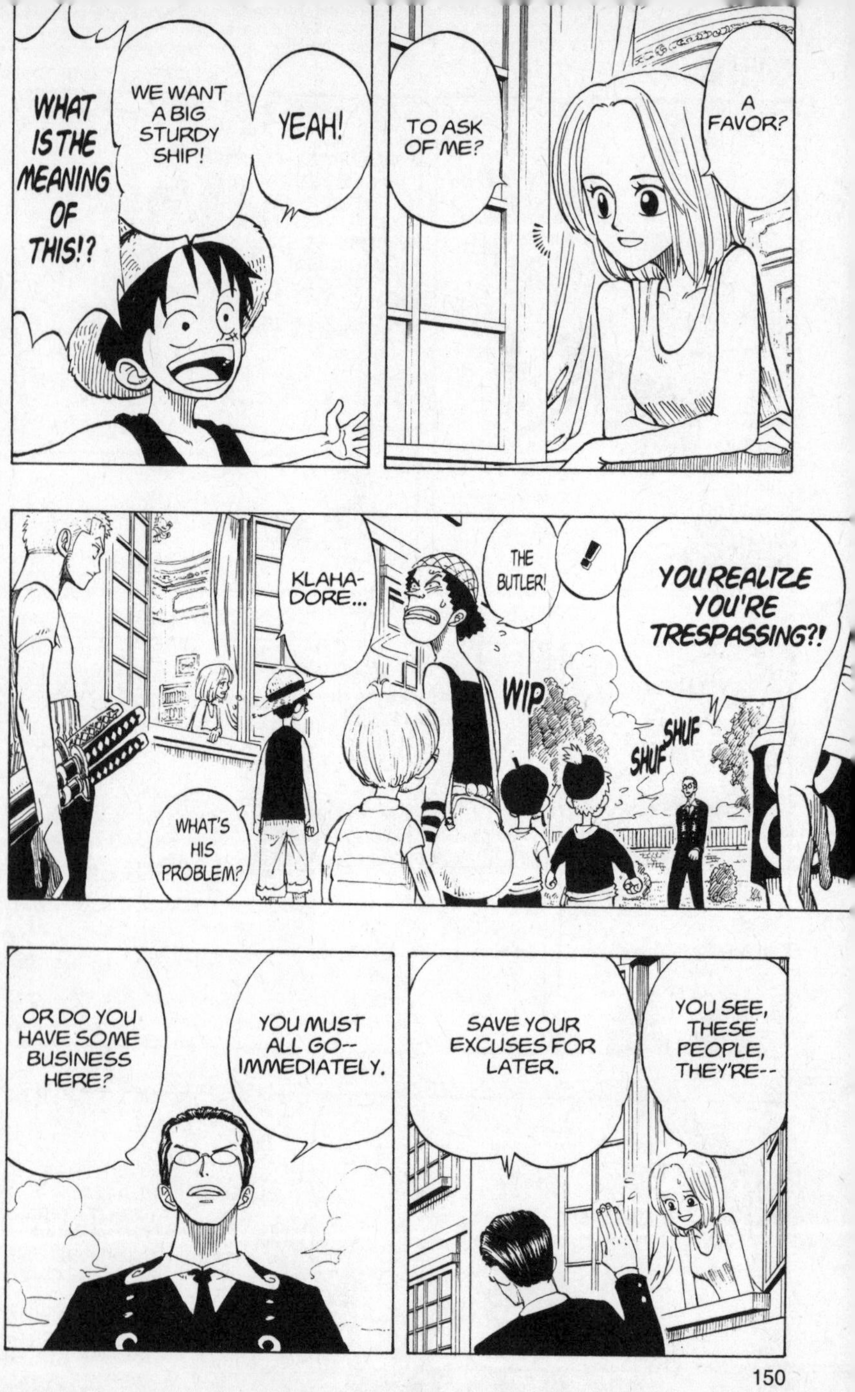
A FAVOR?
TO ASK OF ME?
YEAH!
WE WANT A BIG STURDY SHIP!
WHAT IS THE MEANING OF THIS!?
YOU REALIZE YOU'RE TRESPASSING?!
!
THE BUTLER!
KLAHA-DORE...
WIP
SHUF SHUF
WHAT'S HIS PROBLEM?
YOU SEE, THESE PEOPLE, THEY'RE--
SAVE YOUR EXCUSES FOR LATER.
YOU MUST ALL GO-- IMMEDIATELY.
OR DO YOU HAVE SOME BUSINESS HERE?

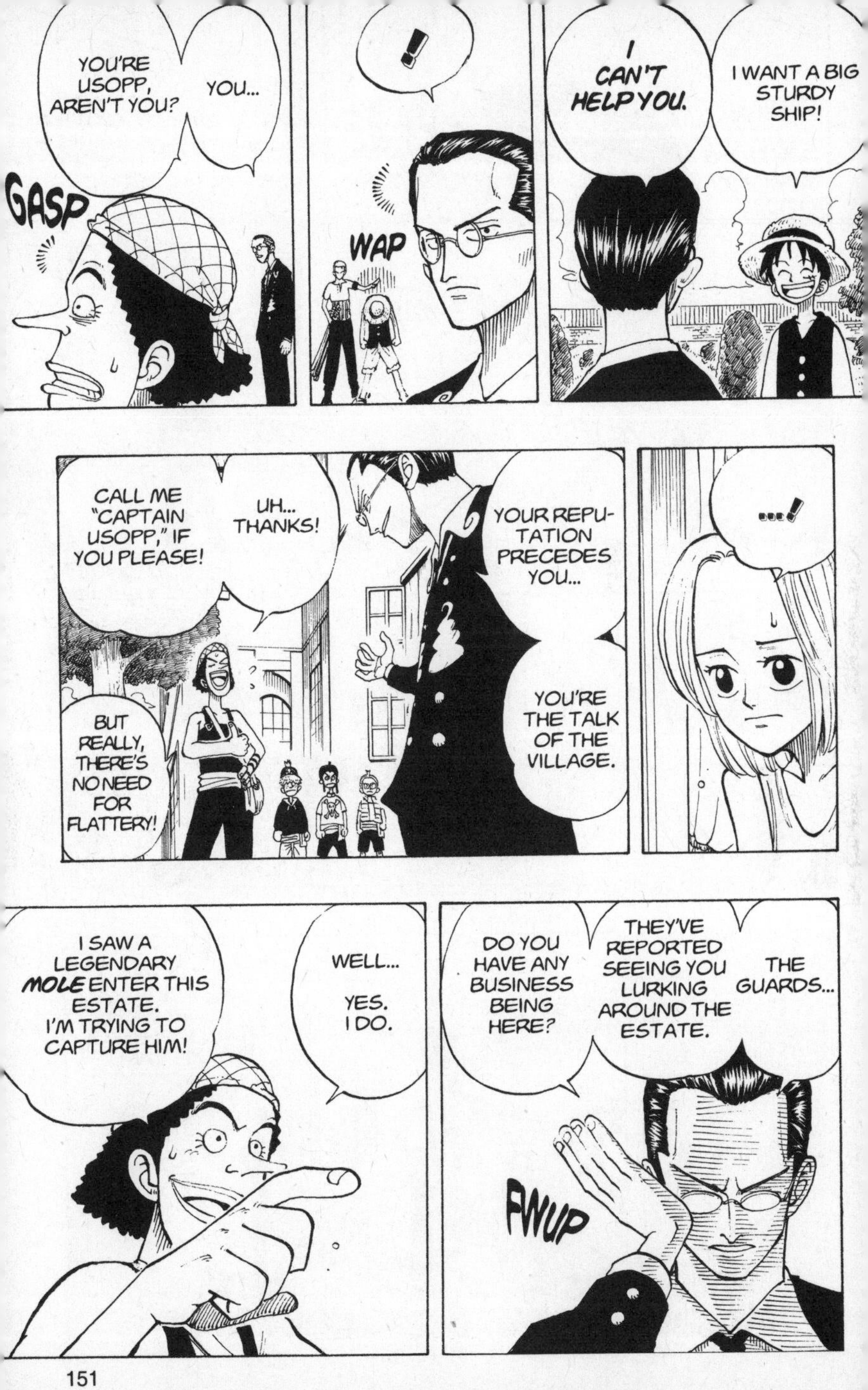

I WANT A BIG STURDY SHIP!
I CAN'T HELP YOU.
!
WAP
YOU...
YOU'RE USOPP, AREN'T YOU?
GASP
...!
YOUR REPU-TATION PRECEDES YOU...
YOU'RE THE TALK OF THE VILLAGE.
UH... THANKS!
CALL ME "CAPTAIN USOPP," IF YOU PLEASE!
BUT REALLY, THERE'S NO NEED FOR FLATTERY!
THE GUARDS...
THEY'VE REPORTED SEEING YOU LURKING AROUND THE ESTATE.
DO YOU HAVE ANY BUSINESS BEING HERE?
FWUP
WELL...
YES. I DO.
I SAW A LEGENDARY MOLE ENTER THIS ESTATE. I'M TRYING TO CAPTURE HIM!

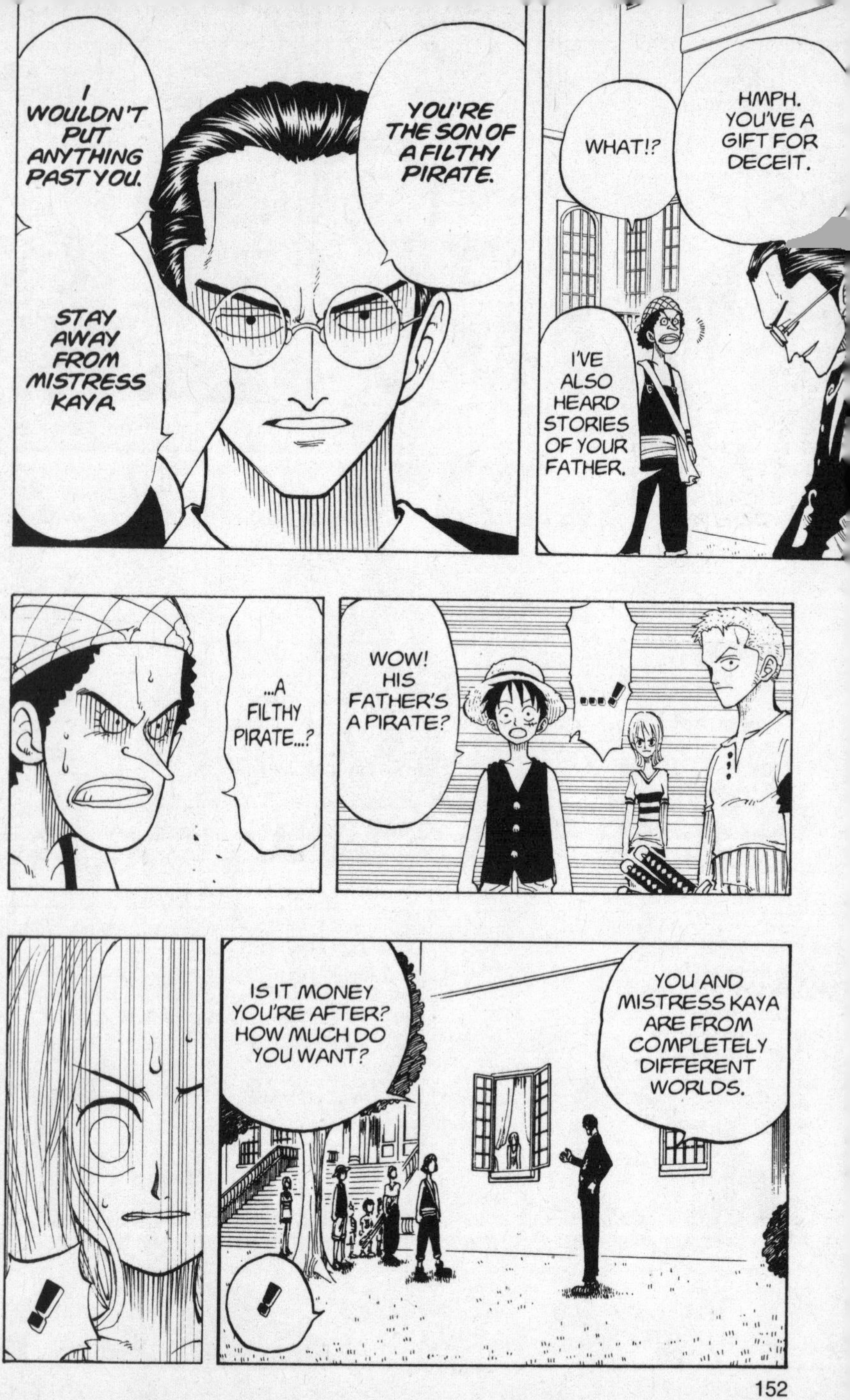
HMPH. YOU'VE A GIFT FOR DECEIT.
WHAT!?
I'VE ALSO HEARD STORIES OF YOUR FATHER.
YOU'RE THE SON OF A FILTHY PIRATE.
I WOULDN'T PUT ANYTHING PAST YOU.
STAY AWAY FROM MISTRESS KAYA.
...!
WOW! HIS FATHER'S A PIRATE?
...A FILTHY PIRATE...?
YOU AND MISTRESS KAYA ARE FROM COMPLETELY DIFFERENT WORLDS.
IS IT MONEY YOU'RE AFTER? HOW MUCH DO YOU WANT?
!
!

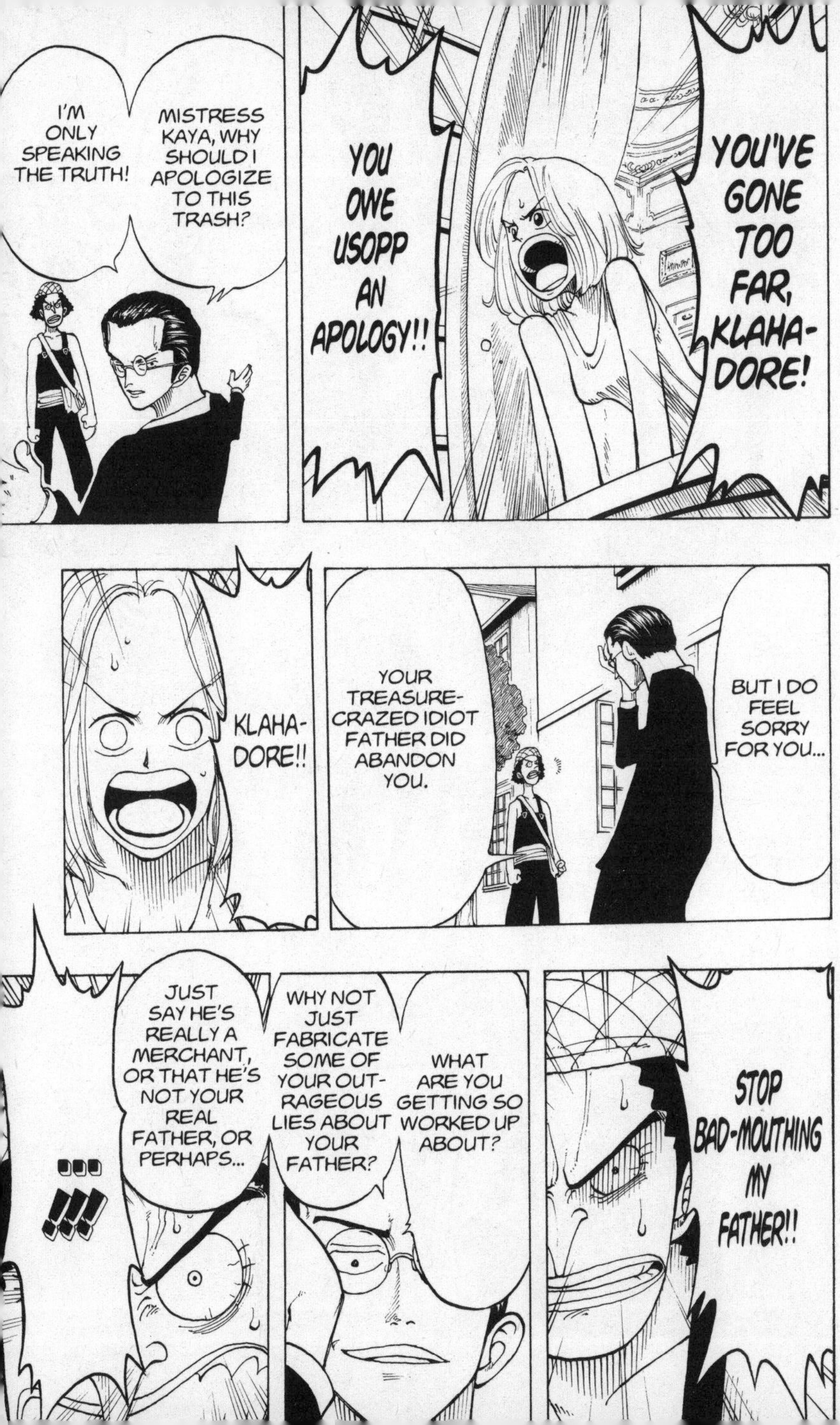

YOU'VE GONE TOO FAR, KLAHA-DORE!
YOU OWE USOPP AN APOLOGY!!
MISTRESS KAYA, WHY SHOULD I APOLOGIZE TO THIS TRASH?
I'M ONLY SPEAKING THE TRUTH!
BUT I DO FEEL SORRY FOR YOU...
YOUR TREASURE-CRAZED IDIOT FATHER DID ABANDON YOU.
KLAHA-DORE!!
STOP BAD-MOUTHING MY FATHER!!
WHAT ARE YOU GETTING SO WORKED UP ABOUT?
WHY NOT JUST FABRICATE SOME OF YOUR OUT-RAGEOUS LIES ABOUT YOUR FATHER?
JUST SAY HE'S REALLY A MERCHANT, OR THAT HE'S NOT YOUR REAL FATHER, OR PERHAPS...
...!!!!

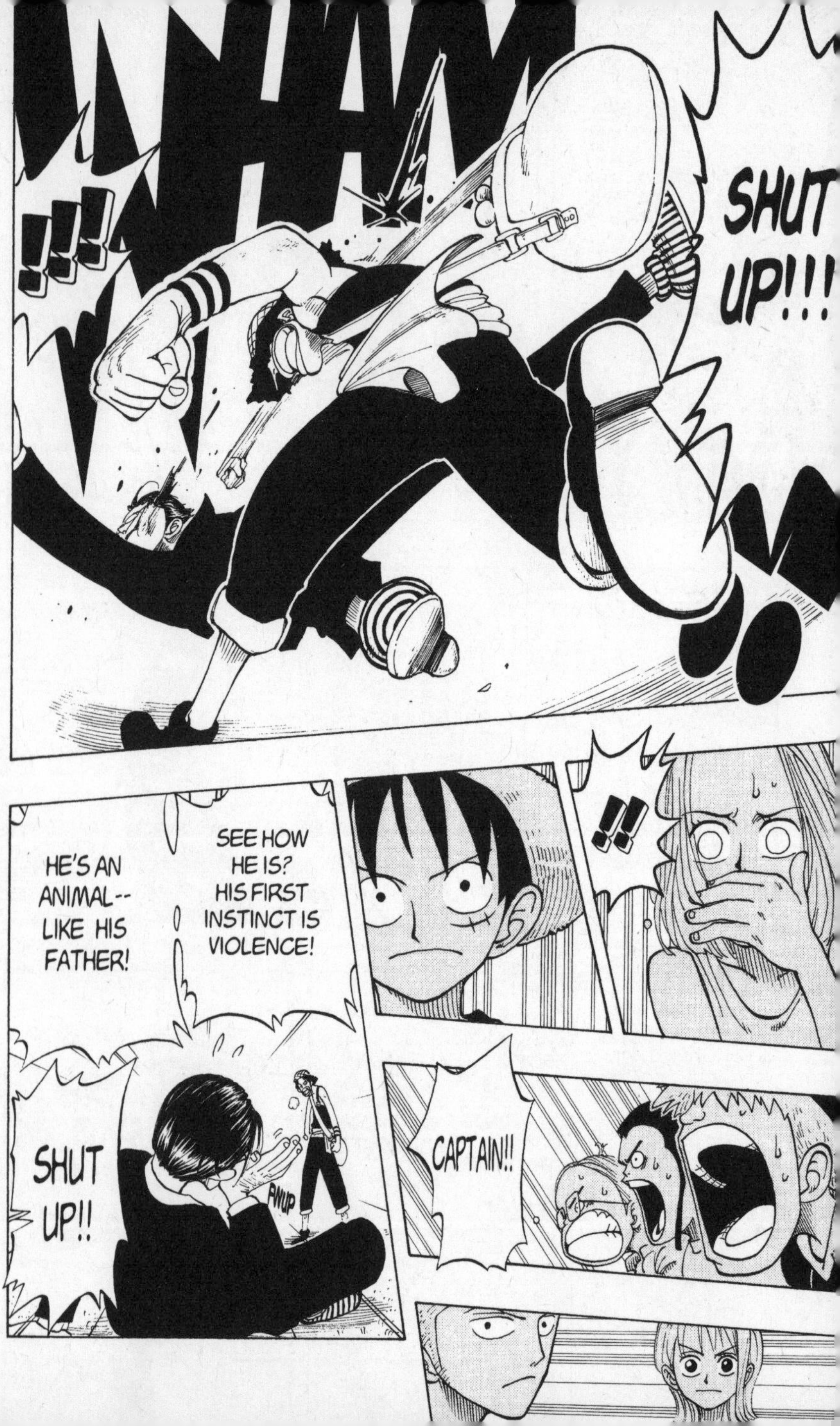
SHUT UP!!!
!!!
!!
SEE HOW HE IS? HIS FIRST INSTINCT IS VIOLENCE!
HE'S AN ANIMAL-- LIKE HIS FATHER!
CAPTAIN!!
SHUT UP!!
PWUP

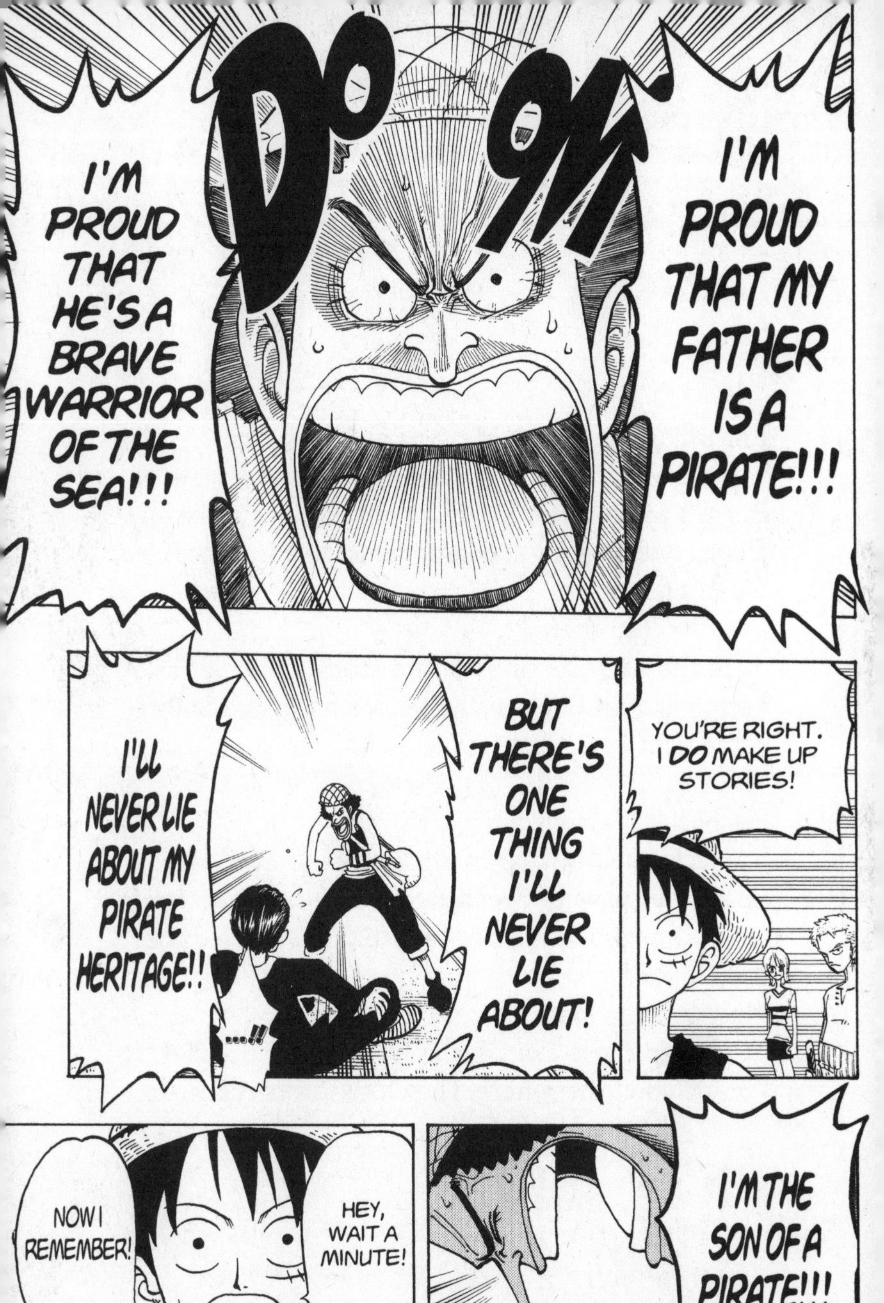
I'M PROUD THAT MY FATHER IS A PIRATE!!!
DOOM
I'M PROUD THAT HE'S A BRAVE WARRIOR OF THE SEA!!!
YOU'RE RIGHT. I DO MAKE UP STORIES!
BUT THERE'S ONE THING I'LL NEVER LIE ABOUT!
I'LL NEVER LIE ABOUT MY PIRATE HERITAGE!!
....!!
I'M THE SON OF A PIRATE!!!
HEY, WAIT A MINUTE!
NOW I REMEMBER!

The Path To Becoming a Manga Character!

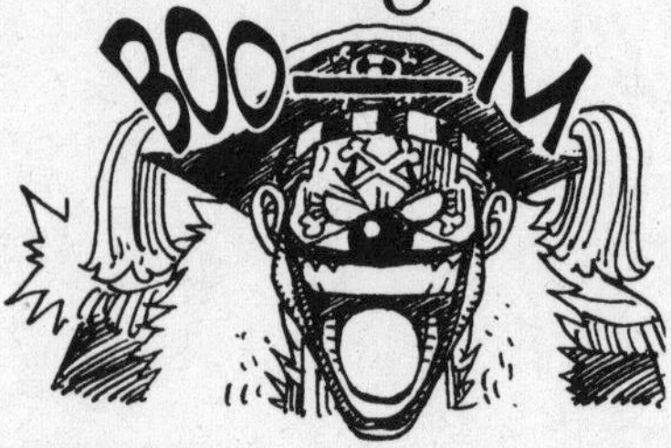
BOO—M

Part 2

Regarding the drawings on page 136:

This was the second draft of sketches I drew of Buggy's pirate crew. At this point I didn't make any changes to Buggy's appearance, so he's not included on this page.

Why is Zolo there?

In the early versions of the story, Zolo was a bodyguard on Buggy's ship before he joined Luffy. After a lot of thought, I decided not to do it that way.

Hachi the Messenger

Hachi the Messenger is a carrier pigeon. He relays messages between Buggy and his crew. He is an Opo bird, and his natural habitat appears to be the Grand Line.

Mohji Design Ideas

I found these sketches in my book of doodles, so I've included them here. They look pretty cool, too!

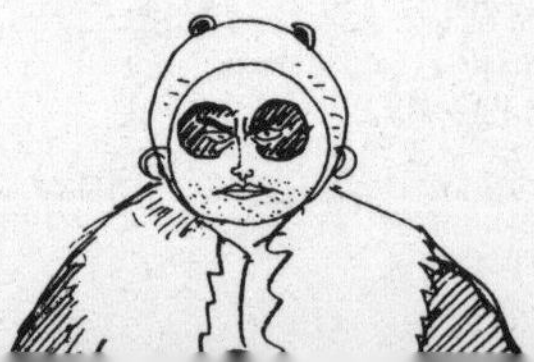

Chapter 25:
LIES

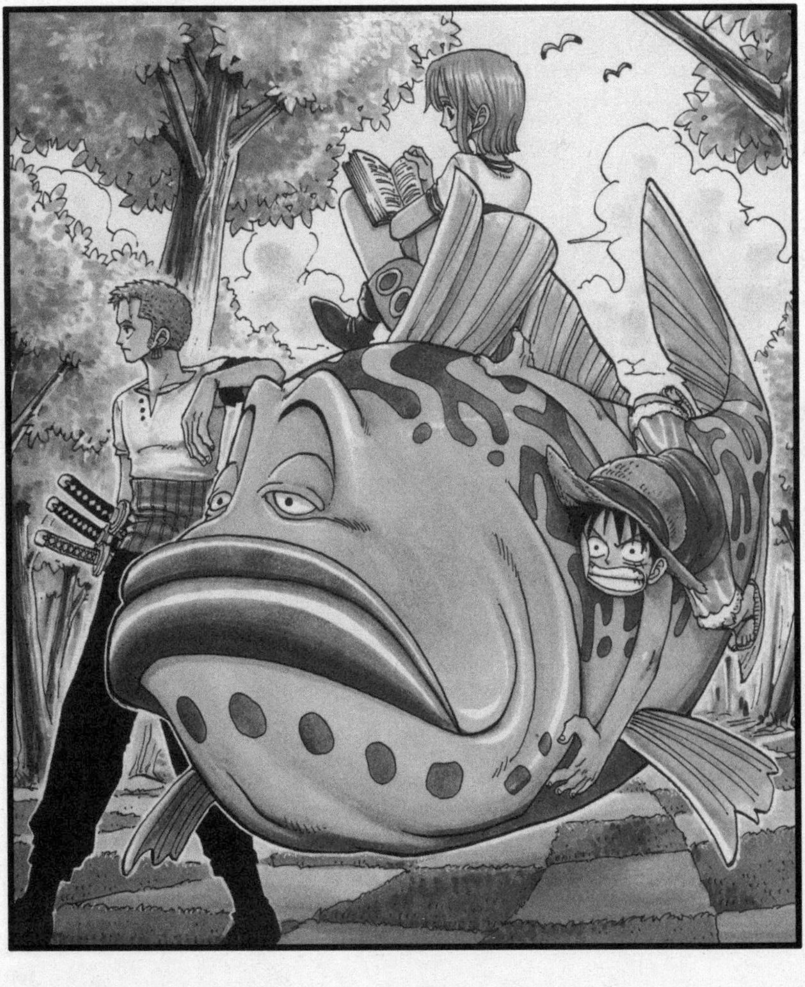

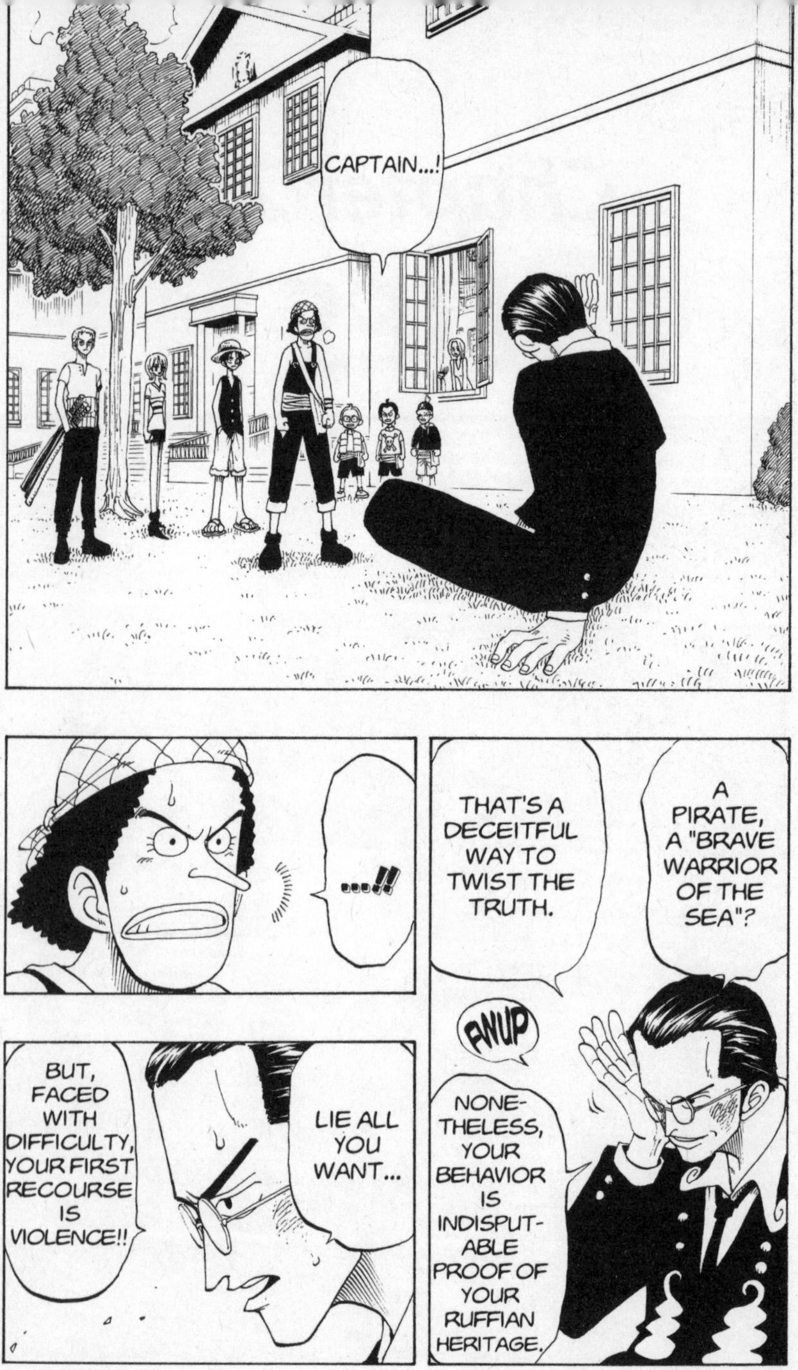
CAPTAIN...!
A PIRATE, A "BRAVE WARRIOR OF THE SEA"?
THAT'S A DECEITFUL WAY TO TWIST THE TRUTH.
FWUP
NONE-THELESS, YOUR BEHAVIOR IS INDISPUT-ABLE PROOF OF YOUR RUFFIAN HERITAGE.
...!!
LIE ALL YOU WANT...
BUT, FACED WITH DIFFICULTY, YOUR FIRST RECOURSE IS VIOLENCE!!

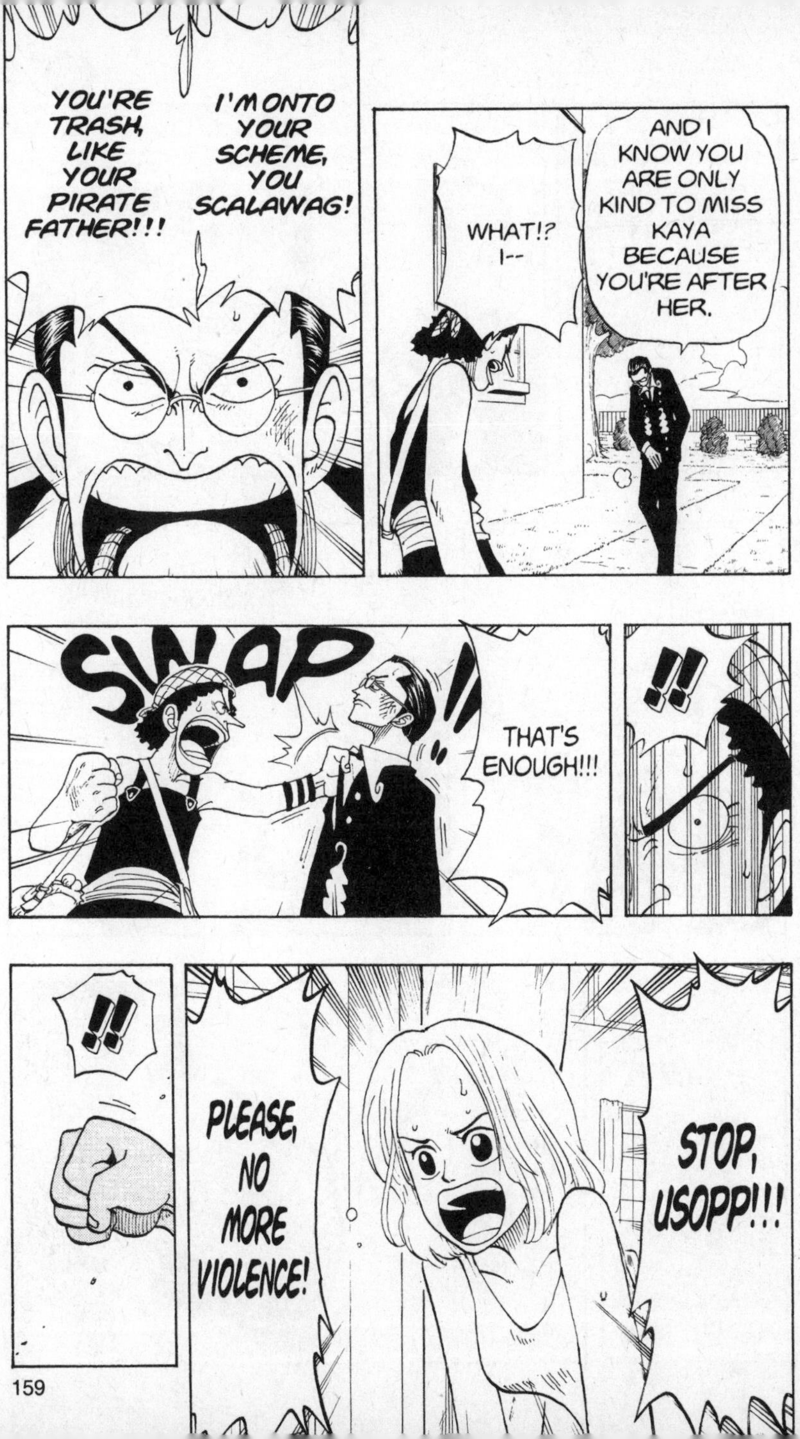
AND I KNOW YOU ARE ONLY KIND TO MISS KAYA BECAUSE YOU'RE AFTER HER.
WHAT!? I--
I'M ONTO YOUR SCHEME, YOU SCALAWAG!
YOU'RE TRASH, LIKE YOUR PIRATE FATHER!!!
!!
THAT'S ENOUGH!!!
SWAP!!
STOP, USOPP!!!
PLEASE, NO MORE VIOLENCE!
!!

READ THIS WAY

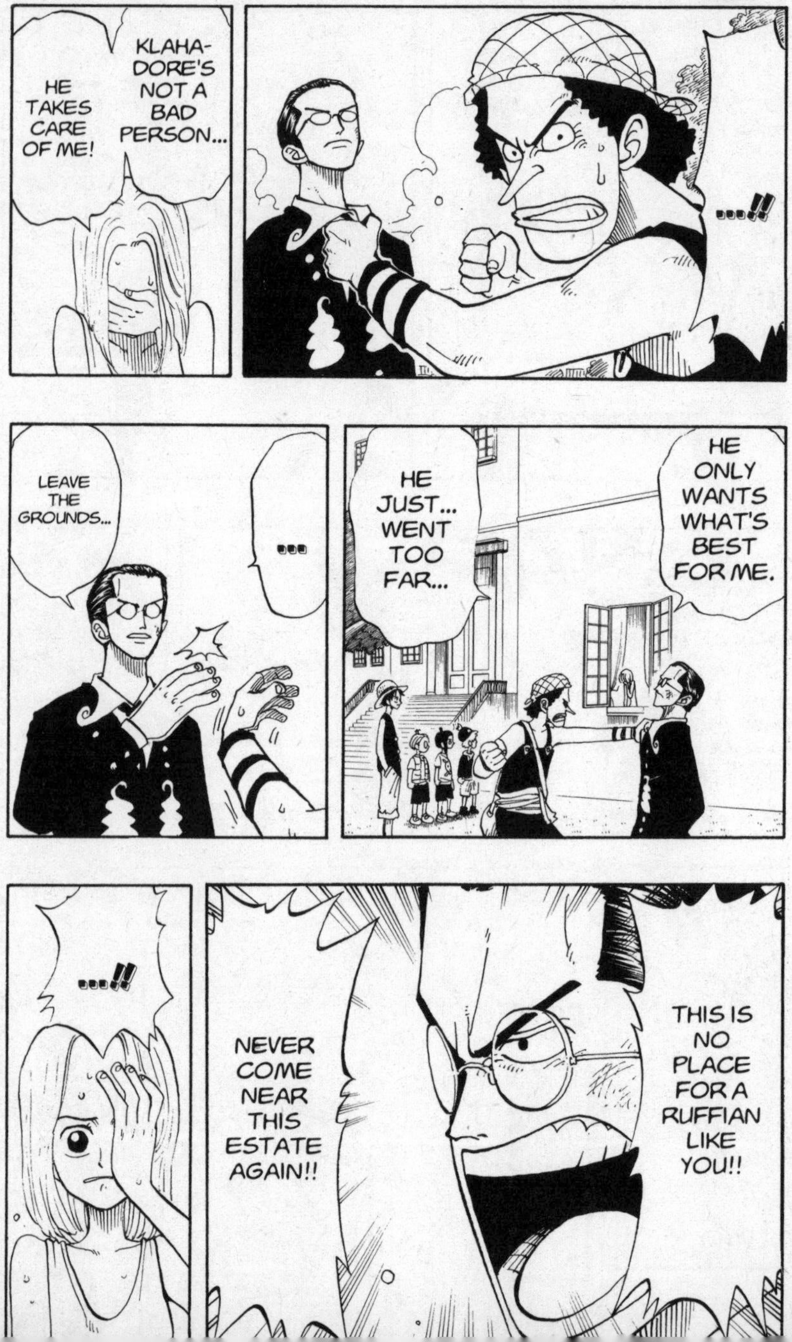
...!!
KLAHA-DORE'S NOT A BAD PERSON...
HE TAKES CARE OF ME!
HE ONLY WANTS WHAT'S BEST FOR ME.
HE JUST... WENT TOO FAR...
...
LEAVE THE GROUNDS...
THIS IS NO PLACE FOR A RUFFIAN LIKE YOU!!
NEVER COME NEAR THIS ESTATE AGAIN!!
...!!

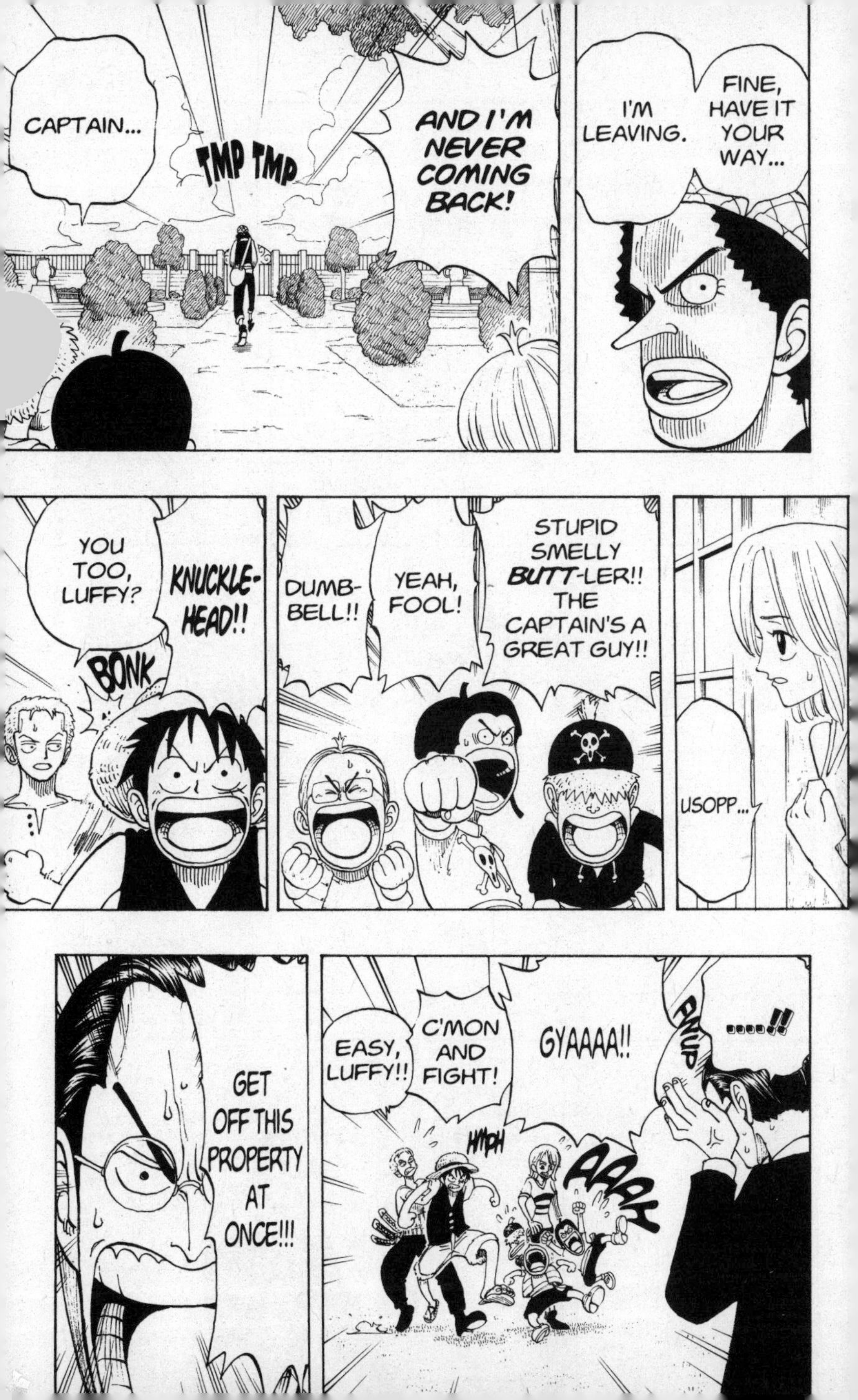
FINE, HAVE IT YOUR WAY...
I'M LEAVING.
AND I'M NEVER COMING BACK!
TMP TMP
CAPTAIN...
USOPP...
STUPID SMELLY BUTT-LER!! THE CAPTAIN'S A GREAT GUY!!
YEAH, FOOL!
DUMB-BELL!!
KNUCKLE-HEAD!!
YOU TOO, LUFFY?
BONK
....!!
FWUP
GYAAAA!!
C'MON AND FIGHT!
EASY, LUFFY!!
HMPH
AAAH
GET OFF THIS PROPERTY AT ONCE!!!

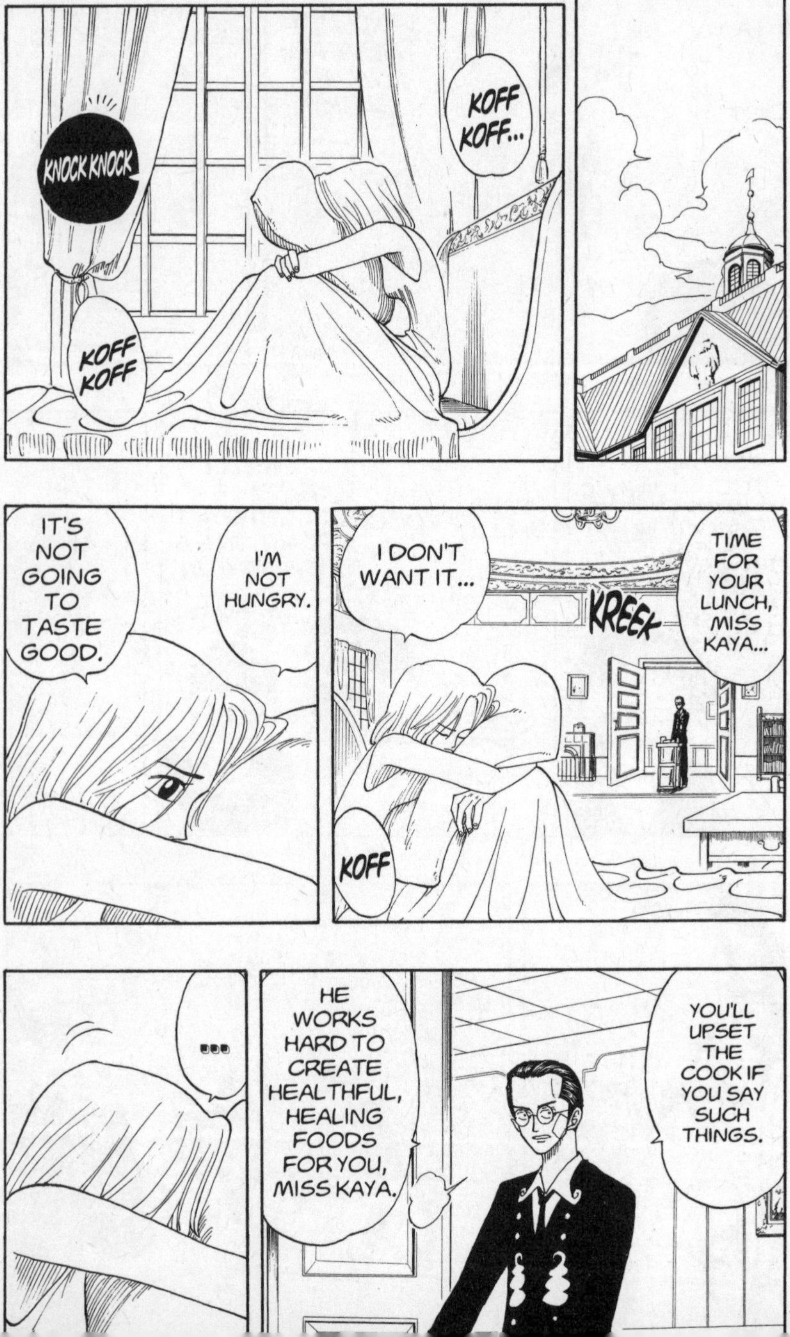
KOFF KOFF...
KNOCK KNOCK
KOFF KOFF
TIME FOR YOUR LUNCH, MISS KAYA...
KREEK
I DON'T WANT IT...
KOFF
I'M NOT HUNGRY.
IT'S NOT GOING TO TASTE GOOD.
YOU'LL UPSET THE COOK IF YOU SAY SUCH THINGS.
HE WORKS HARD TO CREATE HEALTHFUL, HEALING FOODS FOR YOU, MISS KAYA.
...

READ THIS WAY

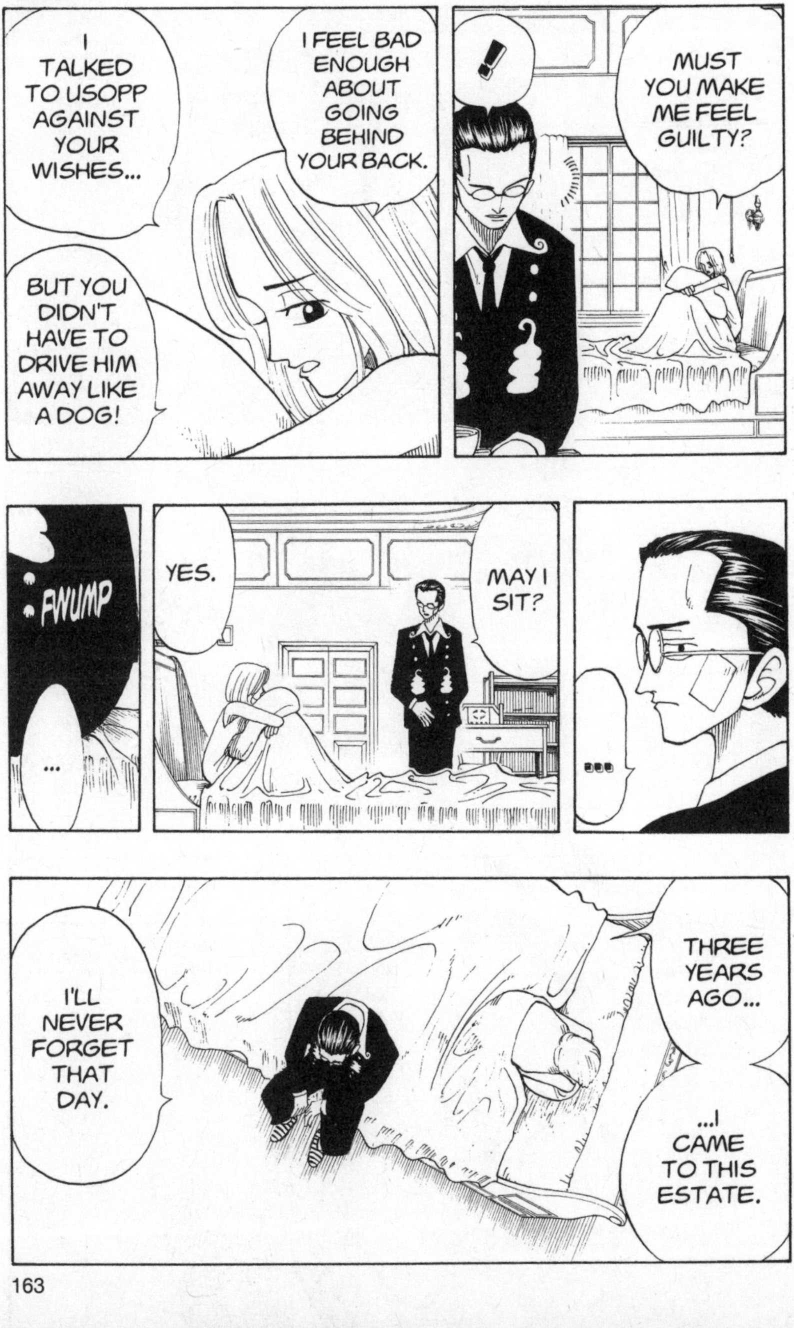
!
MUST YOU MAKE ME FEEL GUILTY?
I FEEL BAD ENOUGH ABOUT GOING BEHIND YOUR BACK.
I TALKED TO USOPP AGAINST YOUR WISHES...
BUT YOU DIDN'T HAVE TO DRIVE HIM AWAY LIKE A DOG!
...
MAY I SIT?
YES.
FWUMP
...
THREE YEARS AGO...
...I CAME TO THIS ESTATE.
I'LL NEVER FORGET THAT DAY.

READ THIS WAY

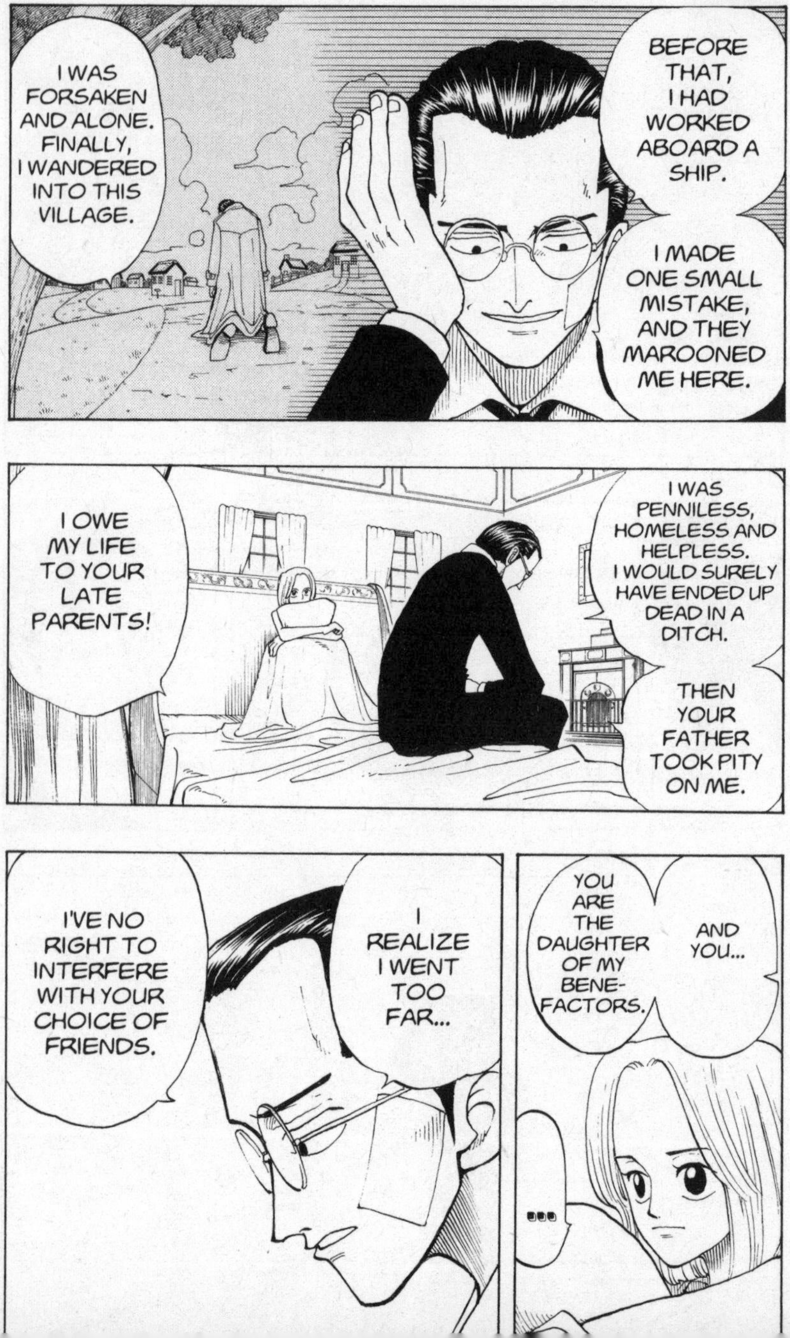
BEFORE THAT, I HAD WORKED ABOARD A SHIP.
I MADE ONE SMALL MISTAKE, AND THEY MAROONED ME HERE.
I WAS FORSAKEN AND ALONE. FINALLY, I WANDERED INTO THIS VILLAGE.
I WAS PENNILESS, HOMELESS AND HELPLESS. I WOULD SURELY HAVE ENDED UP DEAD IN A DITCH.
THEN YOUR FATHER TOOK PITY ON ME.
I OWE MY LIFE TO YOUR LATE PARENTS!
AND YOU...
YOU ARE THE DAUGHTER OF MY BENE-FACTORS.
...
I REALIZE I WENT TOO FAR...
I'VE NO RIGHT TO INTERFERE WITH YOUR CHOICE OF FRIENDS.

READ THIS WAY

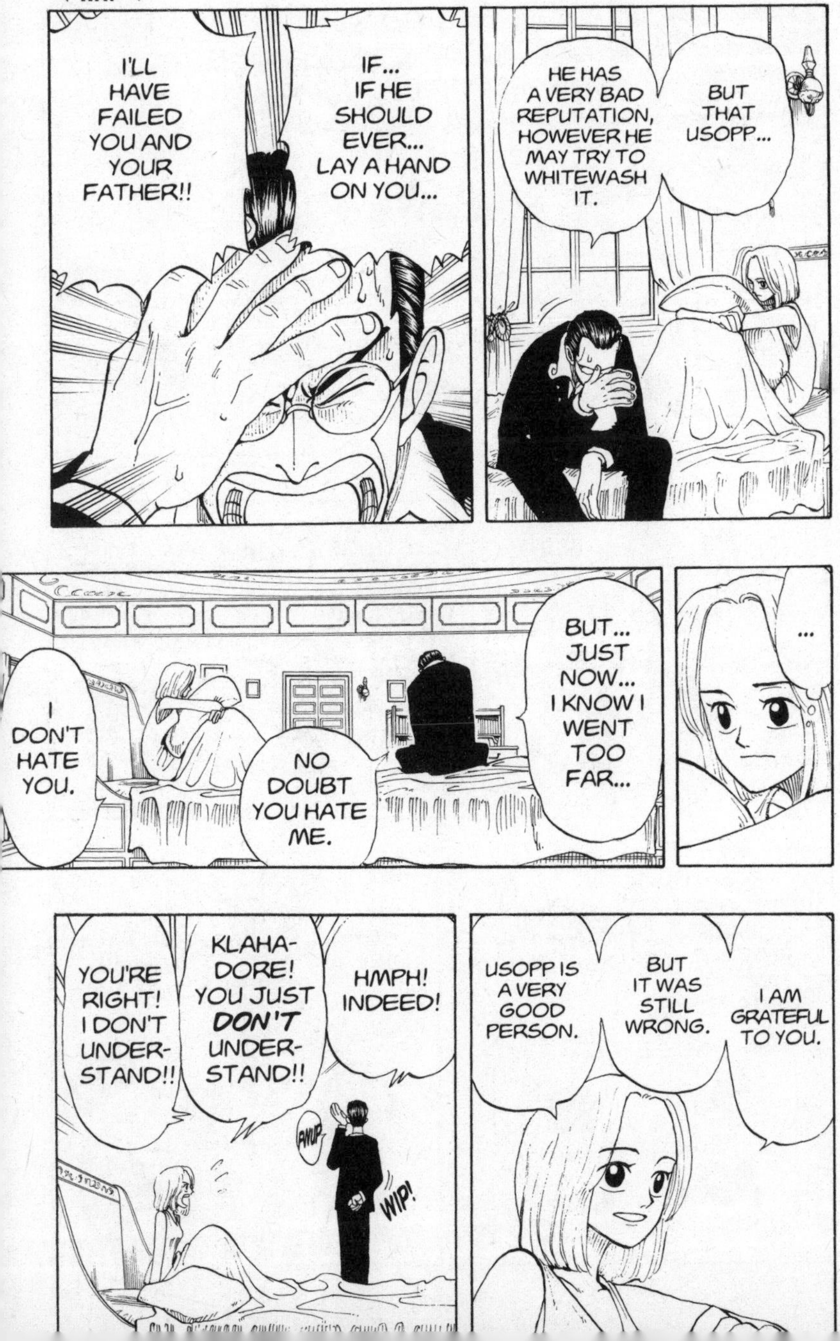
BUT THAT USOPP...
HE HAS A VERY BAD REPUTATION, HOWEVER HE MAY TRY TO WHITEWASH IT.
IF... IF HE SHOULD EVER... LAY A HAND ON YOU...
I'LL HAVE FAILED YOU AND YOUR FATHER!!
...
BUT... JUST NOW... I KNOW I WENT TOO FAR...
NO DOUBT YOU HATE ME.
I DON'T HATE YOU.
I AM GRATEFUL TO YOU.
BUT IT WAS STILL WRONG.
USOPP IS A VERY GOOD PERSON.
HMPH! INDEED!
KLAHA-DORE! YOU JUST **DON'T** UNDER-STAND!!
YOU'RE RIGHT! I DON'T UNDER-STAND!!
FWUP
WIP!

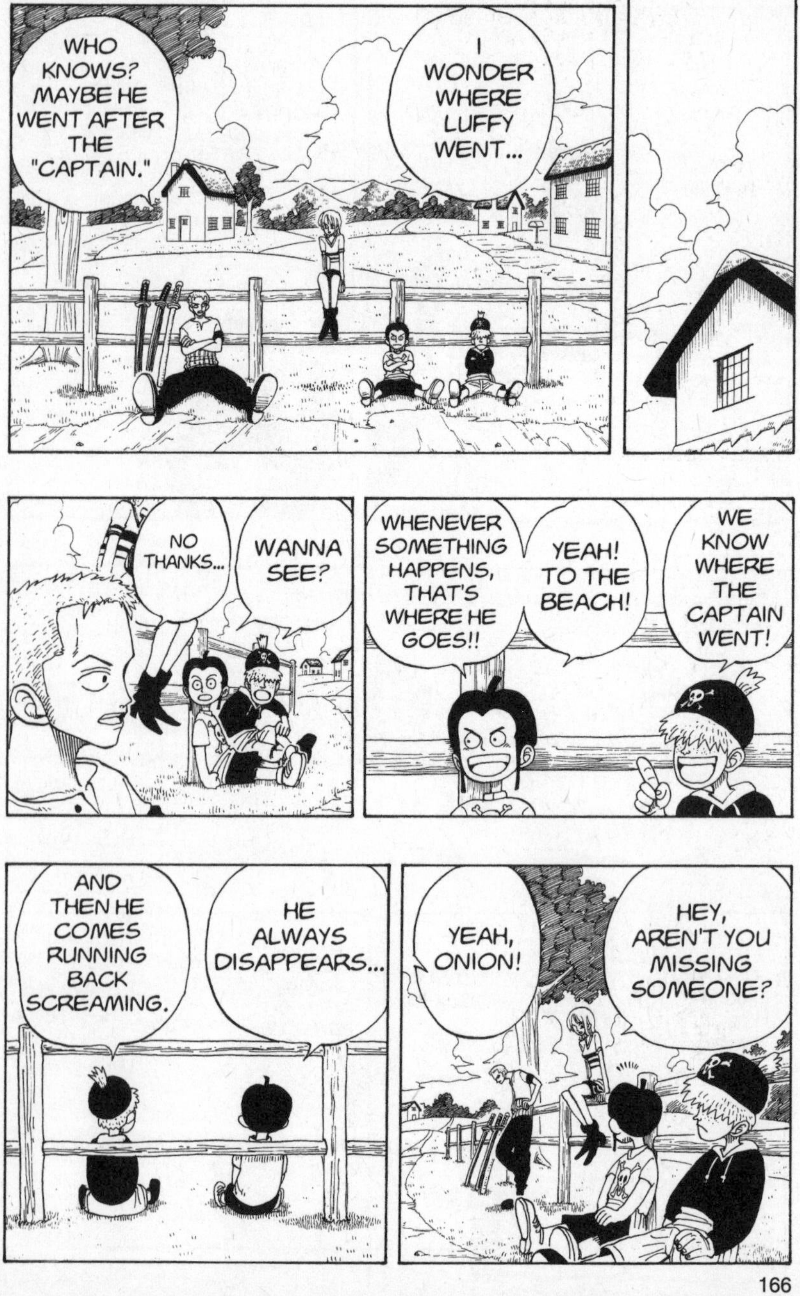
I WONDER WHERE LUFFY WENT...
WHO KNOWS? MAYBE HE WENT AFTER THE "CAPTAIN."
WE KNOW WHERE THE CAPTAIN WENT!
YEAH! TO THE BEACH!
WHENEVER SOMETHING HAPPENS, THAT'S WHERE HE GOES!!
WANNA SEE?
NO THANKS...
HEY, AREN'T YOU MISSING SOMEONE?
YEAH, ONION!
HE ALWAYS DISAPPEARS...
AND THEN HE COMES RUNNING BACK SCREAMING.

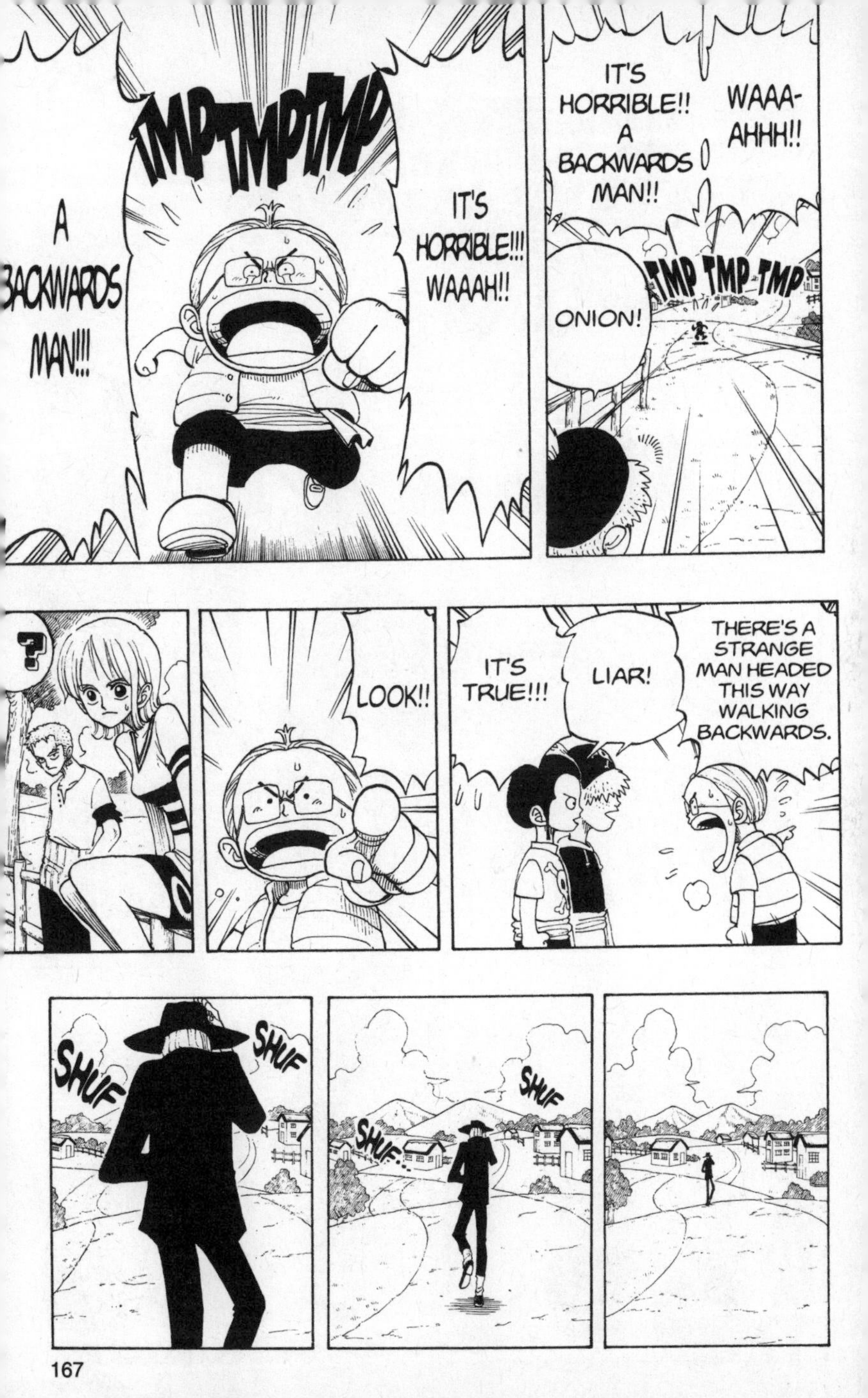
WAAA-AHHH!!
IT'S HORRIBLE!! A BACKWARDS MAN!!
TMP TMP TMP
ONION!
TMPTMPTMP
IT'S HORRIBLE!!! WAAAH!!
A BACKWARDS MAN!!!
THERE'S A STRANGE MAN HEADED THIS WAY WALKING BACKWARDS.
LIAR!
IT'S TRUE!!!
LOOK!!
?
SHUF
SHUF...
SHUF
SHUF

READ THIS WAY

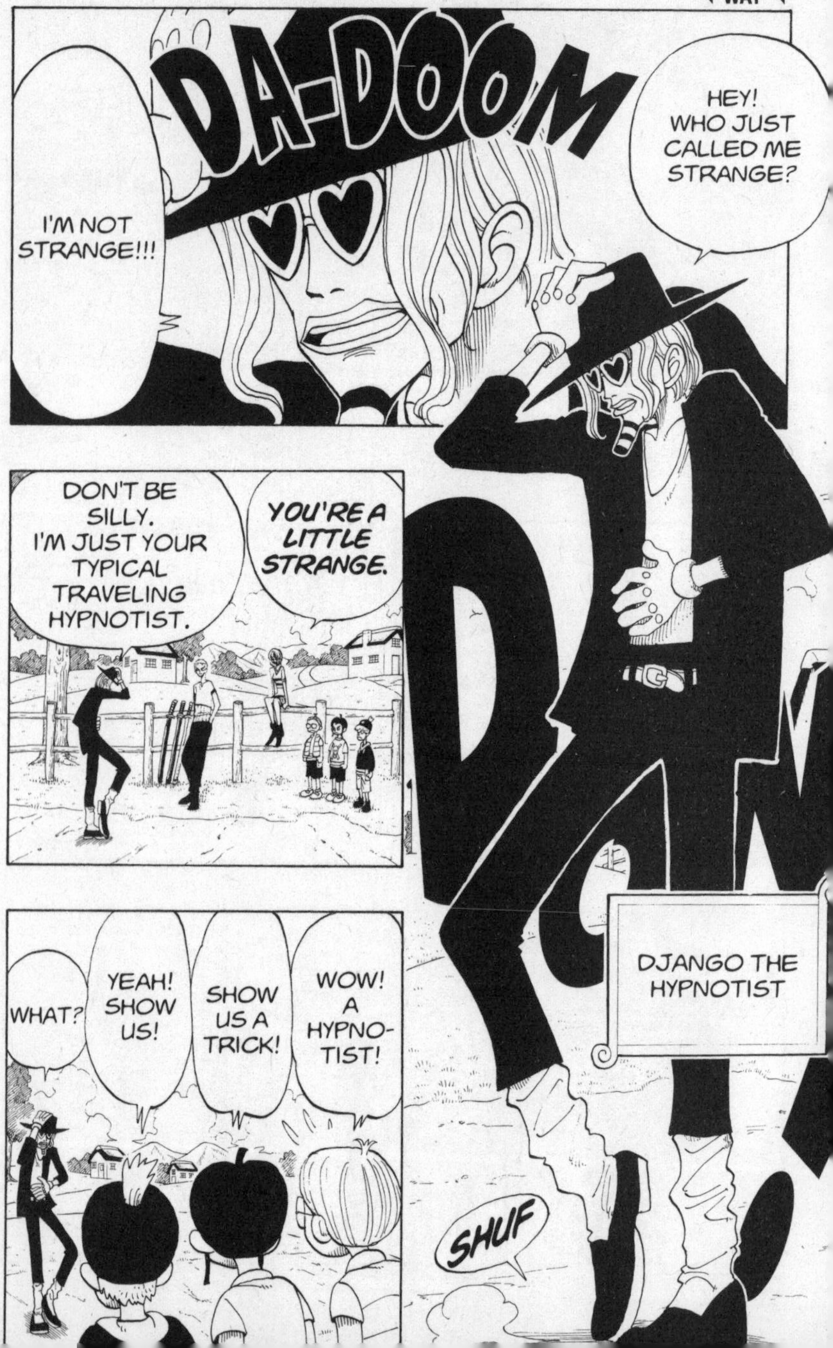
HEY! WHO JUST CALLED ME STRANGE?
DA-DOOM
I'M NOT STRANGE!!!
DJANGO THE HYPNOTIST
SHUF
YOU'RE A LITTLE STRANGE.
DON'T BE SILLY. I'M JUST YOUR TYPICAL TRAVELING HYPNOTIST.
WOW! A HYPNO-TIST!
SHOW US A TRICK!
YEAH! SHOW US!
WHAT?

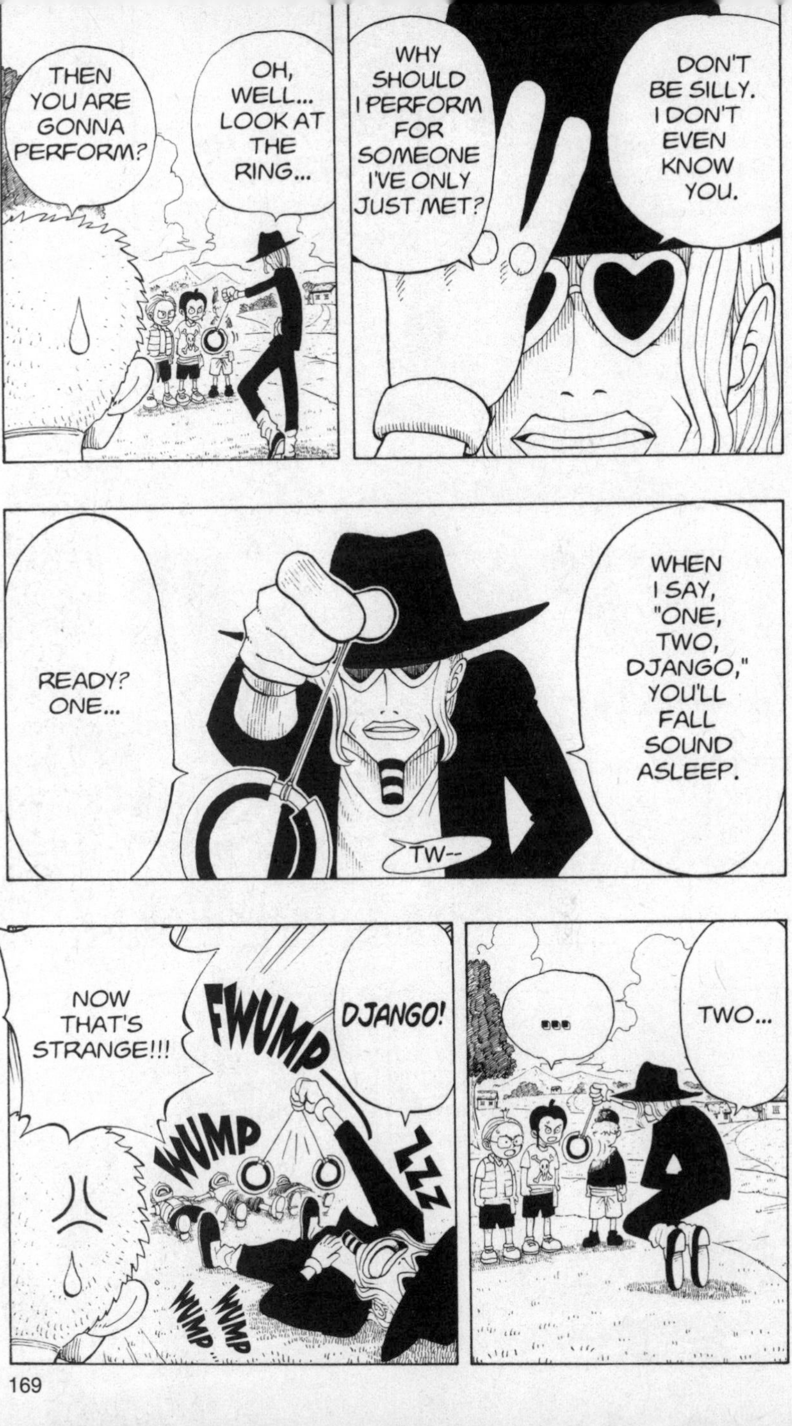
DON'T BE SILLY. I DON'T EVEN KNOW YOU.
WHY SHOULD I PERFORM FOR SOMEONE I'VE ONLY JUST MET?
OH, WELL... LOOK AT THE RING...
THEN YOU ARE GONNA PERFORM?
WHEN I SAY, "ONE, TWO, DJANGO," YOU'LL FALL SOUND ASLEEP.
READY? ONE...
TW--
TWO...
...
DJANGO!
ZZZ
FWUMP
WUMP
NOW THAT'S STRANGE!!!
WUMP
WUMP...

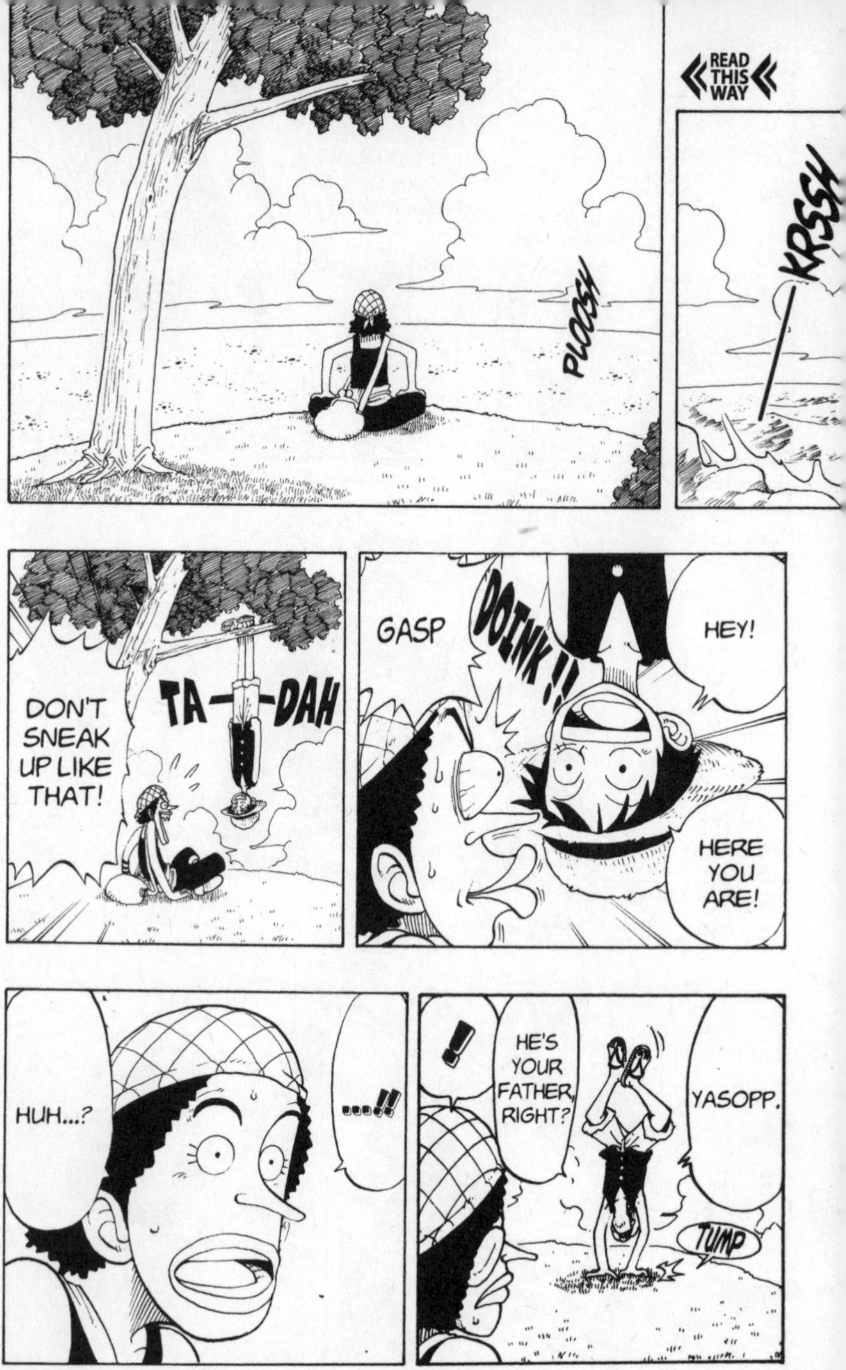
READ THIS WAY
KRSSH
PLOOSH
HEY!
DOINK!!
GASP
HERE YOU ARE!
TA--DAH
DON'T SNEAK UP LIKE THAT!
YASOPP.
HE'S YOUR FATHER, RIGHT?
!
TUMP
...!!
HUH...?

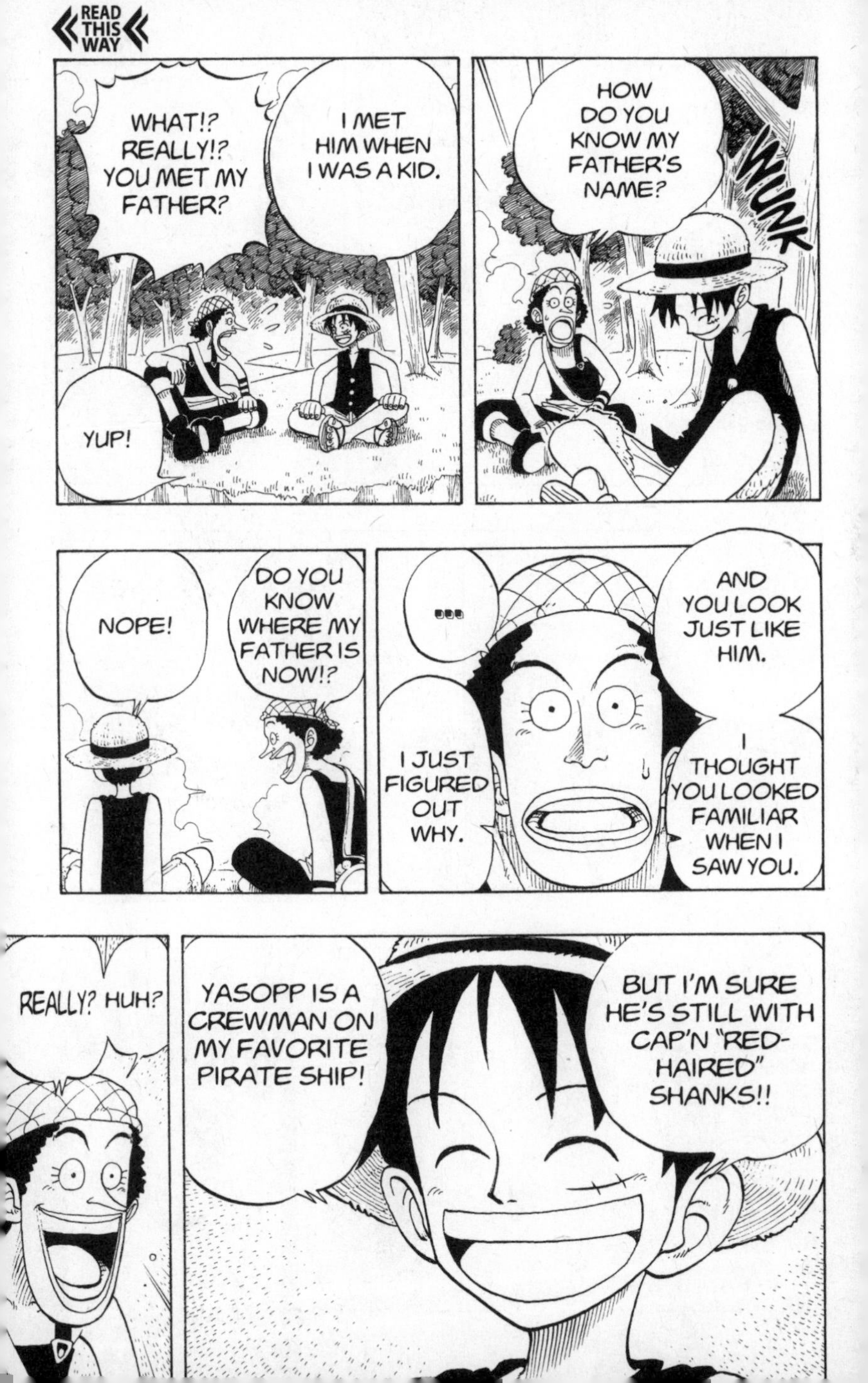
READ THIS WAY
HOW DO YOU KNOW MY FATHER'S NAME?
WUNK
I MET HIM WHEN I WAS A KID.
WHAT!? REALLY!? YOU MET MY FATHER?
YUP!
AND YOU LOOK JUST LIKE HIM.
I THOUGHT YOU LOOKED FAMILIAR WHEN I SAW YOU.
...
I JUST FIGURED OUT WHY.
DO YOU KNOW WHERE MY FATHER IS NOW!?
NOPE!
BUT I'M SURE HE'S STILL WITH CAP'N "RED-HAIRED" SHANKS!!
YASOPP IS A CREWMAN ON MY FAVORITE PIRATE SHIP!
REALLY? HUH?

READ THIS WAY

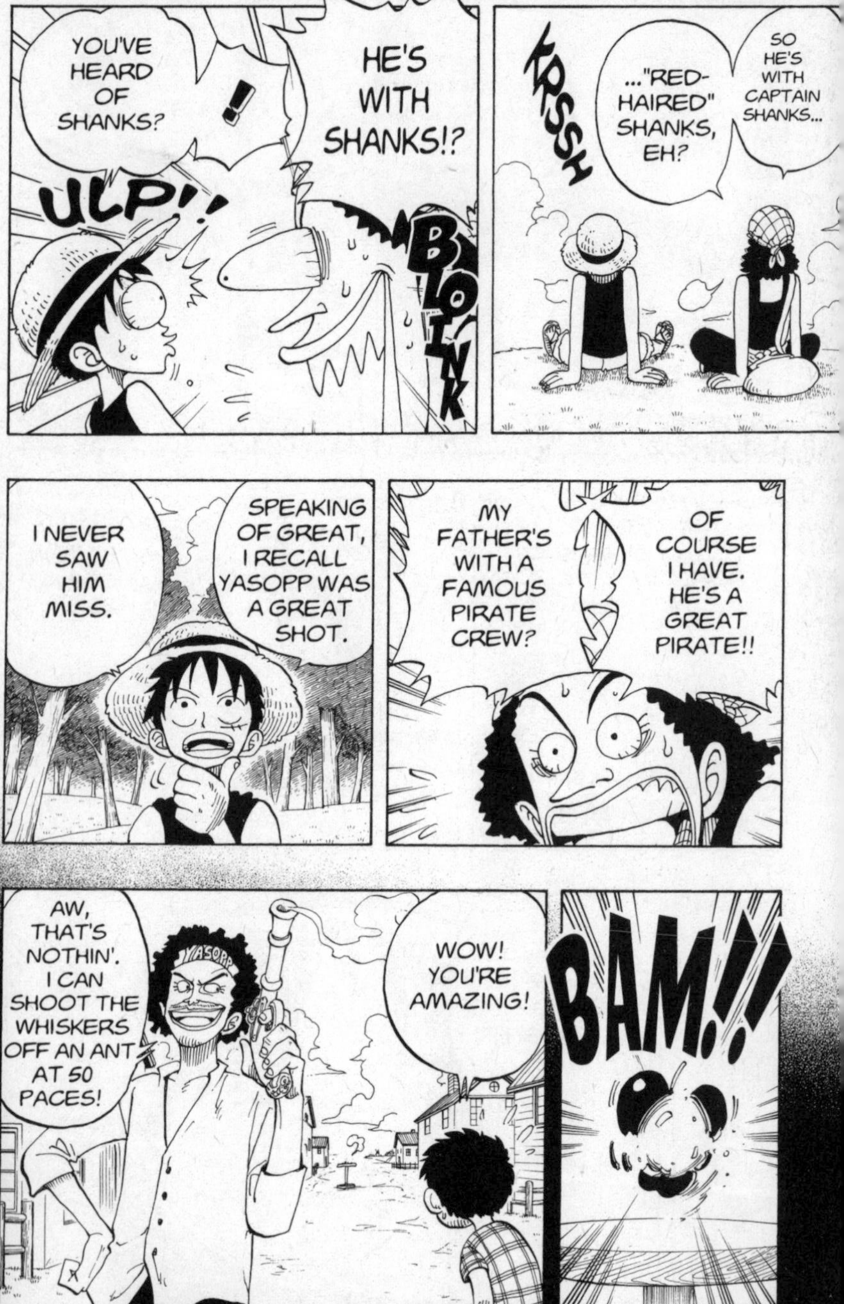
SO HE'S WITH CAPTAIN SHANKS...
..."RED-HAIRED" SHANKS, EH?
KRSSH
HE'S WITH SHANKS!?
BLOINK
!
YOU'VE HEARD OF SHANKS?
ULP!!
OF COURSE I HAVE. HE'S A GREAT PIRATE!!
MY FATHER'S WITH A FAMOUS PIRATE CREW?
SPEAKING OF GREAT, I RECALL YASOPP WAS A GREAT SHOT.
I NEVER SAW HIM MISS.
BAM!!
WOW! YOU'RE AMAZING!
AW, THAT'S NOTHIN'. I CAN SHOOT THE WHISKERS OFF AN ANT AT 50 PACES!
YASOPP

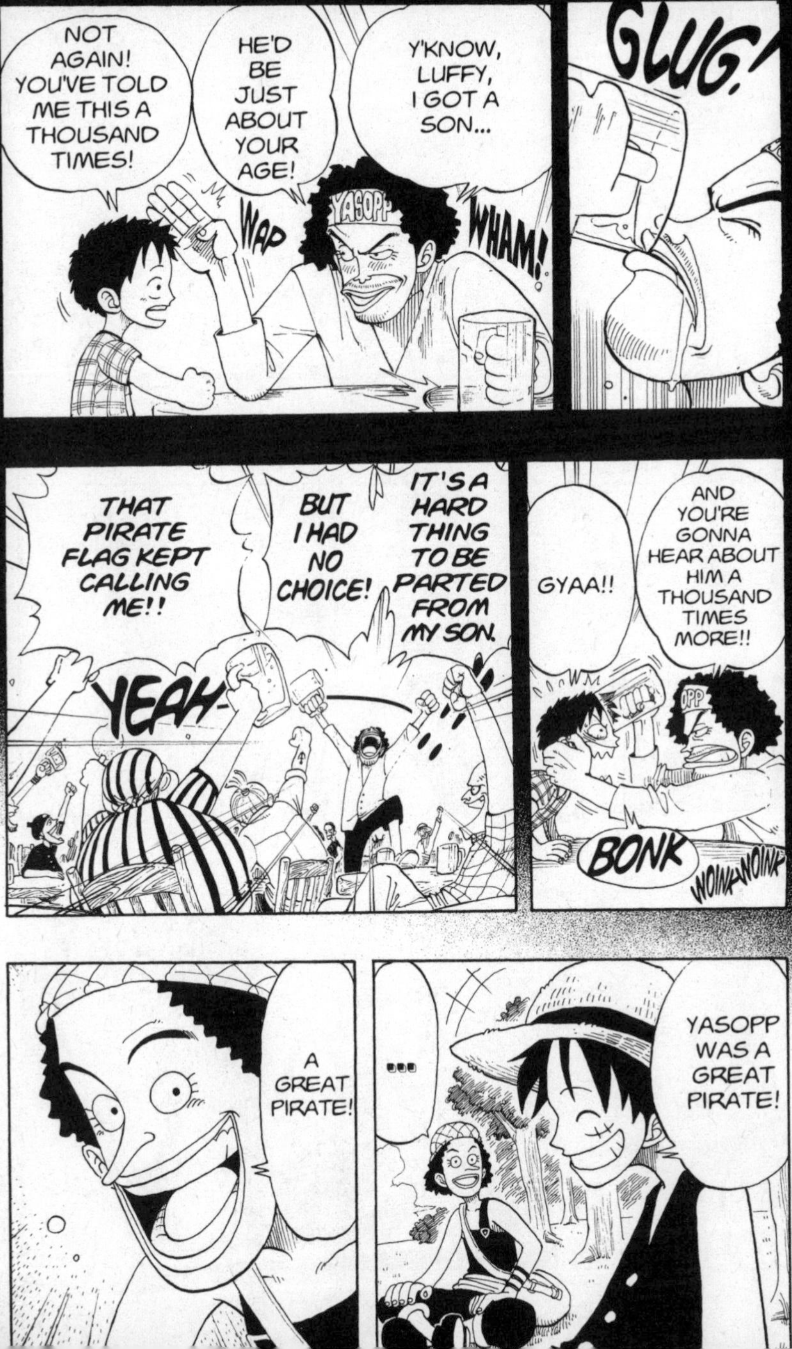
GLUG!
Y'KNOW, LUFFY, I GOT A SON...
HE'D BE JUST ABOUT YOUR AGE!
WHAM!
NOT AGAIN! YOU'VE TOLD ME THIS A THOUSAND TIMES!
WAP
AND YOU'RE GONNA HEAR ABOUT HIM A THOUSAND TIMES MORE!!
GYAA!!
BONK
WOINK WOINK
IT'S A HARD THING TO BE PARTED FROM MY SON.
BUT I HAD NO CHOICE!
THAT PIRATE FLAG KEPT CALLING ME!!
YEAH-
YASOPP WAS A GREAT PIRATE!
...
A GREAT PIRATE!

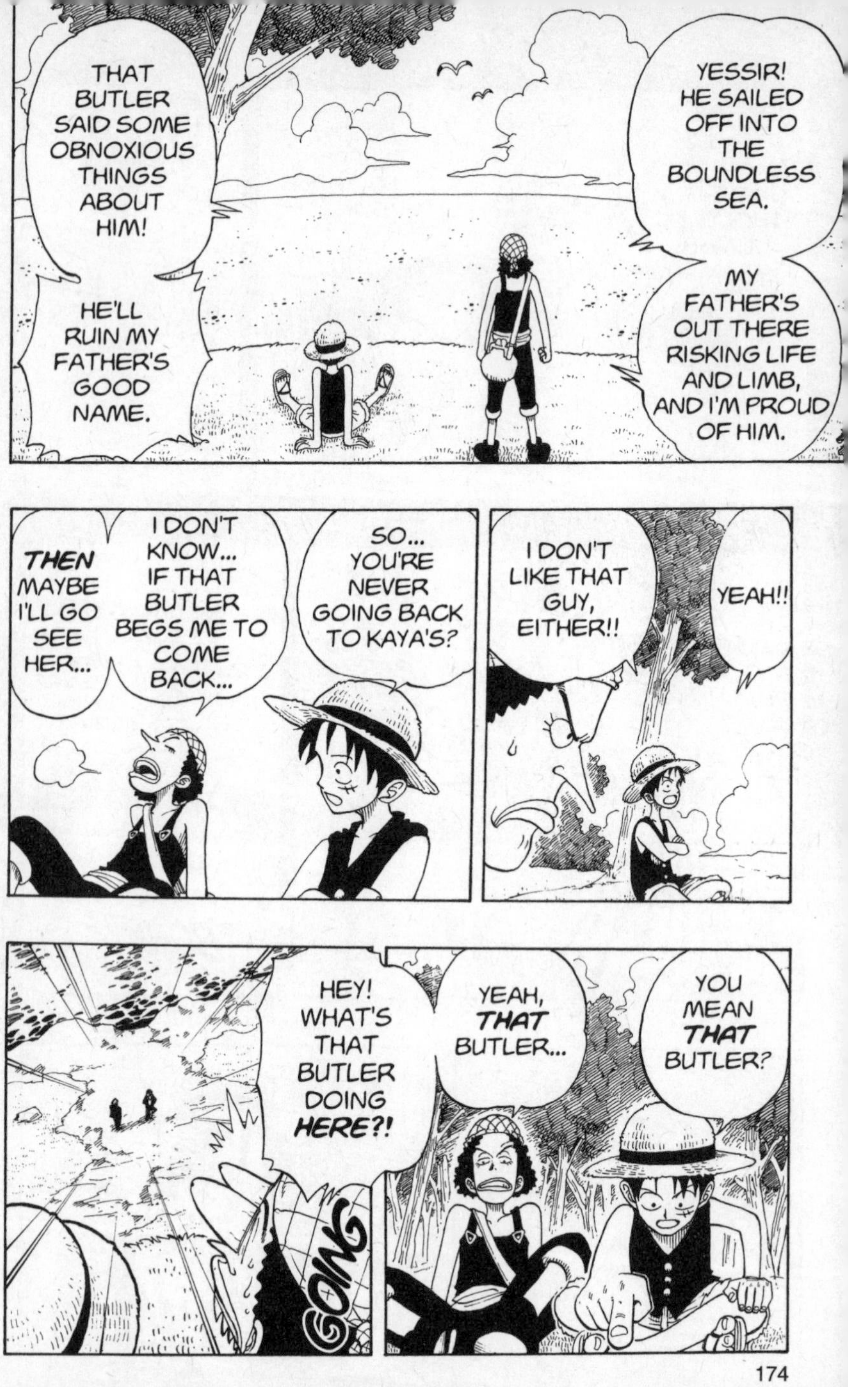
YESSIR! HE SAILED OFF INTO THE BOUNDLESS SEA.
MY FATHER'S OUT THERE RISKING LIFE AND LIMB, AND I'M PROUD OF HIM.
THAT BUTLER SAID SOME OBNOXIOUS THINGS ABOUT HIM!
HE'LL RUIN MY FATHER'S GOOD NAME.
YEAH!!
I DON'T LIKE THAT GUY, EITHER!!
SO... YOU'RE NEVER GOING BACK TO KAYA'S?
I DON'T KNOW... IF THAT BUTLER BEGS ME TO COME BACK...
THEN MAYBE I'LL GO SEE HER...
YOU MEAN *THAT* BUTLER?
YEAH, *THAT* BUTLER...
HEY! WHAT'S THAT BUTLER DOING *HERE?!*
GOING

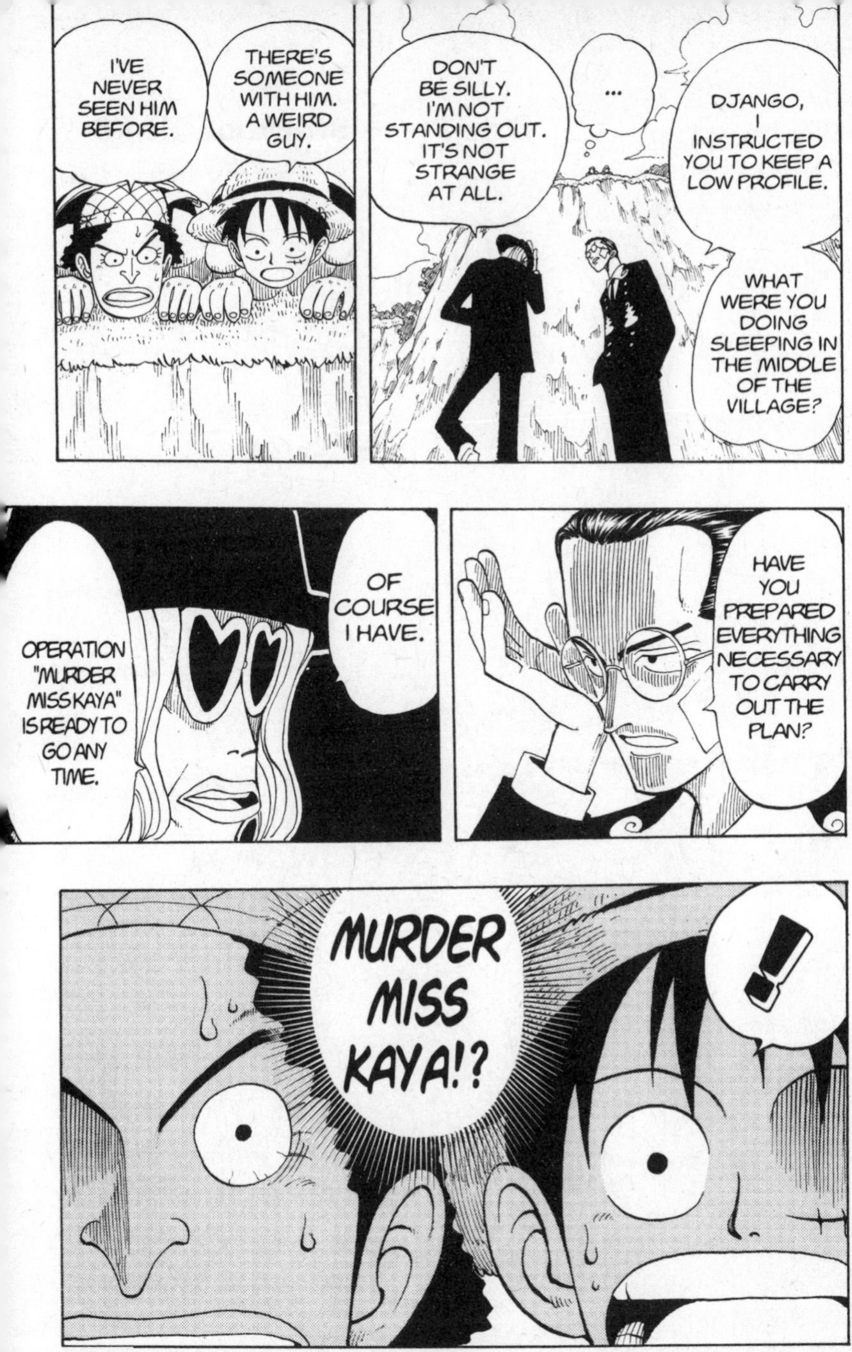
DJANGO, I INSTRUCTED YOU TO KEEP A LOW PROFILE.
...
WHAT WERE YOU DOING SLEEPING IN THE MIDDLE OF THE VILLAGE?
DON'T BE SILLY. I'M NOT STANDING OUT. IT'S NOT STRANGE AT ALL.
THERE'S SOMEONE WITH HIM. A WEIRD GUY.
I'VE NEVER SEEN HIM BEFORE.
HAVE YOU PREPARED EVERYTHING NECESSARY TO CARRY OUT THE PLAN?
OF COURSE I HAVE.
OPERATION "MURDER MISS KAYA" IS READY TO GO ANY TIME.
!
MURDER MISS KAYA!?

One Piece Storyboards #8

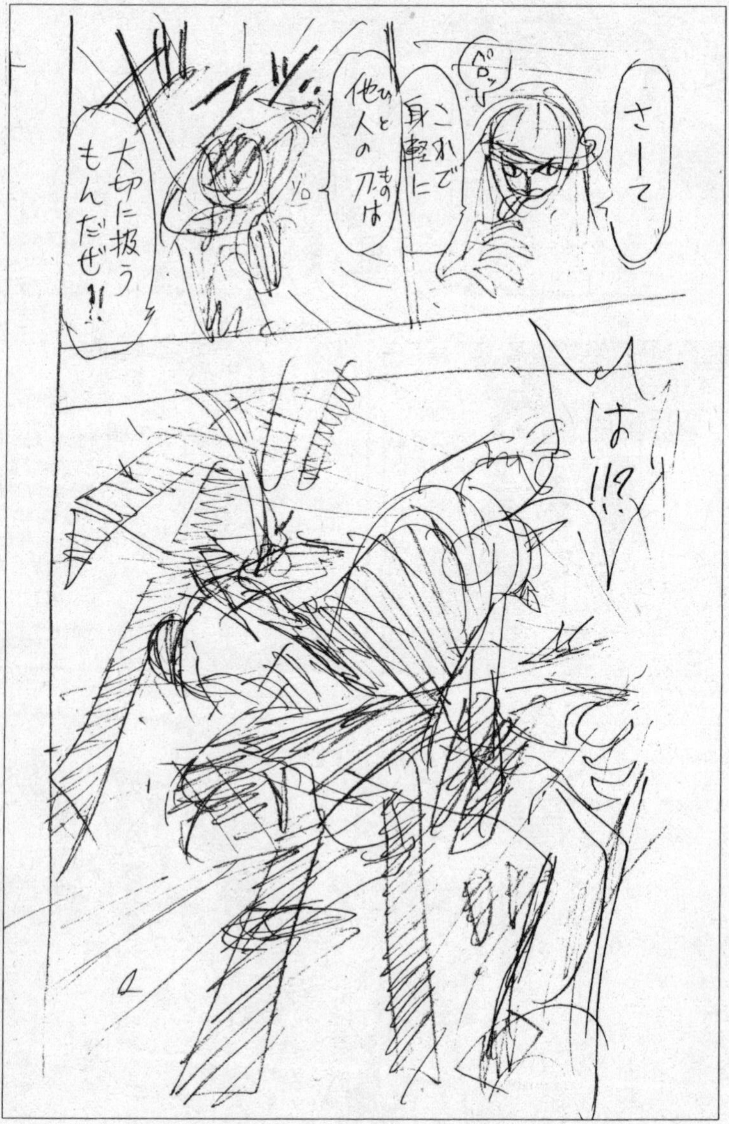

さーて
ペロッ
これで身軽に
他人の刀は
大切に扱うもんだぜ!!
は!!?

Chapter 26:
CAPTAIN KURO'S PLAN

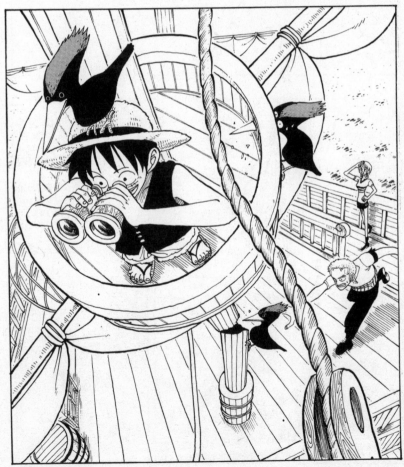

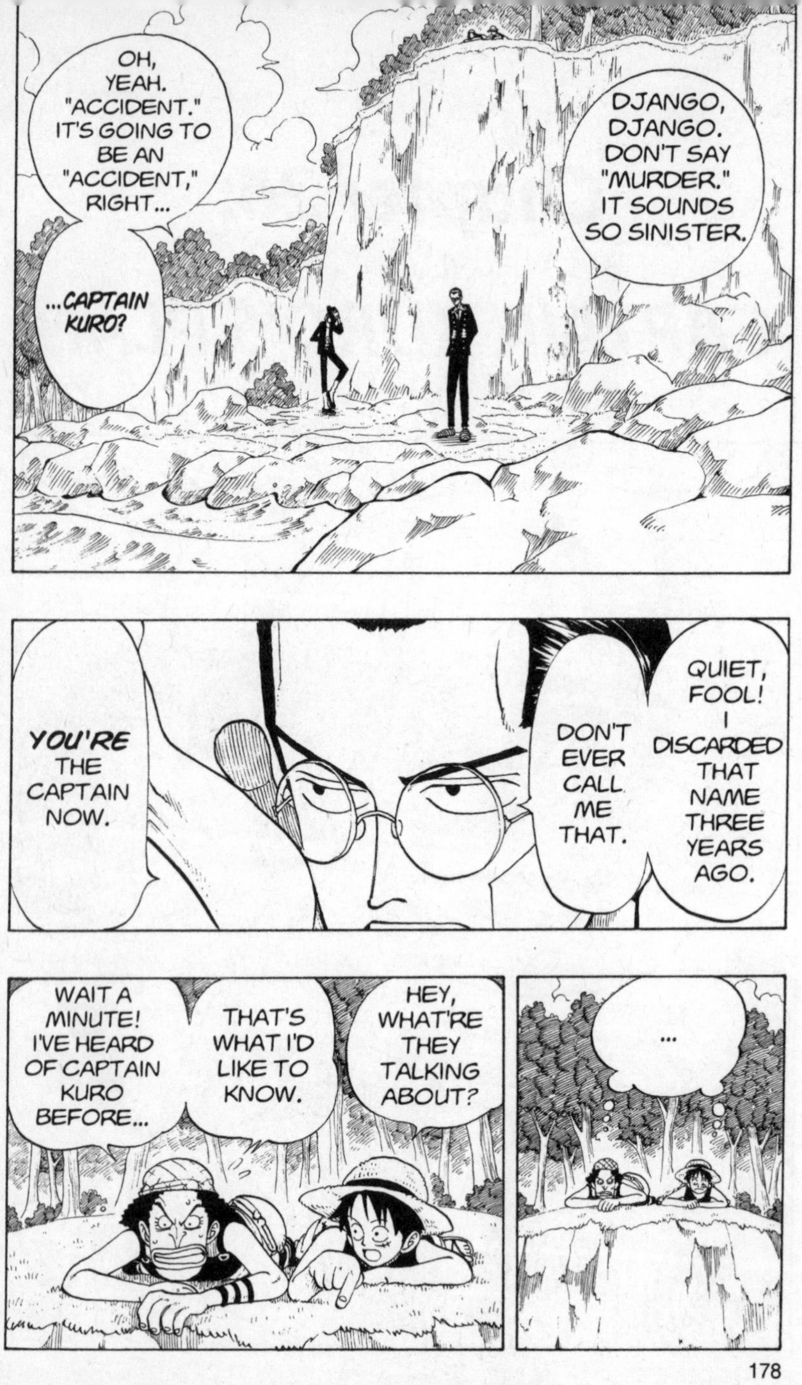
DJANGO, DJANGO. DON'T SAY "MURDER." IT SOUNDS SO SINISTER.
OH, YEAH. "ACCIDENT." IT'S GOING TO BE AN "ACCIDENT," RIGHT...
...CAPTAIN KURO?
QUIET, FOOL! I DISCARDED THAT NAME THREE YEARS AGO.
DON'T EVER CALL ME THAT.
YOU'RE THE CAPTAIN NOW.
...
HEY, WHAT'RE THEY TALKING ABOUT?
THAT'S WHAT I'D LIKE TO KNOW.
WAIT A MINUTE! I'VE HEARD OF CAPTAIN KURO BEFORE...

READ THIS WAY

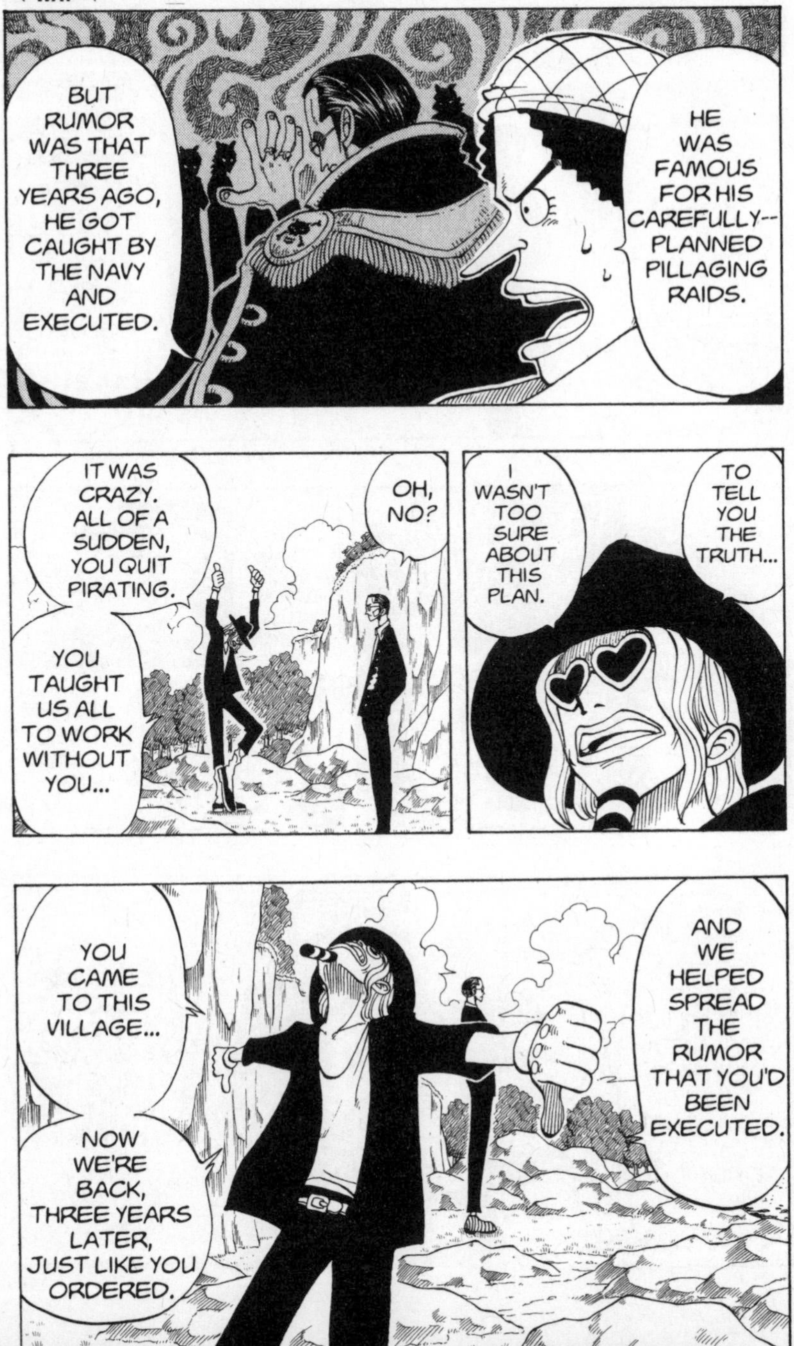
HE WAS FAMOUS FOR HIS CAREFULLY-- PLANNED PILLAGING RAIDS.
BUT RUMOR WAS THAT THREE YEARS AGO, HE GOT CAUGHT BY THE NAVY AND EXECUTED.
TO TELL YOU THE TRUTH...
I WASN'T TOO SURE ABOUT THIS PLAN.
OH, NO?
IT WAS CRAZY. ALL OF A SUDDEN, YOU QUIT PIRATING.
YOU TAUGHT US ALL TO WORK WITHOUT YOU...
YOU CAME TO THIS VILLAGE...
AND WE HELPED SPREAD THE RUMOR THAT YOU'D BEEN EXECUTED.
NOW WE'RE BACK, THREE YEARS LATER, JUST LIKE YOU ORDERED.

READ THIS WAY

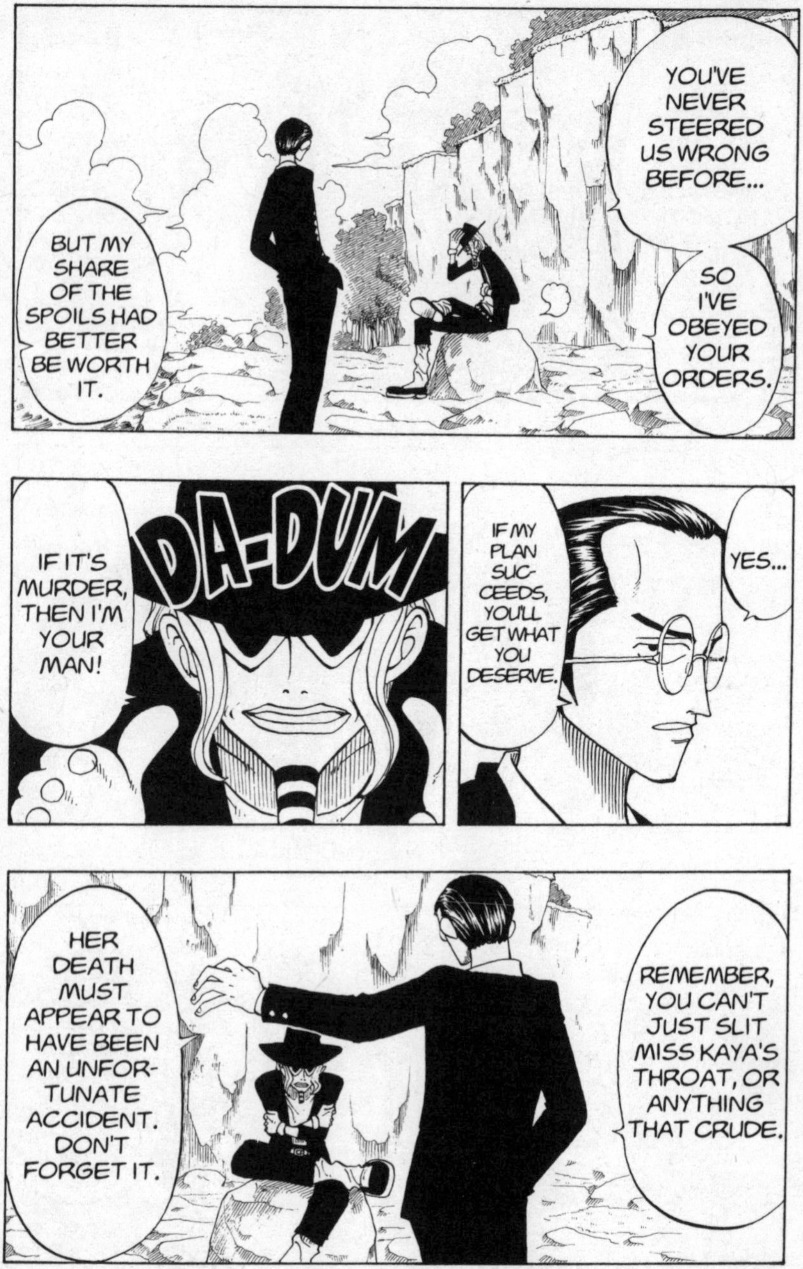
YOU'VE NEVER STEERED US WRONG BEFORE...
SO I'VE OBEYED YOUR ORDERS.
BUT MY SHARE OF THE SPOILS HAD BETTER BE WORTH IT.
YES...
IF MY PLAN SUC-CEEDS, YOU'LL GET WHAT YOU DESERVE.
DA-DUM
IF IT'S MURDER, THEN I'M YOUR MAN!
REMEMBER, YOU CAN'T JUST SLIT MISS KAYA'S THROAT, OR ANYTHING THAT CRUDE.
HER DEATH MUST APPEAR TO HAVE BEEN AN UNFOR-TUNATE ACCIDENT. DON'T FORGET IT.

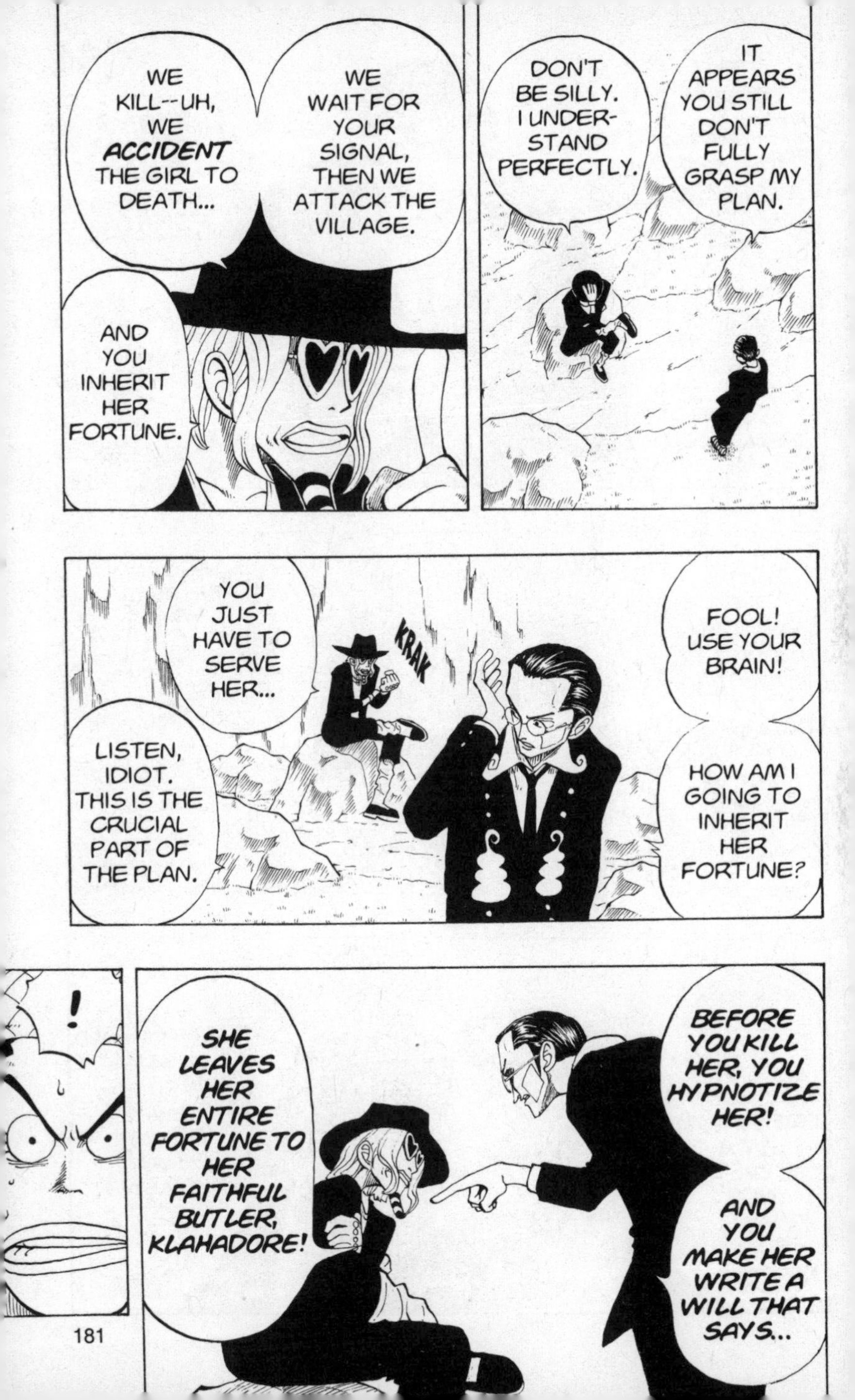
IT APPEARS YOU STILL DON'T FULLY GRASP MY PLAN.
DON'T BE SILLY. I UNDERSTAND PERFECTLY.
WE WAIT FOR YOUR SIGNAL, THEN WE ATTACK THE VILLAGE.
WE KILL--UH, WE ACCIDENT THE GIRL TO DEATH...
AND YOU INHERIT HER FORTUNE.
FOOL! USE YOUR BRAIN!
HOW AM I GOING TO INHERIT HER FORTUNE?
KRAK
YOU JUST HAVE TO SERVE HER...
LISTEN, IDIOT. THIS IS THE CRUCIAL PART OF THE PLAN.
BEFORE YOU KILL HER, YOU HYPNOTIZE HER!
AND YOU MAKE HER WRITE A WILL THAT SAYS...
SHE LEAVES HER ENTIRE FORTUNE TO HER FAITHFUL BUTLER, KLAHADORE!
!

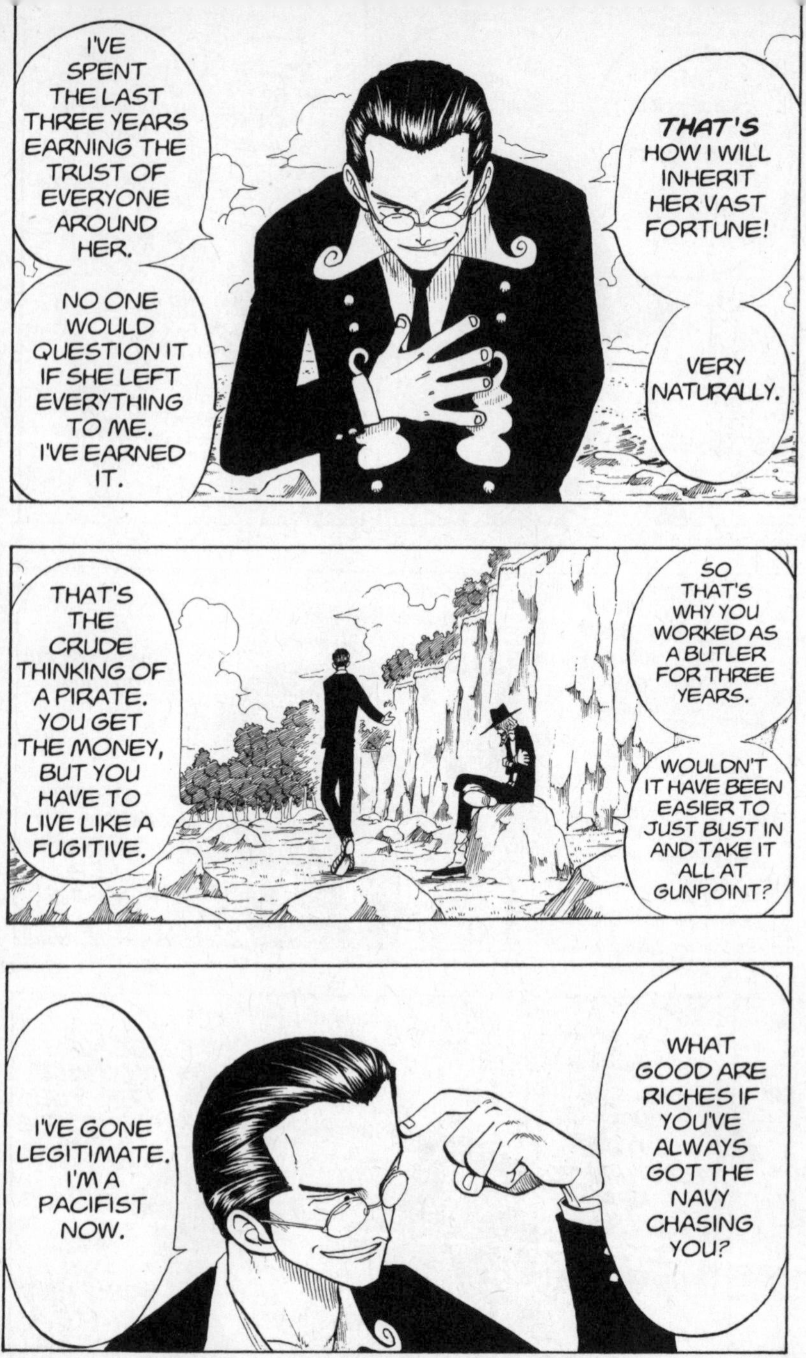
THAT'S HOW I WILL INHERIT HER VAST FORTUNE!
VERY NATURALLY.
I'VE SPENT THE LAST THREE YEARS EARNING THE TRUST OF EVERYONE AROUND HER.
NO ONE WOULD QUESTION IT IF SHE LEFT EVERYTHING TO ME. I'VE EARNED IT.
SO THAT'S WHY YOU WORKED AS A BUTLER FOR THREE YEARS.
WOULDN'T IT HAVE BEEN EASIER TO JUST BUST IN AND TAKE IT ALL AT GUNPOINT?
THAT'S THE CRUDE THINKING OF A PIRATE. YOU GET THE MONEY, BUT YOU HAVE TO LIVE LIKE A FUGITIVE.
WHAT GOOD ARE RICHES IF YOU'VE ALWAYS GOT THE NAVY CHASING YOU?
I'VE GONE LEGITIMATE. I'M A PACIFIST NOW.

READ THIS WAY

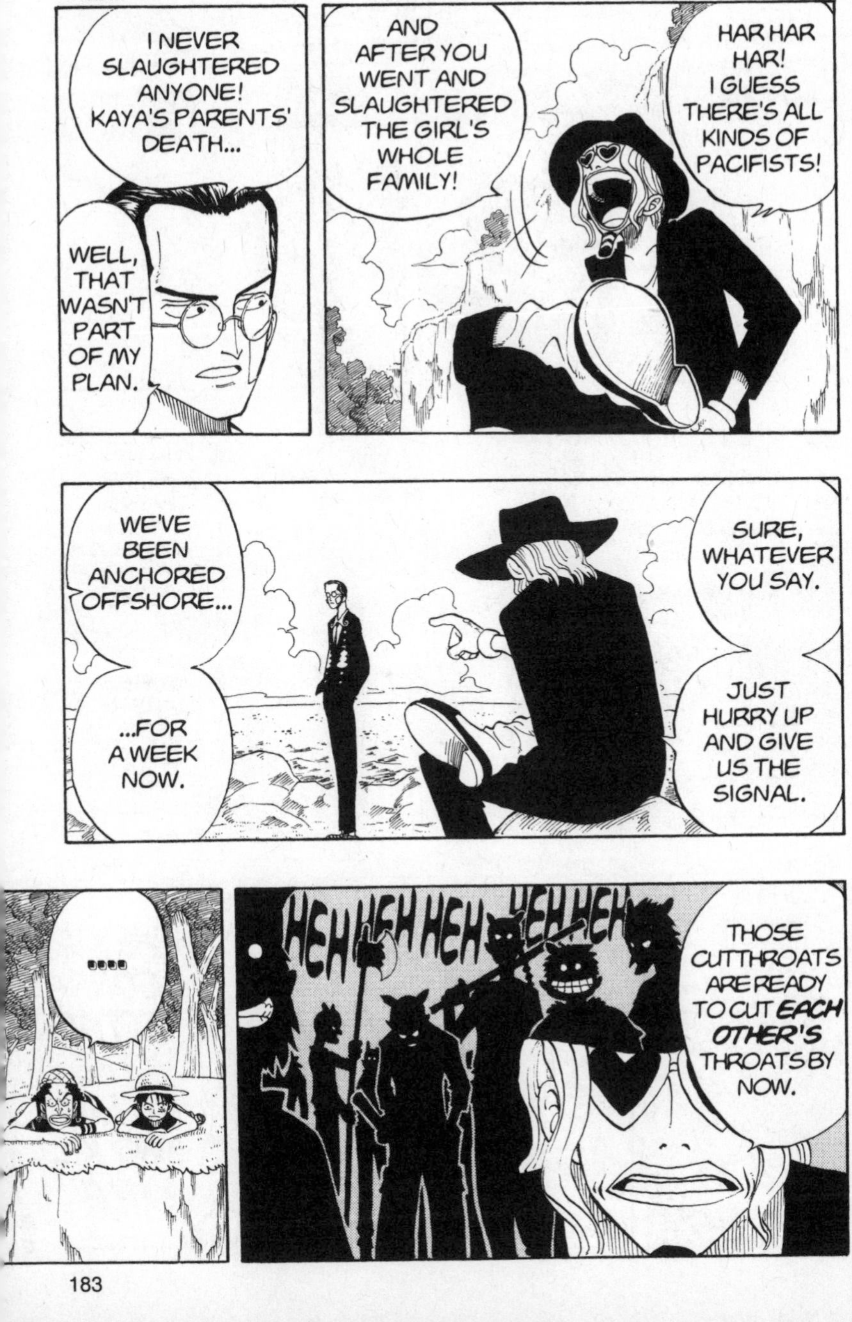
HAR HAR HAR! I GUESS THERE'S ALL KINDS OF PACIFISTS!
AND AFTER YOU WENT AND SLAUGHTERED THE GIRL'S WHOLE FAMILY!
I NEVER SLAUGHTERED ANYONE! KAYA'S PARENTS' DEATH...
WELL, THAT WASN'T PART OF MY PLAN.
SURE, WHATEVER YOU SAY.
JUST HURRY UP AND GIVE US THE SIGNAL.
WE'VE BEEN ANCHORED OFFSHORE...
...FOR A WEEK NOW.
HEH HEH HEH HEH HEH HEH
THOSE CUTTHROATS ARE READY TO CUT *EACH OTHER'S* THROATS BY NOW.
....

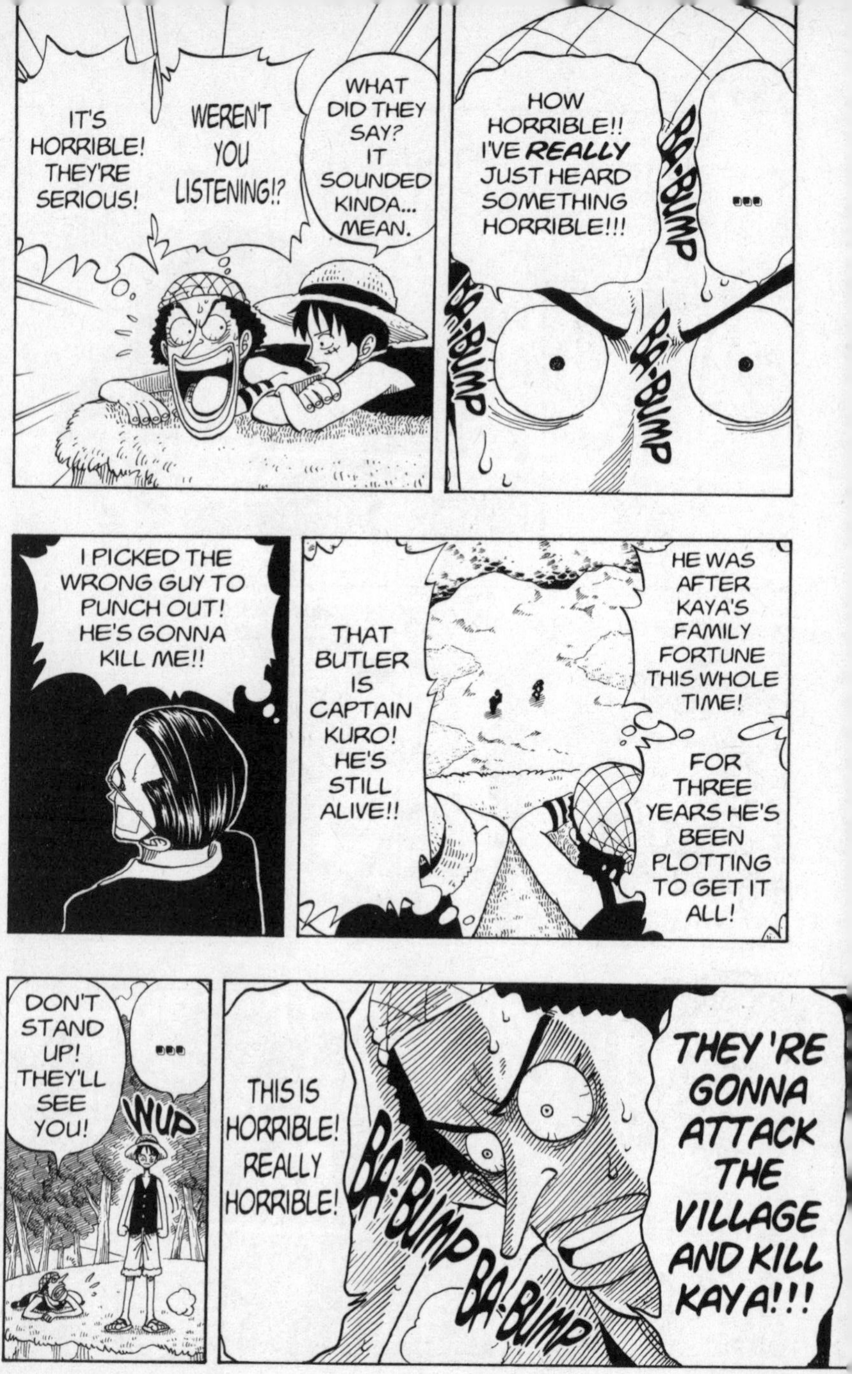
...
HOW HORRIBLE!! I'VE **REALLY** JUST HEARD SOMETHING HORRIBLE!!!
BA-BUMP
BA-BUMP
BA-BUMP
WHAT DID THEY SAY? IT SOUNDED KINDA... MEAN.
WEREN'T YOU LISTENING!?
IT'S HORRIBLE! THEY'RE SERIOUS!
HE WAS AFTER KAYA'S FAMILY FORTUNE THIS WHOLE TIME!
FOR THREE YEARS HE'S BEEN PLOTTING TO GET IT ALL!
THAT BUTLER IS CAPTAIN KURO! HE'S STILL ALIVE!!
I PICKED THE WRONG GUY TO PUNCH OUT! HE'S GONNA KILL ME!!
THEY'RE GONNA ATTACK THE VILLAGE AND KILL KAYA!!!
BA-BUMP
BA-BUMP
THIS IS HORRIBLE! REALLY HORRIBLE!
...
DON'T STAND UP! THEY'LL SEE YOU!
WUP

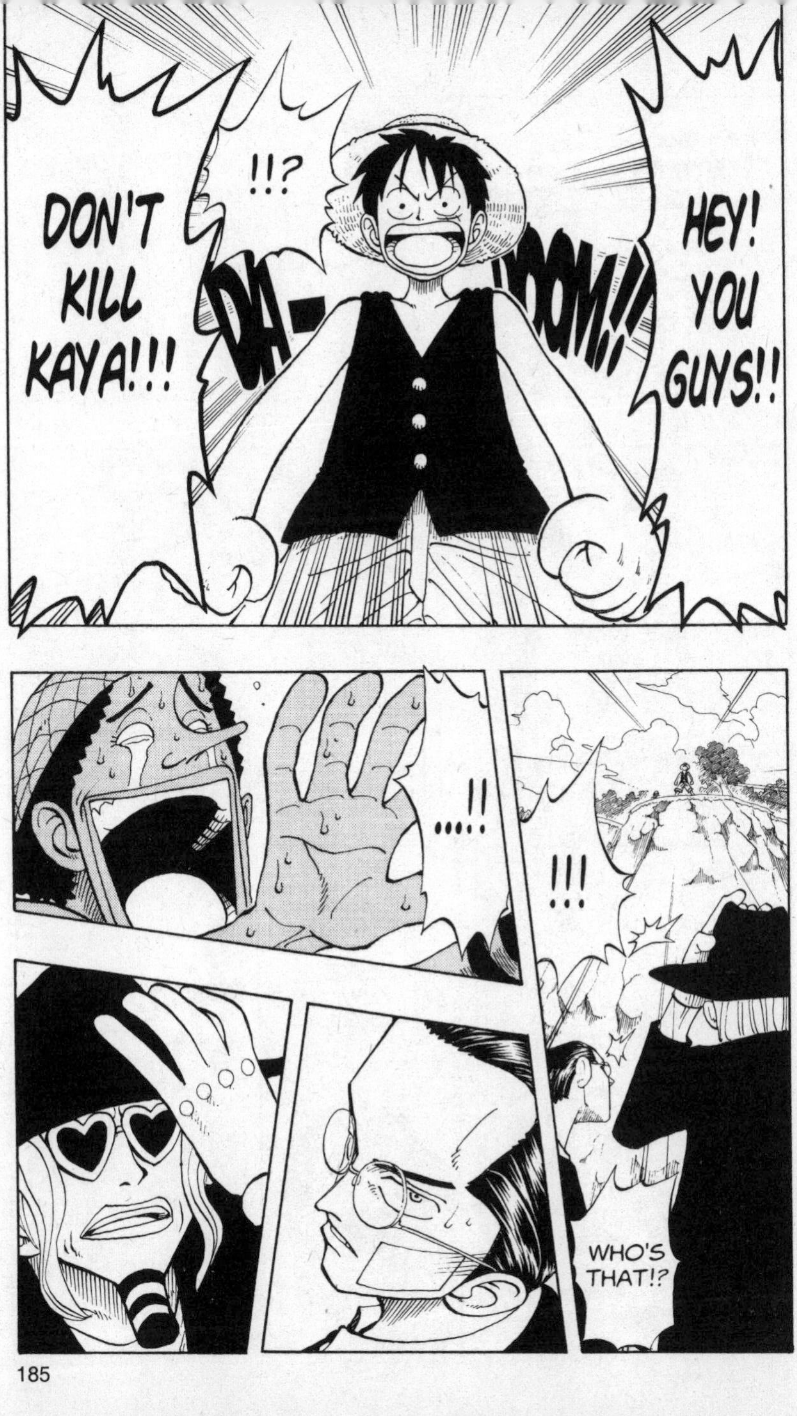
HEY! YOU GUYS!!
!!?
DA-DOOM!!
DON'T KILL KAYA!!!
!!!
WHO'S THAT!?
....!!

READ THIS WAY

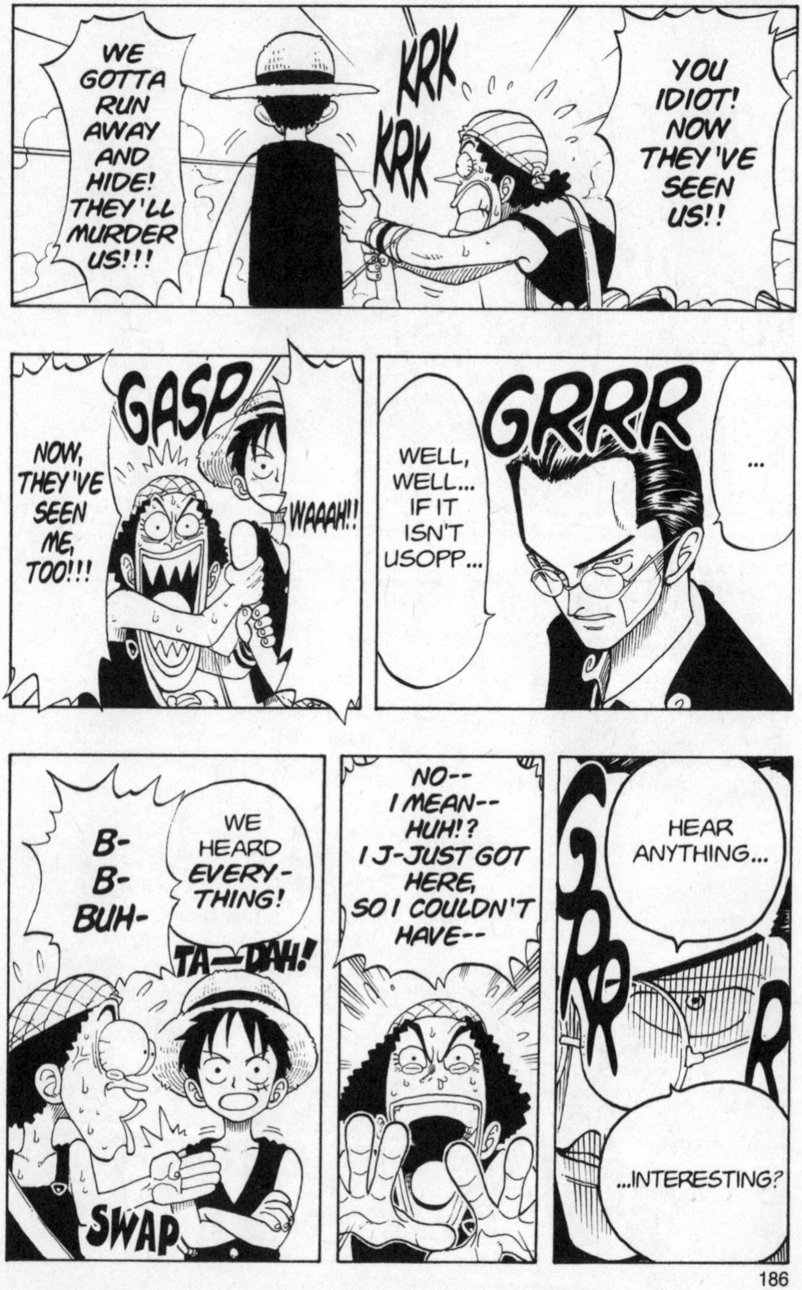
YOU IDIOT! NOW THEY'VE SEEN US!!
KRK KRK
WE GOTTA RUN AWAY AND HIDE! THEY'LL MURDER US!!!
GRRRR
...
WELL, WELL... IF IT ISN'T USOPP...
GASP
WAAAH!!
NOW, THEY'VE SEEN ME, TOO!!!
HEAR ANYTHING...
GRRRR
...INTERESTING?
NO-- I MEAN-- HUH!? I J-JUST GOT HERE, SO I COULDN'T HAVE--
WE HEARD EVERY-THING!
B-B-BUH-
TA-DAH!
SWAP

READ THIS WAY

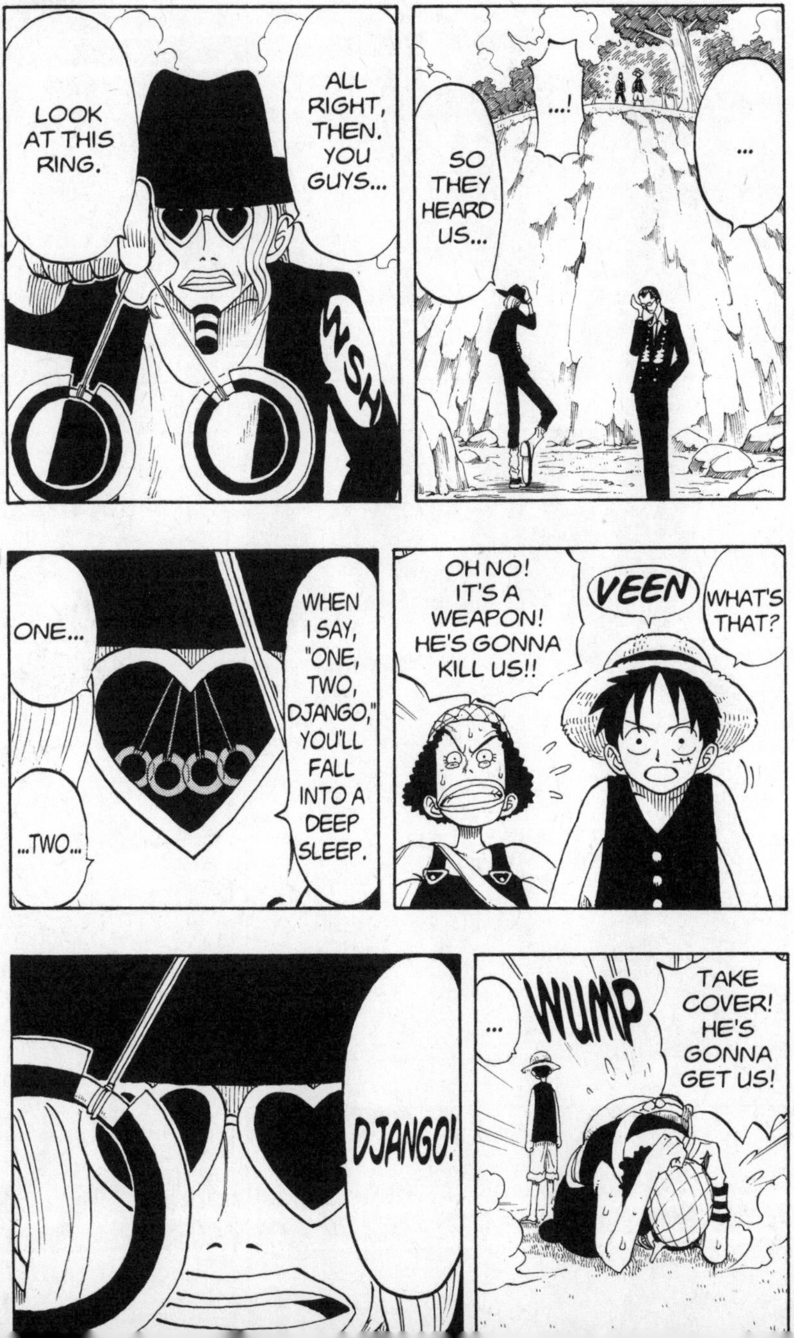
...
...!
SO THEY HEARD US...
ALL RIGHT, THEN. YOU GUYS...
LOOK AT THIS RING.
WSH
WHAT'S THAT?
VEEN
OH NO! IT'S A WEAPON! HE'S GONNA KILL US!!
WHEN I SAY, "ONE, TWO, DJANGO," YOU'LL FALL INTO A DEEP SLEEP.
ONE...
...TWO...
TAKE COVER! HE'S GONNA GET US!
WUMP
...
DJANGO!

READ THIS WAY

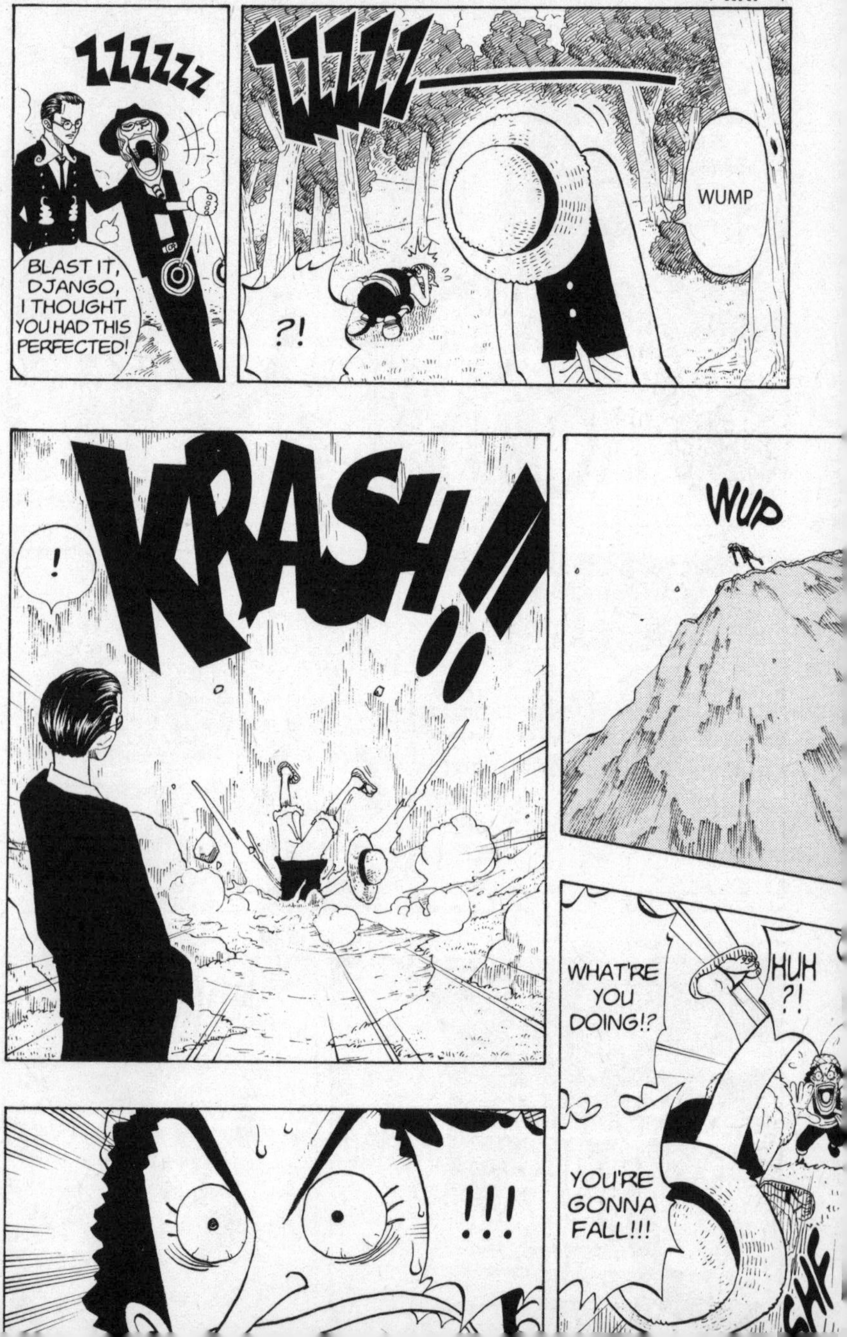
WUMP
ZZZZZ
?!
ZZZZZZ
BLAST IT, DJANGO, I THOUGHT YOU HAD THIS PERFECTED!
WUP
HUH ?!
WHAT'RE YOU DOING!?
YOU'RE GONNA FALL!!!
SHF
!
KRASH!!
!!!

READ THIS WAY

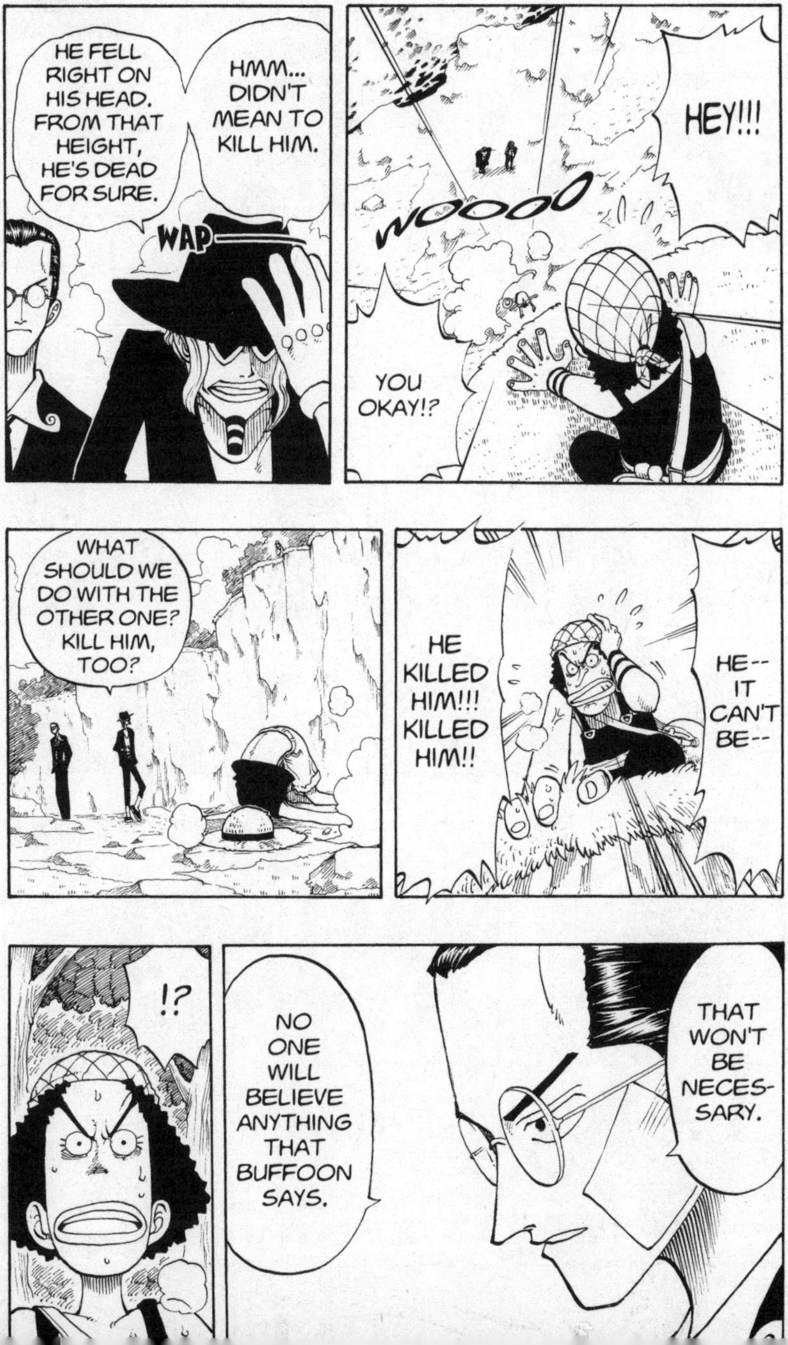
HEY!!!
WOOOOO
YOU OKAY!?
HMM... DIDN'T MEAN TO KILL HIM.
HE FELL RIGHT ON HIS HEAD. FROM THAT HEIGHT, HE'S DEAD FOR SURE.
WAP
HE-- IT CAN'T BE--
HE KILLED HIM!!! KILLED HIM!!
WHAT SHOULD WE DO WITH THE OTHER ONE? KILL HIM, TOO?
THAT WON'T BE NECES-SARY.
NO ONE WILL BELIEVE ANYTHING THAT BUFFOON SAYS.
!?

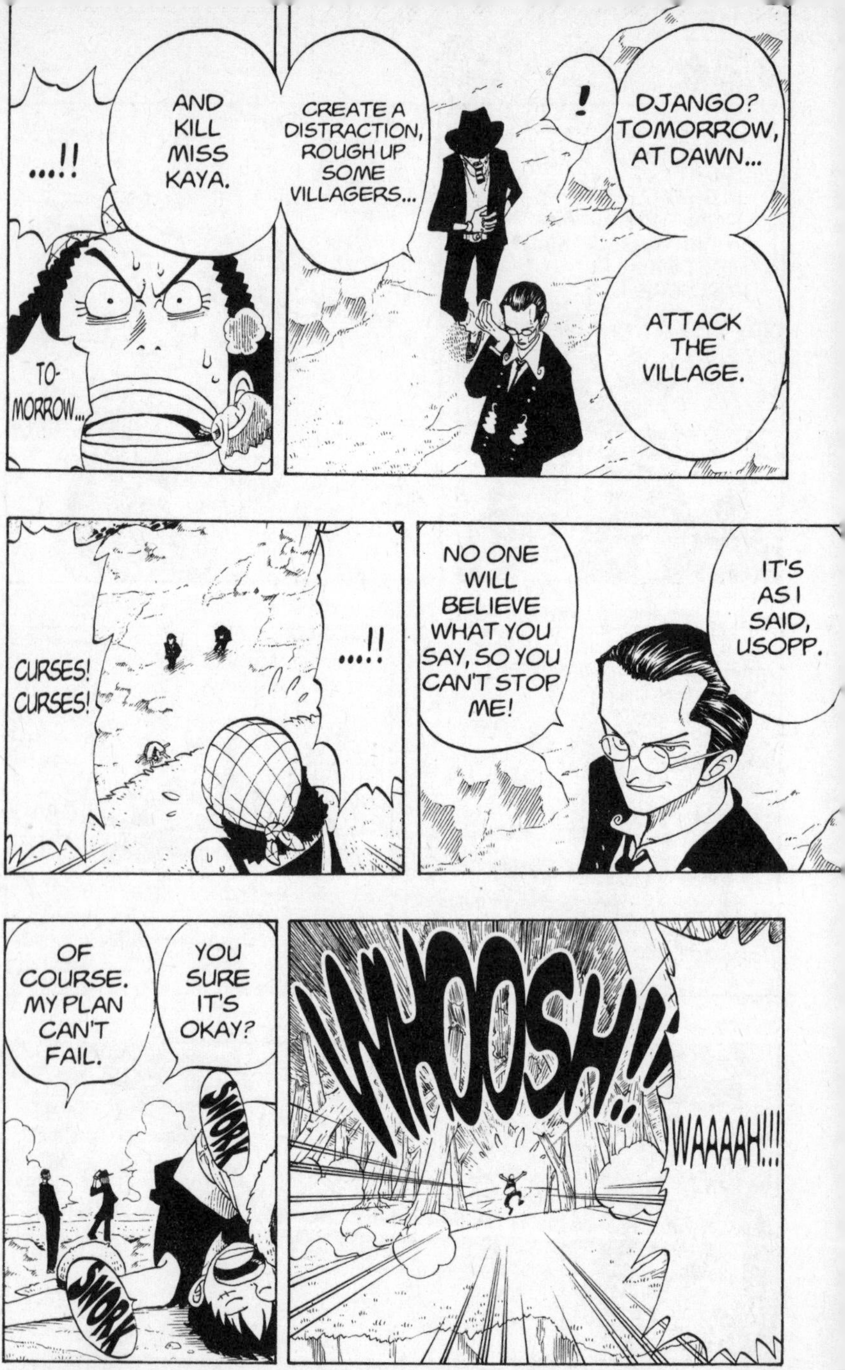
!
DJANGO? TOMORROW, AT DAWN...
ATTACK THE VILLAGE.
CREATE A DISTRACTION, ROUGH UP SOME VILLAGERS...
AND KILL MISS KAYA.
...!!
TO-MORROW...
IT'S AS I SAID, USOPP.
NO ONE WILL BELIEVE WHAT YOU SAY, SO YOU CAN'T STOP ME!
...!!
CURSES! CURSES!
WHOOSH!!
WAAAAH!!!
YOU SURE IT'S OKAY?
OF COURSE. MY PLAN CAN'T FAIL.
SNORK
SNORK

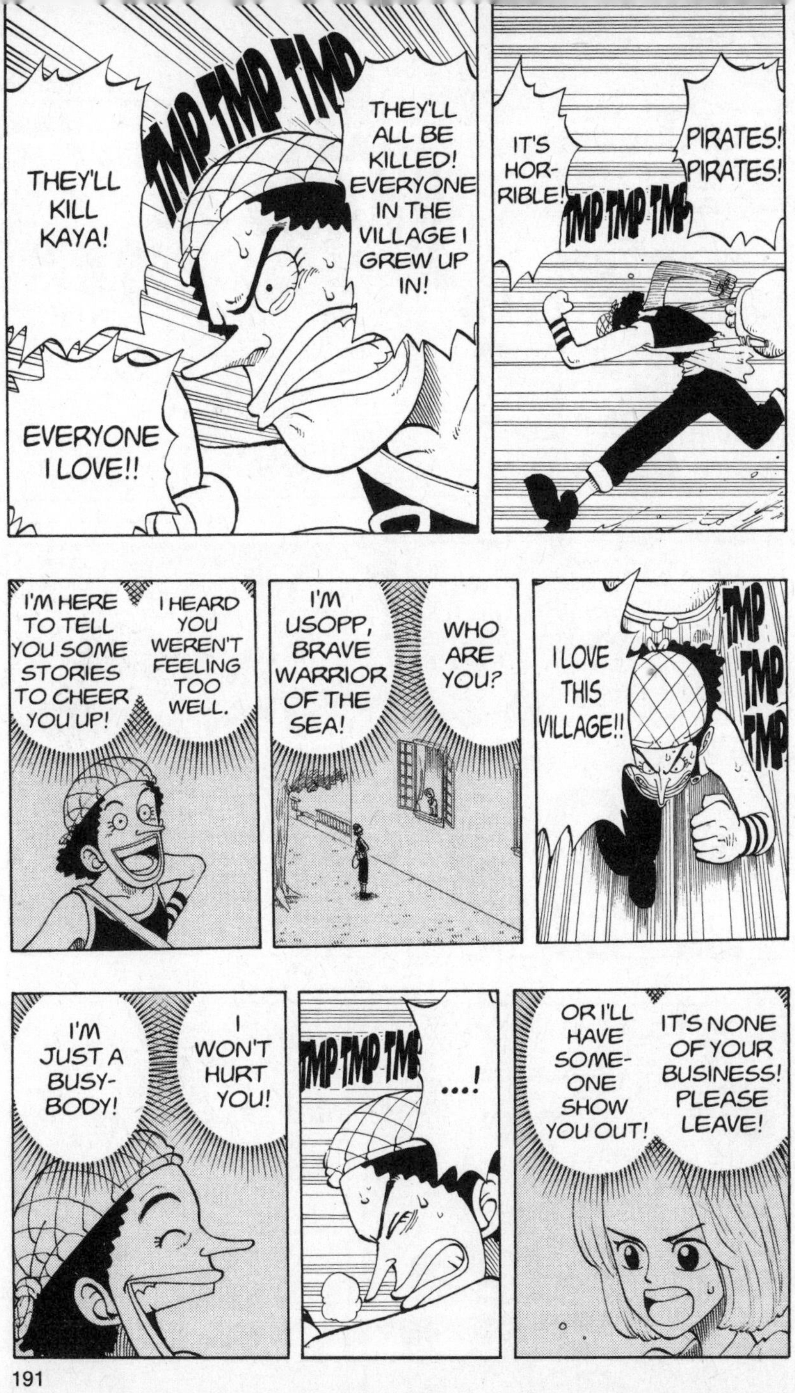
PIRATES! PIRATES!
IT'S HORRIBLE!
TMP TMP TMP
TMP TMP TMP
THEY'LL ALL BE KILLED! EVERYONE IN THE VILLAGE I GREW UP IN!
THEY'LL KILL KAYA!
EVERYONE I LOVE!!
TMP TMP TMP
I LOVE THIS VILLAGE!!
WHO ARE YOU?
I'M USOPP, BRAVE WARRIOR OF THE SEA!
I HEARD YOU WEREN'T FEELING TOO WELL.
I'M HERE TO TELL YOU SOME STORIES TO CHEER YOU UP!
IT'S NONE OF YOUR BUSINESS! PLEASE LEAVE!
OR I'LL HAVE SOME-ONE SHOW YOU OUT!
...!
TMP TMP TMP
I WON'T HURT YOU!
I'M JUST A BUSY-BODY!

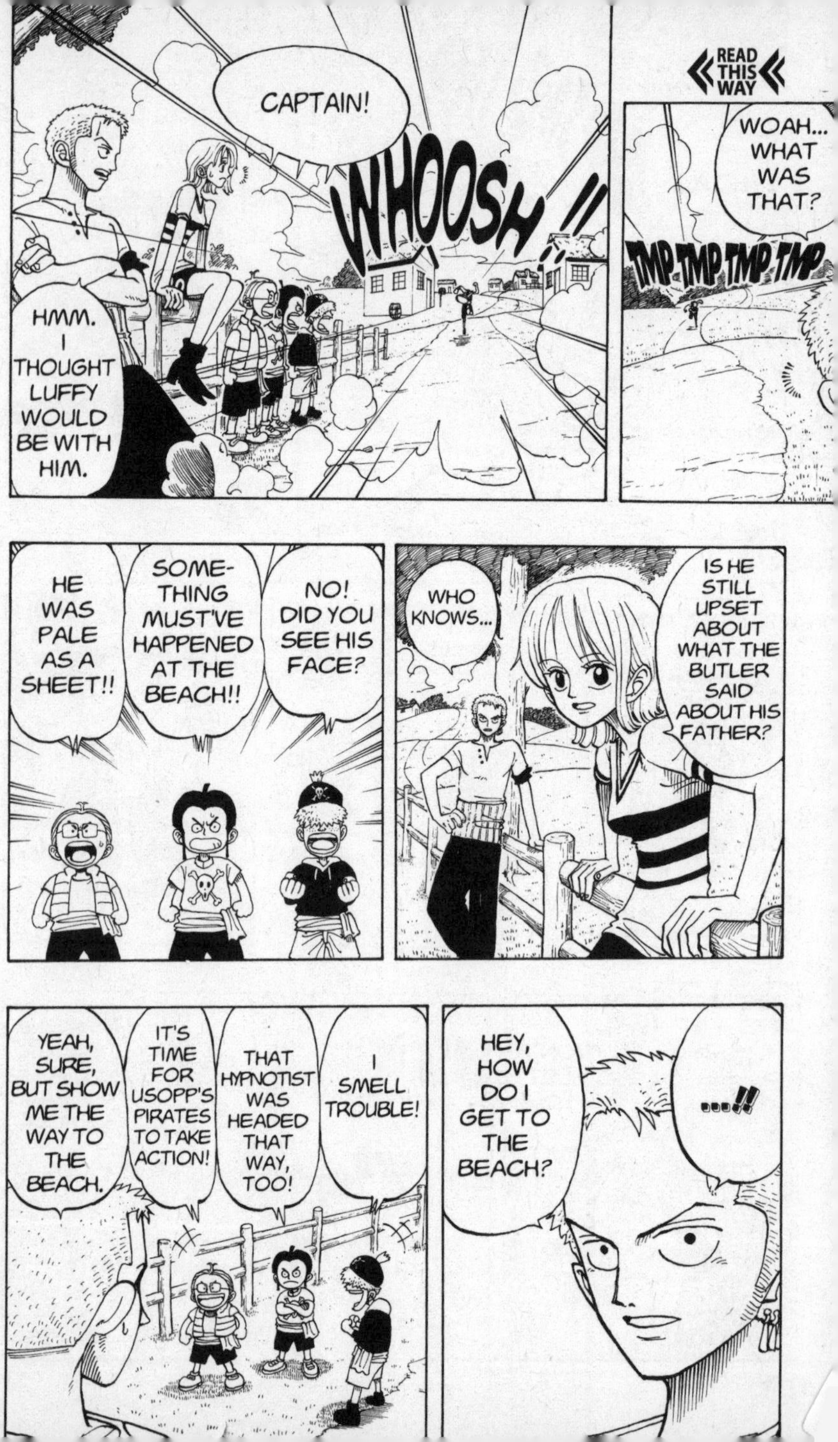
READ THIS WAY
WOAH... WHAT WAS THAT?
TMP TMP TMP TMP
CAPTAIN!
WHOOSH!!
HMM. I THOUGHT LUFFY WOULD BE WITH HIM.
IS HE STILL UPSET ABOUT WHAT THE BUTLER SAID ABOUT HIS FATHER?
WHO KNOWS...
NO! DID YOU SEE HIS FACE?
SOME-THING MUST'VE HAPPENED AT THE BEACH!!
HE WAS PALE AS A SHEET!!
...!!
HEY, HOW DO I GET TO THE BEACH?
I SMELL TROUBLE!
THAT HYPNOTIST WAS HEADED THAT WAY, TOO!
IT'S TIME FOR USOPP'S PIRATES TO TAKE ACTION!
YEAH, SURE, BUT SHOW ME THE WAY TO THE BEACH.

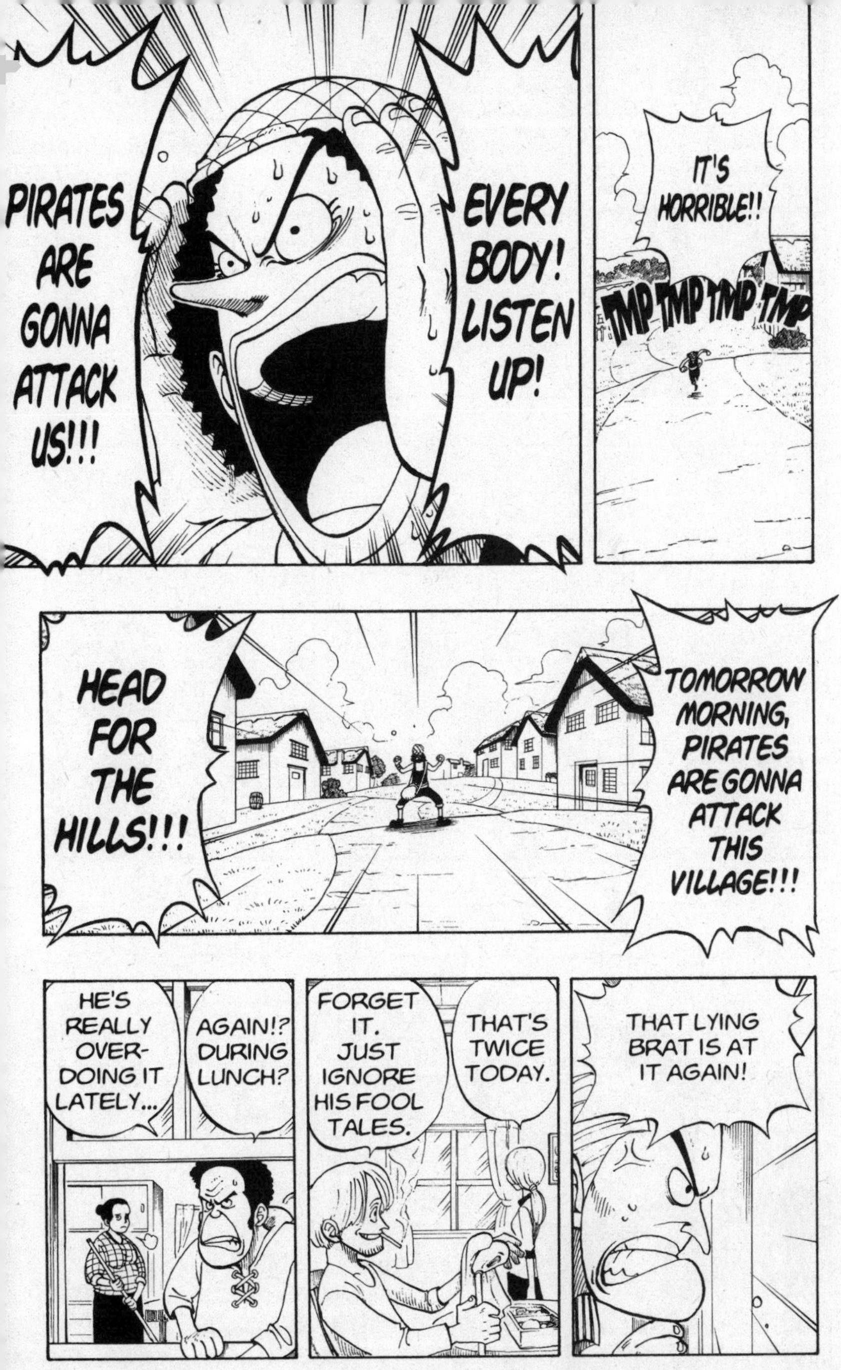
IT'S HORRIBLE!!
TMP TMP TMP TMP
EVERY BODY! LISTEN UP!
PIRATES ARE GONNA ATTACK US!!!
TOMORROW MORNING, PIRATES ARE GONNA ATTACK THIS VILLAGE!!!
HEAD FOR THE HILLS!!!
THAT LYING BRAT IS AT IT AGAIN!
THAT'S TWICE TODAY.
FORGET IT. JUST IGNORE HIS FOOL TALES.
AGAIN!? DURING LUNCH?
HE'S REALLY OVER-DOING IT LATELY...

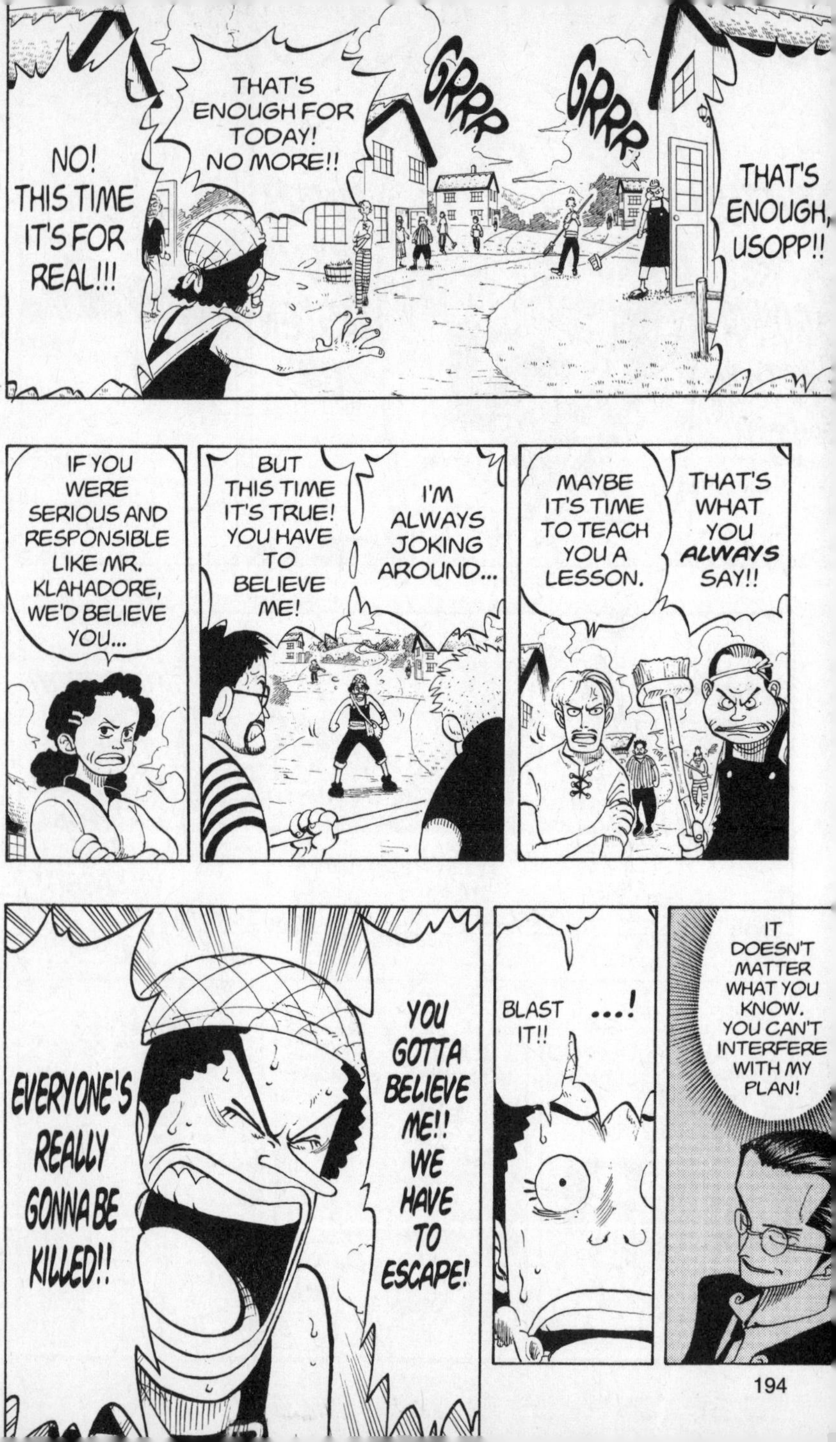
THAT'S ENOUGH, USOPP!!
GRRR
GRRR
THAT'S ENOUGH FOR TODAY! NO MORE!!
NO! THIS TIME IT'S FOR REAL!!!
THAT'S WHAT YOU ALWAYS SAY!!
MAYBE IT'S TIME TO TEACH YOU A LESSON.
I'M ALWAYS JOKING AROUND...
BUT THIS TIME IT'S TRUE! YOU HAVE TO BELIEVE ME!
IF YOU WERE SERIOUS AND RESPONSIBLE LIKE MR. KLAHADORE, WE'D BELIEVE YOU...
IT DOESN'T MATTER WHAT YOU KNOW. YOU CAN'T INTERFERE WITH MY PLAN!
...!
BLAST IT!!
YOU GOTTA BELIEVE ME!! WE HAVE TO ESCAPE!
EVERYONE'S REALLY GONNA BE KILLED!!

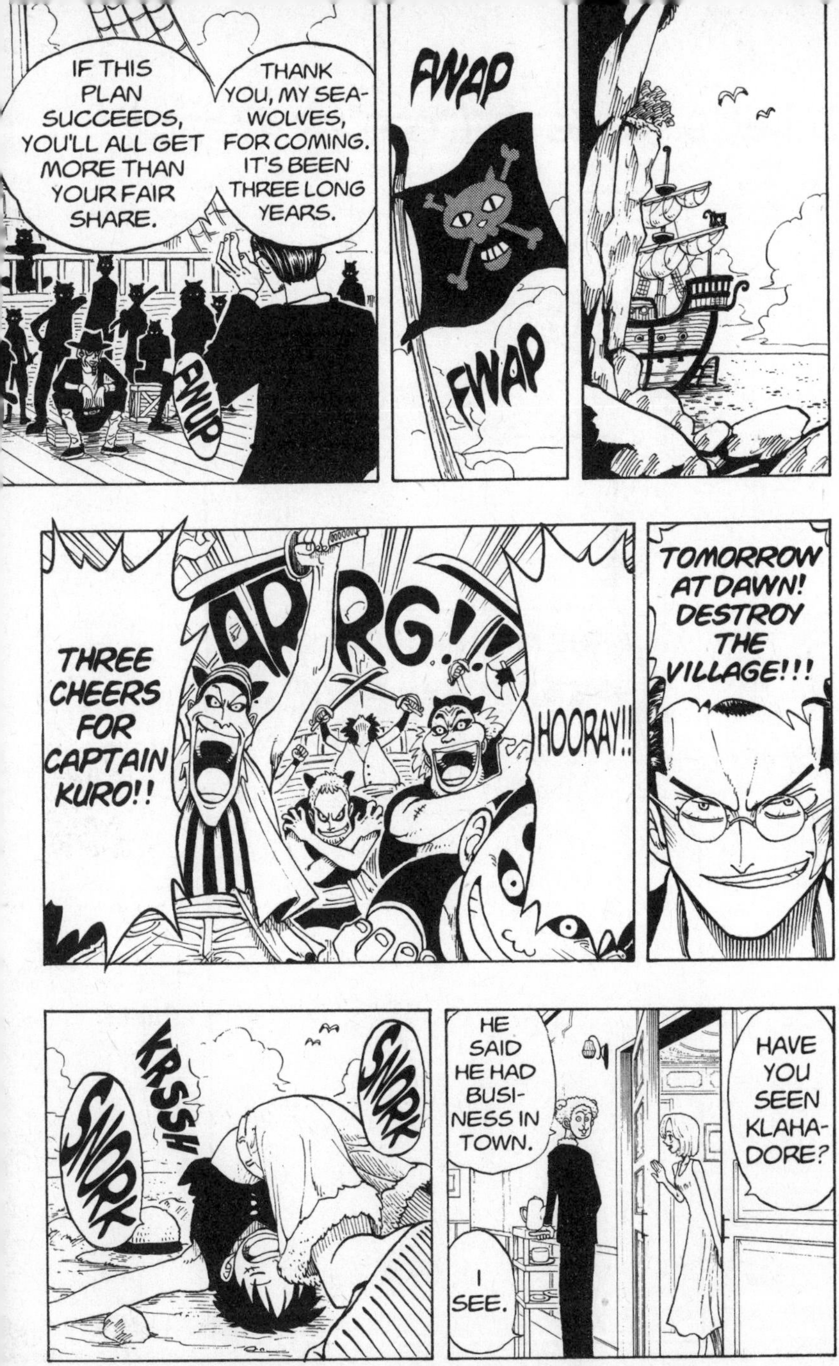
FWAP
FWAP
THANK YOU, MY SEA-WOLVES, FOR COMING. IT'S BEEN THREE LONG YEARS.
IF THIS PLAN SUCCEEDS, YOU'LL ALL GET MORE THAN YOUR FAIR SHARE.
FWUP
TOMORROW AT DAWN! DESTROY THE VILLAGE!!!
ARRG!!
HOORAY!!
THREE CHEERS FOR CAPTAIN KURO!!
HAVE YOU SEEN KLAHA-DORE?
HE SAID HE HAD BUSI-NESS IN TOWN.
I SEE.
SNORK
KRSSH
SNORK

TO BE CONTINUED IN *ONE PIECE* VOL. 4!

Let's Make a Treasure Theater!

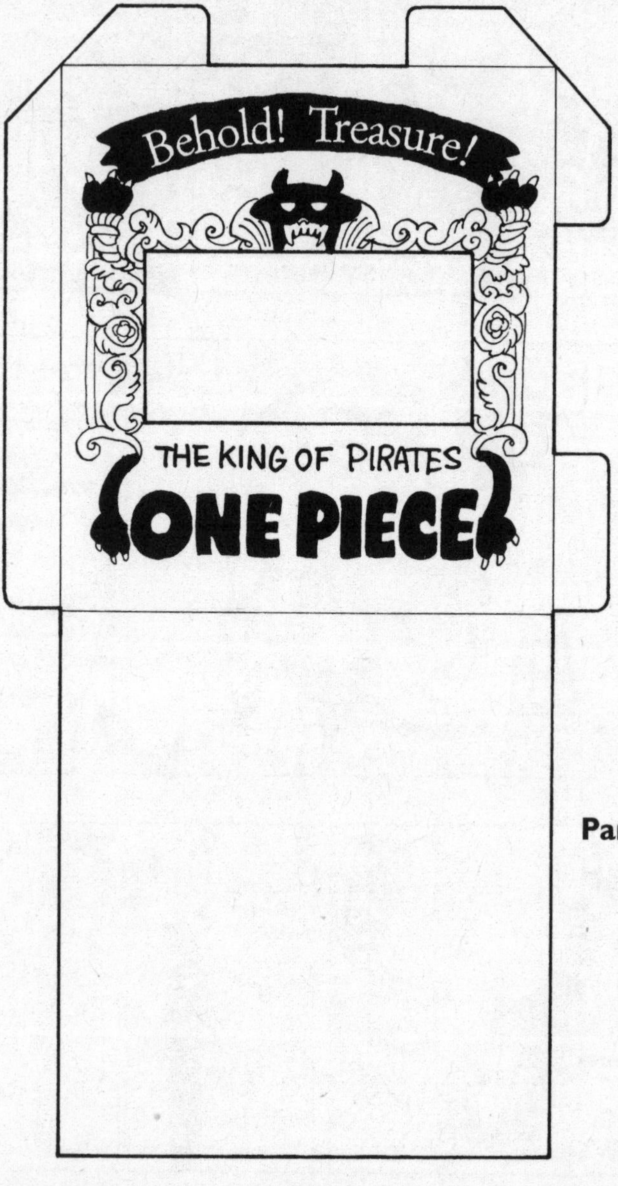
Behold! Treasure!
THE KING OF PIRATES
ONE PIECE

Part1

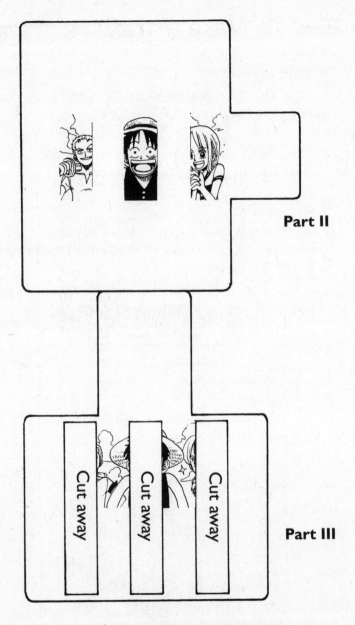

Part II

Cut away

Cut away

Cut away

Part III

⇐ See next page for assembly instructions!!

How To Make a Treasure Theater

✤ You'll need:
Scissors, cutter, glue or paste, a pen, stiff paper (on the thin side)

✤ You won't need:
Tea. (Please don't go to the trouble.)

✤ Instructions:
1. Glue. (To be cancelled in event of rain.)
Glue the pages containing Part II and Part III to a piece of the stiff paper.

Shloop!

(Use a photocopy if you don't want to cut up your book.)
2. Cut.
Cut out Part I, Part II, and Part III. Be careful when cutting out the slots.

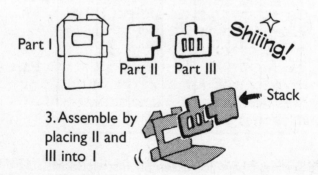

Part I

Part II Part III

Shiiing!

Stack

3. Assemble by placing II and III into I

4. More glue.
Fold over Part I and apply glue.

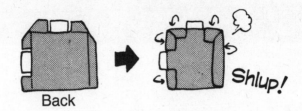

Back

Shlup!

5. Draw in the "Treasure."

Ta-Daa!

When you pull the tab…a white surface appears!
Draw in the picture or words that you'd like, and
your Treasure Theater is complete!!
(It'll be even nicer if you color it.)

✳✳✳✳ L.A. Corner!! (Little Apology) ✳✳✳✳

I'm sorry. About what? About the Q&A
Corner that I promised would be in this
volume. Due to the production timeline
of the comics, it couldn't be done. Will
you forgive me if I say it'll be in the
next volume? Aw, don't get mad. Don't
cry. Don't hit me. I'll do it. Really, I will.
Just wait for volume 4!

COMING NEXT VOLUME:

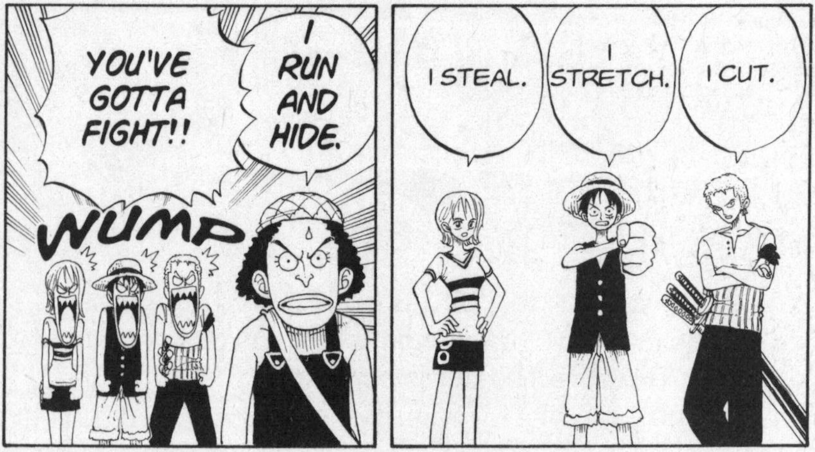
I CUT.
I STRETCH.
I STEAL.
I RUN AND HIDE.
YOU'VE GOTTA FIGHT!!
WUMP

The Black Cat Pirates have landed… but if they want the village, they'll have to go through Luffy and his crew! How will Usopp's slingshot, Zolo's swords, Nami's cunning, and Luffy's elastic punch fare against the twisted mind and razor-sharp claws of Captain Kuro?

AVAILABLE NOW

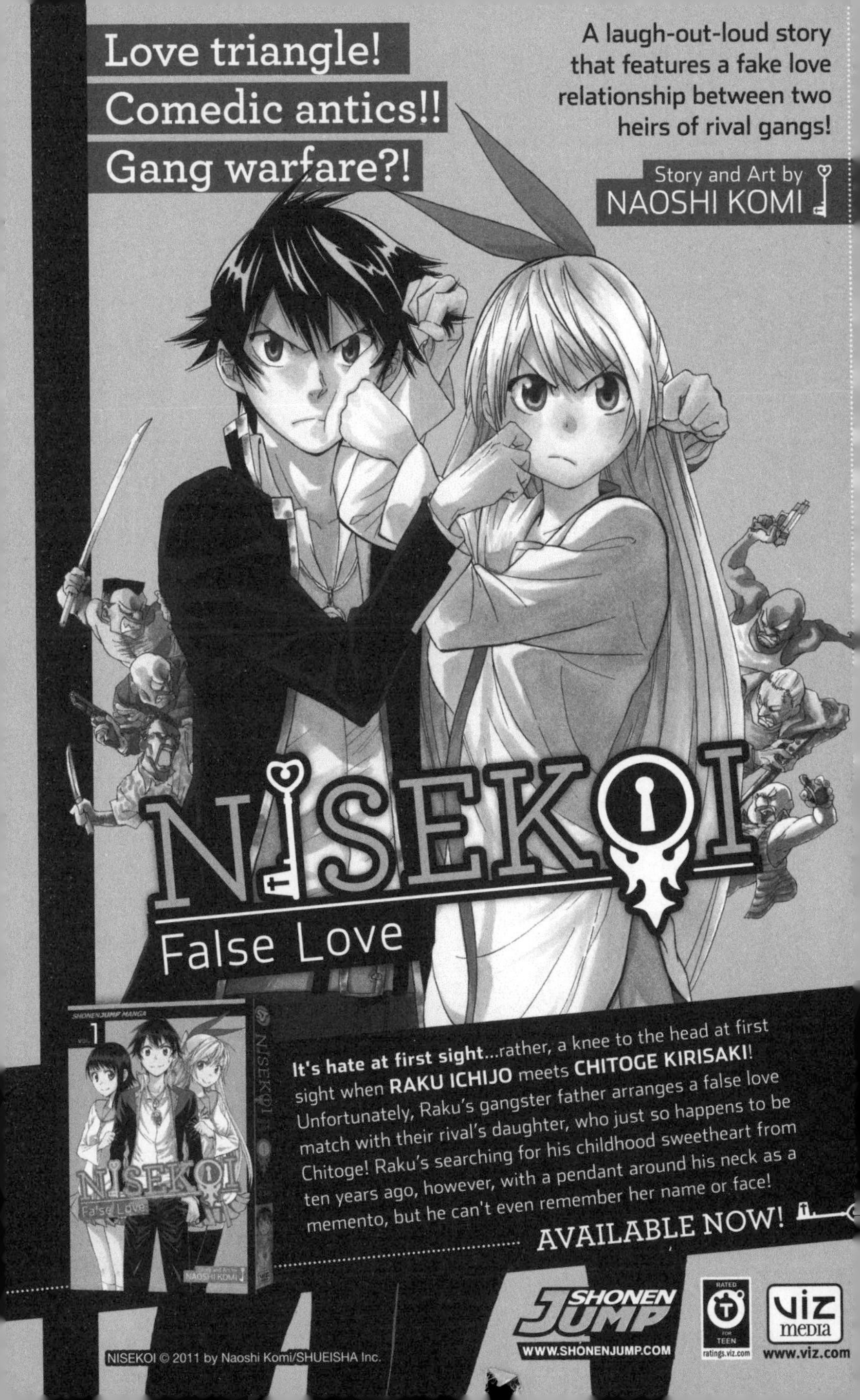
Love triangle!
Comedic antics!!
Gang warfare?!
A laugh-out-loud story that features a fake love relationship between two heirs of rival gangs!
Story and Art by NAOSHI KOMI
NISEKOI
False Love
SHONEN JUMP MANGA
NISEKOI False Love
It's hate at first sight...rather, a knee to the head at first sight when RAKU ICHIJO meets CHITOGE KIRISAKI! Unfortunately, Raku's gangster father arranges a false love match with their rival's daughter, who just so happens to be Chitoge! Raku's searching for his childhood sweetheart from ten years ago, however, with a pendant around his neck as a memento, but he can't even remember her name or face!
AVAILABLE NOW!
SHONEN JUMP
WWW.SHONENJUMP.COM
RATED T FOR TEEN
ratings.viz.com
viz media
www.viz.com
NISEKOI © 2011 by Naoshi Komi/SHUEISHA Inc.

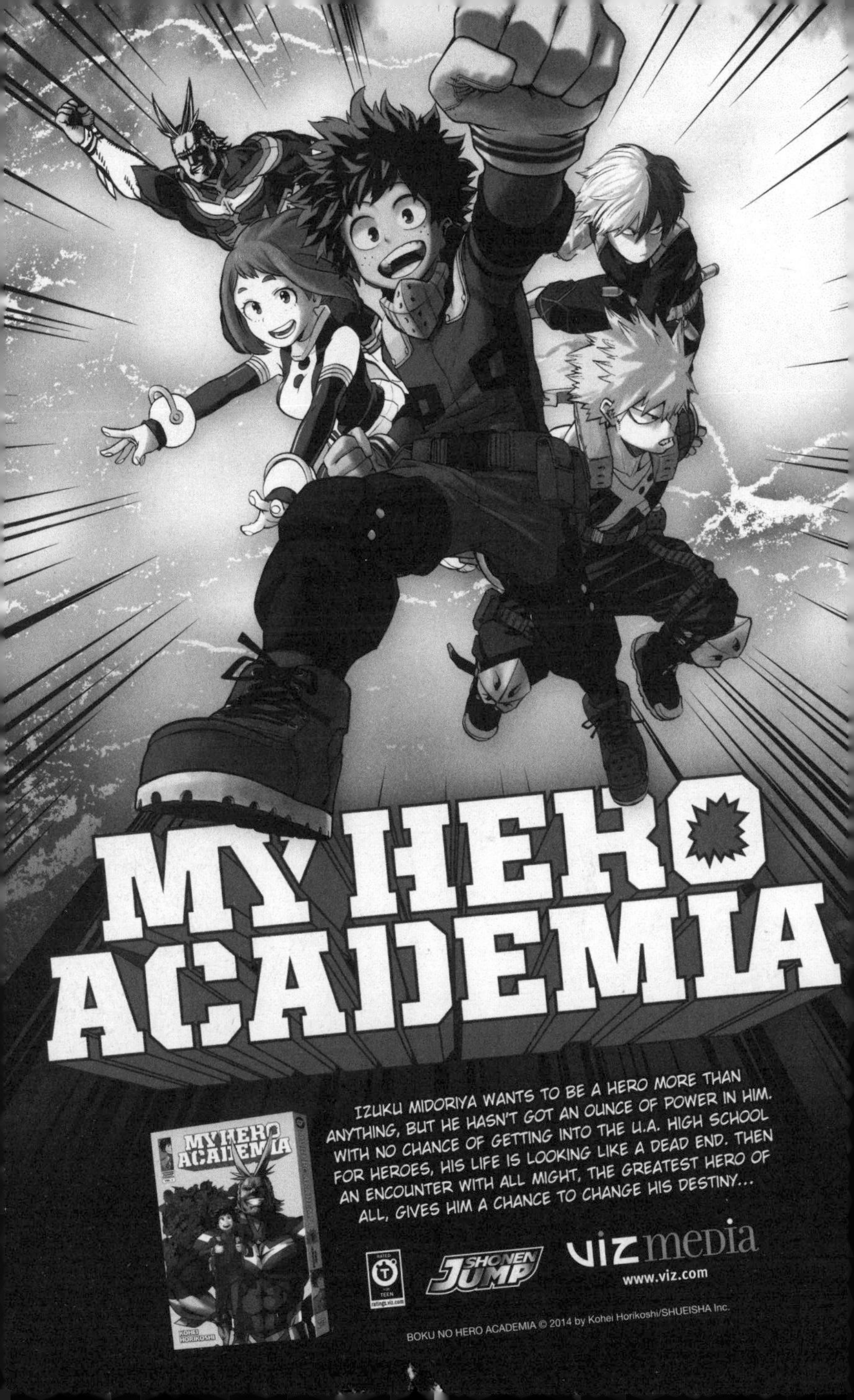
MY HERO ACADEMIA
IZUKU MIDORIYA WANTS TO BE A HERO MORE THAN ANYTHING, BUT HE HASN'T GOT AN OUNCE OF POWER IN HIM. WITH NO CHANCE OF GETTING INTO THE U.A. HIGH SCHOOL FOR HEROES, HIS LIFE IS LOOKING LIKE A DEAD END. THEN AN ENCOUNTER WITH ALL MIGHT, THE GREATEST HERO OF ALL, GIVES HIM A CHANCE TO CHANGE HIS DESTINY...
MY HERO ACADEMIA
KOHEI HORIKOSHI
RATED T TEEN
ratings.viz.com
SHONEN JUMP
viz media
www.viz.com
BOKU NO HERO ACADEMIA © 2014 by Kohei Horikoshi/SHUEISHA Inc.

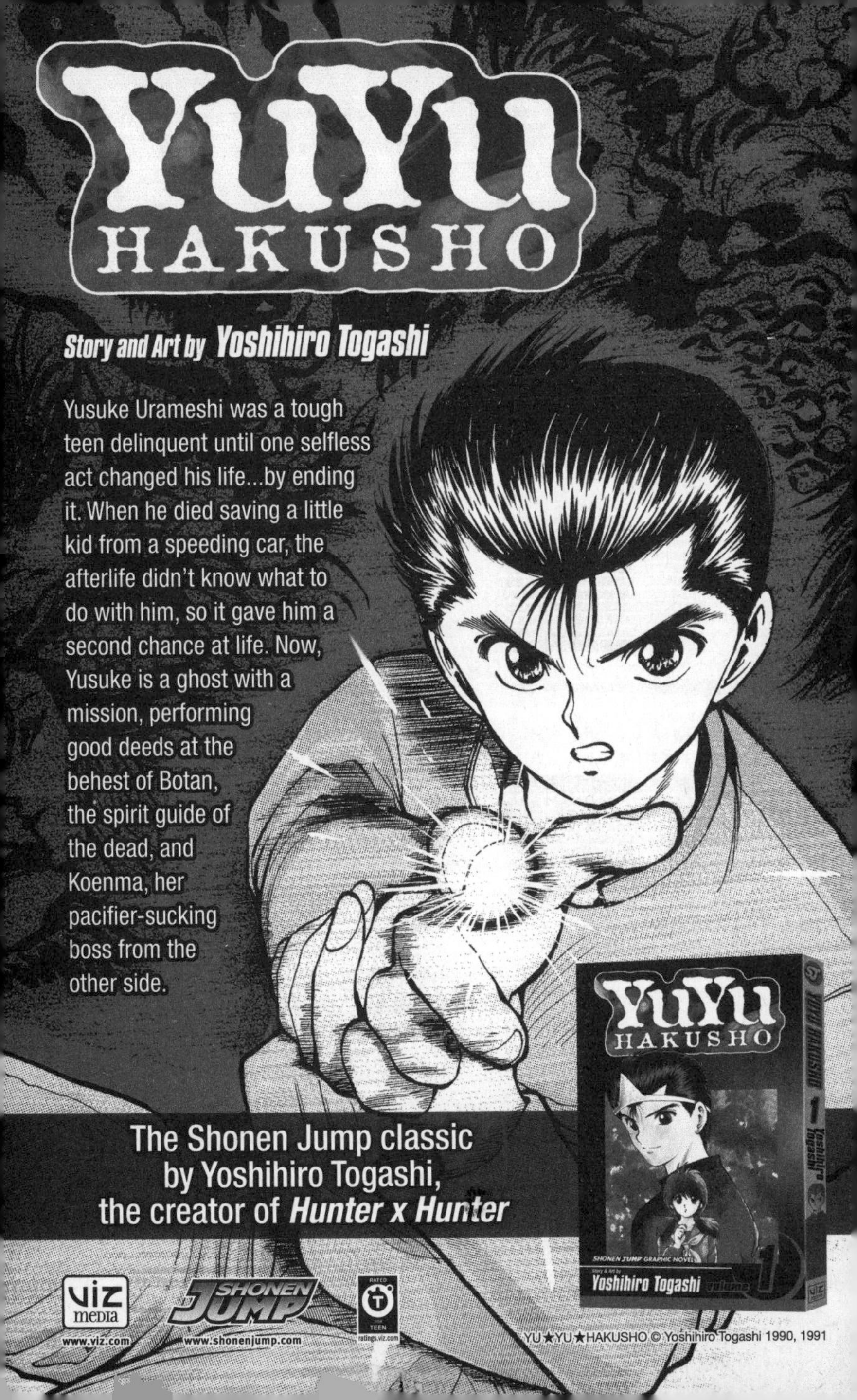
YuYu HAKUSHO
Story and Art by Yoshihiro Togashi
Yusuke Urameshi was a tough teen delinquent until one selfless act changed his life...by ending it. When he died saving a little kid from a speeding car, the afterlife didn't know what to do with him, so it gave him a second chance at life. Now, Yusuke is a ghost with a mission, performing good deeds at the behest of Botan, the spirit guide of the dead, and Koenma, her pacifier-sucking boss from the other side.
The Shonen Jump classic by Yoshihiro Togashi, the creator of *Hunter x Hunter*
YuYu HAKUSHO
SHONEN JUMP GRAPHIC NOVEL
Yoshihiro Togashi
viz media
www.viz.com
SHONEN JUMP
www.shonenjump.com
RATED T FOR TEEN
ratings.viz.com
YU★YU★HAKUSHO © Yoshihiro Togashi 1990, 1991

You're Reading in the Wrong Direction!!

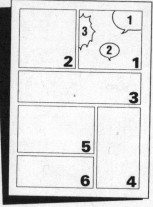

Whoops! Guess what? You're starting at the wrong end of the comic!

...It's true! In keeping with the original Japanese format, **One Piece** is meant to be read from right to left, starting in the upper-right corner.

Unlike English, which is read from left to right, Japanese is read from right to left, meaning that action, sound effects and word-balloon order are completely reversed...something which can make readers unfamiliar with Japanese feel pretty backwards themselves. For this reason, manga or Japanese comics published in the U.S. in English have sometimes been published "flopped"—that is, printed in exact reverse order, as though seen from the other side of a mirror.

By flopping pages, U.S. publishers can avoid confusing readers, but the compromise is not without its downside. For one thing, a character in a flopped manga series who once wore in the original Japanese version a T-shirt emblazoned with "M A Y" (as in "the merry month of") now wears one which reads "Y A M"! Additionally, many manga creators in Japan are themselves unhappy with the process, as some feel the mirror-imaging of their art skews their original intentions.

We are proud to bring you Eiichiro Oda's **One Piece** in the original unflopped format. For now, though, turn to the other side of the book and let the journey begin...!

—Editor

JUL